OPEN QUESTIONS

HELEN MOLESWORTH

OPEN QUESTIONS

THIRTY YEARS OF WRITING ABOUT ART

Edited by Donna Wingate

OPEN QUESTIONS

I was in my mid-twenties when I started to ask myself the question "Why write?" This is hardly unusual; most writers, at some point, are compelled to write about why they write. It's both solipsistic and completely structural to the endeavor: writing is a form of thinking, hence (the tautology continues), writing is the activity and the medium that allows writers to think. Thinking—both as a process and as a set of results—is as malleable and sclerotic as humans themselves, which is to say soft, muscular, rigid, fluid, et cetera, et cetera. (I can hear Morrissey singing in my inner ear . . .)

I did not feel the calling that some writers have felt; I did not have hypergraphia. I was not burning with a compulsion to write. I never managed to keep a journal with even a modicum of success. I didn't know what to say to those empty pages. In this regard, I didn't write "for myself"; I wrote on assignment, not in a journalistic sense, since I was more in control of my choices than I may have understood at the beginning. I wrote to figure things out. I wrote as a way of coming to terms with the art that pleased, confused, bothered, disturbed, or confounded me. This is another way of saying that for me art was the engine; writing was the caboose.

I spent my adolescence loafing around in Manhattan's museums, old movie houses, and art galleries. In the early 1980s, I was an inveterate truant; I frequently found myself slipping out the side door of my Lower East Side high school to go to the Met or catch a midafternoon double feature at the Quad or Theatre 80 St. Marks. I did all of this alone, and my solitariness was an essential part of the situation. Hindsight allowed me to see that I have always enjoyed being alone with others. Often, in my early days of museumgoing, I found myself in a fugue state, characterized by a kind of aimless, distracted attention. Floating outside of my body, I would watch myself drifting, taking in the whole scene: the carved marble steps, the herringbone wood floors, the gilt frames, the picture rail, the people coming and going, the looking, the searching. All of this was suffused with blankness. I experienced art as a kind of muteness. It never occurred to me that I might one day live in this world: the world of museums and galleries seemed as unscalable as a mountain—partly due to my class position, but just as equally due to the way in which it felt like that world was already all sorted out, timeless, not in need of anything new or young. It certainly did not appear deficient in anything a nerdy teenage girl from Queens might bring to the table.

That changed a little in college. One wintry morning during my freshman year a wonderful professor asked one of those horribly straightforward, 100 percent too-obvious questions: Would someone please describe the slide being projected on the screen? It was a Rembrandt painting of an old bearded white man reading a book. This benign bit of pedagogy produced an excruciating silence. Surely this was a trick. For some reason (probably to stem the discomfort), I raised my hand and began to say out loud what I was seeing. When I stopped, the professor was smiling. He took what I said and unfurled the class in its wake. A few weeks later, I gathered the temerity to visit him during office hours, not something I had ever done up until that point, and he told me that I had "it." When I asked what, precisely, "it" was, he offered a vague formulation that I half remember at best. My takeaway was that I was someone who looked at pictures and saw things other people didn't see. It would be years before I realized how true this was. There would be countless encounters in my professional life in museums in which I would "merely" describe what I saw only to be swarmed after the talk and regaled with the most outrageous compliments, all of which shared the structure of revelation: *I never would have seen that without you.*

The ego does love to be stroked.

Such commotion belies the reality that alone I was blank. Whenever I looked at pictures, the inside of my brain was curiously quiet, whereas in front of an audience, with an interlocutor, or sitting at my computer, I could think. That's how the writing started. I needed a ground from which to push off. I needed the promise of a reader. In the beginning, I wrote, as many students write, with very specifically imagined readers in my head. In my sophomoric imagination, these readers were my teachers, my elders. As I wrote, I imagined their responses and adjusted my text accordingly. Luckily, I had a very smart friend who admonished me early on. "Don't write for people older than you," she said. "You can't change their minds. Write for people younger than you and help shape their conversation." I was deeply turned on by this formulation, partly because it helped crack the protective carapace of writing for someone else's approval, but more so because it staked out a claim for writing as a form of conversation. Conversation implicated me in a relationship with my reader, and that, in turn, opened up the problem of ethics. If there was a reader, they had to be, as any "other" must be, accounted for, accommodated, addressed. How to speak to others, particularly others I did not know, was at the heart of the matter. In the beginning, I was looking for language that would be both open and erudite, accessible and advanced, open-ended and persuasive. Perhaps this search for language carried an extra charge for me because I didn't know what to say until I started writing. I still don't.

Part of why I don't know what I think before I write is because writing about art presents me with a profound dilemma. One of the reasons I assume people like myself (and maybe you, the reader), are interested in pictures is because pictures condense an enormous amount of information into one highly compacted image. Pictures, by virtue of their gestalt, happen "all at once." Even pictures that reveal themselves gradually happen all at once. One walks into a room and has an encounter. The encounter can be a slow simmer, or it can be a thunderbolt: however it occurs, it is nonlinear, and your brain is doing all sorts of work without you necessarily being aware of it. It's organizing perceptions of form. The nervous system kicks in to augment or challenge or support those perceptions; both body and mind start metabolizing the information and experience of the artwork before the cognitive, linguistic brain kicks into gear. At any rate, this is how I experience art objects.

When I find myself "on assignment," I start writing. Books, their spines splayed open to the pages with pictures, are spread out on a large table. My laptop screen is a stream of images, sometimes gathered into a PowerPoint presentation that I mindlessly advance, the pointer finger of my right hand lazily poking at the arrow key, letting the images come and go. When the writing begins, it often feels perverse. Even though I love art because of its capacity to condense meaning and affect into nonlinear form, when I write, I translate it into one of the most linear forms we have, a written text. A text in which one sentence follows another until they accrue into paragraphs and an argument that, by virtue of the temporality of reading, has a beginning, middle, and end.

An artwork has none of those things. An artwork is a network of ideas, feelings, form, history, and subjectivity condensed such that its syntax is one of accumulation, accretion, conglomeration. My desire to understand is so ruthless that I undo the thing I love. I "uncondense" all the information and make it linear. I do this so I can comprehend how the thing I love functions, how it behaves. The writing is often simultaneously an interpretation and a translation.

A by-product of this activity was a growing awareness of the contours of my own mind—my own interests, problems, concerns, as well as my blind spots and my intellectual and psychic limitations. This became part of writing's ethical conditions for me. Fairly early on, I was aware that if one effect of the writing was self-discovery, then I needed to be honest about that in the text. I decided to make things self-consciously "personal." I use the first person. I talk about my childhood. I include the deductive process as part of the text. I let the reader see the mess of me trying to figure it out. Since I have been coming to terms with who I am in relationship to a category of objects—art—that has been produced in a highly authored manner, it seems only fair to try and match the intensity/vulnerability/self-reflection of the artist in my text.

I've asked myself fairly regularly over the past three decades, "Why do I love art?" I love art because it's difficult. I think the world is an incredibly complex place, and art is an amazing lever for cracking the case. Art is a form of knowledge. It's a practice of investigation (science, journalism, observation) married to the human capacity for and drive toward play. (More condensation.) Art is a site where contradictions are engines rather than obstacles. Indeed, art may be one of our most beautifully designed tools for permitting, managing, and valorizing contradiction. I love that art maintains an aura of impenetrability, of obscurity. I love the way art acts like it's a secret but often does so in public space. I love the way art condenses the feeling, time, and space—to a point of mutual imbrication—of the agency of the person who makes it with the agency of the person who looks at it. I love art because I love artists; they're the last people in the world who get to say no with impunity. I love the ethics of being an artist—to decide every day that you are one, that you have to be one, and that you, and only you, determine what that means.

For all of the reasons enumerated above, art helps me understand, think through, and enact love and freedom. These two big ideas are my intellectual and affective lodestars. Art doesn't merely represent those things for me; it enacts them. It *is* them. Art is not a picture of love—it *is* love. The acts of making it, preserving it, displaying it, writing about it—all of these are events in which one makes oneself permeable to the other. This vulnerability is sometimes draped in elitism or obscurantist language, but I find those affects or responses to be brittle, designed to protect the truth that the desire of art is to exceed oneself and to meet an "other" on mutual terms. This is central to the event of art, and that impulse is one I associate with love. Similarly, art is not a picture of freedom—it *is* freedom. To say this is to register that art doesn't "merely" represent things: art behaves; it does things. For me, art is not inert. It is constantly active, in ways both intellectual and animistic. It's terribly romantic to think of the artist as someone involved in unalienated labor. By now, we are all far too familiar with the commodifiability of everything, even the moon. And yet part of art's DNA, part of its power, comes from the pocket of resistance, or denial, or rejection of the gnawing forces of repression (state, social, financial, psychic) that structure our daily lives. For all of the reasons art is a form of love, it is also a form of freedom.

I've come to believe that freedom and love are each impossible without the other. To be free is to know the unsayable within oneself; it is to know that things are unsayable because language escapes this mandate. Art can shatter our defenses about the unsayable. (This is why right-wing extremists *always* hate art: they understand its core power is the twinning of love and freedom.) Enter poetry, music, pictures, dance—at their most extraordinary (and sometimes at their most ordinary). Art is the form and activity we have for producing knowledge from the unsayable. Art is where the syntactical arrangements of everyday life (be they grammar, or class, or race, or gender) are allowed to be provisionally suspended and rearranged.

I also love art because it's the closest I can get to time travel. When I look at something from the ancient period or from the early twentieth century, I'm keenly aware that it is coming to me from another space-time continuum we conveniently call "the past." (As if the past were all done and dusted; as if the past weren't always ongoing, traveling alongside us, acting as the engine that propels us toward its equally abstract companion "the future.")

The promise of time travel is not unidirectional; its potential is embedded in the art of today. I am terribly aware when I look at contemporary art—art made by my contemporaries, art made in the space-time continuum we call "the present"—that even though I am its implicit audience, that's just the ego talking. The art of today is also lying in wait for its future audiences. Just as paintings made today are in dialogue with work made hundreds of years ago, so too I think of my writing as a contribution to the equally long textual conversation engendered by the history of art. The essays in this book are signposts along the way, cartographic notations for an unknown future reader, more akin to a recipe—a way of thinking and assembling the knowledge I have been able to glean through my experience.

Another way of thinking about art's futurity is to wonder whether the object in question can withstand the pressure of time travel. One way of describing the force and greatness of Manet's *A Bar at the Folies-Bergère* is to acknowledge the degree to which it has withstood the distance—in both time and space—between 1882 and now. It has done so in large measure due to its reliance on the primary institution that regulates art's time travel in the West: the museum. Even though, over the course of my professional life, I became increasingly disenchanted with the museum as an instrument of the patriarchal and colonial project, my belief in art and artists remains steadfast. Humans have been making objects and images for millennia. The framework for those endeavors has changed demonstrably over time. I happen to have been born into an era in which the museum is the hegemonic tool for the display, interpretation, and management of art. And thus, I fell in love with the museum. Like many, I have been navigating a tricky balancing act between critique and love of art's major institution for quite some time. This balancing act is crucial, as much of what I think about art would simply be impossible without museums. And almost all of the art discussed in these pages was made with a deep awareness of and imbrication in the idea of the museum as art's final repository. Now I find myself in a bind: while

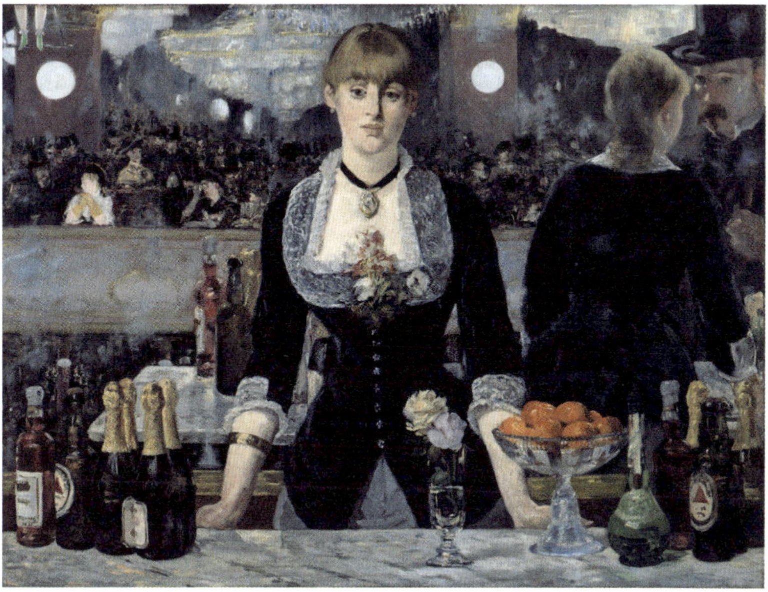

Édouard Manet, *A Bar at the Folies-Bergère*, 1882, oil on canvas, 37¾ x 51⅛ in. (96 x 130 cm)

I believe in art, I have lost considerable faith in the museum.

My disenchantment with the museum, my shaken faith, has led me to think about how all of the different ways I love art could be described under the umbrella of faith. It's been pretty uncool to think about the intimate relationship between art and faith for quite some time. The trifecta of the Enlightenment, modernism, and the avant-garde did an excellent job of ripping the two ideas asunder. And yet, I remain aware that more than any other human activity, it's art that allows me to have faith—in the future, in humanity, in ideas, in our capacity to think about things larger than ourselves. I have faith that art changes our consciousness. I have faith that art slips unnoticed into many rooms and shifts cultural discussions. I have faith that some of the art made today will mean something to someone a hundred years from now. Even if and when museums as we know them cease to exist, I have faith that there will continue to be artists who work to make things, and that in turn some people will continue to value those things. I have faith that all of this will happen even if the audience for these things is comprised of people I can't imagine, even if the framework for display is unrecognizable to me, even if the systems of value are different from those we share today.

When art pulled away from structures of faith, it did so in concert with the museum. When the Enlightenment-era museum performed a perfectly reasonable *détournement* of the religious into the secular, it replaced the values and activities associated with "belief" or "faith" with the behaviors and values associated with "knowledge." I have long advocated for art as a form of knowledge (rather than, let's say, art as an asset class, or art as entertainment, or art as healer, all of which can also accurately describe the category). Art's condensation of information, perception, and feeling into form is one of humanity's most profound reservoirs of knowledge. Nevertheless, I also understand the structure of faith to be an essential part of art's work in the world.

When I say that I think some of the art of our time will exist in the future, to have an encounter with a radically unknown other, and that possibly some infinitesimal part of that future encounter might carry with it some of the interpretative framework I offer in these various essays—when I say all that, I am suggesting, tacitly, that I believe in the future and have faith in the ongoing potential of the communicative, knowledge-based enterprise I am involved in. I see this conviction on my part as a display of my faith that some of the choices I've made, or some of the enterprises I've engaged in, will have a life beyond me, a life beyond this life, a life beyond this time. The structure of such beliefs are deeply rooted in the West's historical association of art and religion (associations, it's worth noting, shared by almost every culture on earth). While I am not a religious person, I recognize that my belief structure in art is completely analogous to the deep structure of religious belief, if for no other reason than that *I believe in things I cannot prove.* If one of the things I love about art is its capacity to present us with diametrically opposed concepts simultaneously, then one of those antinomies is surely the fact that I think art is a form of knowledge bound up in the mysteries of faith.

What I find slightly surprising, now that I am a woman of a certain age, is the degree to which I've staked an ethics on this submerged structure of belief and faith, and I wonder what would happen if I were able to deal with this conjunction more explicitly. I'm still not sure how to do this. As I assembled these essays, written over the course of three decades, I found myself returning to an encounter I had a few years ago in front of the aforementioned time traveler, Manet's *A Bar at the Folies-Bergère*, when, overwhelmed by the intensity of communication and connection this painting was capable of some 140 years after it was made, I found myself in tears in a room at the Courtauld Gallery in London. In the intervening years I've tried to make sense of those tears. I cried because I missed my grandmother, whose love of work lives on in me in ways both seen and unseen. I cried because the art historian T. J. Clark's writing about this painting opened a whole world for me. I cried because the museum job I had at the time was lonely and difficult. I cried because sometimes I'm tired of being a white woman. I'm weary of withstanding all the pressures of a category I didn't choose but that nevertheless has fully circumscribed my existence. I cried because the painting's still life of Bass Ale bottles and the crystal-footed bowl filled with oranges on the white marble bar says *plus ça change* to me. I cried because the mysterious reflection in the mirror is an inside painterly joke that stems from the invention of portable panel painting. I cried because I identify with the white woman working behind the bar. I feel related to her—materially, physically, and conceptually. I cried because our society is arranged such that life depends on us selling our most precious thing—our time. I cried because this picture helps me realize that, even though I don't believe in progress, time is both linear and cyclical. I cried because I realized how much this painting mattered to me, how much I carry it around as an image in my mind's eye. I cried because in the church of art these times are trying, and my faith has been tested. (There have been days when I flirted with not believing anymore.) I cried because this painting stokes my faith on the days I find it hard to maintain my faith. I cried because this painting allows me to reassemble my belief—because without a framework of belief, there's only cynicism. And I cannot abide cynicism.

For years I felt embarrassed by the tears—so dramatic, so maudlin, so consummately uncool. But now I see them as a registration of vulnerability, which is OK with me, as I've come to understand that part of the ethical contract of art requires its viewers to be consistently vulnerable to the other. (It's worth repeating: this is why art is perennially threatening to totalitarian, authoritarian, and fascist regimes.) Related to this implicit demand for vulnerability, on the part of both viewer and artist, is the way art is sometimes offered in the spirit of repair. The world is a horrible, cruel, unfair, violent, and vicious place. Sometimes art is doing the work of mending some of the damage. This may be another way of saying that I cried in front of *A Bar at the Folies-Bergère* because sometimes we go to museums to have an intensely private experience in public space.

Art is interesting in large measure due to its public dimension. (Or, to be more precise, I am particularly interested in the publicness of art.) The beginning of the reparative act happens when art commands public space and the viewer's time. Art permits us to say the unsayable, feel the ineffable, and think the difficult in public. The writings compiled in this volume all partake of this dimension of the art experience: each essay is a record of an individual having a private experience in public. Each is a transcript of how I perceive and understand a particular set of objects. The essays share the framework of the disciplinary expertise of art history, crossed with the love of a fan, mixed with the zeal of a true believer. Knowledge can lead one to be calcified and jaded, or labile and curious. I am familiar with both paths. Even though these essays are written in the spirit of interpretation and exposition, I want to make a passionate plea for retaining one's curiosity, because to be curious is also to be vulnerable. To be curious is to not know and to want to know. And when it comes to art, the more you know, the more you'll see. The more you know, the more complex it becomes. The more complex it is, the more you realize how much you don't know. A life lived with art is neither linear nor progressive. It is meandering and recursive, forever folding back on itself. Art is perpetually tidal, receding and coming forth.

My hope is that these essays cohere into a set of working assumptions about how to be curious in front of works of art. I hope they offer a submerged, tacit methodology about how to let a work of art guide you through both itself and you, and the ineffable mixture of the two. I believe, as Marcel Duchamp famously said, that when it comes to art, "the viewer completes the work." What an awesome task. What an ethical responsibility. What a generous offer. And because he says "the viewer" rather than "a viewer," then that means you too. And if there's a "you," then, however provisionally, there's also an "us." Or at least that's how I understand the entire proposition of art: an object is made, an audience gathers, the encounter occurs, one thinks, feels, and writes in the wake of this encounter. The work of art lives in the space of the gerund. It is ongoing. Its completion is permanently stalled; it is forever an open question.

THE EARLIEST SHOTS ACROSS THE BOW

For most of the 1990s I was in graduate school pursuing my art history PhD, and the following three essays exemplify my search for a writerly voice that felt authentic—though I never used that word at the time. While I enjoyed reading art history, I found the heavily armored language of most academic writing off-putting. I had an inchoate desire for a more readerly text, one that preserved my fandom while also allowing me to flex my critical chops.

Early on, I had a sense that artists might be my ideal audience. I craved approval from the artists I knew far more than I did from my professors. I was hip to the kind of self-searching questions the artists around me had been asking of themselves and of their work. There have always been artists' artists. I certainly had aspirations to be an artists' curator. I remember wondering if I could write with the same mixture of passion, intensity, self-reflection, and criticality as my fellow artists. Could I turn self-exploration into rigorous form? Could I write in a way that was as self-aware and transparent as an artist at work in their studio? Could I implicate my own desire—for ideas, for objects—in the text? Could I write a text that was simultaneously strong enough to function in the world without me and open enough to register my vulnerability? Could I write in a way that incorporated my doubt, my unknowing? Could I write in a way that telegraphed all the mastery (disciplinary, writerly) I was developing, while still allowing the reader to be witness to the very process of my thinking? Could the text read as if it were an unfolding of my own thoughts, while still retaining some of the magic, the aura—indeed, the inscrutability—of the artwork itself? Could I write about the things I loved without leaving them dissected on the table? Could I write about the things I loved in a way that amplified my love for them as much as, if not more than, a text that "explained" the artwork in question? Enter fragments of dreams, snippets of song lyrics, a liberal use of the first person, and a shying away from jargon and/or professional language.

I'm not sure I've ever answered these questions, but these early tactics—through tenacity and force of habit—have, over the intervening decades, become a strategy that helps me enjoy the pleasures of insider baseball (knowledge fully metabolized) while preserving the mixture of love and curiosity that comes with beginner's eyes.

Robert Rauschenberg: Before *Bed*

Originally published in *October* 63 (Winter 1993): 68–82.

Like the smell of a barn: when I see only the bust of the sitters (Hendrijke, in the Berlin Museum) or only the head, I cannot refrain from imagining them standing on manure. The chests breathe. The hands are warm. Bony, knotted, but warm. The table in The Syndics *rests on straw, the five men smell of cow dung. Under Hendrijke's skirts, under the fur-edged coats, under the painter's extravagant robe, the bodies are performing their functions: they digest, they are warm, they are heavy, they smell, they shit. However delicate her face and serious her expression,* The Jewish Bride *has an ass. You can tell. She can raise her skirts at any moment. She can sit down, she has what it takes.*
—Jean Genet, "What Remains of a Rembrandt Torn in Four Equal Pieces, and Flushed Down the Toilet . . ."

The *White Paintings*: simple, rectangular canvases, painted a flat, strokeless white and hung side by side, their edges butting tightly up against one another. Robert Rauschenberg made them in 1951 during his second sojourn at Black Mountain College. They were painted after a prolific summer during which he completed the *Night Blooming* series (1951): large canvases six by eight feet that Rauschenberg took outside, saturated with wet oil paint, and pressed into the ground, where they picked up the heavy gravel from the road. Night blooming in North Carolina . . . jasmine, honeysuckle, sweet gardenia.

John Cage once wrote, "The white paintings caught whatever fell on them; why did I not look at them with my magnifying glass?"[1] They hung on the wall ready for viewers to cast their shadows upon them. Cage's question was incomplete, for dust played second fiddle to shadows. The completion of the *White Paintings* demanded the mark of a bodily form—why else would they have needed to be so large? so smooth? so supplicant? so available? Ultimately, shadows would not be enough, not because they were too arbitrary but rather because they were too ephemeral. They lacked the full texture and the heady smell of the *Night Bloomers*. The first black painting, made at Black Mountain in 1951, mimicked its white counterparts: black matte paint applied to the canvas with a roller. Rauschenberg knew an uninteresting failure when

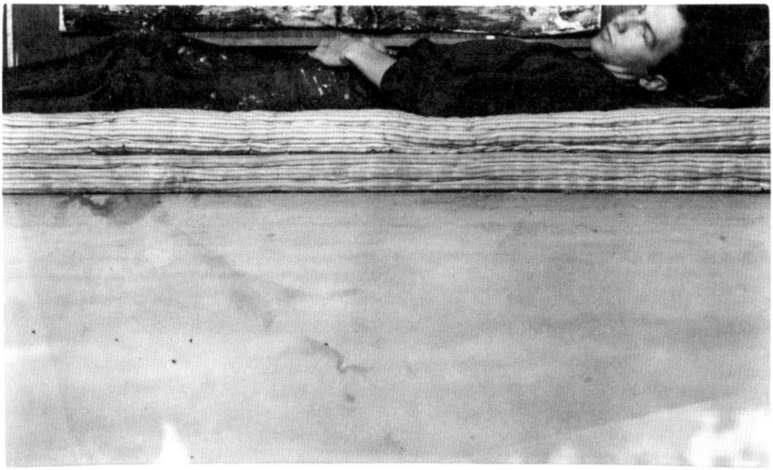

Robert Rauschenberg, *Postcard Self-Portrait, Black Mountain (II)*, 1952–80, gelatin silver print, 3¼ x 5½ in. (8.3 x 14 cm)

he saw one. He quickly returned to texture for a sense of touch, an excitation of the senses. The problem emerged: How to create a texture more bodily in nature than gravel, to register the body more concretely than a shadow?

First produced at Black Mountain between 1951 and 1952 and then, after a nine-month hiatus, in 1953, the black paintings are patterned canvases with dense, crackling surfaces, laboriously made by tearing sheets of newspaper, dipping them in glue, and affixing them to the canvas in a random fashion, where they would be covered by several hues of viscous black paint.[2] In the earliest paintings, the newspaper remains hidden under thick paint, resulting in an ambiguous surface texture. *Untitled (Asheville Citizen)* (ca. 1952), was the first work to expose the newspaper. Rotating the sports and classified pages of the local paper 180 degrees, Rauschenberg spread the full sheets across two joined canvases and painted matte black around their edges. Revealing the newspaper opened a whole new register of meaning for the paintings. For the newspaper is a paradigm of an economy of endless repetition marked by daily consumption and disposability, perhaps best explicated by the popular expression "same shit, different day." Its disposability ensures its dailiness, repetition, and regularity. In the *Asheville Citizen* painting, Rauschenberg exaggerates these aspects of the newspaper by using the sports and classified sections, perhaps the most daily parts of the newspaper (they contain information pertinent only to the immediate present). The black paintings became quite repetitious in both appearance and production, mirroring the structure of their ground.[3] Given the number of paintings, the shadowy newspaper datelines, which almost always remain legible, impart a diaristic quality to the works, linking them even more directly to the dailiness and repetition of the newspaper.

Robert Rauschenberg, *Untitled (Asheville Citizen)*, ca. 1952,
oil and newspaper on two canvases, 74 x 28½ in. (188 x 72.4 cm)

Simultaneously, Rauschenberg assiduously photographed the progress of the black paintings. The photograph's ability to repeat endlessly and the need to repeat the painting through a photograph of it, as well as the indexical capability of the photograph to record the specificity of time and place, has a parallel relation to the newspaper's signification of dailiness. For this purpose, Rauschenberg continually framed the black paintings in doorways and doorframes. "More than simple scaling devices," Walter Hopps has remarked, "they suggest human presence and establish a literal conjunction of abstract art and the physical factum of everyday life."[4] Is the "physical factum of everyday life" merely newspapers and doorways? Or do those traces stand in for dailiness and "human presence" in another form?

It is hard for me to overlook the way the paintings' textures and colors resonate with fecal matter: the smeared quality of the paint, the varying degrees of viscosity, and the color—shit brown and black. After all, repetition and cycles of consumption and disposal have as much to do with anality as they do with newspapers. And the relation between the two is not so far-fetched. Ernest Jones's landmark 1918 essay "Anal-Erotic Character Traits" discusses the various objects that can signify excrement in unconscious life, with newspapers prominent among them (think of those black smudges left on your hands). "Books and other printed matter are a curious symbol of feces," he writes, "presumably through the association with paper and the idea of pressing (smearing, imprinting)."[5] The dirtiness and dailiness, the visual similitude, and the compulsive documenting of the paintings against heavily textured brick walls suggest an "excremental reading" of these works.

In this essay, I give an account of Rauschenberg's early work that engages the uneasiness and disgust that accompany the intense visual pleasure of these paintings. I will also attempt to recapture the profound sense of experimentation with which these works were undertaken. Furthermore, I hope to challenge the codification of several standard formalist/biographical/descriptive/iconographical readings of Rauschenberg.[6] My intention is not to psychoanalyze Rauschenberg or to conflate anality with his sexuality. On the contrary, I feel that "the body" is presented in Rauschenberg's oeuvre as polymorphously perverse. In this regard, my reading engages certain questions concerning the body and the anxieties, fantasies, and problems it raises (arouses), especially in the work of artists during the 1950s.[7] Despite the dearth of literature on the topic,[8] Rauschenberg was not alone in this exploration; the problem of registering the body was shared by (at least) two other key figures at Black Mountain, John Cage and Charles Olson.[9]

"The white paintings came first," Cage wrote. "My silent piece came later."[10] Yet the exact chronology is not as important as the concern with how to mediate and discuss the body within artistic production. In this regard, Cage's recollection of his discovery of silence in a soundproof chamber at Harvard University is striking:

> I entered one at Harvard University several years ago and heard two sounds, one high and one low. When I described them to the engineer in charge, he informed me that the high one was my nervous system in operation, the low one my blood in circulation. Until I die there will be sounds. And they will continue following my death. One need not fear about the future of music.[11]

This revelation locates Cage's most generative musical, artistic, and compositional idea within the body itself—more importantly, within the interior of the body, the nervous and circulatory systems, realms of bodily experience of which we are usually not aware. Cage's silence is both located within and driven by the desire to know the body more intimately, to listen to its interior.

Olson takes up the question of the body in a prose poem titled "Proprioception" (1959).[12] The text has fanciful moments when Olson longs to (re)attribute specific organs' emotional characteristics, such as desire to the heart, sympathy to the bowels. Speculating on the possibility of the unconscious being situated in the "cavity of the body, in which the organs are slung," as opposed to the brain, the poem puzzles over the meanings that our bodies present to us. The viscosity of the poem turns violent at times when it explores the possibility (and perhaps the ramifications) of gathering information from the body:

	Violence: knives/anything, to get the body in.
To which	the data of depth sensibility/the 'body' of us as
PROPRIOCEPTION:	object which spontaneously or of its own order
	produces experience of, 'depth' Viz
	SENSIBILITY WITHIN THE ORGANISM

BY MOVEMENT OF ITS OWN TISSUES[13]

Here the body is a source of experience. Similar to Cage's work, the external surface of the body is less important than its hidden interior, an interior that is marvelous as it both produces and stores experience as information.

It is within this historical milieu that the black paintings were first exhibited at the Stable Gallery in New York in 1953, where Dore Ashton's review saw them as "black as beasts . . . they stir up vaguely primordial sensations, and anxiety. But that is all."[14] A decade later, the Jewish Museum gave Rauschenberg his first retrospective. In the catalogue essay, Alan Solomon discussed the paintings' use of color: "It supplies an enigmatic field, at once opaque and deep to the furthest reach of space. Shadowed and secretive, it proposes all and discloses nothing, and it became the plasma out of which his present style was formed."[15] The excremental look of these paintings lay barely beneath the surface of these sensual and tentative descriptions of the "deep" and the "primordial"—but the "anxiety" that it produces is dismissed (Ashton's "But that is all"; Solomon's it "discloses nothing").

Rauschenberg's anxiety took a rather different form. Telling an interviewer he went to Black Mountain to be disciplined by Josef Albers, he says:

> I could have gone on painting with my hands, I think, and making messes forever because I really loved painting. I guess the physicality of my personality was emerging, and so I had to paint with my hands. I couldn't stand a brush coming between me and the canvas. Naturally I cleaned my "brushes," which were my hands, on my clothes.[16]

Rauschenberg does not want to be in the painting—as in Jackson Pollock's famous pronouncement that he could "literally be *in* the painting"—as much as he wants to have the painting be on his body and, conversely, to have his physicality be on the canvas.[17]

EXCREMENTAL FANTASIES

In Dennis Cooper's novel *Frisk* (1991), the main character (also named Dennis) finds his ultimate sexual pleasure in the murder of other young men. Or so it would seem, for in *Frisk* it is all a fantasy, elaborated through letter writing, the great literary form of self-disclosure. Beyond the trope of sex and death (better known as "sex 'n' meth" in certain punk film quarters), there lies a deeper probing in this novel. The title gives it all away: what Dennis wants is knowledge. Sitting in a hotel room with hooker/porn star Pierre, Dennis combs every inch of his body with his mouth, gathering minute pieces of information: tastes, smells, changes in skin texture. He is logging them for future reference. Dennis requests that Pierre shit and not flush; this too is information he desires.

> "I'm not being abject," I say. "It's not, 'Ooh, shit, piss, how wicked,' or anything. It's, like I said, information." Pierre nods. "Then what are you going to do with it?" he asks. "I don't mean with my shit, I mean with the information." My face scrunches up. "Uh, create a mental world . . . uh, wait. Or a situation where I could kill you and understand . . ."[18]

Yet Cooper is fully cognizant as to how such information refuses to add up; certainly in the novel it never equals a satisfactory situation for murder. But what drives *Frisk*'s main character is the fantasy of knowing another person so thoroughly that one would be intimate with the interior of that body. "I'm sure I've idealized brutality, murder, dismemberment, etc.," Dennis says to Pierre during their second hotel meeting. "But even slicked up, there's an unknowableness there that's so profound or whatever, especially when I combine it with sex."[19] Sex, that fantasy moment where two bodies merge as one, is an idealized form of the desire to know the inside, or to be inside someone else's body. The act is the idealized form of gathering knowledge about the other. But murder offers another version of "getting to know you"; it offers the "real" stuff, the secret hidden stuff that no one else knows, not even its subject. An existentialist novel, *Frisk* is about the aching desire to know the self and the ultimate impossibility of self-knowledge. No amount of nausea, it seems, reduces the foreignness of one's own body. What is in there, what is it doing, what relation does it have to me and I to it?

For Freud, desire for knowledge awakens when the child asks: Where do babies come from?[20] Initially, these "infantile sexual researches" center on the mother's body, with the child assuming that babies are born from her bowels. Yet, Freud argues, the child has a vague notion of birth's sexual component, although the child is unable to understand it fully. The problem of information exceeding comprehension continues throughout adult life (accounting, he adds, for the brooding of many intellectuals); but it is reactivated most importantly for Freud in the Oedipal conflict.[21]

Perhaps the experience of representing the body through excrement in the black paintings (both for the viewer and for the maker) problematizes the speed with which Freud passes over the child's relation to the interior of the mother's body in his rush to get to the genital and Oedipal configurations of the subject. Melanie Klein, however, lingers and elaborates upon the young child's fantasies regarding the interior of the mother's body. For Klein, the child's earliest relationship to the mother is one of "sucking and scooping" at the breast, voiding the mother of her interior substances. Soon the child begins to take pleasure in its ability to master the process of defecation, a pleasure derived from the interior of its own body. When the child learns that it came out of the mother's body, the initial fascination with the mother's interior becomes interwoven with the child's pleasurable sense of its own. Hence, the child equates itself and excrement as products of the mother's body. "In the imagination of the small child these multiple objects are situated inside his mother's body and this place is also the chief objective of his destructive and libidinal tendencies and also of his awakening *epistemophilic impulses*" (emphasis added).[22]

The child's desire to explore the interior of the mother's body, a desire that extends to the child's relationship to his or her own body and its products, is the awakening of *epistemophilic impulses*. It is on this crucial point that Freud and Klein diverge. For Klein sees the activation of the desire for knowledge as intensely and intrinsically related to the body and the question of its interior and its by-products. Freud does not engage the child's relation to its own or the mother's body outside of the realm of the genitalia. The interior of the body and the mystery that surrounds it, for both the child and the adult, are never quite broached.

For Western civilization, however, the body ultimately is an obstacle to be overcome. Civilization, as Freud has noted, requires the control of bodily functions and the sublimation of instinctual drives. In *Civilization and Its Discontents* he writes: "The diminution of the olfactory stimuli seems itself to be a consequence of man's raising himself from the ground, of his assumption of an upright gait."[23] By pulling his nose away from the ground, Freud argues, man lifts his senses away from the smells of excrement and genitalia, divorcing his senses from his body. Likewise, children are taught to repress their initial means of gathering information: groping, sucking, smearing. Subsequently, the drive for knowledge that prompts the questions "Where do babies come from?" and "Where do I come from?" will need to be sublimated.

But if we read the black paintings as excremental, as the daily expulsion from the body's interior, can the implications of this instance of *de*sublimation, an instance of a body not successfully overcome, transform the question "Where do I come from?" into "What is inside of me?" They manifest the desire to explore the interior body through what might be called "bodily knowledge"—the knowledge, pleasure, curiosity, and disgust surrounding that primary bodily product: shit.

Rauschenberg has indeed attempted to turn himself inside out to mark his own body on the canvas.[24] His immersion in an indexical art practice can be well documented by surveying his investment in imprinting the corporeal senses onto the artistic surface. Placing a nude body directly onto light-sensitive paper, Rauschenberg and Susan Weil made the "blueprints" (1949–51). Taking the wet paintings outside and pressing them in the dirt, he made the *Night Blooming* series. But the questions the black paintings ask are: What kind of knowledge do our bodies produce about ourselves? Can knowledge be desublimated and "returned" to its origin? These are the questions that the black paintings end up sharing with *Frisk*. The black paintings mark the canvas with the body in the basest of ways. "The body begins to exist where it *repugnates*, repulses, yet wants to devour what disgusts it and exploits that taste for distaste."[25] The paintings enact the body liberated through excretion. They are a narcissistic fantasy of self-birth; they give way to the delirium of the body producing its own knowledge.

THE STAIN

A macchiato is an Italian espresso, preferably quite strong. The black coffee is tinged by dark brown that rims the cup; a dollop of light airy foam from steamed milk floats on top. *Macchiato* comes from the Italian word *macchia*, which means "stain." (See antonym: *immacolato*, meaning "immaculate," as in the Conception.)

At the end of a summer of black paintings at Black Mountain, Rauschenberg and Cy Twombly left together for Rome. During the seven-month trip, which included a stay in North Africa, Rauschenberg made Joseph Cornell-like boxes, fetishes that he threw into the Arno River, and a series of collages that he packed up and didn't exhibit for more than twenty years. These delicate collages (all are untitled and dated to 1952) fall between the two periods of the black paintings. Repetitive in size, structure, and material, the collages pull back from the initial viscous explosion onto the canvas of Rauschenberg's interior. The mottled paperboards were collected from the insides of shirts as they were freshly returned from the cleaners: the very support for these collages is bodily through contact and scale. The cardboard is preciously torn, rough edges insisting upon the hand that ripped it; each is topped by a sheet of fluttering paper. Engraved images culled from old books that Rauschenberg found at the local flea markets are pasted on top, the lumpy glue creasing the fine paper or staining the thin cardboard. The images are decidedly "scientific," an eccentric dictionary of various animals, body parts, and microorganisms. The scientific dissections are brief glimpses into biological interiors: interiors devoid of any fluids, interiors that are dry and empty, interiors where the space between skin and bones is discreetly marked off as a void—as nonpresence. Yet the glue stains on the cardboard are an indexical moment of the artist's hand smearing and pressing in the act of collage. Ernest Jones postulates that the sublimation of the smearing impulse leads to the "impulse to stain or contaminate."[26] The stain implies uncleanliness: sweat, semen, mucus, the remains of sex on linen or clothing.

With regard to the Shroud of Turin, Georges Didi-Huberman has argued that it is through "the absence of figuration therefore [that the stain] serves as proof of existence. Contact having occurred, figuration would appear false."[27] The use of the stain as an index, Didi-Huberman insists, affirms the place of contact as a place of origin. These simple early collages are, in this sense, a pedantic object lesson. The origin of the work of art is the artist's body—in the pressing and the smearing, in the dailiness of bodily functions, in the question "What kinds of marks can I make?" If, as Didi-Huberman argues, collage is indexical, then, for Rauschenberg, the absence that the collage signifies is the body of its maker.

TOWARD *BED*

The intolerance for disorder is closely related to another trait, the intolerance for waste. This has more than one source. It represents a dislike of anything being thrown away (really from the person)—a manifestation of the retaining tendency under consideration—and also a dislike of the waste product because it represents refuse—i.e., dirt—so that every effort is made to make use of it. Such people are always pleased at discovering or hearing of new process for converting waste products into useful material, in sewage farms, coal-tar manufactories, and the like.
—Ernest Jones, "Anal-Erotic Character Traits"

The *Red Paintings* (1953–54) begin Rauschenberg's lifelong investment in found objects. Moving beyond printed matter, the paintings incorporate a large array of fabrics, found wood, and trinkets. When asked why he used the color red, Rauschenberg replied, "I was trying to move away from the black and white.... So I picked the most difficult color for me to work in. If you're not careful, red turns to black when you're dealing with it."[28]

The Latin root of *scrutiny* is *scruta*, meaning "rags" or "trash." Originally, to scrutinize an area meant to investigate so thoroughly as to search through the rags. The domestic nature of the use of fabrics such as lace and brocade in the *Red Paintings* has been noted by several critics. That these traditional emblems of femininity should be so inundated within the bloody surface of these paintings gives pause in light of this text. If the black paintings are an attempt to know the interior through the autoerotic pleasures of shit, then the *Red Paintings* are the horror of the body exploded, dispersed, and flowing over the surfaces of everything. The extreme agitation of the *Red Paintings* is perversely heightened by the attempts to modulate their "bloodiness." Their grounds are built up from cartoons and comic strips. The playful polka-dot fabric in *Yoicks* (1954) or the three childlike hearts drawn into the surface of *Red Import* (1954) seem to make the violence more macabre. Their viscosity oozes even beyond that of the black paintings, and their incorporation of found objects blurs any clear distinction of interior/exterior, found object/painting. As Andrew Forge has put it, "The frames and battens of *Charlene* (1954) articulate the *inside* of the picture; they also throw its boundaries far and wide."[29] This struggle over boundaries is what is continued so persuasively in the Combines (1954–64), and perhaps *Bed* (1955) is the ultimate moment of blissful and terrifying confusion.

Anality is less a matter of actual feces than of the fantasies surrounding them—their production and disposal.[30] If one of sublimation's definitions is the displacement of the low functions of the body onto its higher faculties, then Rauschenberg radically reinserts the lower body into art. He desublimates the hand of the artist, allowing it to smear and rub, press and glue, privileging tactility over sight. Rauschenberg's work catalogued the body through its products—shit, stain, blood—but ultimately the body produces a limited amount of knowledge about itself. Rauschenberg even told Billy Klüver that the black paintings interested him "in their complexity without their revealing anything—the fact that there was a lot to see but not much showing."[31]

"Sublimation is a search in the outside world for the lost body of childhood," Norman O. Brown has written. Rauschenberg's art is this search. And yet this body is not reconstituted until the advent of the *Red Paintings*. They start to participate in "the totality of the disorder in the human body."[32] For anality is never isolated; it, too, is being continually displaced onto other sites in the body. The body's entire sexual organization is one of displacement from one region and/or function to another.[33] In this regard, the *Red Paintings*, and subsequently the Combines, come closer than the black paintings to "knowing" the body, by enacting its nonhierarchical displacement onto a conglomerate of heterogeneous objects. Inasmuch as they achieve this, they simulate the fantasy space that surrounds the body's functions, desires, and organization. For it is there, in the realm of fantasies which surround the interior body, that "body knowledge" is actually constructed.

Brown argues that culture functions dualistically: as a denial of the body and as a projection of that repressed body into things. Despite this, "the child knows consciously, and the adult unconsciously, that we are nothing but body" and that "all values are bodily values."[34] Rauschenberg's radical inclusion of "things" in the *Red Paintings* allows the body to be reconstituted at its *limit*, in the space of fantastic disorganization. Perhaps the *Red Paintings* are best described by a passage from Roland Barthes: "Collages are not decorative, they do not juxtapose, they conglomerate . . . their truth is etymological, they take literally the *colle*, the glue at the origin of their name; what they produce is the glutinous, alimentary paste, luxuriant and nauseating."[35]

A DREAM

I dreamt that after reading in bed I fell asleep, book across my chest. My lover came to bed and woke me. He seduced me and entered me from behind. Never having had intercourse this way before, I was surprised. Afterward I felt elation, lightness; for by having this sex my lover had voided me of all my interior substances. He had emptied me, and I drifted off into a sleep more peaceful than any I had ever known.

Special acknowledgments must be made to the invaluable comments and criticisms of Roddy Bogawa and Miwon Kwon.

Postscript

I remain enthralled by the work of Robert Rauschenberg. Pop artists such as Andy Warhol and James Rosenquist suggested that postwar life was an elaborate negotiation between the consumer and the razzle-dazzle promises of the shiny new commodity object; it turns out I preferred Rauschenberg's understanding of the self through the cast-off, the discarded, the flotsam and detritus of the everyday rather than the shiny promise of a tomorrow forever deferred.

Even though this text strikes me as a touch choppy (all cutting, no glue!), I recognize my youthful attempt to write in a manner that feels parallel to how his black and red paintings actually work. If Rauschenberg was trying to assimilate all the parts of himself into an object, then I was similarly trying equally hard to incorporate psychoanalytic theory into art writing. The psychoanalytic part seems hopelessly out of fashion at the moment—universalizing in a way that is incommensurate with our current understanding of the specificity of subjectivity and the colonialist underpinnings of almost all Enlightenment forms of knowledge. Problematic as it might be, I still think psychoanalysis offers us an architecture of language and ideas for thinking through the unconscious—for identifying its arrivals and departures in our thoughts, feelings, and behaviors. I also know of no better way to account for ambivalence; Freud says that the structure of dreams is never either/or, it is only "and." Since one of art's great strengths is its ability to sustain contradiction (rather than eliminate it), the capacity to think psychoanalytically about the kinds of questions staged by art objects remains trenchant. The trick, it seems to me, is to leave out the narrative connective tissue that wants to securely tie an interpretation of the work to a given psychoanalytic text. This essay was an early attempt at seeing what happens when you suspend any kind of cause and effect when it comes to discussing artworks and their makers, as a way of acknowledging everything that you can't know about those relationships.

Why Is the Sky Blue and Other Questions Regarding Writing

Originally published in *Documents*, no. 7 (Fall 1996): 16–19.

A version of this paper was given at the panel "The Voices of Criticism," organized by Janet Kraynak and held at Basilico Fine Arts, New York, on June 27, 1996.

As a question, "What is criticism?" is on par with "Why is the sky blue?" I know I know the answer, but I can never remember it. When confronted with the question, I often experience a kind of sputtering effect; my sentences become punctuated with "and" and "but." So my remarks here will operate in that manner: they will take the form of numbered ruminations, the conjunctions between which may be somewhat associative.

1. I never describe myself as an art critic or a cultural critic, although I have performed acts that people associate with those roles. I like to think of myself as a writer before any other institutional affiliation. I write in large part because I love to read. I love reading because I like to experience how other people's minds work. This is also, by the way, why I like art. I write something that corresponds to the term *criticism* because it is often the best way to figure out what I think. I tend to write about things that I don't fully understand because writing helps me to understand them better. I also write about things I love. I have a bad habit of falling in love with art objects.

2. The writing that appeals to me the most tends to capture a series of seemingly opposed terms. Doing so, it seems to acknowledge some of the problems bound up in the notion of criticism. I am drawn to writing that embodies the texture of the everyday but also has an acute sense of the historical (and because it seems appropriate to name names, I will give examples as I go; here, Edmund Wilson's *To the Finland Station*). I like writing that straddles the divide between subjective immersion in the material and a more traditional sense of objectivity between itself and its object of inquiry, writing that exhibits a personal sensibility, yet is also somewhat aloof (Leo Steinberg's essay "Other Criteria," Roland Barthes's *Camera Lucida*). I prefer criticism

that is generative of questions and possibilities to criticism that is prohibitive or corrective (Miwon Kwon and Dave Hickey).

What I desire most from criticism, and is often the hardest thing to find, is writing that is highly tuned to the problematics of the relational. By this I mean writing that is aware of the difficulties of positing and/or describing the relations between art objects, their makers, their historical conditions of possibility, and their various interlocutors. In other words, work that pays close attention to what happens when you put something called theory or history next to something called an art object (Mark Seltzer's *Bodies and Machines*, Carol Armstrong's *Odd Man Out*, Molly Nesbit's essays on Duchamp). This is to suggest what criticism is, for me.

3. Terry Eagleton begins his book *The Function of Criticism* with the assertion that criticism has no function. He argues that criticism developed as a form of protest against an absolutist state, and that its historical transformations have tended to be intertwined with changing systems and formations of power and state apparatuses. In other words, criticism has an intimate relation to the public sphere, both making it possible and helping to bring about its demise. Eagleton ends his book by stating that while criticism currently has no function, it must create one for itself, and that its task should be to fight the bourgeois state.

The problem with this argument and others like it is that we don't live in a bourgeois state. The terms of our world are structured by multinational global conglomerate capital. There is, in this regard, no public sphere (in the broadly Habermasian terms in which Eagleton understands it) for criticism to operate in or against. This may be one of the reasons for the development of cultural studies, an academic interdiscipline which sets out to examine the "anti-public sphere" of the entertainment industry. The impulse behind cultural studies is not wrong, especially the notion that consumers can be active rather than simply passive participants in their culture. The problem is that cultural studies has largely taken as its field an extremely narrow, albeit incredibly popular, segment of cultural expression. It sees popularity or numbers as generating interest as such. In so doing, it frames practices that have smaller fields of interest, expertise, or constituents as either elitist or uninteresting. Or, conversely, cultural studies discourse has tended to privilege the marginal as such, assuming a kind of inherent radicality in subcultural or youth culture formations.

Unfortunately, many art historians and critics feel threatened by the development of cultural studies (an anxiety felt in other disciplines as well). Certainly art magazines have turned to fashion and everything under the sun but art in order to be as hip as cultural studies. This is slightly confusing, given the fact that art is more popular now than ever before. Even though the culture wars are evil and ridiculous, they have focused an incredible amount of energy on art. And we need only think of the Vermeer and Cézanne shows, and the use of contemporary art in city festivals and tourist junkets, to see how "in demand" art is at the moment. These developments should not be read merely as cynical, corporate-sponsored gestures designed to dupe the public through an elaborate public relations ruse.

They are that, of course, but the public is also flocking to see "art." And while we need to remain aware of what "use" art is put to, if we imagine it put to no use or not open for ideological manipulation, then perhaps we have imagined art to exist in a separate sphere after all. But both cultural studies and art specialists have made a common error, of not seeing the interrelations between various manifestations of visual culture. We have set up an either/or situation instead of an apparatus that is able, or willing, to account for "both."

4. Historically, America has been suspicious of intellectuals. Leo Steinberg has argued that American artists have often wanted to be seen as "workers," doing everything they could to distance themselves from the notion of "art." Critics have been similar, billing themselves as "cultural workers" and preaching high political value for their articles. This means we have not embraced terms like *uncertainty* or *failure* in our writing or in the way we approach objects and problems. We want to explain, to convince, more than we want to ask questions or pose problems.

Given the absence of a viable public sphere, the task may not be to resuscitate an older, corrective model of criticism but to be more open and inventive in our current approaches to culture, for its terms, too, have changed dramatically. And if in fact criticism has no function, then perhaps we shouldn't try to defend it on the grounds of functionality. After all, do acts of interpretation need to be justified as such? Do we need to make huge claims for the status or function of criticism?

5. We live in a culture that rewards stupidity and mediocrity. We live in a nation of increasing homogeneity and "surburbification." We live in a culture that equates being smart with being elitist. We live in a country, and especially this state and city, that has no regard for education. In my (relatively short) lifetime, I have seen the dismantling of public and state school systems, as well as federal aid to students. This has been accompanied by the rise of the star academic, whose major concern is not pedagogy but, borrowing terminology from the sciences, "research" (i.e., the lecture circuit). These phenomena have contributed to the intense isolation of academic debates and concerns, as well as the sense of threat or danger felt on many campuses by humanities programs. (Perhaps the "crisis" or "threat" of "interdisciplinarity" is a straw man in this regard, a stand-in for the real possibility—indeed, actuality—of disciplinary elimination, in the form of the wholesale cutting of departments.) Universities have for the most part stopped teaching students how to think, let alone think critically, and instead have opted for preparing them for vocations. The university has become, in large degree, a training center.

What is to be done? A lot and not much. I think we live in a period in which the Big Questions are not so productive. I think we live in an era of the small gesture. In the Jewish faith, people are supposed to make a mitzvah every day. A mitzvah is a good deed, for in Judaism the task of faith is to make the world we live in a better place, not to put all our effort toward an afterlife. In some senses I feel that criticism, art making, writing, and teaching are like mitzvahs. In a culture that actively promotes stupidity, to express a thought, to contribute to intellectual dialogue is itself a form of struggle against the status quo. But to allow that we might "contribute to intellectual dialogue" is in some way to posit a public sphere that earlier I said doesn't really exist. Contradiction. The traditional public sphere doesn't exist; neither does the role of public intellectual. So we have to recognize, on one hand, that when we write or make art we do so in and for microcommunities, at best. On the other hand, we have to recognize that our little communities are part of the culture, that they overlap with each other, and that our friends sometimes talk to people we don't know.

To sum up, the first point that I would emphasize is that for me the series of "crises" posed by the fall of criticism, the rise of interdisciplinarity, the isolation of the art world, etc., can be traced back to the larger problem of the lack of importance education has in our culture in general. The second is that to say that what I do (write, and write criticism) has no function is not necessarily to say something cynical. I often experience this with great freedom: if it has no function, then I can do what I want with it. But then, I'm not the only person involved; usually there is an artist (and if they are alive you can count on at least one reader). To take this into consideration generates a certain obligation to write with respect and kindness, terms that in the last instance I find much more compelling than "criticism."

Postscript

I quit smoking (three packs a day) cold turkey the day after my thirtieth birthday, making this the first essay I ever wrote as a nonsmoker. It was also written when I still assumed I would be a professor. In the '90s, cultural studies, visual studies, and interdisciplinarity were some of the most charged buzzwords to be found in the university. They signaled a growing discontent with academic fields created in the eighteenth century, and a need for many to justify their "nontraditional" objects of study—ranging from television shows, vernacular photography, advertising imagery, and popular culture writ large. At the time, many of my professors were dismissive of these new ideas. I wasn't particularly bothered. It seemed to me that as long as the writing about the thing was intelligent, then anything, and everything, could be an object of study. (This was for me the import of a writer such as Greg Tate, RIP.)

Today, I suppose, this might all seem a bit quaint, though I suspect that the structure of the opposition—which was largely generational—still exists. In other words, emergent generations can't help but extend and discard the fights, language, and interests of their elders. Now that I am on the elder side of the equation, I endeavor to remember this now faded "crisis" of criticism when listening to my peers express their fears and anxieties about what will be lost as new forms of knowledge and new objects of study become ascendant.

Kerry James Marshall: Project America

Originally published in *frieze*, no. 40 (May 1998): 72–75.

According to the survey undertaken by Komar and Melamid in their recent *People's Choice* project (1994–97), the painting the average American would most like to see would consist of a landscape with an expansive blue sky, inhabited by a group of figures at leisure, all painted in vibrant shades. Perversely enough, this could be a schematic description of the work of Kerry James Marshall, whose colorful landscapes are populated by jet-black figures at leisure in the all-too-familiar housing projects that punctuate the African American neighborhoods of America's large cities. Whereas the resultant painting made by Komar and Melamid was a rather stylized, kitsch image, Marshall's work is a lush jumble of painterly styles and allusions that greatly complicates the Soviet émigrés' vision of America.

Before *People's Choice*, another, stronger version of American painting was set forth in influential articles such as Clement Greenberg's "'American-Type' Painting" (1955) and Michael Fried's "Three American Painters" (1965). Both critics contended that the strengths and virtues of Abstract Expressionism emerged from a particularly American sensibility (albeit one informed by dissident and exiled Europeans, along with some Mexican muralists), akin to the poetry of the nation's laureate Walt Whitman and the "buckeye" painting of American Sunday painters. Hung unframed like tapestries, Marshall's large canvases, often in the eight-by-twelve-foot range, would surely have dismayed Greenberg and Fried, saturated as they are with narrative content, the inclusion of text, and human figures. Nonetheless, the paintings from his *Garden Project* series (1994–95) share many of these critics' concerns. They are emphatically flat (both the figures and the swathes of deep space), and drips, dots, and strokes of paint create a kind of allover pattern effect when the paintings are seen from afar. They are, as Greenberg and Fried demanded, quite self-consciously aware of their status as paintings; indeed, they play out, with a kind of schoolyard glee, one of painting's central problems: the struggle between illusionary space and flatness.

Better Homes, Better Gardens (1994) is in part anchored by the tension between the way in which the flat black figures occupy a three-dimensional space whose surface is covered with scumbles and drips of paint that forever bring the eye to the front of the canvas. Likewise in *Watts 1963* (1995), a pictorial tension is created when the tilt of the flat green space of Nickerson Gardens runs aground at the base of the International Style modernist architecture in the painting's background, simultaneously providing no steady footing for the children in the foreground, all three of whom stare searchingly out at the viewer. Perhaps Greenberg best describes the effect of these paintings when he writes "the flattening surfaces of their canvases compelled them to move along the picture plane laterally and seek in its sheer physical size the space necessary for the telling of their kind of pictorial story."[1] Obviously, Greenberg is referring to canvases made by the men of Abstract Expressionism, and not, say, the flattened outdoor spaces of Jacob Lawrence, similarly populated by flat black figures who often moved laterally across the picture plane.

But Marshall appears equally at home in both métiers, and in his hands, abstraction ceases to be of interest as such, while figuration is hardly retrograde. Rather, to approach the problem by way of an analogy, if the institutional critique of the '80s and '90s (from Hans Haacke to Fred Wilson) can be seen as a complication of the presumed neutrality of the viewer of Minimalist sculpture, so too can Marshall's work be seen as complicating the project of modernist painting, a project that found its apotheosis not in any actual paintings but in the writings of Greenberg and Fried. And herein lies the rub, for Marshall seems to be borrowing (at will) from a variety of artistic modes of production and address, as opposed to merely rejecting out of hand the modernist doctrine set forth by two of its major rhetoricians. Yet his brand of painterly pastiche comes less from a watered-down version of postmodernism and more from the collage sensibility of Romare Bearden and Robert Rauschenberg. Marshall's paintings also appear unworried by recent critical dismissals of the modernist project, which have often manifested themselves in alternately mournful or celebratory reports of the end of painting.

This is not, however, to say that Marshall's work is anti-intellectual or anticritical. On the contrary, Marshall's paintings are a complex affair (in part due to their deceptively "simple" or "folk art" appearance): they disregard wholesale rejections of the various modernist projects in favor of a more complicated version of modernism. Their intricacy is compounded by their status as history paintings whose concerns are contemporary history and the history of painting; and the version of both stories they offer is nuanced, intertwined, and particularly generous. This is all to say that in Marshall's work, modernism is not only the painting championed by Greenberg and Fried, but the reciprocity of such painting with other cultural forms, such as architecture, popular music, and the work of artists like Lawrence and Bearden—a reciprocity continually denied by modernist critics' insistence on the purity of media.

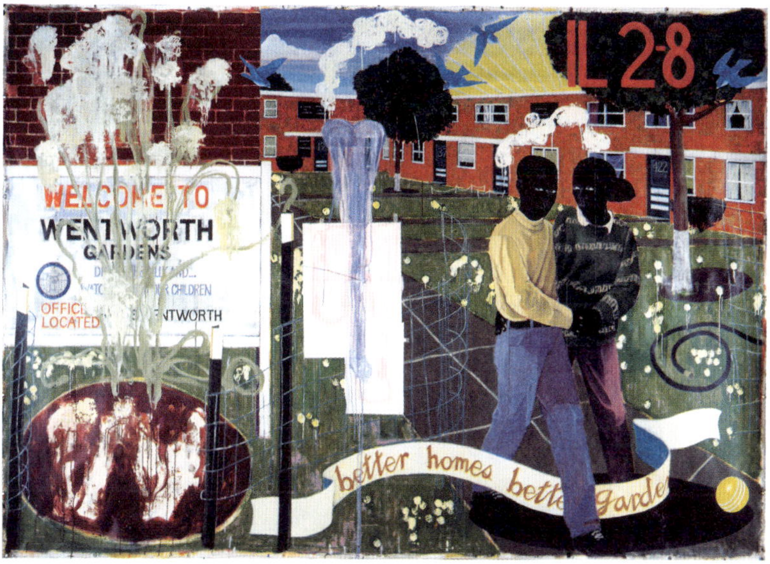

Kerry James Marshall, *Better Homes Better Gardens*, 1994,
acrylic and collage on canvas, 100 x 142 in. (254 x 360.7 cm)

The most obvious connection made by Marshall is that between the ambitions of modernist painting and architecture in postwar America. The projects and gardens that serve as the settings for Marshall's paintings are subjected to a trenchant rhetorical analysis. All the connotations of "project" are conjured up, from the scientific and social experiment to the philosophical and aesthetic. Equally, "garden" runs the associative gamut from Adam and Eve, through Renaissance delights and English country pastimes, up to its use as a common surname for inner-city housing projects. The social experiment in affordable, equitable urban housing degenerated under the continual pressures of capitalist greed and systemic racism, and resulted in one of the most obviously failed moments of modernist ambition. Meanwhile, the rhetoric of painting in modernism led to an endgame strategy that seemed to exhaust the medium's ability to say anything much at all. In these paintings, Marshall draws a morphological similarity between the two "projects"—the rigid geometrical look of International Style architecture summons the flat planes of much late modernist painting. Yet Marshall drapes decorative swirls and layers over both, slyly mocking the antidecorative paranoia of figures such as Le Corbusier and Greenberg.

The utopian desires of postwar painting and architecture are continually flagged by the streamers of text that float through the canvases, often held aloft by Disneyesque bluebirds. Truisms of American life, snippets of the commercial world's promise of continuous goodness and plenty, phrases such as "better homes, better gardens," "our town," and "there's more of everything" turn ironic in the context of housing projects where plenty has been made structurally inaccessible. That irony is a defining characteristic of modernist literature should not surprise us, given Marshall's pillaging of the field. And true to form, his irony is (slightly) modernist in feel, for it is an irony born of having believed or having wanted to believe in the thing now treated ironically, as opposed to the cool irony of contemporary experience that is the belief system or the experience in and of itself.

In different hands, this gambit might have turned cynical or maudlin. Such pitfalls are avoided—but how? It's due, I think, to Marshall's lush meditation upon how the projects of modernism—of painting and architecture—are intertwined. The paintings are about how these projects managed to develop, despite the purported intentions of their makers or the proclamations of their supporters, resolutely embedded in one another, in complex and difficult ways. The ability to articulate the *how* of this embeddedness is problematic and elusive. After all, what cause-and-effect links can we make between the development of project-style housing and the meteoric rise (and equally abrupt decline?) of "American-Type Painting"? Marshall's paintings suggest that perhaps the connective tissue is bound up in the way such histories created spaces and genres that are continually shot through with the stuff of everyday life, filled as they are with people just living their lives, and usually, despite all the odds, enjoying themselves. In *Our Town* (1995), two children careen through the landscape, a boy on a bicycle, a girl in hot pursuit. In *Better Homes, Better Gardens*, a young couple's stroll evokes the lyrics of Meshell Ndegeocello: "Step, step, step into the projects where I found love."

Music is always implicit in Marshall's work; the gorgeous brightness of the colors, the layered styles, and the disjointed space all have a particularly aural effect. And it is invariably popular music: the extreme blackness of the figures evokes Curtis Mayfield's "We the People Who Are Darker than Blue"; the flat blazing sun that rises in the background of many of the paintings recalls Sly and the Family Stone's "Hot Fun in the Summertime." In *Past Times* (1997), the musical undertow is made explicit, as a father and son sit in a park together, listening to music, while the background is ironically populated with African American figures enjoying the stereotypical upper-middle-class white pastimes of golf and waterskiing. The father listens to Smokey Robinson sing "Just My Imagination," while the son's radio dispenses lyrics by Snoop Dogg: "With my mind on my money and my money on my mind."

Looking at Marshall's work, one often finds oneself with snippets of music in one's head, the catchy lyrics that circulate in our minds as we move through time and space. But more importantly, perhaps, is the way in which we are identified generationally by the music that ends up

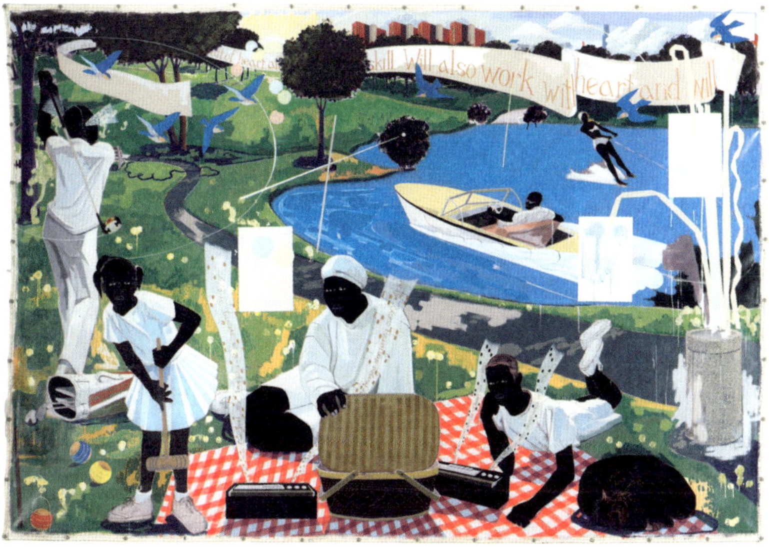

Kerry James Marshall, *Past Times*, 1997, acrylic and collage on canvas, 108 ¼ x 157 in. (275 x 398.8 cm)

revolving in our heads. So that, once again, Marshall has refrained from a monolithic notion, this time of African American identity, and displayed instead the polyphony that is structural to all social and cultural formations.

Dave Hickey has recently written that popular music is the dominant art form of the American twentieth century, so much so, he maintains, that Abstract Expressionism is unthinkable without bebop, and Warhol inconceivable without rock and roll.[2] This seems true of Marshall's mix, for amid the problems of painting and the disastrous results of International Style architecture there remains the continuity of everyday life, which moves along at its own geological pace, a continuity for which the soundtrack is popular music. Part of what these paintings are about, then, are the ways in which different forms such as music, art, and architecture are experienced as coterminous and inextricable from one another. They are also about the utter and complete inextricability of African American history from American history, indeed African American experience from the American experience (whatever that is, as nebulous and expansive as such a category would have to be). If, for Marshall, modernism is disallowed its traditional "purity" of media, so too American experience—be it New York School painting, modernist urban planning, or popular music—is shown to be about the inextricability of Black and white experience. While the powers that be continue to maintain the differences (be they aesthetic or social) in order to protect the privileges garnered by such acts of exclusion,

Marshall's ironic text banners continually gesture toward the promise of equality and the reality of shared experience. And while these ideas may now seem to be a failed utopian vision, his paintings suggest that such a premise should not be abandoned, that the histories of American-type painting, and all of the things that run through and around such a venture, may still be open for revision.

Postscript

The fickleness of the art world can never be underestimated. I have not thought about the Russian conceptual art duo Komar and Melamid in decades; and when this was written they were the popular figures, while Kerry James Marshall was perceived to be "outside" of the dominant conversation.

Modernity, as a project, is no longer the primary frame through which Marshall's work is understood. Now he is seen as the ur-figurative painter. I think if I wrote this essay on Marshall today, I'd be looking much more closely at his use of abstraction. For instance, the extreme blackness of his figures does much to exaggerate the tension between foreground and background, and signals to the viewer that the "black" they see is the black of paint. His use of black is entirely bound up in the act of representation, and not born of a desire for the image as such to be "truthful" and/or "accurate." We can see Marshall's use of color, pattern, and decoration as a set of tactics designed to call the picture plane into question, rather than secure its one-to-one legibility. All this might lead one to argue that his central project is just as much a profound querying of race as a *form* of abstraction, as it is a consolidating of race through, and in, representation.

THINKING ABOUT MARCEL DUCHAMP, OR WHY I THINK A PHD IN ART HISTORY IS STILL A GOOD IDEA

In the fall of 1997, I defended my PhD dissertation at Cornell University in Ithaca, New York. The dissertation was a hybrid: partly monographic, about Marcel Duchamp, and partly problem-based, as it was specifically concerned with the readymade. I was attempting to place Duchamp's readymades within the historical and social context of New York and Paris in the first two decades of the twentieth century. However, I think what I was really after was a means for thinking deeply about what art was, what it did, and what "use" it might serve. I wanted to ask questions about things a lot of folks felt were obvious: How do we decide what is art? Whose interests are served by art? What was the role of museums with relation to art's many meanings?

This was important to me because I was perennially turned on by the twentieth century's avant-garde aims to broker a relationship between art and life. It seemed to me that art historians talked a good game about the art part of that equation, but they frequently left out the "life" part. Since the everyday—and pretty much anything having to do with domesticity and mass consumption—had been relegated to the sphere of "women" (for me an unquestioned term at that time), all of this felt a bit renegade because I was essentially interested in what a feminist take on readymades might look like.

In many ways, I grew up with Duchamp. My earliest essays on his work were about the readymade—complete with their schoolyard puns and broad physical comedy. "Rrose Sélavy Goes Shopping" was part of my dissertation, and in it I was trying to figure out both of us—myself and Duchamp. I was, and still am, deeply enamored with housewifery—I love to cook, decorate, make a home, entertain. None of these forms of labor were given much credence or value, and I (perversely) saw in Duchamp a kind of fellow traveler: he too was interested in the problems of the everyday and in the critical role taste plays with regard to everything from food to fashion to art. As a young adult trying to find my way, I found that Duchamp's oeuvre permitted me to marry my theoretical, aesthetic, and personal interests.

Upon getting my first big museum job, I became concerned with what exactly constituted "work," as I was never quite sure at the end of the day if I had done "enough" work. The fact that Duchamp had actually made art via buying his sculptures already made and then, further, audaciously claimed to have abandoned art for a life of playing chess resonated deeply with me. Thinking about whether or not Duchamp had done enough work became the catalyst for my first big exhibition, *Work Ethic* (2003). It turns out I wasn't the only person wondering whether what I did when I went to the museum and arranged pictures in a room was *work*. Artists were in their studios wondering about what constituted labor as well, at the same time as sociologists were writing about labor as the postwar US economic engine shifted from manufacturing to service/entertainment.

My near-ruthless use of Duchamp's oeuvre to work out my own problems continued. For example, in 2000 I found my one true love, and even though I am a hopeless romantic, because I am queer I never expected to marry. And then the day came when that became possible (my wife and I were married in Massachusetts in 2006), and I turned to Duchamp once more to make sense of it all. I built an entire exhibition, *Part Object Part Sculpture* (2006), around the object Duchamp gave to his wife Teeny Matisse as a wedding present. What could Duchamp's turn to the handmade tell me not only about the history of postwar sculpture but also about repetition and singularity—which, let's face it, is a working definition of marriage? And then, once I got married, and as marriage rights were slowly extended, state by state, to queer folk, I found myself confronting the very serious and extremely adult scenario of the merger of love and desire. Duchamp was there again, and my last Duchamp essay (to date) was written about *Étant donnés*.

Here is my impassioned plea for why I think getting a PhD is one of the best things a person could ever do: although some may see it as a pathway to an academic job, a set of hoops to jump through in the game of professional validation, I learned many other things from the exercise. Graduate school gave me the time (nearly five uninterrupted years!) to read both widely and specifically. At that particular moment in my life, I read everything ever written on Duchamp. That level of expertise is an unparalleled privilege. Full-time employment offers no such luxury. I learned how to tell a big story, how to read tens of thousands of pages so that I could write three hundred. I learned how to edit, how to focus, how to let some details go, and how to amplify others. I learned a lot about myself and what I was capable of. My dissertation taught me to be fearless—because the process of writing it not only taught me what I think but, much more importantly, how to think. And last but not least, a dissertation can be a gold mine of ideas. Mine led to a handful of articles, two major exhibitions—*Work Ethic* and *Part Object Part Sculpture*—and a lifetime's interest in what we mean when we say "art" or "taste" or "labor."

The artist Lari Pittman once told me that he thought his job as an artist was to go out into the world and report back on his findings. I found that Duchamp had been doing just that. And as he aged, his findings shifted in tenor and affect. I found that as I aged, I could track my experience of adulthood against his. I suspect I'm not done with Duchamp. I reckon there are other experiences he's reported back about that I may not yet be old enough to understand. I do know that his tombstone bears one of my favorite epigrams, and it stands like a beacon of sorts, about the last inevitable experience we all share. It reads, "And besides, it's always the others that die." I know there's an essay in there somewhere.

Work Ethic

Originally published in *Work Ethic*, ed. Helen Molesworth (Baltimore: Baltimore Museum of Art; University Park: Pennsylvania State University Press, 2003), 25–51.

Some people, they like to go out dancing, and other people, they have to work.
—The Velvet Underground

One of the more curious attributes of avant-garde art after World War II was the increasing disregard for traditional artistic skills such as drawing, painting, and sculpting. Robert Rauschenberg's legendary *Erased de Kooning Drawing* (1953) consisted of just that: the artist erasing a drawing by Willem de Kooning. Frank Stella's *Club Onyx* (1959) is a painting of black stripes of house paint; their width is determined by the store-bought brush. And when Robert Morris made *Box with the Sound of Its Own Making* (1961), critic Leo Steinberg described it as:

> A plain wooden box and a tape recording of the sawing and hammering that put it together. The work strips the adverb from the definition of art. A thing done—period.[1]

Steinberg had distilled the problem. Here was a work of art content to be described in the language of *work* as opposed to that of art. Sawing and hammering had replaced drawing and composition. And in replacing the skills of art with the activities of work, artists began to make art that eschewed artifice and illusion and instead presented itself to the world as it was: a box with the sound of its own making, an object insistent upon the labor of its maker.

This essay argues that one unifying principle of the extraordinarily heterogeneous field of post–World War II avant-garde art was a concern with the problematic of artistic labor. A historical convergence had occurred. Just as artists relinquished traditional artistic skills and the production of discrete art objects, the status of labor and the production of goods in the culture at large were also changing profoundly as the American industrial economy, based in manufacturing, shifted to a postindustrial economy rooted in managerial and service labor. The concern with artistic labor manifested itself in implicit and explicit ways as much of the advanced art of the period managed, staged, mimicked, ridiculed, and challenged the cultural and societal anxieties around the shifting terrain and definitions of work.

One of modernism's many promises was that art offered possible resistance to an increasingly regimented and segmented life under the auspices of industrialization. From the Arts and Crafts movement to the Bauhaus, the history of modern art is shot through with the dream of an integration of the realms of art and life, work and leisure, such that the alienation produced by the fragmented nature of modern labor would be ameliorated. This essay argues that in the period following World War II, artists came to see themselves not as artists producing (in) a dream world but as workers in capitalist America.[2] They navigated the avant-garde desire to merge art and life under dramatically different social structures than their modernist predecessors. Artists during the 1960s made art in the midst of the corporatization of American culture, the professionalization of the category of "artist," and a burgeoning New York market for contemporary art. These sociohistorical forces placed extraordinary pressures on artists to redefine themselves and their work, and often they did so by thinking through and acting out the profound transformations of late-twentieth-century labor in their work.

It is a well-worn tale that the end of World War II ushered in an era of remarkable economic growth for the American economy. Just as the manufacturing base quickly reconfigured itself to meet the needs of a wartime economy, with similar ease it transformed into a manufacturing economy of commodities for an increasingly affluent and mobile middle class. This, in turn, was accompanied by the rise of the managerial class, whose labor was no longer defined by the production of objects. Rather, the work of management was to oversee the labor of others, and it often involved making representations of work, such as diagrams, graphs, and flowcharts.[3] Paul Osterman and the other authors of *Working in America* describe how "at least since the New Deal, a clear view of how work is organized has been embedded both in law and policy. On that view, there is a sharp and identifiable divide between the activities of managers and those of workers, the former being responsible for conception and planning and the latter for execution."[4] Joseph Pine and James Gilmore note in *The Experience Economy*, however, that "it was in the 1950s when services first employed more than 50 percent of the US population, that the Service Economy overtook the Industrial (although this was not recognized until long after the fact)."[5] While the recognition of the change in labor demographics from a manufacturing to a service economy may have been slow in coming, management's cultural ascendancy aided this shift. Hence, Pine and Gilmore argue that with the codification and rise of management, the work executed by workers has also been transformed from goods ("tangible products that companies standardize and then inventory") into services ("intangible activities performed for a particular client").[6] While the manufacturing base of the United States was diminishing, the production of goods increasingly happened elsewhere—usually in "unseen" faraway places such as China, Korea, Japan, Malaysia, and India, and, as the decades wore on, in places such as Mexico, closer to home but still just as much out of sight. Ironically, the manufactured commodity's vanishing in America was accompanied by the disappearance of the traditional art object as well; the changing economy had a significant impact on how postwar art was made. This

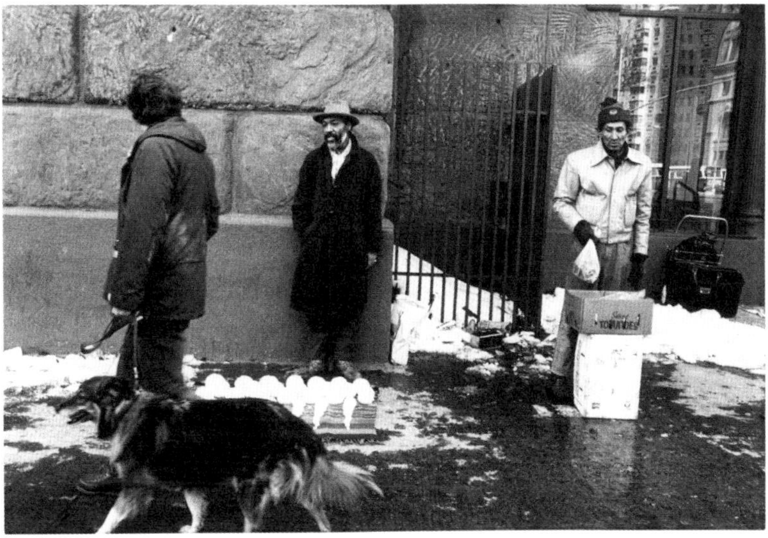

Dawoud Bey, *David Hammons, Bliz-aard Ball Sale, Cooper Square, New York*, 1983, resin-coated print, 8 x 10 in. (20.3 x 25.4 cm)

economic transformation was accompanied by an artistic one that further shaped artists' exploration of the problem of artistic labor: the increasing influence and importance of the work of Marcel Duchamp.

Conceivably, no twentieth-century artist was more ambivalent about artistic labor than Duchamp. In the teens, he purchased mass-produced commodities (most famously a urinal he titled *Fountain* [1917]) and dubbed them "readymades." The readymades defied two historical definitions of art: namely that art should be unique and that it should be produced by a highly trained artist with a requisite set of learned skills. By challenging the necessity of traditional artistic labor and the value of unique objects and by establishing a potential continuum between the space and activities of everyday life and the rarified realm of art, Duchamp's readymades constituted the most serious attack on the category of art since the Renaissance.

Far from destroying art, Duchamp's profound challenge ultimately served to create an enormous field of aesthetic possibility. It helped liberate artists from conventional modes of working, contributing to a climate that permitted and rewarded an increasingly porous idea of art's possibilities. Artists no longer needed to content themselves with the production of visually aesthetic objects. Art became a realm of ideas. This freedom did not come immediately; the most important reception of Duchamp in the United States occurred in the late 1950s through John Cage, Jasper Johns, and Robert Rauschenberg, all of whom rejected the supposed purity and emotionalism of Abstract Expressionism and enabled a fuller exploration of Duchamp's questioning of skill and labor.[7] Notoriously heterogeneous, the art of the 1960s and 1970s produced a wide range of movements, including Minimalism, Conceptual art, Fluxus, performance, process, feminist art, and Happenings. The new art was described in various ways. It was dematerialized; it pursued the aesthetics of silence; it was anti-illusionistic; it was conceptual; it was anti-commodity; it was democratized. The new art remained, however, extremely difficult for lay viewers to understand or interpret. Its difficulty lay, in large measure, in its double rejection: as artists stopped employing traditional artistic skills, they also stopped making works of art that imagined the museum or the collector's home as their final destination. Instead, artists attempted to make works of art that would actively resist easy assimilation into the realm of the art market, where art was seen to be one luxury commodity among many.[8]

The liberation of art from traditional artistic skills, the production of a unique object, and the primacy of the visual necessitated new aesthetic criteria less focused on appearance and more concerned with ideas. Morris's *Box with the Sound of Its Own Making* and Rauschenberg's oeuvre provided Steinberg with a new hermeneutic, one he went so far as to call postmodern. In his deeply influential essay "Other Criteria" (1968), he stated plainly that new art presents itself not as "art" but as "work," and as such needs to be analyzed in sociocultural terms in addition to those taken from the discourse of art.

Much as the category of art was in question, the role of the artist was being rearticulated. Two texts also important to the formation of postmodern ideas declared the newly problematized author/artist. One was a short speech delivered by Duchamp, "The Creative Act" (1957), and the other was an essay by French theorist Roland Barthes, "The Death of the Author" (1967). Both appeared in the eclectic avant-garde journal *Aspen* in 1967—Duchamp's spoken by the artist and distributed on a floppy record, and Barthes's in its first English translation. Both texts would become legendary. Duchamp's argument became a received idea in art schools across the United States, and Barthes's text would become standard college reading in the humanities.

Duchamp's lecture put forward the then radical idea that "the creative act is not performed by the artist alone." Denying both the autonomy of the artwork and the privileging of the artist's intention, Duchamp instead turned the focus of attention upon the viewer, stating that "the spectator brings the work in contact with the external world by deciphering and interpreting its inner qualifications and thus adds his contribution to the creative act."[9] Barthes similarly challenged the idea that "the explanation of a work is always sought in the man or woman who produced it, as if it were always in the end . . . the voice of a single person, the *author* 'confiding' in us." Citing the public and ideological character of language, he suggested that the author could no longer be seen as an omnipotent, singular, and codified dispenser of meaning. Instead, the reader is the privileged subject, for the "reader is the space on which all the quotations that make up a writing are inscribed. . . . A text's unity lies not in its origin but its destination." Emphatically, Barthes's essay ends with the oft-quoted line, "The birth of the reader must be at the cost of the death of the Author."[10] By positioning the reader as the final destination of a text, Barthes's essay rhymes in spirit with Duchamp's. Both shift the value and emphasis away from the producer of the work of art or literature in favor of the viewer or reader.[11]

"The Death of the Author" crystallized a point of view by succinctly describing an increasingly prevalent form of anti-authorial artistic practice. Many artists and writers in the 1960s found the idea of the author's metaphoric death liberating, and they deployed a variety of means to undermine or downplay their own authorship. Some (e.g., John Cage) used chance operations, feeling that when the conscious choice of the artist was eliminated, so too was artistic intention. Others (e.g., Sol LeWitt) adopted serial systems, reasoning that a predetermined mathematical logic diminished the display of artistic subjectivity. Many artists (e.g., Donald Judd) felt increasingly comfortable turning over the production of their work to paid assistants and fabricators. Still others (e.g., John Baldessari) turned to the camera, hoping that a mechanical tool would lessen any trace of their hand. And then there were those (e.g., Yoko Ono) who turned the completion of the artwork over to the viewer in a literal way, creating participatory proposals that were only considered "art" once engaged by a viewer.

When artists challenged the role of the author, they also, wittingly or not, questioned the status and even value of their labor. In effect, to problematize the role of the author/artist is to place the producer of the text/art object in question. By diminishing traces of their intentionality and subjectivity, attributes of the work of art usually associated with its fabrication were removed: traces of the artist's hand, reliance upon a learned set of skills, a prolonged duration for the creation of a work, a studio complete with tools and equipment. Even though artists embraced these new anti-authorial modes of artistic production, they did so at some peril. Were artists still required, in any subjective or authorial specificity? (Anyone can follow through a serial system, click the shutter on a camera, and throw a pair of dice.) If not, what exactly was their role? What was to constitute their labor? This was felt particularly keenly in the visual arts, where one effect of the ebbing of the authorial role was that the resultant art was often only tenuously an object.

Sol LeWitt, whose work was also included in *Aspen*, discussed the new artistic process in the following way:

> The aim of the artist would not be to instruct the viewer but to give him information. Whether the viewer understands this information is incidental to the artist; he cannot foresee the understanding of all his viewers. He would follow his predetermined premise to its conclusion avoiding subjectivity. . . . The serial artist does not attempt

> to produce a beautiful or mysterious object but functions merely as a clerk cataloguing the results of his premise.[12]

That LeWitt imagines himself a clerk is not surprising. The newly problematized relationship to artistic authorship and its attendant modes of artistic labor hardly happened in a vacuum. America's shift from an industrial to a postindustrial society was to have as profound an effect upon art as it had upon the daily lives of all workers. Far from being a timeless and unchanging entity, art of the 1960s reflected the rise of a highly professionalized managerial class and the simultaneous development of a service economy.

Some art historians have viewed the strategies of anti-authorship, such as LeWitt's imagining of himself as a clerk, as part of the "de-skilling" of the artist. Yet it is more accurate to treat this transformation as a re-skilling, for as artists weathered the change from a manufacturing to a service economy, it stands to reason that the declining value for one set of skills would be accompanied by a rising value for another. So what then were the new sets of skills needed to be an artist? What kinds of artistic labor would come to be seen as legitimate within this new socioeconomic context?

In the early 1940s, there were sixty candidates for graduate degrees in studio art enrolled in eleven American institutions. By 1950–51, there were 322 candidates at thirty-two institutions. The trend continued through the end of the century. Thirty-one new master of fine arts (MFA) programs opened in the 1960s, and forty-four in the 1970s. From 1990 to 1995, ten thousand MFA degrees were awarded in the United States. These numbers are astounding. What do they mean for artists and the art they produce?

In *Art Subjects*, historian Howard Singerman persuasively argues that after World War II, artists were increasingly professionalized in academic art programs in the United States. With the GI Bill fueling the professionalization of degree-granting art departments, the way art was taught changed markedly. This shift is most evident in the diminishing importance accorded to the traditional skill of drawing—long the core of artistic training. The predominance of Abstract Expressionism, with its emphasis on unconscious processes and a highly rigorous version of abstraction, often meant that the technical skill of drawing was no longer encouraged. In this context, Rauschenberg's *Erased de Kooning Drawing* takes on a new (and renewed) significance. Of all of the Abstract Expressionists, de Kooning was renowned for his draftsmanship, something that Rauschenberg was doubtlessly aware of when he asked the artist for a drawing he would subsequently erase. That Rauschenberg should request to erase one of de Kooning's drawings can be seen less as an anti-Oedipal urge and more as an acknowledgment that one form of artistic skill was being supplanted by another—draftsmanship erased in the face of Conceptual art's nascent ascendancy. Despite the lack of technical skill required to erase the drawing, Rauschenberg claimed to have worked very hard to erase the drawing well. And the results of his hard labor are evident: not even the slightest trace of the drawing remains.

As art departments continued their professionalization and artists continued to undermine the significance of technical skill, contradictory ideas emerged about the teaching of art. On the one hand, the idea arose that art could not be systematically taught. On the other, there was a consensus that art could be learned and that it was acquired in large measure by being around artists and listening to them talk. This "talk" took place in the form of the "crit," the guest artist lecture, and the phenomenon of the studio visit, all of which signaled a significant break with traditional academic art training. In such training, the "assignment and product are given in the same language"—life drawing, for instance. In the postwar period, however, a split occurred, and the language of the "assignment" was quite different from the language of the finished product. For example, the assignment might be to "make a void," a kind of problem solving that can take any form.[13] If the separation of mental labor from manual labor is one of the hallmarks of managerial professionalization, then, Singerman argues, postwar artistic training was designed to train artists in a theoretical discourse separate and distinct from manual labor. The result was a generation of college-educated artists whose skills were no longer manual and visual but largely theoretical and verbal. The rise of the MFA artist—an artist trained in large measure to become a teacher in MFA programs and whose proficiencies are mental rather than manual—reflects the shift in labor experienced by the vast majority of American workers. And just as many Americans now earn their livings without ever making a salable commodity, many artists have stopped making commodities such as painting and sculpture designed to be bought and sold on the market.

Yet there was (and remains) a curious resistance to the idea of the professional artist—a person for whom being an artist was a job, a way to make a livelihood (often through teaching) as much as an existential "calling." When Harold Rosenberg, an influential critic of the 1950s and a champion of Abstract Expressionism, wrote "Everyman a Professional" in 1959, he opined:

> Thus the essential mark of a profession is its evolution of a unique language. . . . The more incomprehensible the lingo is to outsiders, the more thoroughly it identifies the profession as such and elevates it out of the reach of mere amateurs and craftsmen.[14]

Even though Rosenberg criticized artists for this development, his commentary supports Singerman's contention that part of what it meant to become an artist in the late 1950s and 1960s was to learn how to talk about art with other art professionals. But the romantic myths of the artist as outcast, the artist as lone genius, the artist as inspired (not trained) or, conversely, the artist as one possessing a highly distinctive set of laboriously learned skills still held sway in the popular imagination. In these scenarios, the rise of the professional artist was viewed as a cynical degradation of art's magical or auratic status. The nostalgia for certain sets of skills was countered, however, by a generation of artists who acknowledged that art and artists are both in and of the world, helping produce it and being produced by it. In this light, the use of a non-object-based art made by an academically trained artist and described in an increasingly professionalized language echoes similar transformations in other forms of production (of both knowledge and objects) from the university to the corporate boardroom, as postwar culture at large came to be dominated by the logic of the management and service sectors of the economy.

The professionalization of the artist did not happen immediately or easily. As artists grappled with the emergent terms of a postindustrial world in which the conditions of labor were changing dramatically, one of their responses was to portray themselves as workers. The Abstract Expressionists maintained and helped to promulgate the largely European myth of the isolated artist in his studio, but, as art historian Caroline Jones argues, they also presented themselves as workers by participating in the creation of a documentary image-world of the artist at work in his studio. These images varied greatly: artists presented themselves as members of the working class, as typified by photographs of Jackson Pollock in his work shirts and blue jeans, and as members of the business class, as seen in Barnett Newman's professional images, complete with suit and bow tie.[15] Yet it was the emergence of Frank Stella and Andy Warhol that set into motion a new set of practices as well as images for the artist as worker-professional. Both Stella and Warhol made art where the interior life of the artist, as expressed through an individualized mark, was utterly absent from the final artistic process. To do so, both adopted a mechanistic production apparatus: Stella developed a highly regimented stripe of paint, equal to the width of the store-bought paintbrush, and Warhol borrowed mass-produced images that he subsequently silk-screened in an assembly-line fashion.

And while Stella shocked the art world with his idea of an "executive artist" who has others do his work for him, Warhol actualized this model when he established the Factory and famously quipped that if people wanted to know about his work, they should ask his assistants. Despite their embrace of the executive model, both artists also flirted with other forms of identification, projecting an affinity with members of the working class. Stella's adoption of house painting's tools and techniques was accompanied by the following recollection: "It sounds a little dramatic, being an 'art worker.' I just wanted to do it and get it over with so I could go home and watch TV."[16] Here, Stella mimed the stance of the hourly worker, not the corporate executive, and it is telling that Hollis Frampton's photographs of Stella painting in the studio are a strictly blue-jeans-and-white-T-shirt affair. According to Jones, Warhol was also ambivalent about his role as either art worker or business executive, which may account for his vacillation between a blue-jeans aesthetic and his position as the head of the Factory.

For some, the idea of the artist as worker-professional was less ambivalently structured. Allan Kaprow's description of the contemporary artist in "Should the Artist Become a Man of the World?" (1964) matter-of-factly states that artists "resemble the personnel in other specialized disciplines and industries in America," so much so that "on the street they are indistinguishable from the middle-class from which they come and towards whose mores—practicality, security, and self-advancement—they tend to gravitate." The problem for Kaprow was not professional status but that the artist must work within a "subtle social complex whose terms he is only beginning to understand."[17]

An important aspect of this new social complex was the post–World War II emergence of New York as the capital of the art world. In addition to the influx of European artists during the war and the rise of an increasingly lucrative art market, part of New York's becoming the mecca of the art world was the phenomenon of loft conversion. Wildly different in scale and effect than the garret apartments of prewar artists, loft spaces were typically found in abandoned light manufacturing buildings. In the illuminating study *Loft Living: Culture and Capital in Urban Change*, Sharon Zukin tracks the rise of SoHo and loft living, demonstrating how artists displaced light manufacturing only to be displaced themselves by members of the elite service industry.[18]

One unique quality of SoHo was that artists from disparate artistic movements lived and worked there simultaneously. Stella occupied a loft space on West Broadway in 1958, and Alison Knowles and George Maciunas, both Fluxus artists, were some of the first artists to buy buildings in SoHo. Kaprow's Happenings took place in SoHo lofts; artists involved in the new sculpture (Donald Judd, Robert Morris, Richard Serra) lived and worked there, as did Conceptual artists (Sol LeWitt, Mel Bochner). This highly abbreviated list suggests that no matter how divergent the aesthetic concerns and practices, the infrastructure of SoHo was a common denominator in putting pressure on artists to perform or stage their work in new ways. For instance, the Artist Tenants Association was formed in 1960–61 in order to protect artists' right to live in lofts zoned for manufacturing. In their attempts to gain the attention of Robert Wagner, then mayor of New York, they threatened to boycott all art exhibitions in the city unless officials stopped their eviction policies. That artists could bond together as professionals and envision themselves as participants in a boycott already conveys a level of professional identity through affiliation. It also suggests that they understood their identities as not only the producers of culture but also its potentially primary consumers. Artists thus straddled the nascent economic transformation from production to consumption within their own professional identities.

The loft laws were resolved to ensure artists' ability to inhabit them. But residency came with a requirement that the spaces be studio-residences: the lofts could not be used only for living (as opposed to living and working).[19] Hence the edict *to work* was in place as a mandatory component of the legal solidity of SoHo as the artists' neighborhood. If one of the most enduring legacies of the early-twentieth-century avant-garde was the desire to blur the boundaries between art and life, then loft living may have furthered this initiative. The combination of the scale and historicity of such spaces, along with the new legalistic imperative to produce at a time when production was very much in question, was bound to have an enormous influence on contemporary art practices.

Artists stood at a crossroads in the 1960s. The influences exerted upon them and their conditions of possibility were extraordinary: the postwar reception of Duchamp, a profound alteration in the conception of the artist's role, the shift in the economic structure of the Western world, the rise of a new type of academic art training, and a dramatic change in the site of artistic production all came to bear on the production and reception of avant-garde culture. This essay has argued that shifts in artistic practice were bound up with a changing economic structure. The transformation from an industrial to a postindustrial society is perhaps best described by Ernest Mandel, who historicized this period as late capitalism. For Mandel, one of late capitalism's most distinctive characteristics is the spread of the logic of work into all areas of life, resulting in an increasingly bureaucratic and disciplinary society. He writes, "Mechanization, standardization, over-specialization and parcelization of labor, which in the past determined only the realm of commodity production in actual industry, now penetrate into all sectors of social life." Mandel continues with a particularly germane example: "The 'profitability' of universities, music academies, and museums starts to be calculated in the same way as that of brick works or screw factories."[20] The visual and plastic arts were particularly well poised to negotiate this historic shift, as the value found in art has traditionally been positioned within a dialectical set of social practices. Produced by both mental and manual labor, it is also a mixed site of leisure and work. Furthermore, throughout the twentieth century the avant-garde has set out to blur the distinctions between art and life. All these factors contribute to contemporary art's increasing porousness to the economic and social conditions of its production as well as its ability to represent and critique these transformations.

At this crossroads, much of the most important and challenging art of the period staged the problem of labor's transformation, its new divisions, and the increasingly blurred boundaries between work and leisure. Generally speaking, artists responded in one of four ways. Some played the part of both manager and worker, restaging the late-nineteenth- and early-twentieth-century division of labor. Others, emboldened by the professionalization of the category of artist and liberated by an economic shift away from manufacturing, simplified things by adopting a purely managerial position. Still others had a prescient understanding that the burgeoning service economy would ultimately give way to a leisure economy based on experience.[21] These artists turned to participatory strategies, directly involving the audience in the art. And finally (although this mapping is by no means chronological), there were those artists who experimented with not working at all, or at least with trying to figure out how to work as little as possible.

Many artists staged the tension of the changing definitions of labor by mimicking the logic of labor's division into mental and manual realms. By establishing a task and then performing it, these artists acted out the roles of both manager and worker. It follows that in the absence of traditional artistic skills and concrete objects, the artist's studio, the space of artistic production, became a highly charged arena. What exactly was an artist supposed to do there? Bruce Nauman laconically presented the problem as follows: "If you see yourself as an artist and you function in a studio . . . you sit in a chair or pace around. And then the question goes back to what is art? And art is what an artist does, just sitting around the studio."[22] Yet Nauman never simply sat. He dictated for himself a set of task-like activities—playing a note on the violin, bouncing balls rhythmically, walking around the studio in an exaggerated manner—all of which were filmed, transforming the studio into a performative arena.

If Nauman's activities betray a literal, futile, and restless quality, then Vito Acconci's *Trademarks* (1970) can be seen as a humorous send-up of some of the anxiety provoked by the studio. In *Trademarks,* Acconci bit himself repeatedly on the arm and leg, trying to make a perfect dental impression on his skin. The impression was inked and "prints" were made, which were subsequently given away as gifts. In a parodic gesture of artistic mark making, Acconci deploys his body as the exclusive agent of artistic production, yet he does so in a way that empties out any particular subjective dimension. Not quite as efficient (or as iconographic) as a thumbprint, *Trademarks* offers an unskilled but physically arduous art activity, suggesting that even though the artwork was just barely an object, it still required a lot of effort to make.

Artists who assigned themselves tasks and then performed them rejected traditional artistic media and their attendant skills and turned instead to a presentation of the work of art in the language of "a thing done," a task performed. In doing so, many developed an obsessive reliance upon documentation.[23] Often the films and photographs produced in this manner are fairly banal, produced with a deadpan lack of affect that is usually quite humorous. Yet the humor masks a certain level of anxiety surrounding the making of the art. When is the work finished? Is it "enough" work? It repeatedly appears that mimicking the strategies of efficient and productive labor in a parodic and deliberately unproductive way both enacts the artist's desire to embody a stereotypical American work ethic while simultaneously critiquing it. Consider Chris Burden's *Honest Labor* (1979), in which the artist himself dug a ditch over a period of three days while acting as a visiting artist at an art school. Typical of much task-based work and process art, the end "product" or result of *Honest Labor* is "useless": a ditch without a purpose. What is valued is the *process* and/or the performance of the artist. Elevating the process was seen as a way to de-emphasize the traditional values—both aesthetic and financial—attributed to the final product or artwork. Here, the artist does an "honest day's work," yet refuses to produce a luxury commodity object.

Artists emphatically suggested in the 1960s that the importance of a work of art lay more in how it was made rather than in the final product. Often referred to as process art, this shift in emphasis was offered as a critique of the commodity status of art and was bound up with artists' desire to retain a degree of autonomy for the artistic act—a last-stand protection of sorts against an increasingly commodified world. Another way to conceptualize "process" is to read it as "artistic labor," for the process through which a thing is made is where its labor resides. So, although we have seen that during the 1960s the art object underwent an internal split between mental and manual labor, with the privilege continually afforded to the realm of thinking, the emphasis on process provided a way for artists to maintain and even give value to the manual labor still inherent in the production of an object. Hence Burden's highly physical activity of ditch digging is ultimately presented as a photograph and a typed description of the activity—manual labor presented in the aesthetic of Conceptual art.

Process art and task-based works were not the only places in which the language and logic of work were mimed by artists. Conceptual artists (perhaps more than any other group) disavowed the final object or product status of art, opting instead to emphasize cognitive processes. In doing so, they often relegated the production of their work to others, replicating the logic of managerial labor. LeWitt seemed to have no trouble in taking a classic white-collar stand in regard to work's production. In his widely read "Paragraphs on Conceptual Art," he states, "When an artist uses a conceptual form of art, it means that all of the planning and decisions are made beforehand and the execution is a perfunctory affair. The idea becomes a machine that makes the art."[24]

But machines do not make LeWitt's wall drawings; assistants do, further completing the professionalized separation of mental and manual forms of artistic labor. As many Conceptual artists relied heavily upon the language and logic of the instruction, they functioned like managers, producing graphs, charts, and diagrams with directions for others on how to perform the labor required to make the object. Art historian Benjamin Buchloh described this aspect of Conceptual art as the "aesthetic of administration," arguing that "this aesthetic identity is structured much the way this class's social identity is, namely, as one of merely administering labor and production (rather than producing) and of the distribution of commodities."[25] In this context, John Baldessari's presentation of himself as a "nine-to-five artist," reflecting his daily routine of going to the studio, takes on a new resonance—even if, when he arrived at the studio one day in 1972, he taped himself singing LeWitt's "Sentences on Conceptual Art" to the tune of "Camptown Races" and other songs.[26] Baldessari's *Commissioned Paintings* (1969) consist of a series of works painted by Sunday painters chosen and approached by Baldessari, who asked each of them to faithfully represent banal snapshots of a friend pointing at objects in a domestic and/or studio space. Each painting was subsequently taken to a sign painter, who "captioned" the paintings with the phrase "This is a painting by Pat Nelson" (or whoever the Sunday painter was). Finally, Baldessari placed his signature on the back of the canvas. The *Commissioned Paintings* are a witty jab at the problem of the artist as genius. They also restage the division of labor inherent in the production of all commodities. Baldessari's critical gesture thus becomes that of drawing attention to the problem of the differentiation in value between the named producer of the painting on the front (in this instance, the "manual laborer") and Baldessari's (managerial/authorial) signature on the back.

The question of the differentiation of value mandated by a division of labor was most problematic, perhaps, for artists influenced by feminism. As shifting definitions of labor came to structure both art and everyday life, the traditionally unpaid labor of housework and child-rearing became material for artists interested in problems of work. That many artists who were women tried to combine their housework and their artwork indicates that the traditional division of labor between manager and worker does not apply to domestic tasks. So, too, it is difficult for the necessary tasks of housework to be rendered parodically as useless or non-commodifiable labor. While Minimalist artists farmed out instructions for sculptures to factories, Martha Rosler turned her video camera on her household tasks. In *Backyard Economy* (1974) we watch the artist mow the lawn and hang out the laundry. Daily, necessary, unpaid chores do double duty: they "get done" while art is being made.[27] To this end, feminist art issued a multilayered critique: one was clearly sociological, drawing attention to the status of women's unpaid labor in the marketplace; another was directed at contemporary "critical" art, inasmuch as the miming of industrial and managerial forms of labor in much Minimal and Conceptual art did not enact the same forms of humor and critique when applied to the women's work that is never done.

All of the above artworks engage the problem of labor through the figure of the artist, either as a combined worker/manager or simply as a manager. But our discussion opened with "the death of the author" and the newly central place of the viewer. The viewer is hardly universal, however, and the type of viewer imagined and interpolated by works of art varies greatly. Some artworks are not complete, though, without viewer participation, and as the viewer is pressed into service, it remains unclear whether the activity is work or play. In each instance, the role of the artist as someone who fabricates something designed to promote contemplation is radically altered: the artist now is someone who provides an experience for an audience.

For instance, Allan Kaprow staged an event in 1967 called *Fluids*. Urged on by simple posters that consisted of a schematic drawing and typed instructions, the work consisted of voluntary participants building a wall of large ice bricks in Southern California and—upon its completion—watching the fruits of their labor melt. Kaprow's works, later called "Happenings," always involved an intense interpenetration of art and life, and his events often were guided by a string of refusals. He provided no discrete or permanent object, no comfortable or passive spectatorship. Instead, *Fluids* offers a highly staged version of "useless" labor. This strategy of refusal continues today: Kaprow disallows the documentation of the Happenings in museums, insisting that they are deeply experiential and cannot be understood adequately through documentation.[28] So while we can surmise that the work of fashioning the ice wall was both physically arduous and pleasurable, distinctly blurring the boundaries between work and leisure, the artist rejects spectatorship that is nonparticipatory.

Fluids negated the logic of art as a commodity object by virtue of the artwork's disappearance, and it questioned the labor of the artist and the leisure of the spectator by virtue of its method of fabrication. Fluxus, a loose grouping of international artists, also explored ideas of uselessness, play, and the blurring of art and life, work and leisure. George Maciunas, the "ringleader" of the group, gathered the ideas of Fluxus artists (which often took the form of instructions for nonsensical and nonproductive behavior) and fashioned them into game boards, little puzzles, and an entire array of Cracker Jack–like trinkets designed to be sold cheaply and actively handled. Creating a veritable cottage industry of game production, Maciunas and his Fluxus counterparts did not reject the commodity form but humorously embraced it, subverting its logic. They also skewered the logic of managerial instruction. Fluxus instructions, or "scores'" (a term they borrowed from musical composition), were often of a bodily nature and silly, such as Mieko Shiomi's "smile" piece, in which the participant was asked to smile as slowly as possible.[29] Even though they were created by a disparate group of artists, Maciunas's games and products had a visual and tactile similarity, relying strongly on the modest means of envelopes, letter printing, small plastic boxes, and colored cardboard. The graphics evoke nineteenth-century American carnivals and circuses, drawing a strong corollary between the role of art and the traditional spaces of play and leisure. Ernest Mandel argues that late capitalism is determined to infiltrate every aspect of our lives with the logic of the commodity. In response to this interpenetration, Fluxus insisted on recreation without a profit motive. This is the spirit that drives one of Maciunas's most endearing works: a series of modified Ping-Pong paddles, one with a gaping hole, one with a tin can, one with a soft doughy substance, and so on. Made to be played with, Maciunas's altered rackets imply that above all, the strategy of Fluxus was to be utterly nonserious (or seriously playful), for the world was serious enough.[30]

Unlike artists who imagined the audience as joyful participants, Yoko Ono and VALIE EXPORT presented the completion of the work of art on the part of the audience as a kind of dilemma. In Ono's *Cut Piece* (1964), audience members were invited to cut off pieces of her clothing, and in VALIE EXPORT's *TAPP und TASTKINO* (*TAP and TOUCH CINEMA*) (1968), viewers were allowed to grope her breasts in public. In both instances, spectators were confronted with desire—their own and that of others—in a negotiation of the (problematic) social boundaries of the human body, especially the female body. In each instance, viewership was presented as an activity bound up with the enacting and solving of ethical situations: Should audience members dissuade other audience members from taking too much of Ono's clothing? Should audience members censure the activities meted out on VALIE EXPORT's available body? In other words, the audience is placed in a fraught situation in which its potential passivity is made manifest.[31] By emphasizing the role of the viewer/participant and the struggle it entails, these performances pressure the category of leisure, questioning whether audience-participatory works are a space of deregulatory release or whether they, too, come with responsibilities. As popular as the ideas of sexual and creative liberation—largely put forth by the German intellectual Herbert Marcuse—were in the 1960s, both performances imply that the refuge from work in leisure activities structured around voyeurism have always had as part of their sexual liberation a hidden "price": the potential subjugation of women.[32]

The artists involved with participatory works imagined or interpolated varied audiences, but they shared a common goal of reinvigorating and enlivening the bureaucratic subject of postindustrial labor. Could the repressive structures of an administered society be loosened without risking an (unwitting?) repression elsewhere? As we have seen, the solution for some artists has been to establish a realm of participatory ludic play. The Duchampian legacy, replete with its ambivalence toward work and art, presented many artists with a humorous conundrum: If what artists make is art, then is anything an artist does art? Numerous artists attempted to blur the distinctions between art and life, work and play, by bestowing the name and value of art upon their everyday "non-art" activities. Often this has looked like nice work if you could get it. For instance, *Smashed* (1972) is a deadpan parody of task-based work, as Gilbert and George offer black-and-white photographs of their drunken antics. Similarly, Tom Marioni held a weekly "performance," *The Act of Drinking Beer with Friends Is the Highest Form of Art* (1970), in which friends and artists came together to drink beer, stacking up their empty bottles as an indexical sculpture, clear evidence of process being more important than product. In these works, the artists suggested that rather than blurring art and life for its own sake (a kind of avant-garde formalism) or parodying the structure of a highly administered workplace (a repetition of business as usual), the encroachment of work into the space of leisure could be effectively countered by creating a situation where leisure overtakes work.

Many, if not all, of the works included in *Work Ethic* possess a utopian dimension. This utopianism was made possible, in part, through the widespread social upheavals of the 1960s—rebellions that, in the words of Michael Hardt and Antonio Negri in *Empire*, created a "massive transvaluation of the values of social production and production of new subjectivities [that] opened the way for a powerful transformation of labor power."[33] Yet the 1960s may have been the end of one historical phase and the slow beginning of another. *Empire* contends that late capitalism is on the wane, as nation-based economies are being supplanted by a globalized economy, and the postindustrial service economy is becoming an information economy. Hardt and Negri propose that in the midst of this massive transformation—one that threatens to leave many behind in its churning wake—a sophisticated and articulate account of labor's changing roles and face is imperative for any kind of social change. They offer a map of labor's metamorphosis from what they term "productive labor" (the production of goods and services during late capitalism) to "immaterial labor" (the production and management of information under our current conditions). Further, they contend that immaterial labor is divisible into three basic types. The first is industrial production rendered as information, where "manufacturing itself is considered a service." The second is the "creative and intelligent manipulations [of information] on the one hand and routine symbolic acts on the other." And the third is labor in the bodily mode, meaning the production and manipulation of affect.[34]

There is an almost uncanny homology between Hardt and Negri's assessment of our current economic transformations and the strategies deployed by artists negotiating the ramifications of labor's prior transformation. Artists who play out the roles of both manager and worker in task-based and process works render the logic of industrial production into aesthetic information. Artists who mime the structure of management both creatively and routinely manipulate information. (What better way to describe serial logic?) And artists who turn to the viewer to complete the work consistently do so in a bodily and affective mode. Given these sympathies, it is perhaps no mistake that Hardt and Negri argue that we need "to recognize *the profound economic power of cultural movements*, or really the increasing indistinguishability of economic and cultural phenomena."[35] All of the artists in this exhibition in some way stage, manage, and/or resolve the cultural and societal anxieties that surround changing definitions and divisions of labor. Some seem to have understood these transformations in an almost prescient manner. This is crucial, as work and professional life constitute an increasingly powerful site of our identity (as much as, if not more than, family, religion, and ethnicity). As we try to cope with the increasing regimentation and administration of our daily lives—both at work and at leisure—artists offer tentative, temporary solutions, stopgap measures, or blockades in the road.

Perhaps we can learn a lesson from the current tendency of contemporary artists to repeat various 1960s practices. While some critics might see Gabriel Orozco's *Ping Pond Table (Mesa de ping-pong con estanque)* (1998) as a mere repetition of Maciunas's altered Ping-Pong paddles, I would like to suggest that artists borrowing 1960s strategies do so precisely because they were so instrumental in thinking through the changing dynamics of labor.[36] *Ping Pond Table* is a particularly powerful contemporary instance of this. Two Ping-Pong tables are spliced together to form the shape of a cross. In the center is a square "pond" containing water lilies. The table comes equipped with four paddles and several balls. Viewers are invited to play. Because there are no preestablished rules, the terms of engagement depend upon the

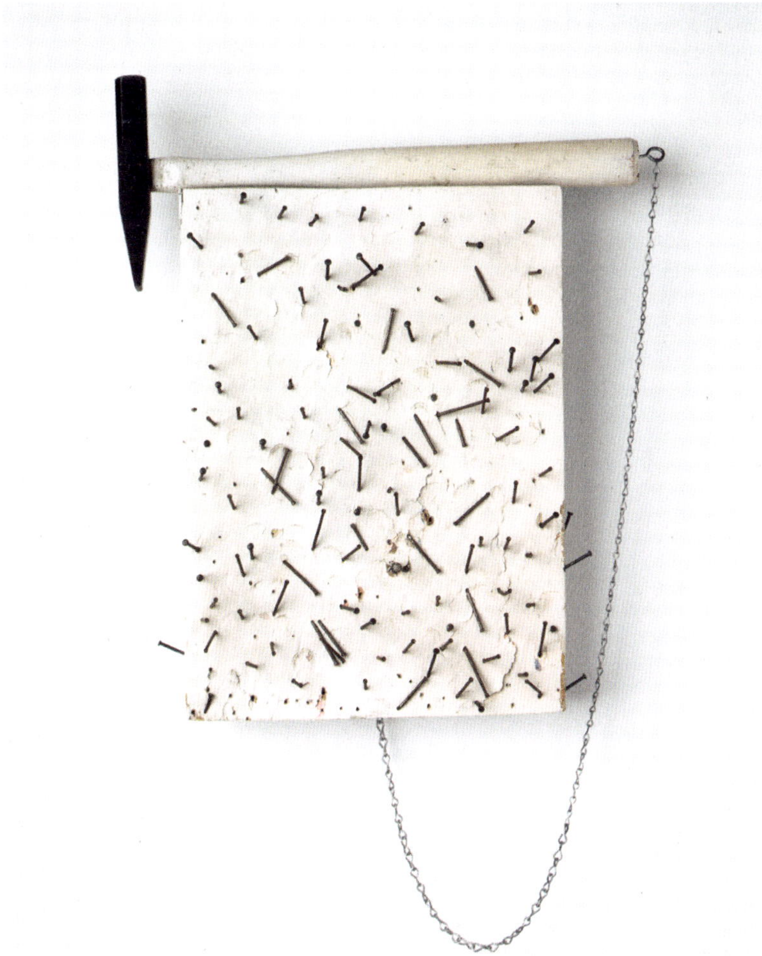

Yoko Ono, *Painting to Hammer a Nail*, 1961/66, painted wood panel, nails, painted hammer, chain, 13 ¾ x 9 ½ x 1 ½ in. (34.9 x 24.1 x 3.8 cm)

participants. The museum's imagining of viewers as solitary is disallowed; instead, a contested (and competitive) public space is offered where participants come together as equals to negotiate a situation. In many regards, Orozco's work offers a utopian microcosm of the traditional public sphere in which disinterested citizens are encouraged to come together to debate the function of their society. Citizens thus bear responsibility for the work of public life. Today, however, such a public sphere has largely ceased to exist, as corporate interests almost entirely shape public debate, and here, debate (or its potential) is substituted with play. Deploying the Fluxus strategies of the nonserious, the game, and the radically altered commodity, Orozco is able to revisit the site of the museum as the primary arbiter of art's role and meaning in society.

Recently, the museum has been discussed in both the popular press and the art media as an institution in crisis. Structured by contradictions, it is a place of work (scholarship and conservation) and leisure (a tourist destination), as well as a site of public service (education) and a place dependent upon private funds (growing corporate support of the arts). Increasingly, the pressures exerted on museums mean that they have become sites of experience as opposed to spaces of interpretation.[37] *Ping Pond Table*, as an object, is both a sculpture and a game, and its dual identity intimates that the space of the museum is a fraught one. As a sculpture, it needs to be interpreted and conserved; as a game, it offers an experience (tellingly, though, the experience it offers is impossible without the active and critical participation of the viewer). In *Ping Pond Table* viewers complete the work, but they are asked to do so in a fashion that is more communal than solitary. *Ping Pond Table* thus suggests that in the face of diminishing spaces for critique and debate within a hyper-commercialized experiential art world, perhaps the space of play can be reclaimed as having a potentially critical dimension. Far from a mere repetition, such a reinvention (provisionally) resists the contemporary forces of global capital—forces that have transformed art into a mere commodity and museums into mandatory tourist destinations—and articulates the potential politics and pleasure in both resisting and shaping new forms of labor and leisure. Contemporary art may hold a key, then, to new identities and to how the conditions of social possibility can be reshaped in the new millennium.

Rrose Sélavy Goes Shopping

Originally published in *The Dada Seminars*, ed. Leah Dickerman (Washington, DC: National Gallery of Art; New York: Distributed Art Publishers, 2005), 173–89.

There are (at least) two versions of the readymades. The readymades of 1917, the objects of New York, were installed in Marcel Duchamp's studio and were lying in wait for an encounter with a visitor. These readymades are the ones that were ultimately lost, or misplaced, or forgotten, but not before they were photographed, playfully, lovingly, by Man Ray or Duchamp, or Alfred Stieglitz, even. These were the readymades purchased by Duchamp, an artist who went into a hardware store, a plumbing manufacturer's shop, or another place of business, and proceeded to look, choose, and, finally, buy one commodity object among many. This artist, the Duchamp of the teens, plucked the readymades (however innocently is up for debate) out of the stream of commodity exchange (where all values are equivalent) and put them down in another place—a studio, an apartment, a gallery, an art show—where, through their migration, their use value was altered and their exchange value temporarily halted.

This Duchamp was different from the Duchamp who emerged, nascently triumphant, after World War II. This Duchamp went to art openings in New York, after Surrealism had been forced from Europe's shores. This Duchamp was friends with Peggy Guggenheim and quietly watched the rise of Abstract Expressionism. This was the Duchamp who sat on a panel at the Museum of Modern Art in 1961 and read "Apropos of Readymades," in which he stated: "The point I want very much to establish is that the choice of these Readymades was *never* dictated by an aesthetic delectation. The choice was based on a reaction of *visual indifference* with at the same time a total absence of good or bad taste."[1] Yet, ironically, this Duchamp no longer visited hardware stores to buy readymades. Quite the contrary, this Duchamp authorized others to do so. Thus Sidney Janis and Ulf Linde both purchased urinals in Duchamp's name. Certainly, these readymades were acquired with Duchamp's "visual indifference." But after seeing his works brought together in his American retrospective exhibition organized by Walter Hopps in 1963, Duchamp revised his position on letting others do the shopping for him and instead allowed Arturo Schwarz to refabricate, by hand, a set of readymades. Their specifications were taken not from the present condition of the objects but rather were drawn from those loving photographs of the readymades taken by Man Ray and Stieglitz so many decades earlier. In other words, the Duchamp who spoke of visual indifference had long since relinquished the dilemma of choosing one object over another; he had long since abandoned the problem of the Duchamp of the teens.

Art historical accounts of Duchamp and the readymades usually neglect to make the distinction between the readymades of the teens and the readymades of the postwar period. Instead, Duchamp's postwar version of the readymades stands as their explanation and justification tout court. As such, we have grown accustomed to thinking of the readymades as mass-produced objects chosen with visual indifference. The problem with such accounts is that they leave out the wrinkles of internal contradiction. Ignored is the possibility of Duchamp's self-revision, and forgotten is the Duchamp of 1913 who wrote of his experience in front of a shop window, the Duchamp who confronted the dilemma posed by the "glass pane with one or many objects of the shop window," in the face of which he felt, "the demands of the shop windows, from the inevitable response to shop windows, my choice is determined."[2] Plotting a course, a pattern all too familiar to any shopper, Duchamp maps the progression from dilemma, to demand, to penalty, which "consists in cutting the pane and in feeling regret as soon as the session is consummated."[3]

Despite Duchamp's early displays of consumerist angst, most discussions of the readymade avoid the problem of mass consumption, preferring to focus on the industrially produced quality of the readymades. One reason for this lacuna may be that we lack an account of consumption as sophisticated as our accounts of production. Perhaps it is because shopping, in large part, was and remains a daily activity whose burdens and pleasures fall primarily upon women. Or it may be that art history has tended to focus on the means of production, separating them, untenably and undialectically, from the experience of consumption. Yet it is precisely this quintessentially twentieth-century experience of shopping that Duchamp introduced into the realm of art, and he did so at a time when its conventions and discourses were relatively nascent. Ever canny, he was quick to describe the experience as one distinguished by a dilemma: the problem of how to choose one thing over another. While commodity acquisition remains the goal of shopping, the consumer first must navigate the perilous waters of taste—both hers and others. Shoppers must decide what commodity is best for them; unlike mass production, the experience of mass consumption is largely dependent upon the activity of choice.

The Duchamp of the teens was emphatic about the problem of choice. Writing in *The Blind Man*, a Dada manifesto designed to justify the artistic legitimacy of the recently suppressed *Fountain* (1917), "Whether Mr. Mutt with his own hands made the fountain or not has no importance. He CHOSE it."[4] The typographical emphasis on choosing is set up in opposition to the more traditional artistic labor of making. Choice was a new form of artistic labor, and as such needed to be foregrounded, enlarged, emphasized, and, ultimately, legitimated. The role of choice in the artistic process found in *The Blind Man* had a corollary in Duchamp's counsel to his friend Beatrice

Wood, a precocious young artist also submitting an entry to the *First Annual Exhibition* of the Society of Independent Artists in New York in 1917. She recalls the following piece of advice: "I sent in a painting of a nude woman taking a bath, with only her torso showing and a piece of real soap covering a certain part of her anatomy, like a fig leaf. The piece of real soap was Marcel's idea: 'Be sure to choose the right shape and color,' he advised."[5]

It appears that two readymades were submitted to this exhibition: both mass-produced, both purchased, and both, it seems, chosen with deliberation and care. Perhaps both were chosen with a sense that shopping was an activity bound up with desire and regret, and that choosing an object out of a shop window, particularly the right object, was no easy task. But what makes choosing and shopping so arduous? The complexity of these activities is that deciding what one likes, establishing one's preferences, cobbling them together over a period of trial and error into one's taste, is in many ways synonymous with the creation and presentation of the self.

In his epic study *Distinction: A Social Critique of the Judgment of Taste*, French sociologist Pierre Bourdieu states his case plainly: "Taste is the basis of all that one has—people and things—and all that one is for others, whereby one classifies oneself and is classified by others."[6] Bourdieu suggests that taste, hardly a fixed system with strict class correlations, is formed through an elaborate mixture of public and private forces, a combination of educational and cultural capital. For Bourdieu, educational capital is the public domain of taste, taught in schools, in the media, and in a variety of public institutions, whereas cultural capital is the taste of the home. The bedrock of one's personal taste begins and ends with one's family, inasmuch as the taste one grows up with is always the taste against which all other forms of taste are measured. Hence taste is a mechanism through which individuals distinguish or align themselves from and with others. Additionally, taste is a calibrating axis along which individuals negotiate or manage the spheres of public and private.

If taste is thus defined, then how does it function? The combination of public and private taste—educational and cultural capital—form a matrix of what Bourdieu calls "perceived needs." This is not the basic need for human shelter and sustenance but the need that evolves in front of shop windows, the "need" for things we want. Nowhere is the problem of taste more evident than with perceived needs. Here our tastes are translated into our preferences, which we subsequently experience as constitutive of the self. Yet our "preferences" are always subject to our conditions, becoming what Bourdieu calls the "taste for the necessary." We do not recognize our conditions as constrictions and forms of classification as such; rather we continually read these systems of distinction to be our own, as manifestations of our preference. A taste for the necessary implies that no matter how much effort goes into our choices, no matter how much we experience our choices as public manifestations of ourselves, our choices are determined as much from the outside as from within.[7] It is this ineluctable mixture of forces, of educational and cultural capital, combined with access to actual capital, that creates a nexus of taste, which, Bourdieu writes,

> continuously transforms necessities into strategies, constraints into performances, and, without any mechanical determination, it generates the set of "choices" constituting life-styles, which derive their meaning, i.e. their value, from their position in a system of operations and correlations. It is a virtue made of necessity which continuously transforms necessity into virtue by inducing "choices" which correspond to the condition of which it is the product.[8]

Perhaps this is what Duchamp felt when he wrote in 1913: "From the demands of the shop windows, from the inevitable response to shop windows, my choice is determined."[9]

What kinds of demands were in play when Duchamp stood in front of shop windows, and how might they have determined his choices? When Duchamp set out shopping in New York, two distinct forces were at work shaping the taste of the American consumer: a lively sense of competition between the museums and the new department stores and the invention of the trademark. During the first three decades of the century, American taste was a topic of active debate between the museums and the big department stores. American museums, founded primarily as educational institutions, dedicated themselves to raising the standards of production and consumption of both commodity goods and art objects. Early-twentieth-century museums in particular championed themselves as educators (and specifically elevators) in matters of the tastes of the people, and most museums had technical and craft schools that were designed to aid and abet in this endeavor. Yet the rise of department stores dramatically shook the museum's sense of its societal role. Historian Neil Harris maintains that "changes in the architecture and display methods of . . . retailers lessened the effectiveness of museum displays, raised public expectations, and so rendered the museum less powerful as a force shaping that abstraction called public taste."[10] By the early decades of the twentieth century, department stores had effectively "stolen" the discourse of taste from the museum, establishing themselves as the preeminent teachers and edifiers of the American public.

One of the ways the department stores were so effective in establishing their role as public educators of taste was their use of "high" (and sometimes explicitly "modern") art. In fact, some of the most radical paintings of Duchamp's day were displayed in department stores. After the success of the 1913 Armory Show, where Duchamp's *Nude Descending a Staircase (No.2)* (1912) was first shown in New York, Gimbels department store mounted the first exhibition of Cubist paintings in the country. The big department stores also offered their customers an ideology not so far removed from the avant-garde rhetoric of the merging of art and life, although with very different political implications. Consider the chapter titled "Art" in the *Golden Book of the Wanamaker Stores*, in which John Wanamaker, a department store magnate, espouses the following philosophy:

> The truth is that the quality of art comes out in everything we do. Whatever is well done, with sincerity and the love of work and a feeling for beauty, is art. Whatever is badly done, with pretense or half-heartedness and clumsiness, is far from being art. It is not only the person whose soul sings through his lips, or who puts his thoughts on canvas with a brush, who is an artist. The vehicle of expression does not matter. It is the spirit that counts. The woman who arranges a room charmingly, who dresses to express her personality, or serves a dinner with grace; the man who binds a book in good taste or turns out a chair that is a pleasure, or lays out a garden to give delight—all are artists in their way. So, too, is the store that lives up to its highest ideal.[11]

Many museums responded to the department stores' success in merchandising and their monopoly of the discourse of taste with a form of mimicry. Curators Stewart Culin of the Brooklyn Museum and John Cotton Dana of the Newark Museum were notable among those who emulated the department stores by changing both their display strategies and the types of exhibitions they mounted. In 1917, Culin, then curator at the American Museum of Natural History, New York, and editor at *Women's Wear*, filled the museum with the textiles of native peoples, collected on expeditions sponsored by John Wanamaker. Culin's self-stated goal was to create a "'laboratory of taste' for our most successful [clothing] designers."[12] Far from perceiving any contradiction between Wanamaker and himself, he championed department stores as "the greatest influences for culture and taste that exist today."[13]

While Culin was in direct collusion with Wanamaker, his counterpart, John Cotton Dana, was a more independent spirit. Founder and curator of the Newark Museum, Dana was as progressive a museum thinker as Duchamp was an artist. In 1917, he wrote a short volume titled *The Gloom of the Museum*, which bemoaned the far remove the average art museum held between its content and its patron. Going so far as to challenge the "undue reverence for oil paint," Dana felt passionately that department stores were "filled with objects closely associated with the life of the people."[14] The task of the museum was to learn from department stores the value of contemporary, machine-made objects. In what must have seemed as heretical as Duchamp's submission of a urinal to the 1917 exhibition, Dana suggested:

> This fact in time will be recognized and acted upon, that the oil painting has no such close relation to the development of good taste and refinement as have countless objects of daily use. The genius and skill

which have gone into adornment and perfecting of familiar household objects will then receive the same recognition as do now the genius and skill of the painter in oils.[15]

This maverick sensibility, combined with progressivist politics, allowed Dana to open the Newark Museum to what he believed were the democratic principles of the department stores.[16] He sought to disabuse people of the notion that the handcrafted object was superior to the mass-produced one. As early as 1912 he was mounting exhibits of industrial design, and one of his favorite tricks was to install machine-made goods with wall labels indicating they were made by hand. By the late 1920s, he was to mount an exhibition of plumbing fixtures. While there is no evidence that points to Dana and Duchamp knowing of one another's institutional and ideological challenges, the high degree of porosity between department stores and museums, and subsequently art and commodities, indicates, if nothing else, that Duchamp's readymade practice occurred within a historical field marked by a debate over who would have the "rights" to high art, who would govern taste, and ultimately, who would negotiate the relationship between art and the ready-made goods.

It's not as if readymade goods were easily negotiated in and of themselves. In the emerging period of American mass-consumerism (roughly 1890 to 1920) the activity of shopping changed dramatically. The consumption of daily goods so thoroughly replaced the production of goods in the majority of American homes that "the home economics profession reclassified housework from a production to a consumption activity."[17] Shopping took place in the new venue of the department store, and women now needed to be able to negotiate an extraordinary array of new products. Advice on how to shop proliferated in books and magazines, primarily encouraging women to buy frugally, to buy products that reflected their identities or personalities, and to choose things in good taste. Shopping was staged as a site of desire through the increase of advertising, women's magazines, and the sensory stimulation of the department stores. It simultaneously offered the paradoxical promise that mass consumption would be able to create a highly individuated subject.[18] A question emerged: if an individuated subject had to be created through the purchase of mass-produced goods, how might the goods be personalized or individuated?

One answer was the development of the trademark. The trademark, established in 1905, differs from a copyright or patent. The copyright is the exclusive right to reproduce a specific product, usually one with some form of "artistic" merit. A patent is the legal acknowledgment of an invention (which is sometimes protected by a trademark). A trademark, however, is the slogan and/or logo identified with a commodity. The typeface and script of "Coca-Cola" establish it as a trademark, and the accompanying slogan, "It's the real thing," is also a trademark. This slogan is particularly apt because it defines the very purpose of the trademark: to guarantee that the commodity in question is authentic. In effect, the trademark is like a signature on a work of art or a check; it signifies the maker's authority to guarantee the authenticity of the product. The dictionary definition of *trademark* is "a distinguishing characteristic or feature firmly associated with a person or thing,"[19] and the elision of "person" and "thing" is crucial as the trademark was designed to give the commodity an identity, a personality.[20]

While the trademark was a device designed to win market shares for the producer, it was presented to the consumer as a helpful facilitator of choice. Given the new variety of readymade goods, producers were relatively quick to bestow identities upon their commodities. The identities or trademark were designed to ease the transition from a more intimate form of consumption when consumers knew the shopkeeper (and perhaps even those who made the product they were buying) to an era of burgeoning national market and increasingly anonymous service and products. As Susan Strasser argues, "A population accustomed to homemade product and unbranded merchandise had to be converted into a national market for standardized, advertised, brand name goods in general."[21] The trademark was an integral part of advertising strategies that linked product with slogans and with fictional characters (such as Quaker Oats). Trademarks, with their guarantee of authenticity, created the impression of providing a consumer choice that emanated from the inside of the individual shopping subject while, in fact, helping to determine choice from the outside.

Duchamp's first artistic foray into the arena of the trademark came with *Apolinère Enameled* (1916–17), in which he consciously manipulated an advertisement for a national brand of paint. Duchamp placed the role of the trademark and advertising front and center—the image of a young girl painting her bedposts seems to imply a correlation between the activity of artists and shopper that ran deeper than previously understood. (Importantly, on the recto of the work, an original label for the Sapolin display remains. It contains a gnomelike figure that suggests the easel will aid sales of Sapolin decorative specialties, complete with the slogan, "It pays to advertise Sapolin.")

In the bedroom-redecorating scene of *Apolinère Enameled*, the great critic of art and the purveyor of home improvement stand side by side, suggesting that Duchamp understood trademarks might be part of the continuity between museums and department stores, inasmuch as all three institutions were motivated by the desire to influence the choices and tastes of the American consumer. When Duchamp wrote in *The Blind Man*, "Whether Mr. Mutt with his own hands made the fountain or not has no importance. He CHOSE it," he insisted upon choice and choice alone as the sufficient criterion to qualify something as an art object. The typographical emphasis on choosing which established the justification for the readymades certainly implies that Duchamp bought these objects. Yet to buy a urinal in 1917 would not necessarily have been an easy task. The urinal in question was elected from the J. L. Mott Iron Works showroom in New York City. The company's promotional catalogue offered myriad types of urinals.[22] By buying from a nationally known maker, Duchamp once again inserted himself into the discourse of trademarks and choice.

Furthermore, he manipulated the idea of the trademark by signing the urinal with a new "trademark," R. Mutt. Yet R. Mutt is not your average trademark; it is an abandonment of or affront to everything the trademark stands for. J. L. Mott because of name recognition may have guaranteed the authenticity of the urinal, but in its rotational transformation into an art object R. Mutt's signature does not guarantee much. Instead it is a joke, a visual pun on the similarity between the signature of the artist and the trademark of consumer culture. By fraying the logic of the trademark, Duchamp rendered his readymades authentically inauthentic.

Further exploring the logic of the trademark, Duchamp invented an alter ego who is also a trademark, Rrose Sélavy, created in 1920, the year women gained the vote. She was an easily identifiable image and brand name; an identity for a given set of products, an identity shielding the identity of her "parent company." The placement of her name or image on works "authenticated" them. The version of authenticity being offered, however, is a puzzling one, for our surest belief in Rrose Sélavy comes not from Duchamp, but from Man Ray's famous portrait of her. In a sense, Man Ray's collaboration on the project made him the "ad man," creator of the Sélavy image, which Duchamp then affixed, trademark-style, onto products. We need only think of the readymade *Belle Haleine, Eau de Voilette* (1921). Here Duchamp took a perfume bottle and manufactured a label replete with his own brand name, which he verified with his trademark, Rrose Sélavy. Later, this bottle was photographed and used as the cover of *New York Dada*, running this time as a sort of print ad.

The Rrose Sélavy trademark makes a telling appearance in Duchamp's best advertisement for himself, *Wanted: $2,000 Reward* (1923). In this readymade, Duchamp pasted two grainy mug shot–style photographs of himself into a joke "Wanted" poster. While the caption promises a reward for information leading to the arrest of George W. Welch, Duchamp offers proof of his "real" identity by exposing Welch's alias as none other than Rrose Sélavy. Why this guise of Duchamp is wanted remains unclear, but the detail that "Welch" was operating a "bucket shop" under the names "HOOKE, LYON and CINQUER" intimates that shady business dealings and false advertising were the crimes. The confusing narrative turns amusing vis-à-vis issues of forensic identification, as the figure of Welch/Sélavy/Duchamp is described as having "complexion medium, eyes same." The consumer's difficulty in distinguishing among things mutates into an inability to make distinctions between persons.

Duchamp used the logic of the trademark to disarticulate his own identity, to fracture its seamless surface with a variety of aliases—R. Mutt, Rrose Sélavy, and George W. Welch—and products, or "readymades," as he called them: *Fountain* (signed by R. Mutt), as well as *Belle Haleine* (1920) and *La Bagarre d'Austerlitz* (1921) (both signed by Rrose Sélavy). This scenario, however, is slightly more complicated than an easy one-to-one association of a trademark with a product, for Rrose Sélavy's best-known product is Rrose Sélavy; she is both an identity without a product and she is the product. Duchamp shows how the trademark ultimately stands for itself, and its logic works regardless of whether a product actually exists.

Authorship, legitimation, and product are all set into flux by Duchamp's seemingly simple gesture of producing aliases. When Duchamp looked back upon his artistic career, he seemed to understand the terms he had unmoored. For example, in the poster for the 1963 retrospective of Duchamp's work at the Pasadena Museum, Duchamp, underneath a reproduction of *Wanted: $2,000 Reward*, wrote the slogan "By or of Marcel Duchamp or Rrose Sélavy" in his own hand.[23] The play between "by" and "of" is pointed in its ambiguity regarding the relationship of agency, or, even more simply, *manufacture*, of the maker/artist to the artistic oeuvre in question. Who stands for what? Who or what is the product of the exhibition, the maker or the objects? Who is the agent of artistic production, Duchamp or Rrose Sélavy (or Man Ray)? This confusion between the role of the maker and the product found in Duchamp's practice resembles the confusion in commodity culture of the boundaries between the persons and things, a confusion maintained by the logic of the trademark.

One consequence of the blurred distinction between persons and things is that in consumer culture, what we buy and what we choose comes to stand for who we are. That is, what we choose is governed by our taste, and taste is one of the strongest mechanisms through which the consumer subject differentiates herself from others (and her objects from those of others). The trademark shores up these distinctions, couching nearly imperceptible differences in terms of preference. Duchamp was one of the first artists to address the thorny issue of preference and taste through his engagement with shopping and the trademark. He also did so through his many identities or alter egos.

If, as Bourdieu suggests, the choice of objects is bound up with the production of the self (however illusory such a practice might be), then what or who is the Duchamp who emerges from his various shopping forays? When he wrote in 1913 that in front of shop windows his "choice is determined," which version of himself was being spoken for? Ironically, it appears not to be Duchamp at all. Bourdieu and Duchamp both propose that choice, the manifestation of taste, does not flow exclusively from the individual to the object, but that objects choose the individual as well (a further blurring of the boundaries between persons and things). Objects can choose because taste is public. (Taste is formed and choice occurs, after all, on the street, in front of the shop window, or in the crowded bustle of the department store.) Objects manufactured with identities (objects complete with trademarks) take on an uncanny ability to interpolate subjects whose perceived needs fit the bill. Duchamp exploits the fact that objects can choose an individual: the urinal did not choose Duchamp, it chose R. Mutt, and the window of *Fresh*

Widow (1920), chose Rrose Sélavy. While Duchamp appears to have been aware of the constraints that are always already placed upon his choice, he also tried to mitigate such a determination; not in the name of a kind of radical individuality, but rather as a way to counteract the logic of an identity that comes replete with an authority bestowed upon it through the proper choice of objects. Like Bourdieu, he suggests that taste is more likely to be a manifestation of social conditions than a display of our interiority or individuation. One fallacy of commodity culture is that we believe our taste is a marker of our personality, character, or identity. There is a way in which our taste bespeaks us—it is simultaneously ours and not ours. As Bourdieu says, "Taste is the basis of all that one has—people and things—and all that one is for others, whereby one classifies oneself and is classified by others."[24] How Duchamp was to be classified by others lay at the heart of the scandal surrounding the 1917 exhibition.

THE 1917 EXHIBITION SCANDAL RECONSIDERED

In light of the complex relationship between museums, department stores, and the discourse of taste, let us reconsider the slogan of the 1917 exhibition by the Society of Independent Artists: "No Jury, No Prizes." Could this slogan embody the desire of the organizers to coordinate an exhibition that functioned without taste, preference, or distinction? Did they wish to democratize the art exhibition, to make it as accessible as the department store? (After all, the exhibition was compared to both the circus and a popular Sunday revival meeting by the contemporary press.[25]) What the organizers of the exhibition did not seem to understand was that they were about to set a crisis in motion by their desire to eliminate taste—a crisis that had at its heart the tension between the dependence of taste on a legitimator and the inherently arbitrary nature of legitimation as such.

The story is well known: Duchamp, under the alias R. Mutt, submitted an inverted urinal; the hanging committee refused to show it; the object was "hidden" behind a partition; and Duchamp and Walter Arensberg resigned in protest. The decision not to exhibit the urinal came from two camps, personified in this argument by George Bellows and Katherine Dreier. Both, oddly enough in the face of the "No Jury, No Prizes" slogan, employ the rhetoric of taste to justify their refusal to legitimate *Fountain* as art. The arguments for showing the urinal also relied on the rhetoric of taste, albeit somewhat unwittingly.

Ashcan School painter Bellows's reaction was perhaps the more predictable of the two objections to the exhibition of *Fountain*. For Bellows, the urinal was a tasteless object, an affront to bourgeois propriety and sensibility.[26] "It is indecent!" he roared upon seeing it for the first time.[27] Arensberg, however, responded, "A lovely form has been revealed," employing the language of aesthetics to back his argument. Their responses seem fairly typical, reflecting Victorian prudery on the one hand and the timeless association of beauty and art on the other.

Dreier's response was more complicated. In a letter to Duchamp regarding the course of events that led to his resignation, she wrote the following:

> When I voted "No," I voted on the question of originality—I did not see anything pertaining to originality in it; that does not mean that if my attention had been drawn to what was original by those who could see it, that I could not also have seen it. To me no other question came up: it was simply a question of whether a person has the right to buy a ready-made object and show it with their name attached at an exhibition? Arensberg tells me that it was in accord with you [*sic*] "Readymades," and I told him that was a new thought to me as the only "readymades" I saw were groups which were extremely original in their handling. I did not know that you had conceived of single objects.[28]

On the surface, it appears as if Dreier's objection was based on the criterion of originality, but as her letter progresses, this position becomes increasingly untenable. Dreier had already been exposed to Duchamp's readymades; she was therefore familiar with their existence and perhaps some of the ideas behind them. But where she experienced them obviously inflected her understanding of them. She saw them in Duchamp's studio—coatrack nailed to the floor, shovel suspended from the ceiling—manifesting their "original handling." More importantly, though, situated in the middle of Duchamp's domestic space, they manifested Duchamp's "sensibility." His placement of objects is analogous to the housewife's artfully arranged living room. In his domestic space, Duchamp "offers" to Dreier an "alternative" version of the domestic interior, one that she reads as being imbued with his taste and his choices. In effect, she reads the readymades as an expression of his lifestyle. Beatrice Wood had a similar reaction to the readymades when she encountered them in Duchamp's studio. In her tribute to him written after his death, Wood says:

> Duchamp's studio was a typical bachelor's niche, with a wall bed, usually unmade, projecting out into the middle of the room, with a chair and table nearby. There were always chocolate bars on the window sill. To my astonishment, ordinary objects were scattered about: a coffee grinder, a bicycle wheel mounted on a box, an advertisement for Sapolin Enamel on the wall.
>
> When I asked why he was keeping such things around, he smiled. They had their purpose, he said, but I should not give them another thought. Once I remember pointing to a square box that had sugar in it. "What is that?" I asked, wanting to be sympathetic with his ideas. "Cela n'a pas d'importance," he would say. And I knew nothing was as important as just being there.[29]

In the same essay, Wood states that, with the exception of *Nude Descending a Staircase*, she did not really understand Duchamp's work. Here again we have a reaction to the oddness of the readymades, their unexpected quality within domestic space, let alone in a gallery or museum. The predominant framework for Dreier and Wood's experience of the readymades is to see them as a manifestation of Duchamp's "artistic sensibility," or taste. The women are hardly to blame. The predominant experience of the readymades was in Duchamp's domicile and studio; they were not exhibited, except for the controversial non-exhibition of *Fountain* and an exhibition where they were shown but never commented upon.[30]

Bellows, Arensberg, and Dreier all seem blind to the crisis of legitimation they are experiencing, for the motto of the show disallowed them (or anyone) from acting as the legitimators of the work, either in terms of decency or aesthetics. Ironically, saying "No Jury, No Prizes" is tantamount to saying, "No Choice." When the organizers of the 1917 show abandoned the institutional role of guaranteeing the authenticity of the art, when they abdicated the right to choose one work over another, the right to express their taste, they unwittingly exposed a much larger problem: the guarantee of the authenticity or legitimacy of art was arbitrary from the very start, because the problem with taste is that it constantly needs a legitimator. Such legitimation, as we have seen, can come in many forms: through the trademark, the instruction of the museum, or the call and response of the department store. Yet Duchamp's sly intervention into the normal workings of taste and legitimation in an art exhibition exposes a much larger problem: If the taste of the museum acts as the legitimator of art, then who legitimates the museum? At the heart of every system of taste lies a moment of arbitrariness, an arbitrariness perpetually covered up by acts of legitimation. In this light, when Dreier and Wood see the readymades within Duchamp's domestic space, they attribute the legitimacy of that space through the function of Duchamp's persona. As lifestyle, they are odd but acceptable; as art, they are confounding and disruptive.

This argument about legitimacy needs to be held in relation to criticism that defines the readymades as a nominalist practice.[31] In such accounts, the artist typically is the sole legitimator of the art object, and Duchamp's emphasis on choice in *The Blind Man* is offered as the ultimate act of artistic legitimation.[32] Yet in actuality, Duchamp did something slightly different. By submitting *Fountain* under an alias, he tried to avoid the use of his personal identity as the legitimator of his practice. Such a position careens dangerously close to Wanamaker's "I shop therefore I am," or rather, "I choose (with taste) therefore I am." Herein lies the context of Dreier's confusion. When the readymades are in the context of an artistic lifestyle, they are art because Duchamp is an artist. R. Mutt, however, was not an artist, because he had not been legitimated as one. In a sense, Duchamp articulated (for the first time?) the problem of what it meant to say that one is an artist. His subsequent "abandonment" of art making is particularly compelling in this light.

In 1921 Marcel Duchamp made *Why Not Sneeze Rose Sélavy?*, a deeply peculiar assemblage of marble cubes that resemble sugar, piled atop one another in a small white cage and accompanied by a thermometer and a piece of cuttlefish. The trademark was making one of her last appearances. Apparently, Dreier's sister Dorothea had grown "a trifle awed by Katherine Dreier's collection"[33] and wanted some art for herself. Katherine acted as the intermediary on her sister's behalf and offered Duchamp three hundred dollars for a commissioned work to be made for her sister. As luck would have it, Dorothea was horrified by the object and returned it to Katherine, who in turn also did not like the work and returned it to Duchamp. For a while in the ownership of Duchamp's good friend Henri-Pierre Roché, it was eventually sold to the Arensbergs for the original price of three hundred dollars. It is well known that Duchamp "abandoned" art making after deciding to leave *The Large Glass* permanently unfinished in 1923. Yet by 1921 the ownership of *The Large Glass* had already passed to Dreier, as the Arensbergs had moved to California that fall. The year 1922 saw no significant artistic activity on the part of Duchamp. It is a moment of pure conjecture, perhaps possible coincidence, but is it possible to think that the Duchamp of the teens was tired of his work not being chosen? The Duchamp of the teens wrote a note to himself asking if it was possible to make works that were not works of art. R. Mutt's submission of *Fountain* seemed to prove that indeed anything could be art; hence it was impossible to make a thing that could not be art. But perhaps the abandonment of art and the subsequent refusal to abide by the logic of choice and taste—the rules of the game set out by the Duchamp of the postwar period—belie a slight variation on the question. Duchamp's radical play with the definition of art finds another corollary in Bourdieu's understanding of taste and legitimation. For Bourdieu,

> the games of artists and aesthetes and their struggles for the monopoly of artistic legitimacy are less innocent than they seem. At stake in every struggle over art there is also the imposition of an art of living, that is, the transmutation of an arbitrary way of living into the legitimate way of life casts every other way of living into arbitrariness.[34]

If Duchamp had tired of his and his aliases' objects not being chosen, or of not being able to make something that is not art (for the rejection of the *Fountain* was in fact what established it as art—even a rejection is a choice), then maybe the true test was to see if one could be an artist without seeking legitimation. Could one be an artist who refused to participate in the game of taste—both one's own and that of others? Could one be an artist underground, like the Duchamp of the postwar period, the Duchamp who worked in complete silence for nearly two decades on a work of art—seeking the choice or taste or legitimation of no one?

My Funny Valentine: *Étant donnés*

Originally published in *Artforum*, January 2010, 164–69.

"You're my favorite work of art . . ."

As you make your way toward Marcel Duchamp's *Étant donnés* at the Philadelphia Museum of Art, you walk down a long hallway with Paul Cézanne's *Les grandes baigneuses* (*The Large Bathers*) (1906) squarely in your sight line. For all its iconic status, it is a bizarre canvas. Its scale is monstrous and not particularly in keeping with its ostensible subject matter: nudes at play in a pastoral landscape. The nudes (or shall we call them women?) proliferate, seated and standing; they arch toward one another like so many windswept trees, forming parentheses around the core of the painting, which remains awkwardly but decidedly empty. The void suggests that something about the very idea of this painting struck Cézanne as potentially ridiculous. It's as if he knew the jig was up: naked women in a landscape? Really? In 1906?

Hang a right at the Cézanne, head down the long, barrel-vaulted hallway, and modernism unfurls before you. Let's face it, the PMA has one of the finest collections of twentieth-century art in the country: Arthur Dove, Man Ray, Constantin Brancusi. This unfolding of the avant-garde dead-ends, as it were, in gallery 183, the room that contains Duchamp's last and most abiding work.

Étant donnés is installed alone in an unlit room whose floor is covered with a worn sisal carpet. You approach a set of massive, weathered wooden double doors, doors canted ever so slightly inward, so that your feet have room to plant themselves as you lower your head a bit to peer through the two peepholes situated just slightly below eye level. Looking through them, you see a nude woman in a landscape bathed in a warm, glowing light.

But I have gotten ahead of myself. Just on the other side of the doors there is a brick wall with a ragged hole broken through it. And it is through this *second* aperture that you witness the mise-en-scène: a headless female mannequin nestled in a pile of dead branches and leaves, legs awkwardly open, labia curiously misplaced as if sliding up the left thigh, left arm outstretched and lifting away from the body, left hand grasping a lantern. The background is an exercise in pastoral kitsch, containing, dutifully, trees against a horizon, clouds, blue sky, a lake, a waterfall. The falls' moving water is simulated by a flickering light that looks as if it were made with

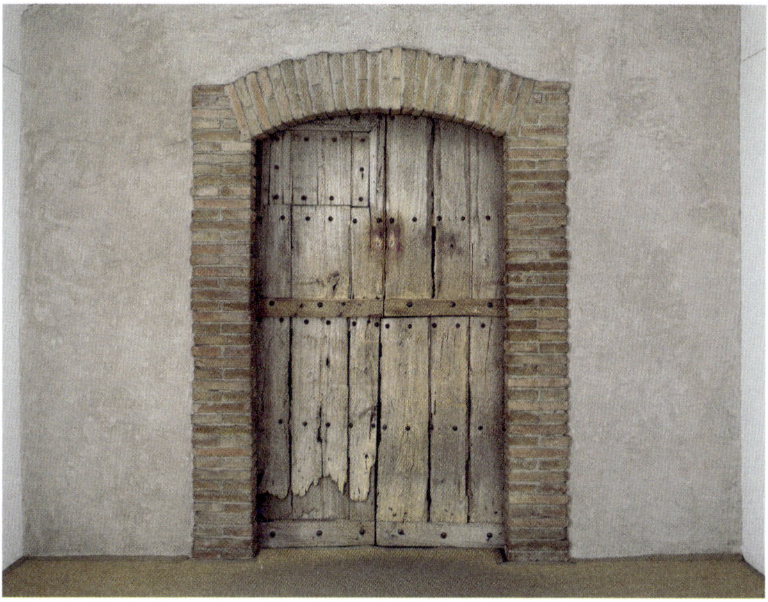

Marcel Duchamp, *Étant donnés: 1° la chute d'eau, 2° le gaz d'éclairage . . . (Given: 1. The Waterfall, 2. The Illuminating Gas . . .)*, 1946–66, mixed-media assemblage: (exterior) wooden door, iron nails, bricks, stucco, 95 ½ x 70 x 49 in. (242.6 x 177.8 x 124.5 cm)

dime-store glitter. It is the only movement in the tableau, its glow echoing that of the lantern. Yet even though both the waterfall and the lantern are included in the work's full title, *Étant donnés: 1° la chute d'eau, 2° le gaz d'éclairage . . . (Given: 1. The Waterfall, 2. The Illuminating Gas . . .)*, neither is the source of the otherworldly, or cinematic, light that illuminates the landscape, the splayed body, and the brick wall.

First-timers often pull back in shock. Those who have been there before frequently linger, puzzled. What is this an image of? Can we even rightly call it an image? What does it mean? How was it made? Can it really be that Duchamp produced, of all things, a diorama? Why did the great advocate of the anti-retinal, the inventor of the readymade, the progenitor of Conceptual art and institutional critique, make *this*?

Étant donnés has been a great mystery for many years. Installed at the PMA in 1969, it was immediately subject to a photographic moratorium: after numerous unsatisfactory attempts to capture the work on film, the curators at the time (notably the late, much-admired, and now deeply missed Anne d'Harnoncourt) decided not to allow any photos of it, concluding that no picture was capable of conveying the visual and physical complexity of the piece. One enduring effect of this decision has been that the reception of the work, by both artists and art historians, has been slow, subject to the hearsay of who saw what when. Ultimately, this contemporary iconoclasm meant that the work hovered like air: crucial but unremarked. Even when the ban was lifted and images of the work began to circulate, people remained quiet—leading Benjamin H. D. Buchloh, in an introduction to a 1994 special issue of *October* dedicated to Duchamp, to bemoan "the near total silence surrounding the hidden enigma in Philadelphia."[1]

This silence may now be broken thanks to the enterprising and extraordinary recent exhibition *Marcel Duchamp: Étant donnés*. Organized by the PMA's curator of modern art, Michael R. Taylor, the show—which marked the fortieth anniversary of the installation of the work at the museum—was at once overdue and timely, bringing us as close as we are ever likely to come to this most reticent of artworks. It gathered every known document, drawing, and object relating to the work, many of which had been sequestered, unknown to the public, in the museum's collection or in the hands of the artist's family for decades. The indispensable and beautifully written catalogue, while purposely light on critical interpretation, outlines the production and reception of *Étant donnés* in exhaustive and riveting detail, as well as reproducing a crucial passage from Duchamp's personal correspondence.[2] The combined effect of the exhibition and the catalogue not only sets the record straight; it makes possible a new conversation.

When it comes to *Étant donnés*, I, too, have been part of the quiet multitude, even though the work has haunted me for years. I first saw it as a teenager on a trip to Philadelphia with my mother and my best friend from high school. I returned to it frequently during the course of writing a dissertation on Duchamp's readymades (although, in the finished dissertation, I never mentioned it!) and later became obsessed with it while working on an exhibition of postwar and contemporary sculpture made in the "tradition" of Duchamp's so-called erotic objects of the 1950s. In the catalogue for that exhibition, *Part Object Part Sculpture* (2005), *Étant donnés* casts a shimmering shadow on the whole project; nonetheless, I still couldn't confront it head-on. Taylor's exhibition and catalogue have enabled me to face what has beguiled and disturbed me over these many years.

What disturbed me most was that, evidently, I wasn't disturbed *enough*. In other words, I never found *Étant donnés* "offensive" or "shocking." As a feminist, I have listened to many a bilious diatribe against it (for many viewers, it is the aftermath of a rape or murder), and I have never *really* been able to articulate why I did not find it antifeminist or misogynist. Certainly, I was able to reproduce Jean-François Lyotard's handy arguments about the piece linking the scopophilia of patriarchy to the development of perspective itself, resulting in the immortal aphorism "*Con celui qui voit*" (He who sees is a cunt).[3] I was also familiar with accounts of the work that read it through the matrix of Lacanian desire; here the figure is centrally marked as castrated, and the viewer is implicated in this abyss of lack. And I was able to convince myself, mildly, of the work's doubly transgressive nature, its simultaneous positioning of the viewer "as essentially carnal," as Rosalind Krauss has phrased it, and

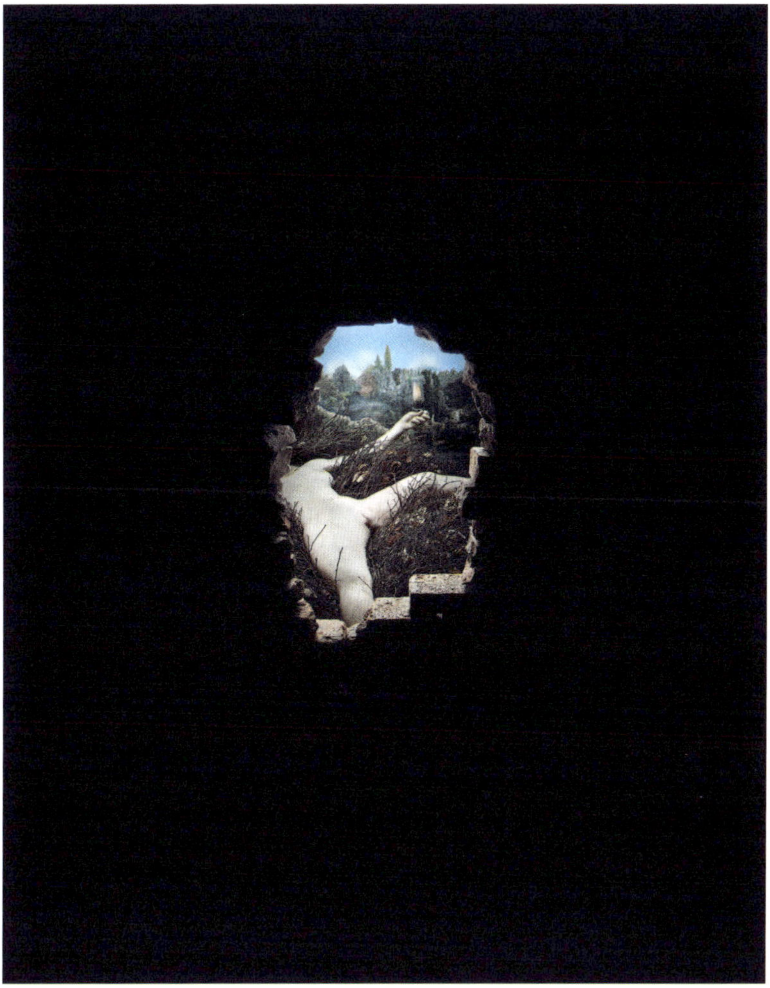

Marcel Duchamp, *Étant donnés: 1° la chute d'eau, 2° le gaz d'éclairage . . . (Given: 1. The Waterfall, 2. The Illuminating Gas . . .)*, 1946–66, mixed-media assemblage: (interior) bricks, velvet, wood, parchment over an armature of lead, steel, brass, synthetic putties and adhesives, aluminum sheet, welded steel-wire screen, and wood; Peg-Board, hair, oil paint, plastic, steel binder clips, plastic clothespins, twigs, leaves, glass, plywood, brass piano hinge, nails, screws, cotton, collotype prints, acrylic varnish, chalk, graphite, paper, cardboard, tape, pen ink, electric light fixtures, gas lamp (Bec Auer type), foam rubber, cork, electric motor, cookie tin, linoleum, 95 ½ x 70 x 49 in. (242.6 x 177.8 x 124.5 cm)

insistence on representation as such.[4] (It's not a woman—it's a sculpture of a woman!) But to be honest, I have always secretly found such accounts, with their insistence on "desire + looking = voyeurism" as the work's primary equation, a bit academic. *Étant donnés*'s intense radicality, indeed its consummate mystery, seemed to elude such formulations. That being said, I shared the sentiment that the work's radicality stems from its evocation of desire—desire for art, for bodies, for images, for sex. Yet beyond that art-historical truism, my thoughts and feelings remained inchoate, particularly when I found myself in its presence.

"Is your mouth a little weak? When you open it to speak, are you smart?..."

Some facts: Among the previously unknown materials revealed by the exhibition is a suite of black-and-white photos of *Étant donnés* installed in Duchamp's studio on Eleventh Street in downtown Manhattan, not long after his death in 1968. They were taken by Denise Hare, the photographer and artist portraitist, at the request of Duchamp's widow, Teeny, in advance of the work's laborious piece-by-piece dismantling, then transfer to and reassembly at the PMA. (It was the second time the work had been moved in less than five years. Duchamp had relocated from his longtime studio on Fourteenth Street in 1965, a victim of rising rents.) The photos are clean and modernist in feel, maintaining a respectful distance even as they knowingly break open Duchamp's great secret. They show us the studio of Duchamp the bricoleur, accumulator of junk, hardware-store scraps, and old chairs, and they give us *Étant donnés* as jury-rigged apparatus: we see the two-by-fours, the drapery, the tangle of coiled and bunched electric wires, the lights, motors, and fans. We see, as well, the full wig of the otherwise headless figure, Duchamp's signature on the body's right arm (until now, hidden from view), and the "empty" studio with its secret door. That's right, a secret door. Duchamp would have people over, and they would leave knowing nothing of his twenty-year project, because all the work was sequestered behind this portal.

Some more facts: Duchamp—who as early as 1921 claimed to have abandoned artmaking for a life of chess and in 1961 infamously stated that he thought the artist of the future would have to "go underground"—worked on *Étant donnés* from 1946 to 1966. During those years, he let only two people know of its existence: his lover the Brazilian artist Maria Martins and, after that relationship ended, his wife, Teeny. A few works relating to *Étant donnés* did make their way into public view in the '50s, but without any indication that they were connected to the clandestine project. Of these, the best known were the erotic objects: *Feuille de vigne femelle* (*Female Fig Leaf*) (1950), *Objet-dard* (*Dart-object*) (1951), and *Coin de chasteté* (*Wedge of Chastity*) (1954), all of which were copied in small bronze editions and reproduced in catalogues as well as exhibited in the '50s and '60s. *Wedge of Chastity*, a bubblegum-pink base with a copper-colored wedge inserted in it, was given to Teeny as a wedding present. When the wedge is lifted, a shocking pink interior, remarkably vaginal in nature, is revealed. According to Duchamp, Teeny used to take it with her when they traveled, leading him to suggest that it was "like a wedding ring."[5] *Female Fig Leaf* looks like a mold of a woman's pussy and was originally given as a gift to Man Ray so that he could make multiples of it for some much-needed cash. *Dart-object* is perhaps the most curious of the trio, simultaneously phallic and scatological, oddly lumpen and inanimate.

Once *Étant donnés* was completed in 1966, a highly select group of PMA trustees and supporters was allowed to see it in order to ensure that it would be accepted into the permanent collection and, further, to guarantee that the work would be placed on permanent public display at the museum, which contains the world's largest collection of works by Duchamp, including the early and crucial *The Bride Stripped Bare by Her Bachelors, Even (The Large Glass)* (1915–23). The work was installed, the fifteen-year photo moratorium was handed down, and gallery 183 was opened. Once it was revealed to the public, it became clear that *Female Fig Leaf* and *Dart-object* were by-products of the casting of the central figure. *Wedge of Chastity*—which is not technically a by-product of *Étant donnés* but, given the way it traffics in playful eroticism and secrecy, belongs among the work's satellites—on the other hand, remained a closed mystery. (The first photo of it "open" was in the *Part Object Part Sculpture* catalogue.)

"Your looks are laughable, unphotographable . . ."

Just as Hare's photos expose some of the physical properties of the work in the studio—as does a series of oddly less evocative photos taken by Duchamp for his meticulous assemblage-instruction manual in 1965—the host of heretofore unknown objects in the exhibition quite literally fill in pieces of the puzzle. Among them are casts of a hand holding the lantern, working body fragments, an array of preparatory drawings, and a marvelous cardboard model of the work with an eye toward its installation in the PMA. The catalogue continues the process of revelation by reproducing not only Hare's and Duchamp's photos but all of Duchamp's letters to Martins, dating from 1946 to 1952, precisely the period he was at work on the large mannequin. The letters are those of a forlorn lover (please write to me) and of a consumed artist recounting his labors in the studio. Every once in a while, they are peppered with revelations of Duchamp's slightly melancholic temperament: "Autumn is quite beautiful here but all the same has a funereal air, like all beautiful autumns—something like a funereal relaxation of things."[6]

One of the most persistent pieces of received wisdom about Duchamp is that he was a paragon of indifference in matters both personal and aesthetic. But this narrative belies another central quality of his character. He had three major romantic relationships: a multidecade affair with the bookbinder and American expatriate Mary Reynolds (she helped the French Resistance during the war), the short-lived affair with Martins, and, late in life, the marriage, by all accounts exceedingly happy, to Teeny. These relationships did not overlap, although Duchamp maintained correspondences and friendships with Reynolds and Martins after their amorous relations had ended. Indeed, he traveled to Paris to be at Reynolds's bedside when she was dying of cancer. Duchamp was nothing if not loyal.

From Taylor's remarkable account of the work's fabrication, we learn, for the first time, that after Reynolds died, her brother provided Duchamp with a trust that gave him enough money to live modestly without having to work; further, Taylor surmises that Duchamp's use of parchment in the molding and casting of the female figure was due to the influence of Reynolds's work as a bookbinder. We also discover that the figure was cast from Martins's body and that the original hair on the mannequin was brown (like Martins's) and was replaced with blond hair after his marriage to Teeny (whose hair was blond). Finally, we learn that one summer it was so hot in New York that the arm holding the illuminating lantern melted and fell off. The break was beyond repair, so it was decided that the limb would be replaced with a cast of Teeny's arm. However, Teeny's arm was larger than Martins's, a discrepancy that contributes to the figure's odd, Ingres-like disjointedness. Each bit of new information, of course, deepens our understanding of *Étant donnés*, but it is these details, above all, that seem to me, finally, to pry open the mysteries of Duchamp's great secret.

"Don't change a hair for me, not if you care for me . . ."

Of course, my long-standing thinking about *Étant donnés* as being, in some way, "about" desire places it in a continuum with *The Large Glass* and is in keeping with the common art historical understanding of Duchamp's entire oeuvre as being "about" desire; nothing new to add here. With this exhibition I felt I was finally able to delineate, in a meaningful way, the stature or quality of that desire. Indeed, the show made me realize the mangy paucity of Duchamp studies (my own included), in that all the talk of desire is always generic (be it capitalist or Lacanian) and never approaches the problem of desire's specificity. It is only now that we can see that "my woman with the open pussy" (from a letter of Duchamp's to Martins) is in fact a complicated composite of three people: Reynolds (the parchment and the money to work), Martins (the original cast and inception), and Teeny (the left arm, the hair, and the completion).[7] The figure is a literal conflation of two bodies, the overall work a palimpsest of, and testament to, three profound love affairs.

An interpretation: I think *Étant donnés* is about love *and* desire, the kind of love you have with another person with whom you are in a desiring relationship. The work's composite nature suggests to me that our capacity for love is infinite; it is not an emotion we run out of or get filled up with. Certainly, it can fade, and often it does. But its possibility for reemergence is continual and ever-present. *Étant donnés* presents us with a quandary, but not the one that has commonly been perceived. Its question is not, How do we make an image of our seemingly unending and unfulfillable desire? but, How do we express this desire when it is also bound up with the infinite quality of love? How do we articulate the tension between the obdurately physical and numinous existential nature of this nexus of love and desire? What is our relationship not only to desire per se but to the other as such? *Étant donnés*'s very immobility, its insistence that you see it on its own terms, is the beginning of the answer. It proposes that love and desire are not portable, available to be moved around at your, our, or my whim. Rather, the work spatializes the idea that when one is in the grip of love and desire, one must meet the other on her own terms. Duchamp's terms are literally to pin me in place; the work holds me at a distance, and I am forever craning my neck to see behind the brick wall, only to find myself, oddly, looking down at my shoes. And isn't that how it so often goes? As hard as we try to "know" the other (our lover), we often end up in a narcissistic loop, talking about ourselves when we mean to be listening.

Étant donnés offers us the encounter with the other in a way that makes it plain we cannot know her. She will remain forever separate. Her muteness is compounded by our inability to remember her accurately, which is how I read the problem of the misplaced labia—as a physicalization of the distortions of memory. Not only is the work unphotographable, it cannot be reproduced in the mind's eye, either. One tends to remember the initial encounter in a general way rather than the kinds of details typically revealed by prolonged looking. Truth be told, long looking is difficult, worried as you are by the thought of being watched by others in the gallery. This is one of the often-remarked ironies of the work—instead of looking at it, we are conscious of being looked at. In the context of this exhibition, I was more conscious than ever of the possibility that I was selfishly taking "too much time." I was acutely aware that when I was looking through the peepholes, someone else couldn't be, and this one-at-a-timeness is analogous to the structure of the monogamous couple, in which only one person can occupy your heart and mind at a time. And coupledom is at the heart of the matter, for no matter how "shocking" or radical *Étant donnés* is, it also suggests that we are never free of the societal conventions of such amorous arrangements, be they the conventions of the affair (Martins was married when she and Duchamp became lovers) or of the marriage—just as we cannot be free of certain pictorial arrangements, whether perspectival viewing or the kitsch of the landscape-as-backdrop.

In *Étant donnés* there is no completion, only encounter. In this sense, it's not so much that the work is shocking (i.e., in some pornographic fashion), but rather that it is shattering, in Leo Bersani's sense of the term. As Bersani says in *The Freudian Body*: "Human sexuality is constituted as a kind of psychic shattering, as a threat to the stability and integrity of the self—a threat which perhaps only the masochistic nature of sexual pleasure allows us to survive."[8] More interpretation: I think *Étant donnés* is an attempt to create an aesthetic experience of shattering that is similar to the alienation from the self we encounter when we fall into the space-time continuum of love and desire. *Étant donnés* is trying to articulate how we arrange ourselves in relation to our own desire for the other. This is where the love part comes in. When we are talking about desire, we easily start talking about objects, for desire is inherently objectifying. When we talk about love, we are discussing the radical interface of (at least) two subjects. With *Étant donnés* we are, it seems to me, a long way from the punning schoolboy humor of Duchamp's early work. We are deep into the problems of adulthood—the time when love and desire are intertwined, the time when our objectifying desire is complicated by the ethics of love.

The work's sensibility is dark. The body is situated among dead branches, and as lifelike as the mannequin is, she is also dead. The viewer is pinned facing the door. Although I think *Étant donnés* is about love and desire (and their working through in coupledom), I also think it produces a kind of tension and ambivalence analogous to marriage's equal summoning of the hope of eternal love and the truth of inevitable death. After all, the *Wedge of Chastity* sat in plain view, establishing both the matrimonial bond and the lie of omission. The secret was established: the couple knows that which those outside it cannot, but internal to the couple there are secrets as well, things that cannot be known. The work's title begins with *Given*, as if a mathematical proof—it begins with the one thing that is irrefutable, the aspect of the problem that cannot be solved but must rather be accepted, as one accepts bedrock. Love and desire are the given; the arrangement we make of them is the challenge. The feminist implications of the work might be that when we come to believe that loving and desirous relations with the other constitute a radical encounter with the self-and not, as we so often think, a completion of the self we are acknowledging our lack of control and authority. The putative violence of the work is possibly a reminder that when we lack control and authority, we risk being damaged or marked—if we return to the mise-en-scène, we will be marked by it, just as we will mark it, leaving our smudged oil marks on the door, an indelible record, a palimpsest of our having been there.

On the walk back, the walk away from *Étant donnés*, nothing looks the same. One glimpses Jasper Johns's sculptures in vitrines, marvelous Joseph Cornell boxes, and Jim Hodges's curtain of flowers, and all of it carries the charge of this encounter with *Étant donnés*, with the given of our loneliness and the funeral quality of our love and desire. *Étant donnés*'s only joke might be about the genre of the nude in the landscape, wherein the rupture of the conventional patriarchal arrangements of women's subservience to men, allegory, aesthetics (just fill in the blank here), cracked open by Cézanne, is completed by Duchamp. If in the Cézanne we see an artist's crisis of faith with such an enterprise, then in *Étant donnés*, a work born of love and desire, completed slowly, in secrecy, and with commitment, we see the great dilemma and shattering pleasure of what it means to be a *subject* of love and desire. It is the viewer who may feel the jig is up and that the task at hand is no longer to produce an image of love and desire, but to render our capacities for those feelings ever more complicated and infinite.

"Each day is Valentine's Day . . ."

Some more facts: as of this writing, thirty-one of the United States of America have legislation that specifically prohibits same-sex marriage. Only five permit same-sex marriage: Connecticut, Iowa, Massachusetts, New Hampshire, and Vermont. The federal government does not recognize the same-sex marriages of these five states, nor does it recognize the same-sex marriages performed in California during the period from June to November 2008, when California deemed it legal for same-sex couples to marry.

FULL-TIME EMPLOYMENT, OR WHEN I REALLY BECAME A FEMINIST

Until I started my professional life, I was a feminist on paper only. Sure, I was all for women's equality and I could easily enumerate the evils of patriarchy, but I was vain in that I thought my successes would belong to me. Like most middle-class white girls born in the USA in the later half of the twentieth century, I fell pretty hard for that whole meritocracy thing. I thought if I did the work, I'd be judged on the work. It wasn't until I left school and embarked on a career path that I began to experience sexism on a daily basis.

I didn't yet have the specific language of "microaggressions" to describe it, but that didn't mean I didn't feel the constant small slights, or that I wasn't aware of how my male colleagues were earning more money than me for doing less work, or that the artwork I was interested in didn't have auction records to justify prices, or that it was infinitely more difficult to land a one-person show of a woman on the exhibition schedule, or that affluent straight white men were forever interested in and confused by my sexuality, and so on.

And there's nothing like walking the halls of a museum every day to drive home the *longue durée* of inequality—in all its sexist and racist manifestations. And yet, every day I went to work I was keenly aware of all the opportunities I had that were literally unimaginable to my grandmother. Every day I went to work I was aware of how firmly in place the glass ceiling (not to mention the lack of access to birth control and abortion) was for women of my mother's generation. Basically, having a job—which means a daily negotiation of power, authority, expertise, and money—meant feminism went from being a set of theoretical problems to being a set of lived daily experiences, with real-life consequences.

Because I believed in the meritocracy, and because I loved to work (my ego was, and remains, very bound up in work), I tried to tackle my experience of sexism by foregrounding the "women" part of the women artists conundrum. I thought if I centered my interests around the artistic production of women, I could make a dent in the patriarchal structure of the museum. I set about, as did a handful of my museum peers, working on, and toward, the feminist process/project of recovery. I attempted on numerous occasions and in many ways to lift women artists out of the benign neglect with which they were treated and demand that we take their work more seriously. I thought that this could be achieved through writing, through acquisition, and through the thoughtful installations of a museum's collection. And because I believe in parity, I thought it was always necessary to look at your lineup of speakers, artists, writers, exhibitions, and say: this list doesn't have enough women on it.

However, the three essays that follow proceed differently. These essays are structured by a somewhat utopian "what if" question: Should you achieve parity, what then? Once I was in the workplace, it was abundantly clear that parity alone was not the answer. And so the real question became: What do we do with recovered women artists' work? How do we tell a story about art, and art history, that acknowledges, rather than papers over, the centuries of inequity? Like many third-generation feminists, I didn't simply want a seat at the table: when it came to the collection, display, and interpretation of art made by women, I wanted a different table.

Despite my good intentions, rereading these essays shows me that they are profoundly lacking in two ways. One is historical in nature—my definition of *woman* is historically bound. When I wrote these essays, I imagined women exclusively as cisgender women. This is a deeply ingrained habit, and I am a profoundly ideological subject in this regard. Rereading these essays, I am unsure of how trans logic might affect them. This is a blind spot. My hope is that, despite my limitations, the essays might be useful for younger scholars and artists, or at the very least, they can function as a kind of step stool for someone to reach higher ground.

The second paucity in these essays dovetails with the first, but at the time of their writing it could have been redressable. Simply put, these are not intersectional essays. When the category "woman" is summoned, it is not marked by/imbricated in race, class, or sexuality. I use the word *woman* in the old-fashioned way: *woman*—literally, invariably—means "white woman." Given that the first essay deals with labor, this feels particularly problematic. I read bell hooks in the late 1980s; I knew better! The hole in these essays is so large that, in the inimitable phraseology of the Texan side of my family, "if it had a nose it would'a bit me." While I am keenly aware of these shortcomings, I still stand by these texts. They have blind spots, and yet they very accurately describe my daily experience (as a cisgender white woman with blind spots) in museums. To me, they feel akin to reading an old diary. They are a record of a curator trying to figure out how to arrange and display artworks and make arguments in ways that were demonstrably different from both her elders and her peers.

Despite their flaws, I think these essays might be some of my best writing because they attempt to take structural absence seriously. These essays don't imagine that a structural absence can be "filled" or "righted." Structural absence means just that—that the situation (the museum, the canon, the Enlightenment, whiteness) is dependent upon absence, so when an absence is "redressed," the structure itself must be altered. Such thinking is most rigorously developed in postcolonial theory, African American studies, and queer theory. And as a result, each of these essays is engaged in a reimagining of art history as an academic discipline, and the museum as the discipline's public facing institution.

And it's their imbrication in institutional thinking that leads me to another reason I stand by these essays. They are each engaged, in increasing explicitness, in the need to rethink the spatial logic of museums. Museums are a great big engine for narrative in three dimensions. Exhibitions are stories told with objects in space, rather than words on a page. These essays are searching for new ways to tell new stories. They explicitly focus on the problem of how and where artworks are installed. They are shot through with an early suspicion of chronological time. They are aware that "history" doesn't benefit the disenfranchised. They are in search of other voices, other rooms. These essays are cognizant that because the arguments made by museums are inherently spatial, that the arrangement of pictures and objects—what we call "the install" in the trade—is not an afterthought; it is a form of thinking in and of itself.

As such, more than any other work I've done, this thinking is what led me to participate in the great experiment of artists Karon and Noah Davis: the Underground Museum. When Noah Davis asked if I would be willing to lend objects from the museum (where I was serving as chief curator) to an artist-run space in the working class, Black and Latinx neighborhood of Arlington

Heights in Los Angeles I was primed to leap at that opportunity because I had already been thinking about how to change the frame. I'd already been thinking about structural absence. I'd already been thinking about power relations. I'd already been thinking about new audiences and what they might need and want. I felt like I was already halfway there.

When Noah and Karon planted the Underground Museum flag, what they offered me was the professional and personal opportunity to alter the logic of the museum, to convert it from one of hoarding and protecting to a structure of asset sharing; from a white, trustee-led space to a Black, artist-led space; and, finally, from my performing the role of titled, paid professional to the opportunity for making the human contribution of what artist Mike Kelley once called "love hours."

If there might be lessons in any of this, I think perhaps one of them would be to seek out in your own work—as well as in the work of others—what renders you the most open to change. No essay or artwork or argument is foolproof, no human is flawless. Perfection is a decoy, a mirage designed to remove you from the far more human path of working toward and contributing to a greater good. Embrace failure, try to see your blind spots, don't let criticism (either your own or others') be corrosive. At the end of the day, for me, feminism was not necessarily about "women" per se. To be more specific, I am not interested in feminism that places women at its center as its exclusive or crowning activity. I'm interested in feminism as a discourse that allows us to query power. Feminism in and of itself is not singular, it is profoundly plural, and as an umbrella term what it encapsulates is a set of tools that help each of us to keep trying to redistribute, circulate, and share any authority, power, and wealth that comes our way. This is why it's so useful at work.

House Work and Art Work

Originally published in *October* 92 (Spring 2000): 71–97.

Laughter in the face of serious categories is indispensable for feminism.
—Judith Butler, *Gender Trouble* (1990)

The much-noted eclecticism of 1990s art practice appears to have been countered only by a steady fascination with and revival of art from the 1970s. This interest, shared by artists, critics, historians, and curators, generated numerous exhibitions and publications dedicated to the feminist work of the period.[1] That such interest in 1970s feminist practice is long overdue perhaps goes without saying, although for many it has emerged as either a mysteriously forgotten moment or the return of the repressed. In both guises many of these stagings have continued, unfortunately, to consolidate a logic of "us" and "them," a structure of bitter binary opposition, an intellectual disjuncture between feminist work based in "theory," poststructuralism, or social constructionism, and work derived from the so-called principles of "essentialism."[2] Far from an attempt to set the record straight, or to ascertain definitively what did or did not happen, this essay is motivated by a need to rearticulate the current reception's account of the relations between these two bodies of work. More precisely, it seeks to reconsider four artists at work in the 1970s—Judy Chicago, Mary Kelly, Mierle Laderman Ukeles, and Martha Rosler—artists whose works have been caught in an interpretive blind spot created by the current reception's perpetuation of the antagonism between feminist art of the 1970s and '80s.[3]

Despite the breadth and complexity of the issues—the diversity of practices within each, somewhat loosely defined, "camp"—a certain reduction has taken place in the current reception of 1970s feminist work, an intellectual fault line broadly described in generational terms. And as the disjuncture between feminist practices from the 1970s and '80s is repeatedly historicized as a permanent rupture, we currently receive these strained relations in the form of a caricature. This situation is perhaps most problematic and prevalent in the classroom, where the debate is often hypostatized into an art historical compare-and-contrast, iconically represented by two seemingly antithetical art works: Judy Chicago's *The Dinner Party* (1974–79) and Mary Kelly's *Post-Partum Document* (1973–79), works taken to be exemplary of an essentialist approach in Chicago's case, and a theory-based feminist practice in Kelly's case. Although both works were completed in 1979, they have been rendered

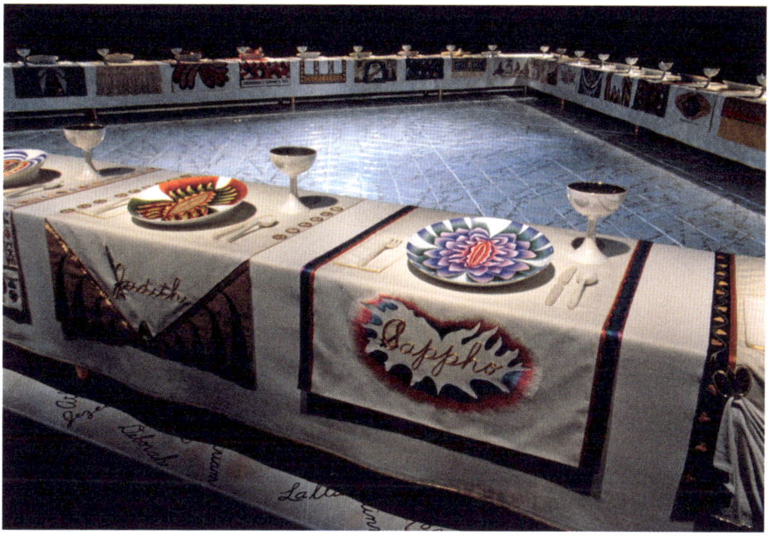

Judy Chicago, *The Dinner Party*, 1974–79, ceramic, porcelain, textile, 576 x 576 in. (1,463 x 1,463 cm)

crudely oppositional and hierarchized, and are often asked to bear the weight of a generational split—from the 1970s to the '80s—as well as presenting, equally self-evidently, the "progression" in feminist art *from* essentialism *to* theory.[4] The language of progress is used across the board; listen as Lisa Tickner argues that the "adolescent vitality of 1970s feminism matured successfully into a body of rigorous 1980s art and criticism."[5] Similarly, Griselda Pollock demarcates a shift from a politics of "liberation" to a "structural mode of analysis."[6] And Faith Wilding, a member of *Womanhouse*, described some 1970s artistic experiments, particularly cunt imagery, as "crude . . . precursors for a new vocabulary for representing female sexuality and the body in art."[7]

The logic of progress has done much to codify this classic pairing of post-1960s art into a stale binarism: all contrast, no comparison. Yet perhaps we can loosen the starched opposition of essentialism "versus" theory by acknowledging that the model of compare-and-contrast need not *only* produce dismissive hierarchies, or generational or oppositional binarisms. It is a model equally well designed to elaborate on moments of affinity and shared concerns (not yet acknowledged), *as well as* moments of contestation and difference (which have been insisted on more forcefully).

Despite various challenges to this generational/progressive frame, it has stiffly endured. The tenacity of the division occludes a more pedestrian question: Why is this particular art historical debate so problematic? For instance, why don't we simply say, "Both sides have strong and weak points," and pluralistically be done with it? As unproductive as this debate has been, merely to paper over significant aesthetic, ideological, and philosophical differences would be to run the risk of consolidating the category heading "feminist art." As a codified "movement" (however internally fractured), feminist art is stripped of its transformative power.[8] Rendered separate and distinct, and hence easier to marginalize, it is unable to challenge and modify our definitions of other artistic categories, the result of which has been to prohibit articulations of the connective tissue between these works and the putatively "dominant" conversations simultaneously being held in the art world.[9] One way, perhaps, to reread the theory/essentialism split is to see artists during the 1980s—in the Pictures group, for instance—as consciously working with ideas such as the theory of representation precisely as a way to avoid the problems of the marginalization of "feminism."[10] So, too, we could see that itacknowledgingwas clearly important for feminists to be able to disagree, and even fight with, previous generations of feminists, as a way both to open the field of inquiry and to proliferate its influence. Currently, however, the continual rehearsing of the theory/essentialism debate, only to choose sides at the end, has disallowed other interpretive formations to arise. For instance, the division may serve to maintain, rather than expand, the rather limited range of feminist theory that operates in the art world. There currently exist critical feminist discourses other than Anglo-American empiricism and continental theory; and the chasm between them has been navigated, most notably, by political philosophers. In other words, we need not only be bound to the interpretive models that have traditionally accompanied each body of work, but we can also look to the tools and interpretive possibilities offered by the feminist critique of political philosophy.

In *Feminism and Philosophy*, Moira Gatens has staged the feminist debate in terms of those who privilege a model of equality and those who think in terms of difference.[11] These terms are analogous to the essentialism/theory split and Gatens astutely problematizes both positions. First, she sets out to dismantle the idea of equality. She argues that the problem with the model of "equality in the public sphere" is that

> the public sphere is dependent upon and developed around a male subject who acts in the public sphere but is maintained in the private sphere, traditionally by women. This is to say that liberal society assumes that its citizens continue to be what they were historically, namely male heads of households who have at their disposal the services of an unpaid domestic worker/mother/wife.[12]

These services have become so naturalized that "clearly, part of the privilege accorded to members of a political body is that their needs, desires, and powers are converted into rights and virtues."[13] In other words, Gatens suggests that the political realm within which women struggle for equality, such as democracy, must be disarticulated, not presumed a priori to be a "neutral" system, except for *its inability to grant women equality*. The system

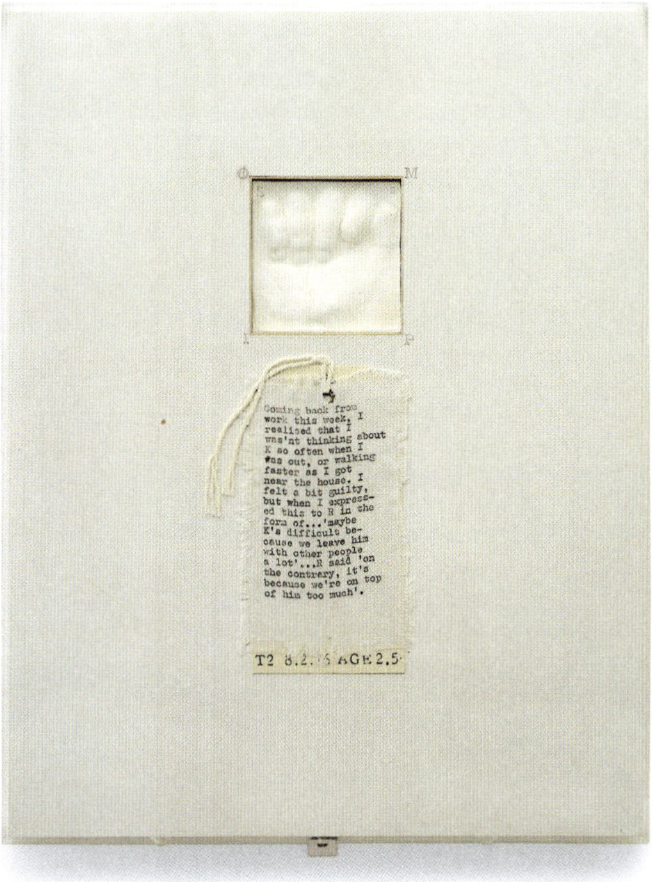

Mary Kelly, *Post-Partum Document: Documentation IV, Transitional Objects, Diary and Diagram* (detail), 1976, Perspex, white card, plaster, cotton fabric, string, 8 units: 14 x 11 in. (35.5 x 28 cm) each

is founded on inequality; hence "equality in this context can involve only the abstract opportunity to become men."[14]

Democracy's dependence upon inequality has been naturalized as the public and private spheres have been used to shore up distinctions and inequities between men and women, particularly in that the private sphere has been "intricate[ly] and extensive[ly] cross-reference[d] . . . with the body, passions, and nature."[15] This critique of equality (as found in much Anglo-American feminist theory) reveals the very notion of equality and its symbolic representation in the public sphere to be historically dependent on the unacknowledged (and unequal) labor of the private sphere.[16]

Gatens is also suspicious of the discursive move from equality to difference. Noting that feminist writing and art practice, after freeing itself from the tyranny of nature, took up explorations of female sexuality, she cautions that such a move runs the risk of reducing women's subjectivity to their sexuality. While Gatens is sympathetic to critical feminist explorations of psychoanalytic models of subjectivity fundamentally rooted in sexuality, she counters the ahistorical logic of psychoanalysis by submitting it to a Foucauldian analysis that conceives of the body as "an effect of socially and historically specific practices."[17] She argues that "bodies are turned into individuals of various kinds" by "discourses and practices [which] create ideologically appropriate subjects" and "practices [which] construct certain kinds of bodies with particular kinds of power and capacity."[18] Furthermore, "to insist on sexual difference as *the* fundamental and eternally immutable difference would be to take for granted the intricate and pervasive ways in which patriarchal culture has made that difference its insignia."[19] She is wary, then, of feminists who place sexuality (as the extension of or outcome of sexual difference) at center stage, theoretically or aesthetically. One effect of Gatens's critique is to register the extent to which *both* groups of feminist work explored issues of sexuality to the exclusion of other attributes of subjectivity and also to the exclusion of political philosophy's critique of the role of the private sphere in the democracy-capitalism covenant.

As Gatens problematizes the equality/difference dichotomy through a feminist analysis of political philosophy, so, too, a similar operation can be performed on the iconic pairing of the *Post-Partum Document* and *The Dinner Party*, by considering them in conjunction with Mierle Laderman Ukeles's *Maintenance Art* performances (1973–74) and Martha Rosler's videos *Semiotics of the Kitchen* (1975) and *Domination and the Everyday* (1978)—works produced around the same time and under similar cultural pressures. Ukeles's and Rosler's work is explicitly concerned with how "ideologically appropriate subjects" are created, in part, through the naturalizing of unpaid and underpaid domestic labor. By placing the *PPD* and *The Dinner Party* within this expanded interpretive field, labor, particularly domestic or maintenance labor, emerges as a thematic shared by these four artists (as well as many others of the period). The introduction of the problem of such labor leads, in turn, to a consideration of the relations between public and private, which emerges as a defining issue in the discussion of 1970s art and the legacy of feminism's intervention in it. The problematic of public and private spheres is, of course, present in both *The Dinner Party* and *Post-Partum Document*, but the essentialism/theory debate has occluded its importance, disallowing the debate to be framed in terms of a political economy as well as a bodily or psychic one.[20]

In her 1969 "Maintenance Art Manifesto," Ukeles divided human labor into two categories: development and maintenance. She writes:

> Development: pure individual creation; the new; change; progress; advance; excitement; flight or fleeing. Maintenance: Keep the dust

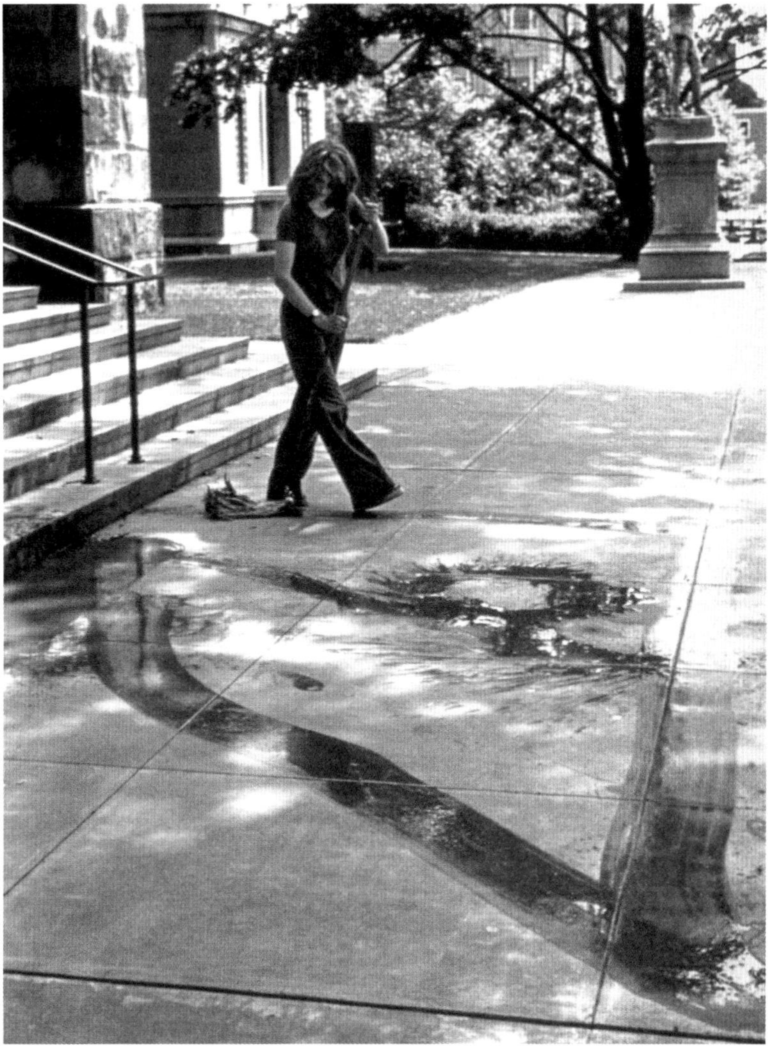
Mierle Laderman Ukeles, *Washing / Tracks / Maintenance: Outside*, 1973, from the *Maintenance Art* performance series, 1973–74. Performance view: Wadsworth Atheneum, Hartford, CT

> off the pure individual creation; preserve the new; sustain the change; protect progress; defend and prolong the advance; renew the excitement; repeat the flight.[21]

Ukeles's manifesto insists that ideals of modernity (progress, change, individual creation) are dependent on the denigrated and boring labor of maintenance (activities that make things possible—cooking, cleaning, shopping, child-rearing, and so forth). Incisively, Ukeles does not refer to maintenance as domestic labor, or housework, for it is evident that such labor is not confined solely to the spaces of domesticity. Included in this manifesto was a proposal that Ukeles live in the museum and perform her maintenance activities; while the gallery might look "empty," she explained that her labor would indeed be the "work."[22] Her offer went unaccepted.

In 1973, however, the Wadsworth Atheneum agreed to the *Maintenance Art* performances. In *Washing / Tracks / Maintenance: Inside*, Ukeles scrubbed and mopped the floor of the museum for four hours. In *Washing / Tracks / Maintenance: Outside*, she cleaned the exterior plaza and steps of the museum. She referred to these activities as "floor paintings." In *Transfer: The Maintenance of the Art Object*, she designated her cleaning of a protective display case as an art work—a "dust painting." Normally this vitrine was cleaned by the janitor; however, once Ukeles's cleaning of the case was designated as "art," the responsibility of the cleaning and maintenance of this case became the job of the conservator. The fourth performance, *The Keeping of the Keys*, consisted of Ukeles taking the museum guards' keys and locking and unlocking galleries and offices, which when locked were subsequently deemed to be works of "maintenance art." In each performance, Ukeles's role as "artist" allowed her to reconfigure the value bestowed upon these otherwise unobtrusive maintenance operations, and to explore the ramifications of making maintenance labor visible in public.

Martha Rosler's videos *Semiotics of the Kitchen* and *Domination and the Everyday* also critically engaged the problem of housewifery. In the relatively new medium of video, *Semiotics of the Kitchen* humorously skewered both the mass-media image of the smiling, middle-class, white housewife and theories of semiotics, suggesting that neither was able to provide an adequate account of the role of wife/mother/maintenance provider. Informed by Marxist and feminist critique, *Domination and the Everyday* considers the everyday household labors of women in tandem with global politics. Like the *Maintenance Art* performances, *Domination* suggests that the domestic chores of cooking and child-rearing are not exclusively private, but, instead, that such labors are intimately connected to public events, and furthermore that unpaid and underpaid maintenance labor needs to be thought of as equivalent to other forms of oppression.

What happens if the *Maintenance Art* performances and Rosler's early video work are insinuated into *The Dinner Party* and *Post-Partum Document* binarism, creating a four-way compare-and-contrast? Might such an expanded field allow us to see previously unacknowledged aspects of each of the works? For instance, as well as seeing the stark contrast between Chicago's cunt-based central core imagery and Kelly's pointed refusal to represent the female body, we might also see that all four artists deal in varying degrees with putatively "private" aspects of women's lives and experience: motherhood, cleaning, cooking, and entertaining. Similarly, as opposed to the intractable

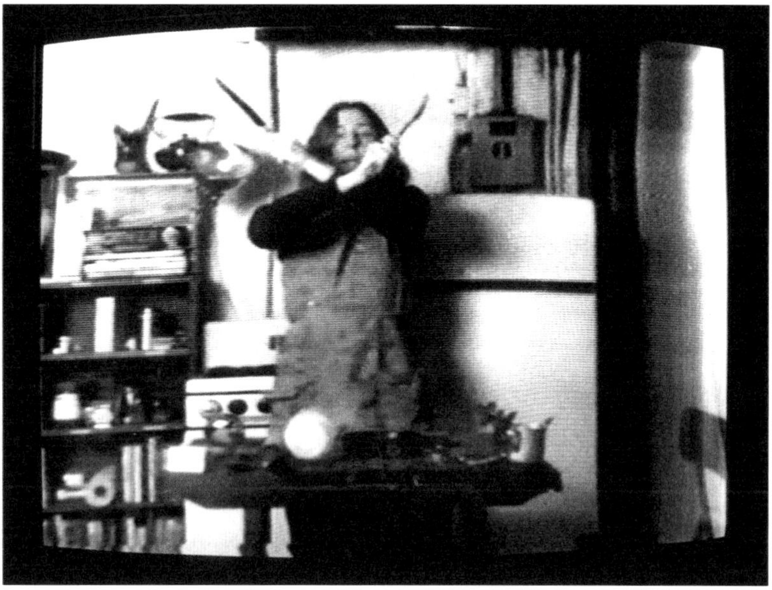

Martha Rosler, *Semiotics of the Kitchen*, 1975 (still), video, black and white, sound, 6:33 min.

contrast between the lush tactile quality of *The Dinner Party* and the diagrammatic aspect of the *Post-Partum Document*, we might see the importance of text in each of the works. The women's names that cover the floor and place settings mean that reading is also integral to viewing *The Dinner Party*. Rosler's *Domination and the Everyday* contains a running text at the bottom of the screen and Ukeles's works contain charts, posted announcements, and the "Maintenance Art" verification stamp. Each artist participated in the assault on the privileged role of vision in aesthetics, as did so many of their 1970s contemporaries. When the binarism is undone, we can see that these works were directly engaged with the most "advanced" artistic practices of the day—Minimalism, performance, and Conceptual art—and that they were also in the process of forming the practice of institutional critique.[23] This is, again, to insist on the linkages between art informed by feminism and most of the advanced or critical artistic practices of the 1960s and '70s that took as part of their inquiry the institutions within which art is encountered. The artists who worked in this manner—whose work's content was bound up with domesticity or maintenance and its structural relation to the public sphere—have been by and large neglected by the historians and archivists of Minimalism, Conceptual art, and institutional critique.[24] Their omission was caused not by active suppression but rather a fundamental *misrecognition* of the terms and strategies they employed. The overtly domestic/maintenance content of such works was read as being equivalent to their meaning.

Therefore, little or no attention was paid to these works' engagement with the Duchampian legacy of art's investigation of its own meaning, value, and institutionality. What has not been fully appreciated are the ways in which this usually "degraded" content actually *permits* an engagement with questions of value and institutionality that critique the conditions of everyday life as well as art. Hence, when we compare *The Dinner Party*, *Semiotics of the Kitchen* and *Domination and the Everyday*, and the *Post-Partum Document* with Ukeles's explicit feminist address of the museum, we are able to reframe them in such a manner as to see that they were each bound up with a critique of the institutional conditions of art. Among the four artists, this critique manifested itself in varying degrees and was shaped by different concerns.

There is no denying that Chicago's work may seem to us now the most problematic of the four, in that her work supports a notion of genius and "artist" in keeping with the ideal model of bourgeois subjectivity offered by the Western art museum. Yet, despite the differences between the works (or because of them), the feminist critique of the institutions of art should no longer be misrecognized, for its understanding of the relations between "private" acts and public institutions will reframe the work of contemporaneous figures in the field. Such a comparison will ultimately expand our notion of institutional critique, precisely because the feminist critique differs so markedly from the paradigmatic works of figures such as Marcel Broodthaers, Daniel Buren, or Hans Haacke. For as we will see, it insisted on the reciprocity and mutual dependence of the categories of private and public.

* * *

Ukeles's performances, by establishing domestic (read: private, natural) labor as "maintenance," help to articulate the structural conditions of the relations between the public and private sphere. It is the "hidden" and unrecognized nature of this labor that permits the myth that the public sphere functions as a self-contained and independent site, a site devoid of interest (in classic Habermasian terms). However, by staging such labors in the museum, a traditional institution of the bourgeois public sphere, Ukeles's work establishes maintenance labor as a subject for public discussion. For, as Rosalyn Deutsche has argued, "what is recognized in public space is the legitimacy of debate about what is legitimate and what is illegitimate."[25] It is the very publicness of art, art's traditional reliance on a public sphere for its legibility and value, that makes art such a rich terrain for feminist critique. Hence Ukeles's performance of maintenance activities, in full view of the museum and its visitors, opens public space to the pressures of what it traditionally excludes, or renders invisible. The work of Chicago, Kelly, and Rosler does this too, each at the level of explicit content (although Kelly and Rosler do considerably more work at the level of form, as well). But when Ukeles renames domestic labor "maintenance," she uses ideas and processes usually deemed "private" to open institutions and ideas usually deemed "public."

This gesture is in obvious sympathy with the 1970s feminist slogan "the personal is political," but, more incisively, it supports political philosopher Carole Pateman's contention that "the public sphere is always assumed to throw light onto the private sphere, rather than vice versa. On the contrary, an understanding of modern patriarchy requires that the employment contract is illuminated by the structure of domestic relations."[26] In other words, one legacy of feminist criticism is to establish that it is the private sphere that can help us to rearticulate the public sphere, as opposed to the other way around. Ukeles's exposure of this problematic animates the content of labor in both *The Dinner Party* and the *Post-Partum Document*, pulling these works away from their more familiar interpretations.

To position this work as negotiating the terrain of public and private is to establish its links to, as opposed to its separation from, other postwar art practices. Chicago's early sculptural activity—in works like *Pasadena Lifesavers* (1969–70)—took the form of repetitive modular units fabricated from industrial materials, objects clearly in dialogue with Minimalism and its West Coast variant, "finish fetish."[27] Chicago's repetitive formal structure, her use of the triangular shaped table, her fetishism of surface and texture, suggest that *The Dinner Party* continued her dialogue with Minimalism. However, by the mid-1970s, Chicago had imported explicit content into these otherwise generic structures. Specifically sexed bodies are offered as opposed to the nonspecific or universal body posited by Minimalism's understanding of phenomenology, and the "private" nature of genitalia, especially the vagina, is rendered spectacularly public. Likewise, historically under-recognized forms of domestic and decorative craft replace the lure (and perhaps just barely veiled decorative aspects) of industrial production. Minimalism also asked for a consideration of the logic of repetition; consider Donald Judd's oft-quoted "one thing after another." Reading *The Dinner Party* through a hermeneutics of maintenance suggests that the logic of repetition is not exclusively bound to industrial production but exists as well—although with vastly different effects—in the perpetual labors of cooking, eating, and cleaning up: the women's work that is never done; work that is conspicuously absent in *The Dinner Party*, effaced as it was by its Minimalist counterparts.[28] And if Minimalism asked its viewers to distinguish what in the room was not sculpture, what in the room constituted institutional space, then *The Dinner Party* potentially asked viewers to articulate what in the room existed in the realm of the private and what belonged in the realm of the public.[29]

By tweaking and pinching Minimalism's suppression of the particularity of gendered bodies, *The Dinner Party* suggested that the (impossible) idea of a generic body helped to enable the historical bourgeois public sphere as a site of (fictional) disinterest, a site bound by the terms of patriarchy. Kelly's *Post-Partum Document* similarly critiqued the terms of Conceptual art. Kelly's early work, done in Britain during the 1970s, was collaborative in nature and focused largely on the struggle for women's equality in the workplace. Two works stand out: the cocurated exhibition *Women and Work:*

A Document on the Division of Labour in Industry (1975) and the collaboratively made film *Nightcleaners* (1975), which documented the organizing of a women's cleaning union but refused the traditional methods of agitprop or documentary, opting for Brechtian strategies of distanciation.[30] *Women and Work* depicted two years of research into the sexual division of labor in a metal-box factory. By conceiving of the exhibition as the artwork itself, *Women and Work* questioned both the autonomy of the art object and the fiction of the disinterested gallery space. The show's refusal of visuality, its negation of the art object as a commodity, and its challenge to the traditional role of the gallery within the distribution system all partook of Conceptual art's assault on art.

It would be *Post-Partum Document*, however, that would launch a more thorough critique of Conceptual art. Following on Minimalism's investigation of the public quality of art, much Conceptual art sought to replace a spatial and visual experience with a linguistic one, or what has been called "the work as analytic proposition."[31] This meant that the art object could be radically de-skilled, potentially democratizing art's production. However, Frazer Ward has argued that while Conceptual art "sought to demystify aesthetic experience and mastery ('Anybody can do that'), [it] maintained the abstraction of content crucial to high modernist art," hence, "if modernist painting was just about painting, Conceptual art was just about art."[32] Just as Chicago exposed Minimalism's abstract viewer, similarly the explicit content of the *Post-Partum Document* complicated Conceptual art's hermeticism.[33]

The *Document*'s numerous graphs and charts, in their standardized frames (a repetition that rhymes with Chicago's), represent the labor of child care, labor normally obscured in Western capitalist culture. One effect of the category of the mother as essential and biological is to naturalize this labor, placing it outside of social conditions. (It is telling that the *PPD* emerges around the time of the idea of the "working mother," as if mothering weren't already a form of work.) Kelly's refusal to image the mother impedes the naturalization of the labor of motherhood (in Gatens's words, "cross referenced with the private"). By submitting this labor to the public and social languages of work and science, the *Document* countermands Conceptual art's maintenance of abstract relations between public and private realms, revealing its continuation of a modernist paradigm of art for art's sake. (Indeed, if one of the primary responses to modernist painting is, "My kid could do that," or, "What is that crap on the walls?" then Kelly's inclusion of her son's soiled diapers could be seen as a joke at the expense of both Conceptual art and modernist painting.) Kelly's inclusion of maintenance labor also functions as an address to the institution of the museum. She has said of the work, "As an installation within a traditional gallery space, the work subscribes to certain modes of presentation; the framing, for example, parodies a familiar type of museum display in so far as it allows my archaeology of the everyday to slip unannounced into the great hall and ask impertinent questions of its keepers."[34] This "archaeology of the everyday" permitted Kelly to represent two forms of labor—artistic and domestic—both of which debunk the myths of nonwork that surround both forms of reproduction (artist as genius, mother as natural). *PPD* stages the relations between artistic and human creation as analogous, and by doing so interrogates the boundaries between public and private realms of experience. And if one premise of Conceptual art is that "anyone can do it," then Kelly's work suggests that the same is true of the labor of mothering, for to denaturalize such labor is to make it non-gender-specific.

While Chicago and Kelly were extensively engaged with the public discursive fields of Minimalism and Conceptual art, Ukeles's explicit address of the museum makes her work an early instance of institutional critique.[35] By taking the normally hidden labor of the private sphere and submitting it to public scrutiny in the institutions of art, *Maintenance Art* explored the fictional quality of the distinction between public and private. The performances demonstrated that the work of maintenance is neither exclusively public nor private; it is the realm of human activities that serves to bind the two. Ukeles's use of performance—her insistence that her "private" body perform "private" activities in public space—seems to suggest that maintenance is a key component of subjectivity. Yet it is one that often goes unrecognized, and instead is naturalized through repetition into the status of "habit," as opposed to being constitutive of identity. So one effect of Ukeles's performances is to show how institutions such as the museum unconsciously help to maintain "the category of artistic individuality that emblematizes bourgeois subjectivity" through its suppression of its dependence on the labors that keep the white cube clean.[36]

However, when the bonding between public and private realms is exposed, or when an identity delineated by maintenance, as opposed to artistic expression, is foregrounded, the "proper" functioning of the public institution is compromised. Ukeles's performances dramatize that when maintenance is put front and center, made visible, given equal value with art objects, the museum chokes and sputters. For instance, *The Keeping of the Keys* wreaked havoc on the museum's normal workday. The piece so infuriated the curators, who felt that their office and floor should be exempt, that when Ukeles announced that their office was to become a piece of "maintenance art," all but one curator ran out of the office, fleeing both the artist and their own work. The work stoppage that resulted from the systematic privileging of maintenance work over other forms of work is a vivid instance of Carole Pateman's argument that it is absolutely structural to patriarchy and capitalism that the labor of maintenance remain *invisible*. When made *visible*, the maintenance work that makes other work possible arrests and stymies the very labor it is designed to maintain.

This work stoppage was not isolated. In *Transfer: The Maintenance of the Art Object*, Ukeles selected a female mummy housed in a glass case from the museum's collection. Traditionally, it was the janitor's job to keep this case clean. In a ceremony staged for the camera, the janitor relinquished his rag and cleaning fluid to Ukeles, who then cleaned the case as a "Maintenance Artist," as opposed to a maintenance person, making what she called a "dust painting." After the mummy case was cleaned, she stamped both it and the cleaning rag with a rubber stamp certifying their new identities as "Maintenance Art Works." The stamped rag and the cleaning fluid were then offered to the museum conservator, in the same ceremonial manner; for the cleaned case, now a work of "Maintenance Art," could only be cleaned (or maintained) by the conservator.

The photographs of *Transfer* are accompanied by a hand-drawn diagram that resembles a low-tech flowchart and details the ramifications of the transfer, mapping how one job (cleaning) had been made the province of three different professionals (janitor, artist, conservator). The goofiness of the chart is a send-up of the clinical "aesthetic of administration" put forth by many Conceptual artists and practitioners of institutional critique, although here the diagram mimes managerial concerns with the division of labor as well.[37] This performance highlights the division of labor that supports the aura of the artist's signature, an aura the museum is dependent on for its legitimacy (and which it in turn legitimates), but in *Transfer*, anyone can use the maintenance art stamp, compromising the value of the artist's signature as a guarantor of art. More importantly, though, by insisting that everyone clean the mummy case, the performance intimates that anyone can perform maintenance. Once again, the public exposure of maintenance gums up the work of the museum, complicating the smooth, seamless, efficient functioning of the institution.

Ukeles's *Maintenance Art* performances combine slapstick humor and serious critique. This aesthetic mixture (Karl Marx meets the Marx Brothers) is also found in the works of Martha Rosler. Rosler is perhaps best known for her two influential Conceptual pieces *The Bowery in two inadequate descriptive systems* (1974–75) and *Vital Statistics of a Citizen, Simply Obtained* (1977), both of which exposed the limits of representation and imported charged political content into the field of Conceptual art. Her early collages and video works are less familiar. Many of these works focused on various aspects of cooking: the disparity between starvation and gourmet meals; the cultural value placed on cooking, and the complicated hierarchies of who cooks and who serves what food. Several works transpose the language of cooking and the language of art, forming a composite that alludes to the similarity between the terms *artwork* and *housework*. In all of these early works—be they videos, film scripts, or postcard pieces—Rosler frames the conviviality of food as a bodily necessity and pleasure that binds all human beings. Yet lest such commonality give rise to humanist myths (as is the case with Chicago's work), she also casts the production of food as a form of maintenance labor, and hence subject to the inequities of race, class, and gender, that cannot be merely swept away under the guise of things "private" or "domestic." Similar to Ukeles's performances in both their rejection of traditional artistic media and their focus on various aspects of maintenance labor, video works such as *Semiotics of the Kitchen* and *Domination and the Everyday* turn a critical eye toward the relations between public and private that shape our daily lives.

Both videos employ various strategies of distanciation, yet, as in Ukeles's performances, such strategies are combined with a sometimes caustic, sometimes slapstick sense of humor. In *Semiotics of the Kitchen*, Rosler stands in a kitchen and names various cooking utensils in alphabetical order and then mimes their uses ("bowl," she declares, and stirs an imaginary substance). Rosler "performs" the role of cook as if the stage directions were written by Bertolt Brecht; straight-faced and purged of emotion, she discourages any identification on the part of the viewer. (However, in the background we can see a large book whose binding reads "MOTHER," suggesting a possible root cause for the character's bizarre behavior.) The tape also lacks a plot, offering a list instead of a story, further blocking "normative" identification. A broadly drawn spoof on television cooking shows, the tape further discourages identification in that there is nothing to cook, no recipe to complete, we are not asked to follow along with her activities. Yet Rosler's deadpan delivery is held in humorous relation to her slapstick-like performance of nonexistent activities (recalling Charlie Chaplin's *Gold Rush*, Rosler ladles an imaginary liquid and then tosses it over her shoulder; instead of "slicing" or "cutting" with the knife, she aggressively stabs at the air). The exaggerated sense of physical labor means that her everyday kitchen gestures border on the calisthenic. The work's humor and deliberate foiling of the maintenance labor of cooking (if the kitchen had any actual food in it, the set would have resembled the aftermath of a food fight) recalls Ukeles's slapstick aesthetic. Indeed, to think of the two works in tandem is to heighten the way in which the works are designed in part to provoke an extremely ambivalent response on the part of the viewer. Should we giggle or shudder at the trapped quality of Rosler's slightly maniacal home cook? Do we laugh knowingly at Ukeles's "floor paintings," with their explicit evocation of the grand painterly gestures of Jackson Pollock, or do we feel a tinge of shame at the public display of a woman who cleans up after us? Responses are rendered ambivalent, in part because both Rosler and Ukeles have combined an aesthetic of identification (traditionally associated with second-wave feminism) with one of distanciation (usually affiliated with poststructuralist feminism); and they have done so, in large measure, by showing us the fault line between things considered private and things considered public.

Rosler deals with this problematic even more rigorously in *Domination and the Everyday*. Self-described as an "artist-mother's 'This is Your Life,'"[38] the tape begins with an image of Chilean dictator Augusto Pinochet. The image track quickly becomes layered, as a steady stream of disparate pictures—family snapshots, mass-media advertising, photographs of political leaders and artists—fills the screen. Scrolling along the bottom of the screen is a dense theoretical text analyzing the problem of class domination and the relation between those who make culture and those with political power, arguing that "the controlling class also controls culture." Deploying a classic strategy of filmic distanciation, the sound and image track are separate. Accompanying this already dense visual field is a similarly doubled soundtrack, as we hear, simultaneously, the real-time conversation between Rosler and her young son as she readies him for bed, and a radio interview with the famous art dealer Irving Blum.

Here the everyday labor of mothering, of feeding, bedtime stories, and cleaning, is laid down next to humanist art discourse, Marxist analysis, and the cruel facts of political domination; their polyvalence renders them, if not entirely equivalent, at least impossible to hierarchize. As one track among many, it is hard to privilege the everyday labor of Rosler's mothering, as hard as it is to keep any one of the tracks in focus above the others, as each interrupts, overlaps, synchronizes, and seems incommensurate with the others. To this end, *Domination and the Everyday* does something slightly different from the *Maintenance Art* performances. Rosler does not isolate the labor in order to show it, nor does she engage the literal public spaces of the museum. Rather, by placing maintenance labor as one competing factor among many, one ingredient among many that blend together to form the everyday, she shows it to be as structuring of our lives as other, seemingly invisible structures—political domination, for instance. For Rosler, the question is how to make the connection between the brutal regime of Pinochet and the ideology of first-world bedtime stories; how to understand the relays between Blum's blather about the genius of Jasper Johns and the laconic address of mother to child, as she slowly persuades the boy to get ready for bed. What do all these things have to do with one another? The tape insinuates that they are related in our inability not only to recognize them (they are too layered; they compete too steadily for our individuated attention), but further, to draw any meaningful connections between them. A sentence scrolls by: "We understand that we have no control over big events; we do not understand HOW and WHY the 'small' events that make up our own lives are controlled as well."

Domination and the Everyday proposes that the public sphere is more than simply the space of the traditional institutions of the bourgeois public sphere (e.g., the museum). Instead, Rosler's work images a public sphere reorganized by, and shot through with, the effects of television (hence her use of video). Eschewing both the traditional venues and mediums of "art," she turned instead to mediums not sanctioned by the art establishment (video, postcards, and performance works), mediums that presented difficulty in terms of distribution—showing distribution to be as important an element in the art process as consumption or production.[39] While Chicago, Kelly, and Ukeles are explicit in their address of more traditionally defined public space, Rosler's work is an early instantiation of the changing parameters of such space, the very despatialization of public space. However, while notions of what constitutes the public may shift, the society of the spectacle hardly operates without the structural role of maintenance labor. And Rosler's works make clear that we not only have to value that labor as such, but that one way we might be able to do that is to articulate the relations among and between different forms of dailiness: the everyday for her being an ineluctable mixture of politics, culture, and maintenance activities. (This is one way Rosler refuses a fetishization of the everyday as a retreat from politics.) To perform this articulation is to be willing to tear away at the layers and veils of ideology that not only separate people from one another but also render various aspects of daily life radically disjointed. And it is here that the function of maintenance as an activity that forms a bond between public and private realms becomes so important. Rosler's work refutes the either unknowing or unwilling acquiescence of people to systems of domination, be they ideological, cultural, or political. Yet such refusals do not operate strictly in the negative, as *Domination and the Everyday* ends on a decidedly utopian note:

> It is in the marketplace alone that we are replaceable, because interchangeable, and until we take control we will always be owned by the culture that imagines us to be replaceable. The truth, of course, is that NO ONE can be replaced . . . but there will always be more of us, more and more of us, willing to struggle to take control of our lives, our culture, our world . . . which to be fully human, we must do and we will.[40]

* * *

My work is a sketch, a line of thinking, a possibility.[41]
—Martha Rosler

I have been arguing that the aspect that binds these works together is their concern with the problems of labor and political economy and their address to the public institutions of art. By importing explicitly domestic or private content (Chicago and Kelly) or by substituting the notion of domestic labor with maintenance labor (Ukeles), or by insisting on the equivalence between maintenance labor and other forms of domination (Rosler), all four artists explore the interpenetration between public and private institutions. This is notable, for in each instance the various institutions of art have wanted precisely to suppress the public address of the works. This is why, for instance, *The Dinner Party* is accused of being too kitschy, for Chicago has smuggled the decorative and the domestic into the modernist museum.[42] So, too, the familiar disparagement of the *PPD*, that it "should be a book," is a desire to deny its place in the public space of the museum, to suppress the nonnaturalness of motherhood as a legitimate public discussion. Rosler's work has received the least "proper" art world attention (she was only recently the subject of a European-initiated museum retrospective). Her explicit desire to envision an art practice that addressed a more diffuse notion of the public sphere and a more expansive notion of art has meant that many of her early video works on food and cooking and her postcard pieces that deal with domestic labor remain difficult to see. Finally, and perhaps most telling of all, the Wadsworth Atheneum kept no records of Ukeles's *Maintenance Art* performances, recalling Miwon Kwon's observation that when the work of maintenance is well accomplished, it goes unseen.[43]

Another aspect that binds these works is that each participates in what Fredric Jameson calls the "laboratory situation" of art.[44] All four works submit various "givens" about the way the world works to a type of laboratory experimentation. For instance, the body and perception are questioned by Minimalism; the status of the art object is queried by Conceptual art; the medium of video places a strain on both art institutions (in terms of distribution) and the viewer (in terms of expectation); and the regimes of power embedded in the museum are articulated by institutional critique. Yet I would contend that these artists add yet another layer to these "laboratory experiments," for embodied in each work is a proposition about how the world might be *differently* organized. Woven into the fabric of each work is the utopian question, "What if the world worked like this?" Chicago offers us the old parlor game of the ideal dinner party, and suggests that the museum could be a site for conviviality, social exchange, and the pleasures of the flesh. Kelly's work intimates the desire for a culture that would bestow equal value on the work of mothering and the labor of the artist; so, too, the work's very existence points toward a different model of the "working mother." Rosler images a polyvalent and dialectical world where the demands of work and pleasure, and the seeming separation between culture and domination, are held in a constant tensile relation to one another. Ukeles's work, again, may be the most explicit in its utopian dimension, its literalness a demand beyond "equal time equal pay" or the "personal is political," for hers is a world where maintenance labor is equal in value to artistic labor—a proposition that would require a radically different organization of the public and private spheres.

Feminism has long operated with the power (and limitations) of utopian thought. It is telling, then, that these artists have dovetailed the "what if" potential of both art and feminism. Yet they have not collapsed the distinction between art and life; rather, they have used art as a form of legitimated public discourse, a conduit through which to enter ideas into public discussion. So while all of the works expose the porosity between public and private spheres, none calls for the dismantling of these formations. Fictional as the division might be, the myth of a private sphere is too dear to relinquish,[45] and the public sphere as a site of discourse and debate is too important a fiction for democracy to disavow. Instead, these pieces have articulated something similar to the utopian thought of feminists like Moira Gatens, and, more recently, Drucilla Cornell. As Gatens argues, "To effect the total insertion of women into capitalist society would involve the acknowledgment of the 'blind spot' of traditional sociopolitical theorizing: that the reproduction of the species, sexual relations, and domestic work are performed under *socially constructed* conditions, not natural ones, and that these tasks are socially and economically necessary."[46] She suggests a new model of the body politic, one that would be able to account for the heterogeneity of its subjects and their *asymmetrical* relations to reproduction, sexuality, and subjectivity.

Such utopian language is vague, and for some time now such vagueness has produced frustration or dismissal. However, this is a utopian language without the problematic prescriptive nature of previous utopian thought.

Similarly, it is not a theoretical language that ends with a description of a system or an ideology. Instead, it offers *speculation*. At the end of *Feminism and Philosophy*, Gatens calls for representations, both symbolic and factual, of future conceptions of sociopolitical and ethical life. And in *At the Heart of Freedom*, Drucilla Cornell writes, "There is a necessary aesthetic dimension to a feminist practice of freedom. Feminism is invariably a symbolic project."[47] It is within the tradition of art as a laboratory experiment that Chicago, Kelly, Rosler, and Ukeles engage in speculative feminist utopian thought, each attempting to rearticulate the terms of public and private in ways that might fashion new possibilities for both spheres and the labor they entail. But this is not a call for a utopian field in which all parties agree on the terms of the discourse, decidedly not. While all four artists are bound by their interest in labor, their address to questions of public and private, and their pointed complications of the (now) standard narratives of postwar advanced art practice, they clearly differ in contentious and important ways. While this essay has valorized a moment of obscured affinity, this is not to say that such affinities should be privileged as such. Difference is crucial for utopian thought, in that utopia (like democracy) has the potential to offer discourses marked precisely by disagreement and contestation. For some time, feminism has labored under equally false ideals of harmony or superiority. What seems increasingly necessary in our putatively "postfeminist" age is a feminism vibrant enough to encourage dissension and conflict without closing off considerations of points of contact, moments of unexpected convergence. That 1970s artwork informed by feminism is currently a site of intellectual energy is perhaps due to the problems of labor that shape our current public sphere: from the "end" of the welfare mother to home officing; from the new threats to privacy made possible by the ever-expanding role of the internet in the lives of people in developed nations to the multinational corporate reorganization of public space. These issues seem to run through the fabric of our daily lives with astounding thoroughness. If the politics of the 1970s were marked by various battles for equality, and the politics of the 1980s were shaped by struggles over the politics of representation under the Reagan/Thatcher era, where the spectacle reigned supreme, then the core of contemporary politics may be shaped largely by the reciprocity and contested relations between the public and private spheres and the forms of labor that support them.

This essay has benefited from many interlocutors. An audience at UCLA asked particularly probing questions, especially Michael Asher, who encouraged me to examine the work of Martha Rosler. Amelia Jones generously shared her thoughts and expertise on *The Dinner Party*. Moyra Davey, Rosalyn Deutsche, Christina Kiaer, Janet Kraynak, Miwon Kwon, Sowon Kwon, Frazer Ward, and Faith Wilding all helped as critical readers. An earlier version of this essay was published as "Cleaning Up in the 1970s: The Work of Judy Chicago, Mary Kelly and Mierle Laderman Ukeles," in *Rewriting Conceptual Art*, ed. Michael Newman and Jon Bird (London: Reaktion Books, 1999), 106–22.

Painting with Ambivalence

Originally published in *WACK!: Art and the Feminist Revolution*, ed. Cornelia Butler and Lisa Gabrielle Mark (Los Angeles: Museum of Contemporary Art; Cambridge, MA: MIT Press, 2007), 428–39.

Although there are virtually no permanent collection galleries dedicated to feminist art in the major museums of modern and contemporary art, it is well known that artists informed by feminism pursued their art practices with particular zeal during the late 1960s and throughout the '70s, the liberation movement of feminism in the social and political arena being an undeniable catalyst for these energies. So, too, the challenges to traditional definitions of art that came from Fluxus, Minimalism, Earth art, Conceptualism, and the like contributed to an abiding sense that business as usual—in both the world at large and the small corner of it called the art world—was coming to an end. It is a well-worn story that the time-honored medium of painting was buffeted by these sea changes. A historical form, shackled by centuries of tradition (from patriarchy to patronage), painting seemed less and less able to account for, demonstrate, or represent the conditions, both aesthetic and political, of the 1960s and '70s. And yet, despite its rumored decline, many women—many feminists—kept painting. At the remove of over thirty years, I find myself increasingly interested in the tenacity of women who continued to paint, despite the seemingly readymade challenges to the medium. What did it mean to be an artist in the 1960s and '70s, to be a woman, a feminist, *and* a painter? If feminism is a methodology, a structure, a way of thinking, as well as a set of contents, then what might feminism do to the category of painting?[1]

For instance, what do we make of a painting by Joan Snyder called *Woman-Child* (1972)? Strokes of dime-store candy colors sit or float on top of a gridded background that resembles a tiled wall. On the one hand, the painting contains the visual expressiveness of Abstract Expressionism; on the other, the conceptual ballast of modernism's grid. The tension between these two modes of painterly address is mirrored in the title's dualism, *Woman-Child*—woman then child, both together, equal or not, autobiographical or universal? The internal balance of the painting signifies a kind of portentous seriousness, one undermined nearly entirely by the everyday banality of the colors. Snyder's work is not alone in its categorical slipperiness. Howardena Pindell's cut-paper collages are equally resistant to proper assignation. Neither paintings nor drawings, these diminutive works comprise small circles of paper

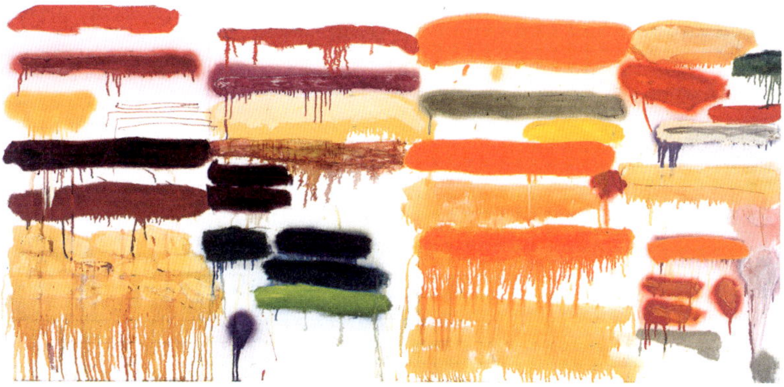

Joan Snyder, *Summer Orange*, 1970, oil, acrylic, pencil, spray enamel on canvas, 42 x 96 in. (106.7 x 243.8 cm)

produced by a hole-puncher affixed with adhesive or string to a submerged grid. Pindell's paintings are a riotous explosion of visual tactility, in which color and texture vie for visual dominance—neither winning. Instead the viewer experiences Pindell's work as a kind of aesthetic stand-off of irreconcilable differences. Then there is Mary Heilmann's *Little 9 x 9* (1973), a monochrome fire engine-red field upon which is draped a grid of black lines. But the lines appear to have been made with a finger as opposed to a brush, and the gridlines switch over and above one another like the warp and weave of tapestry, a conflation of modernism's lofty monochrome with more prosaic forms of mark making.

The three artists discussed above share numerous characteristics: all paint abstractly, all use the grid, and all deploy a strategy of repetition, of both forms and ideas. Additionally, the three women share a strong identification as feminists, all the while participating in the rigorous abstraction associated with modernism. The question of what these paintings might mean—and how feminism might have changed the terms of painting—begins, for me, with an attempt to try and square off some relation between feminism and modernism. The narrative of painting's decline is part of the larger challenges laid at the feet of modernism. Feminism, in all of its disparate political and aesthetic forms, was at the forefront of such challenges. Indeed, feminism's dispute with modernism often led to a blanket condemnation of it generally, and of painting specifically. However, Anne Wagner has supplanted this position by suggesting that "the antipathy of feminist theory toward the reified modernism of its own invention has helped to obscure just those protocols that have made modernism a serviceable, downright expressive choice for female artists."[2] The artists and the modernism that Wagner examined all existed before the strongest challenges to the field occurred. The paintings of Pindell, Snyder, and Heilmann both embody and extend this idea, as each turns to modernism when it is already under siege—from both feminism and the early winds of postmodernism. Hence their version of modernism is already a very complicated affair. Perhaps this is why even though these artists participate in the modernist legacy, their works are rarely discussed in those terms (nor does their work grace many museum walls in this regard). Rather, they find themselves in *WACK!: Art and the Feminist Revolution*, situated in an explicitly feminist context. My argument suggests that paintings that are both abstract and feminist suffer from a kind of illegibility. It is precisely this difficulty I want to address in this essay.

Part of the discomfort aroused by these paintings, part of their unclear historical place, is due to the conditions—social, psychic, and aesthetic—under which women artists pursued painting in the late 1960s through the '70s. I want to propose that the larger umbrella under which women interested in both modernism and feminism operated was one of failure—of both feminism *and* painting. Painting's failure seemed manifest in the near completeness with which so many artists and critics turned away from it.[3] Feminism's failure is a more difficult one to articulate. One aspect of feminism's failure has been (and remains) the reticence of women to come together as such, as defined exclusively by gender. (Why should we, after all?) The putatively sexless nature of art (particularly that of abstract art) was for many women a refuge from the brutal gendering of the world as they knew it.

In her account of the troublesome category of feminist art, Peggy Phelan has argued that the feminist "awakening" was shaped as much by an experience of trauma as of liberation.[4] Such an account helps us to understand why feminism—or, more specifically, an identification based on gender—is so routinely rejected, whether by women artists during the 1960s or by feminist theorists and artists in the 1980s rejecting so-called essentialist feminism. The trauma Phelan described is the trauma of identification with the subaltern position, with the oppressed, with the "weak," with the very precisely sexed. Lucy Lippard, one of the foremost critics of the period, recounted her own feminist/woman aversion in the introduction to her volume of "feminist essays on women's art." In it, she wrote: "One of the first feminist artists' groups—W.A.R.—came out of the Coalition too, but I resisted them for over a year. I was decidedly not accustomed to identifying with female underdogs—with oppressed people and unknown artists, yes, but women—that was too close for comfort. 'I made it as a person, not as a woman,' I kept saying."[5] If the awakening of feminism meant that one had to identify with other women, it also meant that one had to identify oneself as not equal to men—a position some embraced with the proper anger and others avoided with an equally reasonable ambivalence. This lack of equality seeped into discussions of aesthetic quality as well, placing women artists in a double bind—not equal in the society at large, and not equal in the history of art.

Part of the stirring of feminist consciousness in the art world came in the form of Linda Nochlin's now-legendary article of 1971, "Why Have There Been No Great Women Artists?" If the question feels audacious in 2005, one can only imagine the anger and frustration it must have generated thirty years ago. The text is foundational for feminist art history, for it answered its brazen question sociohistorically, offering a detailed account of women's consistent lack of professional training in the arts.[6] Here was a history of art that did not begin and end with transcendental meaning. Quite the contrary, what feminism as a methodology allowed was the unavoidable messiness of the everyday—its politics and procedures.

What Nochlin's essay was also to insist upon (quite bravely) was the answer to her own question—that *yes*, until 1971 there *had* been no great women artists (Eva Hesse still too young to qualify, the impact of Louise Bourgeois not yet understood, perhaps). Certainly Nochlin was quick to bring the fullness of feminist methodology to terms like *great* and *genius*, exposing them for what they are—ideological traps, moments of false consciousness, systems of exclusion designed to protect the status quo. And yet, it was not so easy for her to stop there. While she was prepared to question a "universal" idea of greatness or genius, she was not ready to abandon her own highly developed sense that the world contains deeply meaningful, even superb, works of art and that, as of yet, no woman painter—no matter how interesting or how overlooked—had offered Western civilization anything comparable to Michelangelo, Rembrandt, or Picasso.

Between Nochlin's bald acknowledgment of women artists' historical lack of greatness and Lippard's public acknowledgment that for years she did not take women artists seriously, what could it possibly have felt like to be a woman, working in a painting studio?[7] Clearly, the editors of *ARTnews* were curious as well, as they ran seven responses to Nochlin's text concurrently. The replies were contentious; how could they not have been? The opposition to Nochlin's text began with an anecdote that went to the heart of the matter. Elaine de Kooning did the telling: "Well first—that term, 'women artists.' I was talking to Joan Mitchell at a party about ten years ago when a man came up to us and said, 'What do you women artists think . . .' Joan grabbed my arm and said, 'Elaine, let's get the hell out of here.'"[8] Addressed as a woman artist, Mitchell's reaction is one of consummate rejection and refusal—and not, presumably, of the category "artist." Yet, she does not flee by herself; grabbing de Kooning by the arm is a gesture of solidarity, after all, as artists definitely, but also as women. Nochlin's bracing question, and her devastatingly smart answer, engendered from its inception an avalanche of ambivalence.

I want to argue that this ambivalence was not only felt personally, at New York art world parties or in art magazine interviews, but that the ambivalence about artistic activity, feminism, and modernism seeped into the very groundwater of painting itself. Further, it did so in ways that are difficult to account for and hard to narrate with any "authority," as authority and triumph were two of the words that were being held at bay by women artists of the period. This ambivalence takes center stage in Heilmann's account of how she became a painter: "I was devastated not to be included in *Anti-Illusion*, a turning point show in 1969 at the Whitney. As a result, I abandoned the sculptural work I was doing and, as a rebellious move, switched to the much-maligned practice, painting. Color Field painting was going on, and I hated it then (love it now). What I turned to was a materials-based sort of conceptual, anti-aesthetic, earth-colored, ironic painting that was often hard to look at."[9] Rejected by the avant-garde establishment, her rebellious act was to embrace that which seemed nearly retrograde—Color Field painting. But she was to do so with enormous irony, deploying the colors of contemporary Technicolor cinema and commodity marketing as opposed to colors with putatively transcendental meaning. And yet, while Heilmann's colors may have been chosen tongue in cheek, she appeared radically interested in the very embodied feeling (specifically, the undefined spatial wetness of the tongue pressed against the inside of one's cheek) of how color is always already coded—with culture, with class, and, of course, with gender—and how this sometimes makes things "hard to look at."

Any artist working in New York during the 1960s and '70s did so under the long shadow left by Abstract Expressionism and its critics. Clearly Heilmann, Pindell, and Snyder made work deeply indebted to its legacy—the push-pull of Heilmann, the allover composition of Pindell, and the expressive brushstrokes of Snyder are each impossible to imagine without the aesthetic experimentation enacted by New York School painters. For women artists and for feminists, this was a particularly vexed framework. The freedom Abstract Expressionism embodied was deeply appealing, and the lived reality of the New York School was that it included a great number of women—Helen Frankenthaler, Grace Hartigan, de Kooning, Lee Krasner, and Mitchell, to name only a few. Despite this, Abstract Expressionism remained a boys' club par excellence. A leading example of the patriarchal misapprehension of the situation was the 1969 Metropolitan Museum of Art exhibition of 408 works of art by forty-three artists titled *New York Painting and Sculpture: 1940-1970*. Although the exhibition ended with Pop artists like Robert Rauschenberg, James Rosenquist, and Andy Warhol, it was definitively an exhibition dedicated to the new hegemony of American painting, specifically Abstract Expressionism. Frankenthaler was the only woman included in the exhibition.

Clement Greenberg's essay for the catalogue was a reprint of his 1962 article "After Abstract Expressionism," in which he acknowledged that the problem for painting was the discernment of quality. "The question now asked in their art is no longer what constitutes art, or the act of painting, as such, but what constitutes *good* art as such."[10] Greenberg suggested that the uniqueness of the conception is the bedrock of quality, this in large measure because "skill" had become so easily available (it is no mistake that this period witnesses the rise of the art school). What Greenberg didn't explicitly say is that the language of quality was largely the province of the critic, whose role it was to put forward the robust discourse of affirmation and persuasion. Adjectives and adverbs abound, and quality is not so much stated as insinuated in the process. What this often meant for women artists was a gendered use of language that served to undermine the authority of the works themselves. Using Frankenthaler and the process of staining as a test case, art historian Lisa Saltzman has convincingly argued that the critical reception of Frankenthaler's work differed demonstrably from her male colleagues who used similar techniques (indeed who learned those techniques *from* Frankenthaler). After a careful parsing of the reviews of Frankenthaler's work, Saltzman concluded: "In their attribution of masculinity to canvases painted by male artists and femininity to those painted by female artists, critics asserted the fundamental primacy of sexual difference, and did so at precisely the moment when gender boundaries were seen as being in danger of disappearing, both artistically and socially."[11]

This is all a way of saying that while abstraction in particular, and painting in general, held out the promise of the non-gendered category "artist" to the women who operated within this realm, the audience—critics, curators, collectors, dealers—was not so willing to operate in a state of genderless suspension. Rather, they reinscribed these abstract works in a field of gendered language, insisting consciously or unconsciously upon gender as a primary tool with which to organize the world. Abstraction was not a genderless paradise after all. For Pindell, Snyder, and Heilmann, one aesthetic strategy seemed to be to acknowledge this from the start. In their works, color functions as a kind of preemptive strike against gendered interpretation: it is ever so slightly off, the combinations always a bit odd. The nearly putrid or acidic hues of their palettes suggest that they are willing to perform, in the space of the canvas, the dilemma of whether or not something is a "good painting." By using colors not typically associated with "quality," their paintings stage the problem of how to ascertain it, especially given the fact of their having been made by women. Pindell has recounted her artistic training (in the Josef Albers school of color theory) at Boston University: "Al Held was there and he made fun of the women. He got angry if a woman used certain colors in her work. (A guy could use white mixed with red, which is pink, but if a woman used it he would go into a tirade.)"[12] Pindell continued to use pink, of course, as did Snyder and Heilmann, sometimes to such an extent that their work feels like a bit of a dare—a cocky demand that the viewer look past, or better yet through, the sickly pinks and washy brush strokes of Snyder, or the off-kilter compositions and decidedly domestic references of Heilmann, or the glitter and talcum powder and self-destroyed drawings of Pindell to ascertain just what exactly in the end makes a "good" painting.

While many critics like Greenberg used a Kantian-derived formalism to render the self-expression of artists into a kind of culturally legible public language, this criticism did little to chip away at the desire of many artists to paint in ways that were more personally, physically, and psychically expressive. An alternative understanding of Abstract Expressionism came from Harold Rosenberg's "The American Action Painters" (1952), also reprinted in the Metropolitan's exhibition catalogue, in which he argued that the picture plane was "an arena in which to act" and "the image would be the result of this encounter."[13] This encounter was at its best when an artist was able "just *to paint*. The gesture on the canvas was a gesture of liberation, from Value—political, aesthetic, moral."[14] Like all critics of Abstract Expressionism—for whom the difficulty lay in judging a good work from a bad one—Rosenberg described the criteria thusly: "The test of any of the new paintings is its seriousness—and the test of its seriousness is the degree to which the act on the canvas is an extension of the artist's total effort to make over his experience."[15] Such language is open to a proliferation of interpretations, something Rosenberg seemed to know but only unconsciously, as this sentence is quickly followed by a paragraph in which he worried, deeply, about the encroaching "bad taste in the manner of Park Avenue shop windows"[16] into the field of the new abstract painting.

Snyder's diaristic approach to painting is a supreme example of a canvas being an extension of the artist's experience. Her washy expressive brushstrokes often feel like angry jabs at the canvas, and her flamboyant use of color has been described as producing paintings "drenched with personal pain, stammered with rage."[17] However serious this effort (and I think it was very serious), there is also something about Snyder's work that flirts with bad taste—both in the publicness of such emotions and the disjointed colors. For this reason, her paintings are sometimes discussed with a fair amount of objection; there is a sense in the criticism that Snyder's work borders on the inappropriate. In a recent scathing review, critic Maureen Mullarkey suggested that Snyder's work "illustrate[s] the vulgarity of a movement that traded on the susceptibilities of its audience."[18]

The extremity of judgment that Snyder's paintings engenders is emblematic of art historian T. J. Clark's arguments about Abstract Expressionism. For Clark, Abstract Expressionism's wild exteriorizing of emotion that produced canvases redolent with so-called violent emotion—generated in private studios but displayed on the public's living-room walls—is emblematic of the vulgar. He asked, "To what extent does Abstract Expressionism really belong, at the deepest level—the level of language, of procedure, of presuppositions about world-making—to the bourgeoisie who paid for it and took it on their travels?"[19] His answer, as one might presume, is "pretty fully." For Clark, "Abstract Expressionism . . . is the style of a certain petty bourgeoisie's aspiration to aristocracy, to a totalizing cultural power." (Certainly this account helps to explain how it made it into an exhibition at the Metropolitan Museum of Art so quickly.) He continued: "It is the art of that moment when the petty bourgeoisie thinks it can speak . . . the aristocrat's claim to individuality. Vulgarity is the form of that aspiration."[20] How else, Clark seemed to imply, could the shit browns, bruised yellows, and rococo pinks combined with the swashbuckling flings of house paint and the smarmy smears of impasto have migrated from the bohemia of the studio into the living rooms of Park Avenue, unless they were thought to be expressions of radical individuality? What is deeply interesting about

Howardena Pindell, *Untitled #7*, 1973, pen and ink on punched papers, talcum powder, thread on oak tag paper, 10 1/8 x 8 3/8 in. (25.9 x 21.3 cm)

Clark's account of Abstract Expressionism is how seriously it takes the living room as a site of its reception—the seriousness, that is, with which it takes domestic space, the traditional province of women, being the site of her display of self, of family, of ideology (of the problem that has yet to be named "the problem that has no name"). Clark implied the artists were well aware of their place: "And above all it can have no illusions about its own status as part of that upholstery. It is made out of the materials it deploys. Take them or leave them, these ciphers of plentitude—they are all painting at present has to offer. 'Feeling' has to be fetishized, made dreadfully (obscenely) exterior, if painting is to continue."[21]

What happens to Clark's formulation if we substitute women for the petty bourgeoisie? Were women artists operating within the paradigm of Abstract Expressionism speaking a claim to individuality and personal expression that critics could not help but find threatening, perhaps even vulgar? And did some of the women involved in this enterprise perhaps stage this dilemma—unconsciously or not—in the works themselves? Such that Snyder's strokes look like the work of a crazed censor. Or that Pindell had to first destroy her own drawings with a hole-puncher before reassembling them into a complete work. Or Heilmann, who reimagines Kazimir Malevich's black square as a pink rectangle that threatens to slink off the canvas. Might all of these gestures have about them a bit of canny knowingness? Far from the "pure" expressivity of their Abstract Expressionist forebears, these works instead seem to know that while the personal is political, its expression alone does not guarantee its success; indeed it might be emblematic of a kind of failure or vulgarity.

As fecund and successful as Abstract Expressionism might have been, many artists were suspicious of its overwrought emotionalism (perhaps the vulgarity?) and turned (and returned) to the more cerebral ground of the grid. This was especially the case as the grid remained a protected fiefdom where painting was still permitted and valued by the avant-garde (both artists and critics) of the 1960s and '70s. Its practitioners were able to trace a lineage back to Kazimir Malevich and Piet Mondrian, and its hold on the aesthetic imagination and practice of the day was complete. It dominated what little painting was still deemed important, and it was used as a trope or structural device in much Conceptual art, such that the perversity of the grid as a structure meant that it was used equally by Agnes Martin and Eleanor Antin, Ad Reinhardt and Gilbert and George, Andy Warhol and Louise Nevelson. The list is seemingly endless.

The grid was also subject to a critical enumeration. John Elderfield wrote a zeitgeist-defining article called "Grids" for *Artforum* in 1972 (in which both Snyder and Heilmann were singled out for commentary). So too, Lippard, in a catalogue essay for a 1972 exhibition called *Grids*, wrote: "Perhaps by coincidence, perhaps not, many of the artists who have drawn from the grid's precise strains a particularly unique interpretation are women."[22] She too singled out Snyder for special consideration. Rosalind Krauss was to write the most persuasive and analytical text on the subject. In her 1978 article "Grids," she stated: "The grid announces, among other things, modern art's will to silence, its hostility to literature, to narrative, to discourse."[23] And yet, like all structures, it contains within it the traces of historical forms. So, on the one hand the grid signifies the infinite space of art's autonomy and on the other the symbolist window. She went so far as to say that "behind every twentieth-century grid there lies—like a trauma that must be repressed—a symbolist window."[24] Part of how this trauma manifests itself is the dialectical movement of the grid—both centripetal and centrifugal. The centripetal grid spirals inward, making the frame the content, establishing a quasi-spiritual realm in which art is utterly autonomous, a space for visual contemplation (Martin). The centrifugal model spirals outward, addressing the world and its structure (Warhol). And yet the grid always contains both modalities, such that Martin's paintings are also about the horizon and the sea, and Warhol's are about the unremitting flatness of the picture plane.

Snyder, Pindell, and Heilmann all deployed the self-expressivity, and perhaps the vulgarity, of Abstract Expressionism, and in so doing toyed with the vexed notions of quality that plagued the gendered criticism of the period. Yet they did so while simultaneously exploring the stringency of the grid's refusal or renunciation of language. And they actively took up the depersonalized structure of the grid when the rallying cry of the feminist movement of the 1970s was "the personal is political." The paintings they produced within this framework seem to stage some of the tensions and impossible contradictions enumerated above. Situated between the vulgarity of Abstract Expressionism and the dialectical nature of the grid, between the putative failure of painting and the medium's historical dominance, between the potential of feminist liberation and the entrenched nature of patriarchal power, the paintings of Heilmann, Pindell, and Snyder court notions of failure and abjection; they are rife with ambivalence. In this seeming miasma of theoretical and historical frameworks, many of these paintings have slipped through the cracks of canonicity—not only because they were made by women, but also because they are a bit like what Roland Barthes once called a "message without a code." For Barthes, the medium without a code was photography, but much of his language describes why paintings by Heilmann, Pindell, and Snyder are so difficult to place within the narratives of postwar art offered by most museums and art history textbooks.

For Barthes, the "message without a code" was an image that presents itself as purely denoted (rather than connoted) meaning, in which "the image no longer *illustrates* the words; it is now the words which, structurally, are parasitic on the image."[25] Certainly, this describes the situation of criticism with regards to both Abstract Expressionism and postwar use of the grid. Barthes went on to say images that embody this kind of "pure denotation" are "perhaps not at the level of what ordinary language calls the insignificant, the neutral, the objective, but, on the contrary, at the level of absolutely traumatic images. The trauma is a suspension of language, a blocking of meaning."[26]

The difficulty of interpreting or reading abstraction was hardly a new one, but certainly the wake left by Abstract Expressionism and the decline of painting's prominence made it even harder to do so. That abstraction would be taken up by women who were also invested in feminism seemed to augment this difficulty, partly because of the gendered language used by critics, partly because the artists themselves were carving out new terrain

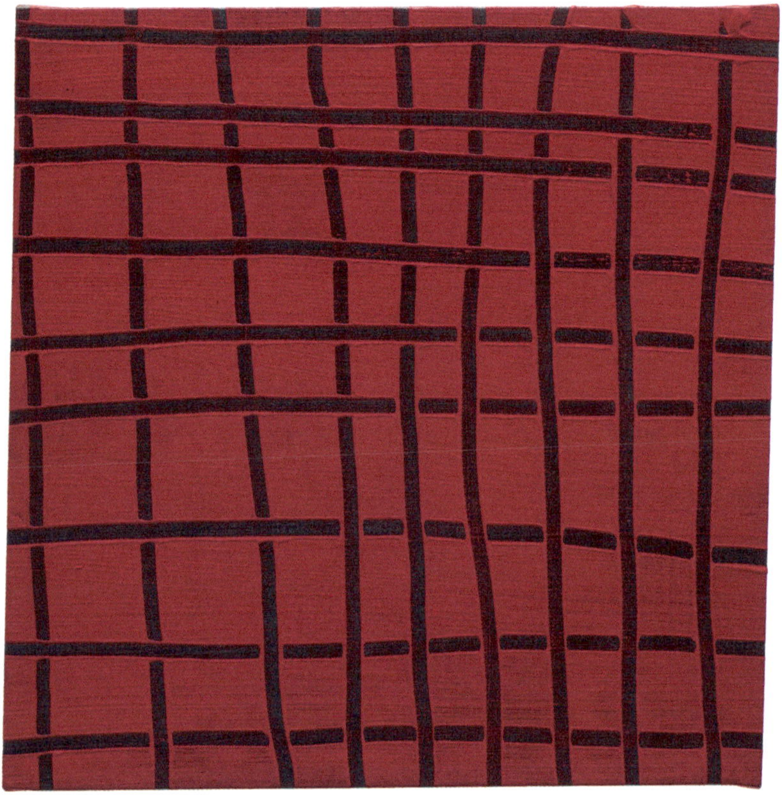

Mary Heilmann, *Little 9 x 9*, 1973, acrylic on canvas, 21⅞ x 21⅞ x 1¾ in. (55.6 x 55.6 x 4.5 cm)

for what their art might mean, that it might in fact be personal—emphatically so, especially as the personal was being contested as being not purely that but political (and public) as well. Oddly, what was public, or political, in these personal gestures was color—particularly abject, vulgar, or gendered hues. Or, to be more precise, these artists explored how *even* color is gendered. The other public dimension of these works was the structure of the grid. Emblematic of modernism, the grid had evolved into the primary signifier for modern art—its coolness, its detached position from worldly concerns, its refusal of the everyday as a consummate statement of art's autonomy. Unlike artists like Martin, Jasper Johns, or Ellsworth Kelly, Pindell, Snyder, and Heilmann weren't using the grid as a way to reject the bombastic aspects of Abstract Expressionism. When they crossed the logic of the grid with that of Abstract Expressionism—these two seemingly antithetical modes of modernism—they created an instance of Barthes's message without a code—a denotative image that courts the traumatic inasmuch as it sits outside of language, particularly the critical languages developed to discuss Abstract Expressionism on the one hand and the use of the grid on the other.

While I don't want to contend that the paintings at hand are exclusively traumatic, I do think that the near-perfect silence surrounding Pindell's paintings from the 1970s, the outright hostility engendered by much of Snyder's work, and the lack of substantive critical and museological attention paid to Heilmann speaks to some kind of repression or inability to process the complication of both the images and the discursive field within which (as enumerated above) they were made. On the other hand, the silence (and repression) seems thorough enough to warrant trauma—especially as it is an almost organic point of contact between Krauss's essay on the grid, Barthes's on the photographic message, and Phelan's on feminist art. It cannot be a mere coincidence that all three theorists resorted to the idea of trauma as a means to express what was happening in image making after World War II. Certainly each writer's use of the term carries a markedly different valence, but the point of contingency merits noting, particularly given the notorious difficulties posed by the category of feminist art, much less feminist abstract painting. While it is traumatic to be outside of language, for many feminists it was equally traumatic to be inside of it (I understand painting here as a kind of language).

Increasingly, I have come to understand the struggle to ascertain the "value" of these paintings (are they "good"?) as bound up with their disturbing use of abstraction and cloying use of color. So too the struggle to interpret these works (what do they "mean"?) is part and parcel of a simultaneous inhabiting and disavowal of the modes or languages of painting under patriarchy and, then more to the point, of patriarchal painting under the siege of feminism. In the end, the struggles for art's meaning and human equality converge in art made by women under the umbrella effects of feminism. Indeed, the struggles for the continuation of modernism's utopian promises and the idealistic promises of modernity—the failure and the absolute necessity of such idealistic pursuits—is splayed across the paintings of innumerable women artists in ways that are still radically difficult to account for or narrate, so much so that the paintings have yet to find their rightful place on the walls of permanent-collection galleries of that other great institution of modernity: the art museum.

How to Install Art as a Feminist

Originally published in *Modern Women: Women Artists at the Museum of Modern Art*, ed. Cornelia Butler and Alexandra Schwartz (New York: Museum of Modern Art, 2010), 498–513.

Let's begin with a working definition. According to Eli Zaretsky, a Marxist historian writing in the 1970s, feminism aspires to "revolutionize the deepest and most universal aspects of life—those of personal relations, love, egotism, sexuality, and our inner emotional lives."[1] I like this definition; it helps me remember that part of what I'm after, as a feminist, is the fundamental reorganization of the institutions that govern us, as well as those that we, in turn, govern. Therefore, thinking about the introduction of feminism into the museum is no small matter. It seems clear that feminist art history has made enormous gains in the academy: we have recovered scores of women artists from oblivion, populated the academy with female professors, established classes on feminist art practices, and entered numerous women artists into the canon, so that your average art history student would be hard-pressed to graduate without knowing at least a smattering of women artists and maybe even a few feminists. But American museums have been slower to encompass feminism's challenges than the academy, despite a workforce largely comprising women. Art history needs its objects of study to be displayed, and thus the history of the museum can be seen in part as a struggle for how to display works of art. This essay looks to recent art historical ideas with the aim of beginning to think through the translation of these new discursive formations into the spatial logic and requirements of the museum. In other words: I feel fairly confident that I know how to write an essay as a feminist, less sure I know how to install art as one.

The pervasive sexism in museums is evidenced by how slow museums of modern and contemporary art were to acquire feminist art of the 1970s. And when they did buy it or accept it as gifts, they were often reticent to exhibit it. Much feminist art in permanent collections, like that of the Museum of Modern Art, rarely, if ever, graces the walls. For instance, MoMA owns two terrific paintings: *Sweet Cathy's Song (for Cathy Elzea)* (1978) by Joan Snyder and an untitled work by Lee Lozano (1963). The Snyder work, acquired the year it was made, has been on view twice: once in an exhibition of new acquisitions in 1979 and then again in a rotation of the collection in 1987. The Lozano work was acquired in 2004 and has been shown just once, in *What Is Painting?* in 2007. I do not wish to engage in the ever-popular

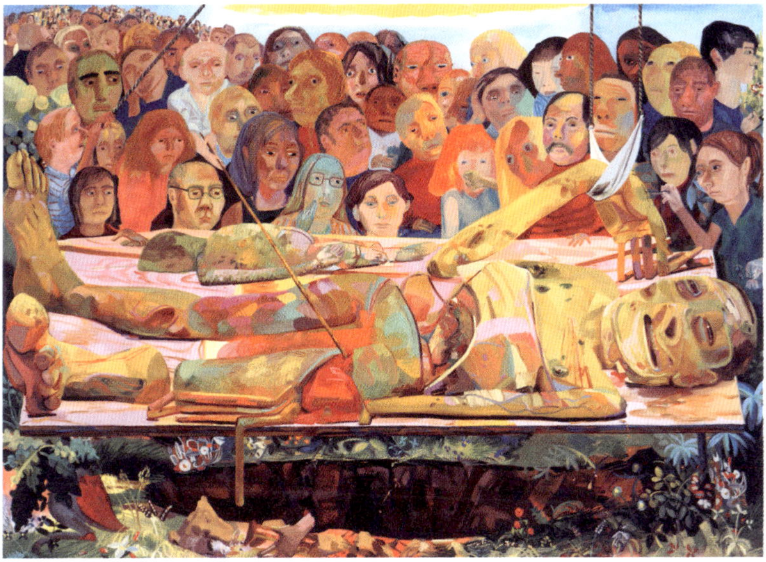

Dana Schutz, *Presentation*, 2005, oil on canvas,
120 x 168 in. (304.8 x 426.7 cm)

sport of MoMA-bashing. There are a million reasons why art objects live lives of quiet desperation in the vault. Rather than simply denounce the status quo, I'd like to ask some questions about the distinct lack of visibility of feminist art production. What are the ramifications for the reception and understanding of contemporary art given the lack of display of earlier feminist work? How do we redress the incomplete history currently on view in most museums? Given that art made by women and subsequently by feminist artists (women and feminists not being the same thing) has been so prominently absent, what forms of history can feminism offer in the space of the museum? And, more specifically, if art objects demand of their viewers various forms of competence for interpretation, what conditions of exhibition does the museum need to establish to create and satisfy those demands? For instance, if feminist works demand that viewers draw on new and different skills to interpret them, how can the museum help create and accommodate those skills?

These questions of history making struck me very strongly in 2005, when MoMA bought and quickly exhibited *Presentation* (2005), a mammoth painting by a young artist named Dana Schutz. Schutz had garnered an enormous amount of press: she was young, a recent graduate of the newly hot master of fine arts program at Columbia University, and she made big, expressive paintings. I confess I was slow to see what was interesting about Schutz's work; I had a typically contrary reaction to a splashy article about her in the *New York Times Magazine*.

I think I had difficulty seeing what was interesting about Schutz largely because she was presented as an ingenue without any *history*, so it is telling that what eventually turned me around were my own scattershot attempts to place her work into some kind of historical trajectory or narrative. For instance, several years after Schutz's meteoric rise to fame, I became interested in Snyder's stroke paintings from the 1970s. These paintings took a modernist grid, with all of its will to silence and impartiality, and combined it with wildly expressive brushstrokes resembling those of an impassioned censor. The combination of expressionism and its disavowal seemed to me emblematic of the feminist struggle to make the personal political. My interest in Snyder was accompanied by an associative—but rather counterintuitive—chain of thoughts about the importance of Willem de Kooning for Amy Sillman. As a feminist trained during the heady days of 1980s theory, I was under the impression that de Kooning paintings were bad—their expressivity garish, their misogyny self-evident. But it became clear to me that Sillman had picked up on the extraordinary use of pink in de Kooning's paintings, which meant that she wasn't having the same problems. Far from feeling compelled to decry de Kooning "the misogynist," Sillman, in her paintings, suggested that in de Kooning one might find a feminized practice of painting in which abstraction is ineluctably linked to the decorative in a non-pejorative way. (I'm thinking of his paintings from the 1970s, the pastoral, frothy, and almost rococo ones, with palettes of rose, cream, and silver.) When I next saw work by Schutz, it was in 2006 in the context of an awful exhibition at the Royal Academy of Arts in London called *USA Today*, a show of recent American art drawn exclusively from Charles Saatchi's collection. Schutz's paintings did not support the exhibition's jingoistic premise (such crass nationalism during wartime was hard to swallow) but unraveled it from the inside. Her oversized, self-devouring figures, awash in a pukey palette, seemed to encapsulate perfectly the horror of America's wartime conditions, particularly the obliteration of rational speech that was a central strategy of George W. Bush's administration.

Perhaps part of the unbridled popular affirmation for Schutz's paintings was due to their energy and vibrancy—a directness of paint on canvas and a disarmingly emotional palate. The paintings display a particularly legible kind of neurosis about power and the body, with devouring and purging mouths desperately spitting out paint—instead of food or words—in an attempt at a kind of pre- or post-linguistic form of communication. Although the body is a perennial feminist subject, Schutz, for the most part, was not discussed in terms of a tradition of feminist work; rather her newness and youth were offered as the primary filters through which to approach her paintings. Part of her meteoric rise, therefore, was tied to the way her work appeared unconnected to artistic precedents. This amnesia, although prevalent in the current market-driven art world in general, is largely not the case with young male artists, who are quickly legitimized into comfortably entrenched art historical narratives, given fathers by their critics.

This makes sense given that the average museum's presentation of its permanent collection is an offering of pluralist harmony (one good picture after another) intermittently punctured by Oedipally inflected narratives of influence, in which sons either make an homage to their fathers (Richard Serra to Jackson Pollock), kill their fathers (Frank Stella to Pollock), or pointedly ignore their fathers (Luc Tuymans to Pollock).

Genealogies for art made by women aren't so clear, largely because they are structured by a shadowy absence. This is why art historians and curators have so often turned to the tasks of recovery and inclusion (we can think here of the recent retrospectives of Snyder, Lozano, and Lee Bontecou, as well as *WACK!: Art and the Feminist Revolution*).[2] The work of recovery is important; I have done it myself and will continue to do so. But I am increasingly puzzled about how to reinsert these absences, repressions, and omissions into the narrative continuum favored by the museum. I know I don't want ghettoized galleries dedicated to art made by women or even a room of "feminist art."[3] But where, for instance, after not exhibiting *Sweet Cathy's Song (For Cathy Elzea)* and Lozano's *Untitled* should MoMA hang these works? Is it really as simple as reinserting them into a chronological narrative that hitherto hasn't accounted for them? Lozano near Philip Guston, Snyder near Brice Marden? The chronological purist in me loves this idea, but I fear it is the nonfeminist in me that desires such a pat formulation: a broken story repaired by insisting that these artists occupy their rightful places in the grand narrative. But is this solution feminist *enough*? Is it a revolution of the deepest order to insert women artists back into rooms that have been structured by their very absence? What would it mean to take this absence as the very historical condition under which the work of women artists is both produced and understood? Might feminism allow us to imagine different genealogies and hence different versions of how we tell the history of art made by women, as well as art made under the influence of feminism?

For instance, I have a fantasy room in which hang works by Snyder, Cindy Sherman, Sillman, Wangechi Mutu, and Schutz. I have an intuition that these works might, as curators say, "talk to each other." My first response to this fantasy is to be made nervous by its ahistorical or potentially essentializing nature, but despite my anxieties, such a room would be true to the kind of associative chain I described earlier, when I moved from Schutz to Snyder to Sillman to de Kooning and back again. Might such a room, organized by the very process of coming to terms with new work, offer a way out of the current impasse created by the opposition of chronological installation (such as that favored by MoMA) versus thematic (favored by Tate Modern, in London)? Instead of coming to terms with Schutz, Snyder, and de Kooning and then putting them back where they "belong," should the museum experiment with other models of history making?

Two art historians, Lisa Tickner and Mignon Nixon, have recently argued, tentatively but with promise, for historical models of influence, production, narration, and interpretation that eschew the two most powerful and familiar in art history: the Oedipal narrative of the son who murders his father (the trumping of one style by another) and the mother-daughter model of the daughter learning through the transmission of oral history (women painters who worked in their fathers' studios; the history of the decorative arts; even some of the mythology surrounding *Womanhouse*).[4] Tickner and Nixon look to another version of family life for models of production and reception, specifically to the relationships of siblings and cousins.

Tickner argues that historically women artists have sought attachment rather than separation, meaning that one of the effects of operating within a genealogy marked by absences and omissions is that you try to seek out your predecessors rather than refute them. She writes that although women may experience "the anxiety of finding oneself a motherless daughter seeking attachment," the discovery of "(real and elective) artist-mothers releases women to deal with their fathers and encounter their siblings on equal terms. Feminism fought for our right to publicly acknowledge cultural expression; it also insists on our place in the patrimony, as equal heirs with our brothers and cousins."[5] This is an interesting idea for two reasons. On the one hand, it moves quickly from a familial narrative to a social one—from a putatively private arrangement to an explicitly public one—in a hallmark of feminist critique: the making public and legible of inequities deemed private. On the other hand, it subverts the potentially pathological nature of familial narratives by insisting on the category of "elective mother." Queer life and theory have offered us increasingly expansive models of the family, and Tickner's argument reaps the benefit of a model developed by those for whom family is established through choice as well as through chance.[6]

To amplify the logic of her argument, Tickner turns to Gilles Deleuze and Félix Guattari's powerful idea of the rhizome as a metaphor for organizing history and knowledge. Unlike the image of the tree—vertical, hierarchical, and evolutionary—the rhizome offers a horizontal, nonlinear structure in which all ideas have the possibility of connecting to all other ideas. Building on this open model of family, she quotes Deleuze and Guattari: "The tree is filiation, but the rhizome is alliance, uniquely alliance."[7] If we think according to the logic of the rhizome, we can see that history is filled with gaps and fissures and moments of connection and synchronicity, and that while there is loss and neglect (as there is regarding the history of art made by women), there are also alliances formed despite geographical distance and temporal incommensurability. Thus an artist seeking an elective mother might not place her in a hierarchical relationship but might instead construct a situation of relative degrees of parity—which might cause those elective mothers a degree of consternation, especially those from the generations of women who fought for the rights we currently take for granted; to them such a synchronic version of history might appear unfair. But a model of history structured by alliance allows us to think about lines of influence and conditions of production that are organized horizontally, by necessarily competing ideas of identification, attachment, sameness, and difference, as opposed to our all too familiar

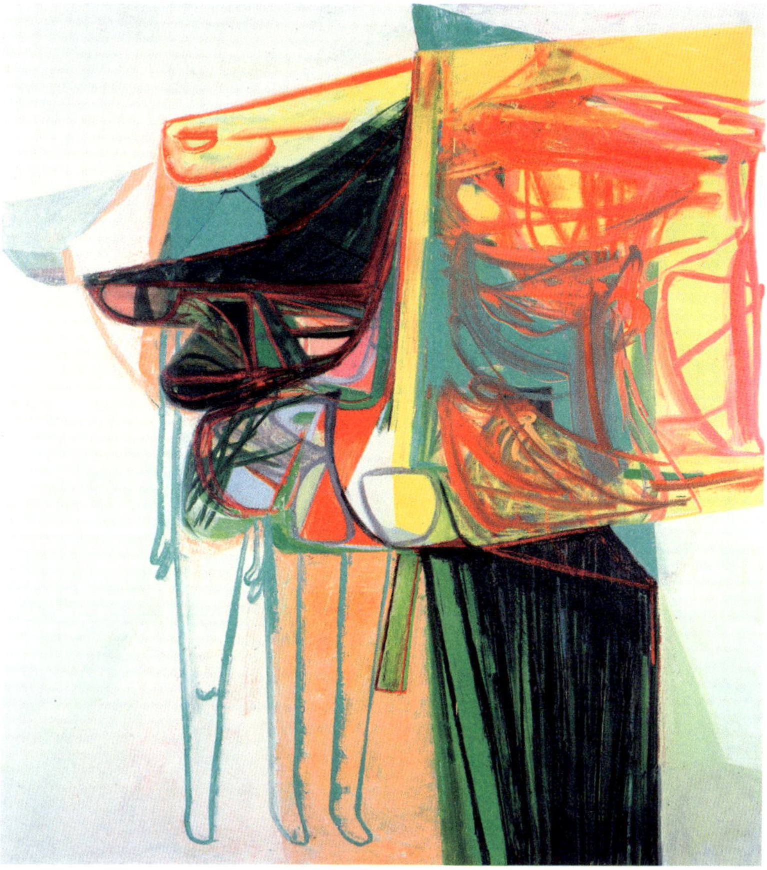

Amy Sillman, *Psychology Today*, 2006, oil on canvas, 84 x 72 in. (213.4 x 182.9 cm)

(vertical) narratives of exclusion, rejection, and triumph. Such a modification in our thinking might, in turn, help us reorganize our institutional dynamics of power.

What would happen if we thought about the museum in this way? After all, it presents its objects simultaneously and equally, while at the same time arranging them chronologically and with an implied tale of progress. Is it possible to privilege the horizontal or rhizomatic aspect over that more powerful vertical spatialization of chronology or those hierarchical family dramas? Better yet, might we be able to highlight or foreground the idea that the model of interconnectedness and the older chronological Oedipal model are already simultaneous with each other? Might we be able to give credence to the deferred and delayed temporality of the recognition of feminist art, to pay better attention to which artists become available and/ or important to us, and at what point? Can we allow this double sense of time and space to have more traction in our ideas about how to present art to contemporary viewers? If we did this, we could better understand the young woman who comes of age as an artist in the halls of MoMA but doesn't see her first Snyder painting until it suddenly emerges at the (corrective) retrospective at the Jewish Museum. Does this young artist, when she encounters an artist heretofore left out of the grand narrative, need the diachronic narrative of mother-daughter or father-son influence in order to incorporate and make sense of the lessons of her discovery? Or does Tickner's model of affiliation and alliance offer other possibilities?

And what new forms of competence would the objects in my fantasy installation, placed in such a configuration with one another, demand of the viewer? In the back-and-forth between the forces of abstraction and representation, between expressionism and its restraint, in the highly affective use of color, might we see a common exploration of non-linguistic communication? Establishing Snyder as an elective mother allows us to see her expressive strokes of enthusiastically colored paint as a rejoinder to the properness of a tastefully muted Minimalist palette, as both a refusal and an embrace of modernism's love of the monochromatic grid. My hope is to suggest that abstraction, expressionism, and beauty or bad taste (depending on your predilection for Snyder's dime-store palette) are not only formal attributes but also constitutive elements in the highly contested field of non-linguistic expression, a form of expression that might have been particularly problematic for artists negotiating the terms of patriarchy (that is, the rules surrounding who gets to speak when about what). Seen in this framework, the tension between Snyder's censorious strokes and demonstrative use of color coheres into a kind of unsolvable contradiction.

Establishing Snyder as an elective mother lets us tease out elements of struggle between silence and expression in all of the works: in Schutz's proliferation of mute figures facing a gaping void; in Sherman's macabre mimicry of Hollywood and fairy-tale narratives, her characters forever silent (despite the prominence she gives to images of mouths); in Mutu's laying bare, with her unwavering cut-and-paste, of women's bodies, particularly her exposure of the colonialist fantasy that is the resplendent, silent, and perpetually available body of color, poised for pleasure and destruction; and in Sillman's neurotic cartoonish figures, delicately sitting on top of powerfully explosive fields of color, begging for captions that never appear. What I see in this installation is an alliance among works formed by a shared disavowal of speech and language and a common ambivalence toward claims of self-expression and toward the privilege afforded such claims by bourgeois capitalism and patriarchy. The internal dynamics of each image show a pictorial struggle to occupy a place in a world structured by language—be it the language of painting, abstraction, color, Hollywood, glossy women's magazines, racism, gender, or family. The combined effect suggests that the artists have entered into these preexisting languages with ambivalence and a degree of difficulty. The works also suggest a perennial feminist dilemma: the simultaneous occupying and denying of these positions (or of our place in these languages). They want expressive power as much as they are critical of it. My hope is that this fantasy room of artworks would make an issue out of the psychic and social conditions of patriarchy, suggesting that not all art by women is the same (the problem created by thematic installation), or that art by women gets progressively better over time and therefore can now be exhibited (the weakness of the chronological installation); it would suggest that these conditions have consistently presented women artists with certain challenges, ranging from the neglect of historical figures to the hierarchy of gender, from the assignation of very strongly defined societal roles to the exclusion of women from the history of painting, and that in this room those challenges and struggles are made visible and become part of the competency required for engaging with art made and installed under the rubric of feminism. The elective mother allows us to see that the silences and absences are indeed part of the history of feminist thought and art-making. By installing a 1970s stroke painting by Snyder in a room with more contemporary works I hope to articulate the temporality of certain art becoming necessary for artists and art historians at certain times. This act is something more than merely rescuing Snyder from the vault. The painting should certainly be shown: it's a great painting (made by a woman), and it's a great feminist painting. By installing it in this way I hope to intimate that "to articulate the past historically does not mean to recognize it 'the way it really was,'" but might mean instead to present it as crucial for recalibrating the effects of the new.[8]

My earlier quandary—how we might create feminist genealogies in the museum—remains. I have declined a ghettoized room of feminist art and refused the simple insertion of women back into canons predicated upon their exclusion. My fantasy room suggests that I am also not interested in rooms where who made the work and under what conditions doesn't matter; it's important to me that these artists are women (important even in the midst of wanting it to not be important: feminism's double bind, its inescapable contradiction). Assembling works of art synchronically through alliance permits them to "talk to each other" about what does matter in our struggle for cultural expression: that women artists, although they might find themselves on what appears to be equal footing with their brothers, still labor under conditions that are demonstrably shaped by patriarchy, and that those conditions and the work they produce can and should be discussed rather than ignored. But lest the model of alliance seem too sunny—everything and everyone happily ensconced in their equality in the benign space of the museum—I want to attend to some of the psychic ramifications of such a model.

Nixon has also been thinking about shifting our interpretation away from the vertical, with a feminist analysis that redirects the hierarchical and vertical family drama of psychoanalysis ("mommy, daddy, and me") toward the horizontal logic of siblings.[9] For Nixon, however, this would not be primarily a model or metaphor for alliance or equality; rather it constitutes a recognition as traumatic as that of sexuality itself, that siblings and cousins are the undeniable proof that one is serial, that one exists in a continuous chain of sameness and difference, of repetition and death. Nixon comes to her argument through *Siblings: Sex and Violence*, a book by the feminist psychoanalytic theorist Juliet Mitchell.[10] Why, Mitchell wonders, do we organize our most powerful narratives of personal identity around our parents rather than our siblings? After all, we know our siblings for our entire lives, and they us. She notes that in Western cultures we talk of liberty, equality, and *fraternity*, and feminists, in upending the gendered logic of democracy, once talked of *sisterhood*. Mitchell contends that while we foreground and even fetishize the hierarchical nature of society, the primary structure of our social organization is lateral, and sibling-based social formations (such as peers, friends, and colleagues) are based on alliances and as a result operate differently from those based on vertical structures (such as parent and child, employer and employee, king and subject). Why, then, do our accounts of selfhood privilege the vertical model to the exclusion of the lateral? Might it be that museums celebrate uniqueness (the genius, the masterpiece) as a way of denying or avoiding the psychological tension produced by the equally strong counter-narrative of sameness? (Let's face it, a lot of those Renaissance altarpieces look alike, as do formal portraits, still lifes, even abstract paintings.) Mitchell proposes that the recognition of sameness—the seriality and repetition implied and instantiated by our siblings and cousins—generates in us a terrifying fantasy of annihilation and of our expendability. Siblings are the traumatic recognition of our mortality. Nixon takes Mitchell's emphasis on repetition in sibling relations and makes an analogy with the serial as a mode of artistic production (from Minimalism and photography to the artist producing her works in editions or series) and suggests that in the hands of someone like Eva Hesse, an artist highly attuned to the activities of her artistic peers, lateral thinking and feeling, rather than Oedipal rivalry, was the very engine for her quirky, medium-extending, bodily engaged, psychically affective work.[11]

I return to my question: is there a way to install works of art so that the artist and the art historian do not experience the space of the museum as the site of one triumph over another? What of the artist who experiences a sisterhood of artists, in which sameness and difference are attributes in constant (pleasurable?) friction with one another? Mitchell, sensing the possibilities her argument has for artists, discusses how artists experience their predecessors "though long dead and buried . . . as the same age as the subject. In other words, these artistic ancestors are 'lateralized.'"[12] Thus it's possible that artists already see the museum as lateralized in that they imagine themselves in a kind of temporal continuity with either Hesse or Albrecht Dürer. Can we permit the fantasy of contemporaneity and the trauma of sameness and its attendant fear of mortality to permeate our museums in a recognizable way? Can we install works of art in ways that permit us this complicated realm of feelings and associations rather than in ways designed to hold such anxieties at bay? Could we reengage with the language of sisterhood, not as a discourse of essentializing sameness but as a complicated narrative of horizontal or lateral thinking?

I have been thinking about relatively new models of thinking (Deleuze and Guattari's horizontal rhizome and Mitchell's lateralization of siblings) and how these are being used by feminist art historians (Tickner and Nixon respectively) to rethink the kinds of stories art history tells us, particularly the stories it tells us about art made by women—stories of exceptionalism or uniqueness, or stories of strays and misfits who simply cannot find their proper place in the gallery. I have been groping around for ways to imagine the fullness of these feminist critiques in the space of the museum, using the installation of the permanent collection as a kind of limit case. Before I close, I want to register a few other instances of lateral thinking, as a way to suggest that the influence of feminist thinking might not always be labeled as such, but we might find it flowing through our discipline nonetheless.

For example, the art historians George Baker and Miwon Kwon have taken up the problem of the post-medium condition. Examining the works of Anthony McCall and Jessica Stockholder, respectively, they have each tried to articulate what is at stake for contemporary artists as they extend and explore the boundaries between and among traditional mediums such as painting, sculpture, and film. Far from celebrating the proliferation of the new post-medium condition for its own expansive sake, they have attempted to make sense of why and how discussions of medium have either fallen into disrepair or become so contentious as to be rendered useless. I have been paying close attention to their language, sifting through the layers of nuance and possibility in the words they chose to describe their objects of study. I listen as Kwon confronts the "tendency toward spatialization in postwar art" and discusses how "three notions of space seem to come together and coexist in her [Stockholder's] installations," meaning that "Stockholder's work asserts (sometimes voraciously) a both/and attitude rather than one of either/or."[13] Consider this alongside Baker's account of the status of medium specificity in McCall's works; he does not insist that they are sculpture, nor that they are film. Baker instead lands upon the seemingly simple word *touch*, as in, "a transgressive model of medium-belonging that sought to take mediums to the limits where they began to touch and shape other forms, but only by 'othering' themselves in the process."[14]

In both of these instances, and notable also in the writing of Briony Fer, a new language has crept into the discourse of art history: an understated but decided move away from dialectical thinking, a tacit refusal to structure arguments in terms of opposition.[15] This art historical generational shift is being mediated neither through "a line of unbroken maternal production" nor "through murderous rivalry either."[16] We are witnessing the replacement of the either/or logic of the dialectic with the conjunction *and*. So, too, the

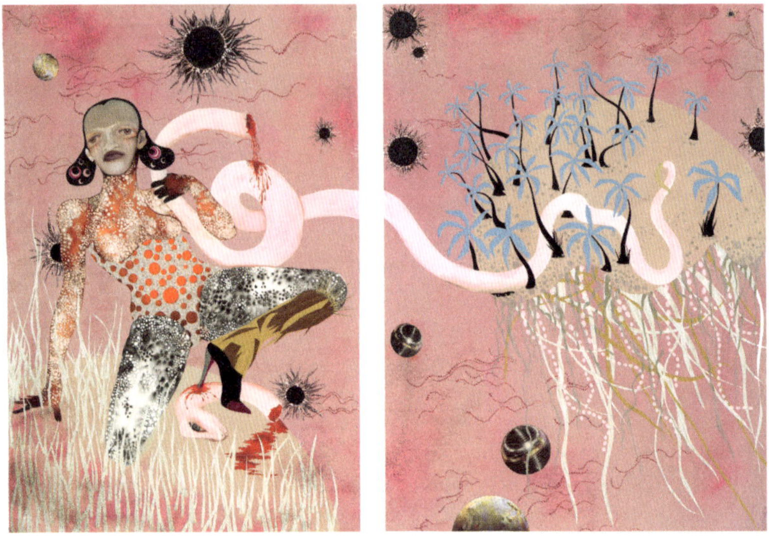

Wangechi Mutu, *Yo Mama*, 2003, ink, mica flakes, pressure-sensitive synthetic polymer sheeting, cut-and-pasted printed paper, painted paper, synthetic polymer paint on paper, 59 1/8 x 85 in. (150.2 x 215.9 cm) overall

go-to structuring word *tension*, used to discuss an artwork, has given way to *touch*. To my ear, such shifts, however delicately deployed, rhyme with the drift away from vertical or hierarchical thinking toward the more lateral and connective rhetorical tissue offered by Tickner and Nixon. "And" and "touch" imply proximity; they are not the language of the inevitable but the contingent, wobbling our routine spatiotemporal conventions, shying away from the hard-and-fast language of causality. They are words that when used in a museum context might offer an opening that would allow us to learn from artists seeking elective mothers in the mode of alliance (as Tickner would have it) or to experience the museum as a site of temporal immediateness (as Mitchell suggests) or to negotiate the psychic ramifications of sameness and difference as they are played out in a field marked by parity (as Nixon proposes). What if we let artworks touch each other in the museum? What if, instead of making demarcations between mediums and artists, we let their mutual otherness act as a kind of contagion? What if, in the next room, around the corner from the Sillman we placed a de Kooning, and maybe next to it a Hesse? (It's worth noting that Hesse was obsessed with de Kooning.) I'd like to install an early Hesse from 1960, one of those not thought to be fully mature—the paintings in which she worked through the logic of one, two, and three. Or, abandoning the language of math, the ones in which she negotiated aloneness, the couple, and the group. What if we made a gallery of paintings by the feminists who were touched by de Kooning, artists for whom there is no either/or between de Kooning and feminism? Could we recover what they found in his work that perhaps now we can no longer see or feel; can we register the artists' sense of alliance; can we enable museum viewers to see their sisterhood?

To close a provisional note: Might there be a way of rethinking the notion of sisterhood—a word so out-of-date it almost sounds cool again? What if sisterhood were not based on essentialist claims of gender? What if it were not dependent on behaving as our mothers or fathers would like us to (or rebelling against them as they expect us to)? What if sisterhood offered a model for forming alliances structured by a loving but skeptical engagement with the new, one that saw the new as part of a larger pattern of seriality and repetition, sameness and difference, annihilation and birth, that defied the logic of chronological or teleological history? Such a model of interpretation, sisterhood, or genealogy would demonstrate that the new does not cancel out the old; it would show us that the new is not a form of triumph but a recalibration of alliances. (Think of the moment a new baby comes home, an arrival that simultaneously produces a mother, a sister, an aunt, and a grandmother: everyone's identity shifts.) In such a model, narratives of influence would be open to a Rashomon-like chorus of voices of nieces, nephews, cousins, sisters, and brothers, opening up single objects to multiple points of alliance, much the way an individual can simultaneously be an aunt, sister, mother, and grandmother. In such a model the seemingly ahistorical installation of Snyder in a room with Schutz, Sillman, and Mutu would allow us to register the affiliations among the artists, to see them as engaged in a common pursuit striated with differences. It might be the beginning of a way of telling history that incorporates the challenges of feminism beyond enumerating which women worked when. So, too, it might be a way of acknowledging the long gaps and absences, the blind spots produced by the vertical narratives of patriarchy, stories so familiar that we often forget that they serve certain interests and not others. Such a room might instead suggest something about how women artists have often forged connections over disjointed periods of space and time, about moving laterally in order to revolutionize the deepest aspects of our lives.

ON WHY I LOVE ARTISTS

One of the art world's dominant conventions is the one-person, or "monographic," show. These exhibitions happen at both the gallery and the museum level. In the gallery, it's meant to display the artist's recent work, from the past two years or so. The focus is on newness, and fundamentally, the setup is a conversational gambit. The artist presents their work, viewers take it in and, as is their prerogative, determine whether or not the artist's recent output is beautiful and/or useful and/or interesting and/or meaningful.

The one-person museum exhibition—the early survey show, or the mid to late-career retrospective—is meant to offer a comprehensive introduction to the development and entirety of an artist's practice. While for the artist such an exhibition bestows the cultural legitimation and critical approbation one might expect, more importantly, it also offers living artists a space to take in the sweep or arc of their work in one location. In this regard, the monographic exhibition is a service to both artist and audience.

Many of the essays in this section were written under the auspices enumerated above, since they were commissioned essays intended to appear in monographic exhibition catalogues. My process to write an essay like this starts with reading everything that has been written on the artist up to that point (in English), as well as looking at as many images as humanly possible. In other words, I engage in total immersion in an attempt to try my hardest to really come to terms with the artist's overall project. This means I test myself and my understanding of the world against their understanding of the world. The search for how to frame their work, and how to gather and compose the very best words to describe what their work was doing—articulating what the work was after—was (and is), for me, an opportunity to understand the work from the inside out. It is not at all dissimilar to taking something apart and putting it back together in order to find out how it works. Each of these essays was written imagining the artist as its first reader, by which I mean I tried to be in dialogue with the artists' work rather than merely describe or interpret it.

Hence, the essays that follow share a searching quality as I try to figure out the very best language to describe why I love the artist's work. These essays allowed me to speak of that love in public, they allowed me to tell the artist I was writing about why their work mattered, and specifically why it mattered to me. There is nothing harder than writing about love, and nothing more important.

Louise Lawler: Just the Facts

Originally published in *Louise Lawler: Twice Untitled and Other Pictures (looking back)*, ed. Helen Molesworth (Columbus, OH: Wexner Center for the Arts; Cambridge, MA: MIT Press, 2006), 143–52.

For Gregg Bordowitz

I'm singing this borrowed tune
I took from the Rolling Stones
Alone in this empty room
Too wasted to write my own

I'm climbing this ladder
My head in the clouds
I hope that it matters
I'm having my doubts
—Neil Young, "Borrowed Tune"

It is tempting to think about writing an essay on Louise Lawler's work made up only of the competing and contradictory quotes of others. One could fantasize that such a process would mime Lawler's own artistic activities: the photographing of artwork made by others in a variety of competing and contradictory situations. For instance, Achim Hochdörfer thinks "Lawler's photographs subtly operate on the borderline between high art and kitsch: when clichés suddenly become authentic and vice versa; or when aggressiveness and moments of shock tum into humor and parody."[1] Bruce Hainley wrote that "a politic can haunt the aesthetic by appearing as a brute blankness, abstraction or even nakedness."[2] Jack Bankowsky writes that "for Lawler, it may be said that there are no facts and nothing speaks entirely for itself."[3] Yet Johannes Meinhardt observes that many of Lawler's images put forward "the seemingly inessential and incidental fact that works of art always occupy a place in a room."[4] One might imagine that the act of appropriating and assembling quotations was in sympathy with the artist's own working process of radically framing and cropping as she photographs art in its various locations. One might imagine that the inevitable disjuncture between the culled quotes would evoke the blank spaces—the walls, doors, and light switches—that almost always appear in between works of art in Lawler's pictures.

And yet the logic of appropriation or pastiche that such an essay would play out in the end doesn't feel quite true to the intricacies and complications of Lawler's oeuvre. It would perhaps reiterate the interpretive misapprehension around her practice that sees it primarily bound up with a critical version of postmodernism that celebrated appropriation as one of its primary modes of working.[5] Isabelle Graw notes that in the process of appropriation, "parasitic behavior replaced the model of the strong subject that creates something new using its own resources."[6] I would like to suggest that this is not a particularly accurate description of what happens in a Lawler photograph. There is, after all, no confusing a Lawler image for one by another artist (as there might be with Sherrie Levine or Richard Prince). They never, for instance, look like the standard publicity shots offered by museums or auction houses, nor do they mime the glossy interior design magazines in which art objects and piles of art books vie for space with the requisite orchids and modernist furniture. Rather, despite the seeming ambivalence in her practice about modernist notions of artistic authorship (her refusal to create something new), the images nonetheless put forward a distinctive way of seeing, one that many writers have recently noted is rife with a kind of poignancy. This suggests that the critical, or ironic, valence of appropriation is not what one finds in Lawler's photographs, at least not exclusively. But what makes Lawler's pictures poignant? What accounts for the emotional affect of these seemingly simple pictures of art in situ? And why has *poignancy* as a term come up so relatively recently in Lawler's reception?[7]

The initial reception of Lawler's work was overwhelmingly positive and saw it as part of a larger critical project, bound up with appropriation as noted earlier, but also with institutional critique. Her photographs titled *Arranged by . . .* of art arranged by others in a variety of spaces from commercial galleries, to corporate offices, to private homes, pointed to the ways in which art is never encountered as such. Lawler's work insisted on the staged and authored nature of those encounters. In an extension of Lawler's dissembling of these domestic and commercial arrangements, she also took pictures of art in museums. Here the arrangements, which are always offered as timeless (and hence pointedly *unauthored* by the institution), are fractured by Lawler's bruising gaze. The extremity of her cropping, her refusal to look at the artwork head on, meant that her pictures often offered an oblique angle such that what was captured was not the work but its reflection in the floor. It is as if Lawler is fundamentally distracted by the elaborate mise-en-scène of the museum and sees always the trees rather than the forest, or, more precisely, sees that the trees are always already the constitutive elements of the forest. She takes seriously the details of the presentation and shows us how power and ideology are carried through in the arrangements of the pictures, as well as in the pictures themselves. For many critics and viewers, the focus on the fragment and on the unseen labor of the situation (the arranging of the pictures, the shine of the floor) was implicitly feminist. Through such gestures one could feel the work slowly but steadily scratching away at the master narratives of institutional power.

Lawler's feminist analysis was perhaps most clearly seen in her photographs of art in domestic interiors. Certainly the importance of institutional critique was to elaborate the ideological and market systems through which art comes to have value. Most often these institutions and processes were deemed to be exclusively public. But, as Andrea Fraser has argued, Lawler doesn't relegate that public function to architecture as such: "rather than situate institutional power in a centralized building (such as a museum) or a powerful elite which can be named, she locates it instead in a systematized set of presentational strategies which name, situate, centralize."[8] In so doing, Lawler became the most serious advocate for the role of art in the putatively private arena of domestic space. Her images of art in the homes of the wealthy not only show us art operating as so many fetishistic trophies of bourgeois ownership, they also show us displays of the arranger's identity or sense of self. Often one feels that the private domestic interiors in Lawler's photographs are arranged for explicitly public consumption, every *i* dotted and *t* crossed in a kind of haiku of self-presentation. This is one way we might read the presentation of a white monochrome flag painting by Jasper Johns hung above a monogrammed bed spread on an impeccably made bed in *Monogram* (1984), where the image of the flag speaks to utter publicness, the Johns painting to highbrow bourgeois taste, and the monogram to the woman's public union (marriage) and identity. The associative chain of meaning offered by the contextualization of art among the décor—where an abstract swirl of paint in a Jackson Pollock painting is not so different from the decorative flourish on a porcelain soup tureen—is a way of saying that art is one artifact among many, part of a set of objects equally available to bear the brunt of our desires or to fade into the background of our everyday lives. In Lawler's photographs, art is often simultaneously banal and unbearably exceptional.

Lawler's pictures of authored arrangements of art in domestic spaces subversively reintroduce private property into "public" circulation. The private ownership of the art objects by private individuals is ever so slightly compromised once her photographs appear in a gallery, art magazine, or museum. But in that appearance another equation is posited: art is a kind of filler (decorative, emotional, financial) whether it's in the gallery or the home. Lawler's works imply, however subtly, that fantasies of ownership belong not only to those who possess the title to the actual objects; the intellectual or artistic class also feels the pull of ownership, albeit of knowledge. The works offer a subtle implication of the viewer who might smugly think, "I understand Jasper Johns even if I don't own one," or, "I understand Johns better than the people who own them." This mode of placing the viewer in her own situation even as she contemplates the arrangement/situation of another is delivered through Lawler's sly titles, particularly the obliqueness with which they interpolate the viewer. As Andrea Fraser has recently noted, Lawler's titles often question the viewer; such titles as *Does Andy Warhol Make You Cry?* or *It Could Be Elvis* "are questioning you on the level of your desire and your interest in looking."[9] I would like to suggest that the image implicates the owner as much as the title implicates the viewer. Some people get to own objects, and through possession feel that they have knowledge of both the objects and themselves; others feel that through knowledge of the object comes what might be called "intellectual possession." Lawler's pictures muddy the waters between these two modalities by staging the problem of desire as reciprocal between them.

And yet Lawler's work does not suggest that the boundaries, however porous, between public and private space don't matter. Indeed, it is telling that Lawler's pictures often focus on works of art by particularly "public" artists whose work has an equally strong "public" dimension: Andy Warhol, Gerhard Richter, and Jeff Koons are recurring subjects.[10] In many ways, the ubiquity of these artists (particularly Warhol) in the public eye compounds the way in which their work seems to be devoid of "private" sentiment but is rather made up of the stuff of a shared culture (be it popular or political). So, too, all three exacerbate and illuminate the tensions between the fantasy of an autonomous realm of art and its intersection with the society of the spectacle (Elvis, the Baader-Meinhof group, and Michael Jackson, respectively) and the cultural ascendancy of the commodity (soup cans, flower paintings, and a stainless-steel bunny in an edition of three, also respectively). Her focus on these artists furthers the simultaneous disjuncture and reciprocity of art's meaning in public and private spaces.

While Lawler is routinely referred to in the list of postmodern artists or artists who use appropriation or artists who practice institutional critique, the emotional affect of her work differs demonstrably from most purveyors of these various practices. For the first decades of her practice, not much was said about the emotional tenor of her work. Her pictures of art in museums or in private homes were seen to be part of a larger critical agenda designed to substantiate how art comes to have value and meaning through acts of exchange and presentation, and to make these attributes of the art situation undeniably evident by redirecting viewers' attention to the framing aspect of the museum, art gallery, and private home. (Part of the early pleasure of Lawler's works was that they "proved" the theories right, which is probably why they were so often used as illustrations in theoretical texts.) It was as if the medium of photography offered a slightly suspect version of every truth except for Lawler's; her skewed framing and "obvious" cropping unveiled the institutional power before our very eyes. But in an interview with Douglas Crimp, one of the very few interviews Lawler has ever given, allergic as she is to statements of artistic intentionality, the emotional affect of her work was registered. In the interview, Crimp opines that the discourse of institutional critique "may be true and accurate about your work," but it doesn't "capture something else that's crucial. There's a word you often use to describe things: 'poignant.'" He continues, "The word 'poignant' means both 'pointed,' 'sharp,' 'focused,' and 'affecting,' 'moving.' So the word captures dimensions of your work compromising not only its pointedness, its criticality, but also something much more difficult to speak about, its emotional effect."[11] To my way of thinking, this poignancy was felt first, and perhaps most strongly, in Lawler's pictures of art at auction.

Lawler took a group of modest black-and-white photographs of the Tremaine collection when it went up for auction at Christie's auction house in 1988. These pictures almost always showed the auction house label adjacent to a very radically cropped work of art and were taken a mere four years after Lawler's now-iconic pictures of the Tremaine collection elegantly arranged in their New York City and Connecticut homes. Of these works, two identical images of a gold tondo of Marilyn Monroe by Andy Warhol, one titled *Does Marilyn Monroe Make You Cry?* and the other *Does Andy Warhol Make You Cry?* (both 1988), are exemplary in registering the kind of pathos that was to emerge in Lawler's pictures. The question that goes unspoken is whether the whole process of the auction might make us cry. Certainly, the auction house is one of the institutions of art in which art's exchange value is privileged above all other forms of value. But that is not what makes Lawler's pictures of art at auction poignant. The emotional intensity comes from the realization that however fancy the trappings of the auction house, and however delirious the bidding, an art auction is nothing more than an extremely fancy garage sale, a collection of cast-off pictures, a grouping of art that is no longer wanted or needed by its owners. Almost a decade later, Lawler would return to the auction house and take two photographs, nearly identical, of the same arrangements of goods for sale, two pieces by Robert Gober, a painting by Damien Hirst, and a photograph by Cindy Sherman. In one, only a fragment of Gober's sculpture of a baby's crib appears; in the other, we can see it in its entirety along with a large photograph by Charles Ray. The picture with the "cropped" sculpture is called *Sentimental*; the other is titled *Unsentimental* (both 1999–2000). The cropped image compresses the two Gobers closer together, the proximity of the severed leg and the child's crib speak to a kind of intense psychic shattering, the frailty of human existence; the wayward hitchhiking girl depicted in the Cindy Sherman *Untitled Film Still* in between them only compounds the effect. As for the Hirst painting, well, it is either a cynical incursion on the scene or benign wallpaper—either way, its emptiness is pushed to the periphery. *Unsentimental* pulls back. The Gobers no longer feel as if they could be in a bedroom; they are "merely" sculptures whose rhythm on the wall is punctuated by photographs—tick tock tick tock. Photography is no longer a lesser medium! It is worth as much as sculpture! All art is equally available in an edition of three or five! If Lawler's pictures show us that the auction house is where the art object's "singular" psychic value gives way to the spectacle of its pure exchange value, then *Unsentimental* seems to ask, "What did you think was going to happen?"

Although Lawler had taken pictures of art at auction before *Sentimental* and *Unsentimental*, the shift to a large color format seemed particularly apposite, as the works act as a witness to the art market boom of the 1990s, which ushered in the apotheosis of photography as a newly expensive (and legitimate) medium. The earlier modest black-and-white photos might have reduced the garishness of the scene, rendered the spectacle too nostalgic. The large color auction pictures also heightened the arbitrariness of the art situation—both in how objects are "installed" for viewing at auction and in the way objects were cycling through the market with increased ease and rapidity. From gallery, to domestic home, to auction, and back again, Lawler's work appeared to be a closed circle of sorts. Art in museums, art in galleries, art in storage, art in domestic space, art in auction houses: her work had exhaustively mapped the system of art's circulation. Like an exercise of declining verbs in a foreign language, Lawler's project was an enumeration of art's various states and of its accumulation of value. And yet the pull of emotional affect, of humor and sadness, derision and melan-choly, was growing in the work, and, as such, the hermeneutics of appropriation or institutional critique seemed to leave out more and more.

To me, a kind of crisis of interpretation seemed to emerge with the pictures in Lawler's first show at the new Metro Pictures gallery in Chelsea in 1997. The photographs in this exhibition documented the renovation of the gallery from an industrial space to a commercial gallery. The images are saturated with color—cadmium and lapis lazuli walls were framed such that they evoked Color Field painting. In *HVAC* (1996), the shiny aluminum surfaces of an uninstalled heating and cooling unit stand propped against the wall like so many would-be Minimalist sculptures. While the pictures certainly partook of a kind of site-specific critique of the production of the white cube, they were also quite abstract. There was nothing specific in the images that would let the viewer know that this was the as-yet-unfinished Metro Pictures. Indeed their saturated color placed them more in the tradition of William Eggleston than Michael Asher. Resignation? Perhaps. This group of pictures pointed to a fault line of sorts, a fissure in the aims or results of a critical art practice—for what was Chelsea if not the possibility of reinventing rather than reinscribing the existing terms of the art world? But a reinscription it was. So where then did the dismantling aims of so much postmodern or critical art reside? What was to be done in the face of what was beginning to look suspiciously like a failure of those ideas and practices?

I don't think Lawler's response to this situation was at all programmatic; in fact, what was ever systematic or programmatic about her project up until this point seemed to become somewhat vulnerable. It is as if the elaboration of art's contextual meaning and systems had rendered things a little too neatly. Or, to put it another way, to borrow the lyrics of Neil Young that opened this essay, the pictures were "hoping it mattered," but were "having their doubts." I don't want to impugn a specific intentionality to Lawler at this moment, but I do think that her pictures have become increasing difficult to read; the situations they depict have become gradually less clear, the titles more oblique, and the overall tenor of her work even more contingent and associative. Two cases in point are *Still Life (Candle)* (2003) and *WAR IS TERROR* (2001/2003).

In *Still Life (Candle)* and *WAR IS TERROR*, we find ourselves looking at art in domestic space. Yet in both instances the spaces do not appear to be exclusively of the wealthy or dominant class. Rather, we encounter an anomaly in Lawler's practice—domestic interiors of the intellectual or creative class, an "our town" of sorts for the critical art viewer. The two pictures form a punctum in Lawler's oeuvre, rare moments of identification and recognition: this is what art looks like when hung by people who feel they own its ideas as well as its actuality. In the diminutive *Still Life (Candle)* (it is only thirteen by ten inches) an inherently modest On Kawara date painting hangs on a wall behind a dining room table. Both the painting and the contents of the table speak of the inevitable passage of time: empty wine glasses, a full ashtray, a used and crumpled napkin, an uncanny silence that lingers in the room after what we imagine might have been lively conversation. Here is an interior not presented for others but used, daily; the finished meal suggests a melancholy mixture of conviviality and necessity. The On Kawara doubles this feeling: the steady continuity indicated by the date of the painting (May 26, 1994) is a testament to the simplicity of his project, still holding forth, still resistant to any kind of spectacle or overblown commodification. There seems to be no denying the fact of the thing. Yes, the date happened; yes, On Kawara painted it on that date; yes, it hangs on a wall. And yet Lawler's title wants to focus our attention on the candle, to bring us back to the table, insisting that the still life on the table register precisely as foreground, that the art in the background is just that, filling space on a wall, filling a space in our mind's eye, relieving our boredom through an appeal to our restless intellect; but, the picture implies, in the end, it is no match for the life that still reigns at the table.

The space of *WAR IS TERROR* is just as intimate as *Still Life (Candle)* as we find ourselves in a bedroom, looking at what appears to be a photograph of Virginia Woolf. The framed portrait in profile is hung half on the wall, half on top of a piece of woodblock print fabric pinned to the wall, like a makeshift headboard—a decorating style redolent of college dormitories and bohemian life. An old steam radiator intrudes on the left side of the picture. The portrait is hung in the way one hangs a photograph of a long-deceased family member or a cultural hero, arranged, that is, not as art, but as a kind of psychic talisman, a mnemonic for hard times, presented less for others than for the self, a reminder of which way to go when the going gets tough. War is terror indeed, and yet the dailiness of life cycles on: beds get made, leaves are raked, pictures are taken. What does it mean to make art during wartime? This was a question that Woolf was to struggle with, a struggle she could not resolve in the end, certainly not win. And yet, for many feminists, Woolf remains a model—her insistence on derision and refusal, so eloquently argued in her antiwar essay *Three Guineas*, remains

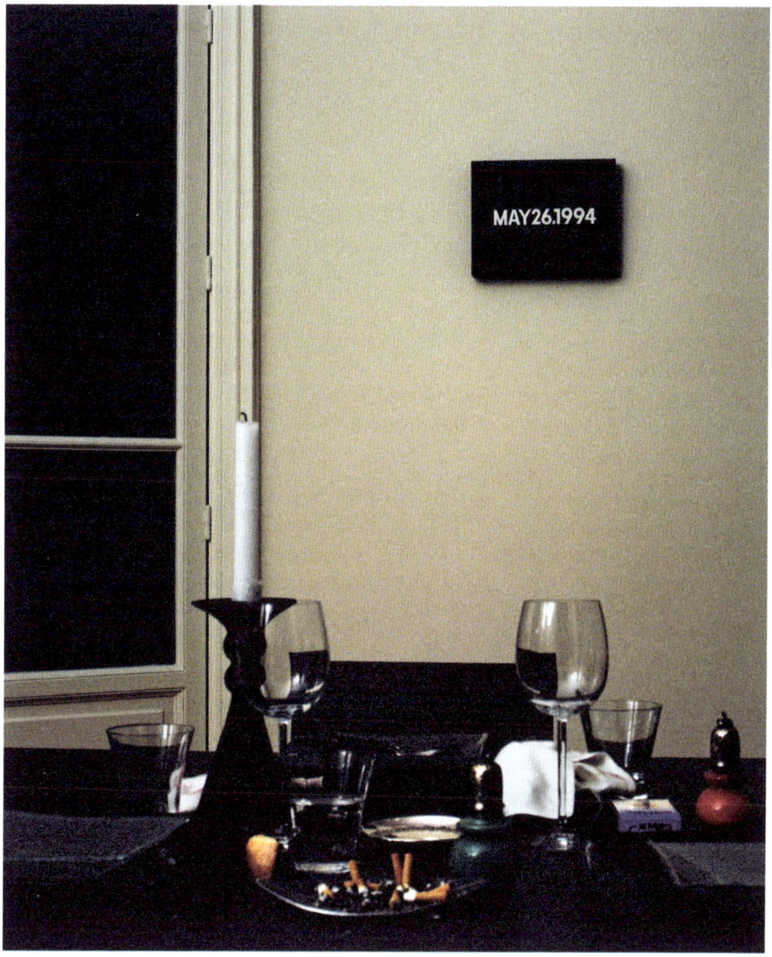

Louise Lawler, *Still Life (Candle)*, 2003, silver dye bleach print on museum box, 13 x 10 ¾ in. (33 x 27.3 cm)

central to feminism—however vexed and ambivalent she may have remained in the face of the collusion of patriarchy and capitalism, a collusion that inevitably culminates in war.[12]

War is Terror. Like Woolf, Lawler appears to be grappling with the enormity of making art during wartime. In this work she flips the logic of the George W. Bush administration back on itself. Not a war on terror, not a war because of terror, but a different factual statement: *WAR IS TERROR*—for both those on whom it is waged and for those in whose name it is waged. In the face of an imperial presidency, both parties are doomed to feel relative degrees of powerlessness. Witness Lawler's 2003 announcement for an exhibition at Metro Pictures that read, "No drinks for those who do not support the anti-war demonstration." And then, printed in the very same announcement: *Four Nudes*, the exhibition's title. Back to business for all those who had forgotten that patriarchy and capitalism combined (again the topic of Woolf's *Three Guineas*) have always led to war and sexism, for as Woolf taught us innumerable times, the two remain inextricably linked.

It's tempting to think about writing an essay now about Lawler's work that is primarily an antiwar essay, using Woolf as a starting point. Then perhaps we could begin to make sense of a picture like *Grieving Mothers (Attachment)* (2005), in which we see the wings of the ancient Greek sculpture *Winged Victory*, which graces the triumphal entrance to the Louvre, lying on the ground. Or the wrapping paper Lawler made in 2004 that had the dollar amounts being offered by the United States government as a reward for Osama Bin Laden's capture. And it would allow us to recall the glasses she installed like so many products on the wall with the phrase "It costs $590,000 a day to operate an aircraft carrier" finely etched into their transparent surfaces. And from there how long would it be before we recalled *Helms Amendment* (1989)? One hundred black-and-white photographs of the kind of plastic drinking cup one gets at the dentist, each standing for one of the senators' votes that denied federal funding for the prevention of AIDS and HIV; a vote that passed with ninety-four yeas, two nays, and four abstentions. How confidently, one imagines, such an essay might progress, claiming for Lawler all of the prominence (given) and authority (taken) of the critical artist and her knowing viewer.

But the facts sometimes do get in the way. The photograph in *WAR IS TERROR* is not of Woolf, but of her mother, Julia Duckworth (the likeness taken by Julia Margaret Cameron).[13] The fallen wings in *Grieving Mothers (Attachment)* are not of the *Winged Victory* in the Louvre, but rather from a plaster cast in a museum in Oslo. What to make of the misrecognitions? Oddly, they only compound my sense of the political quality of these two achingly beautiful pictures. In both the titles are explicitly of our current moment, bringing us back to an awareness of the war. Both images offer the logic of the copy and the promise of limitless reproductions of art—the photograph and the plaster cast. It is difficult, however, to read the potentially infinite reproductions as a challenge to modernist notions of authenticity. In both images, the endlessness of the potential copies appears as a kind of melancholic acknowledgement of the eternal return of the same, the mindlessness of business as usual. Especially as the disjuncture between the titles and the images and the obliqueness of the images also mirror—or track or shadow—the now-daily dissemblance of the truth, or at least the facts. It's as if the pictures can no longer simply, or even confidently, point to the system's ideological fault lines, as if they were somewhere "out there" but they now must recognize that one effect of the current political, economic, and media situation is that those fault lines reside very deeply within our own critical practices. It's as if by making the pictures harder to interpret

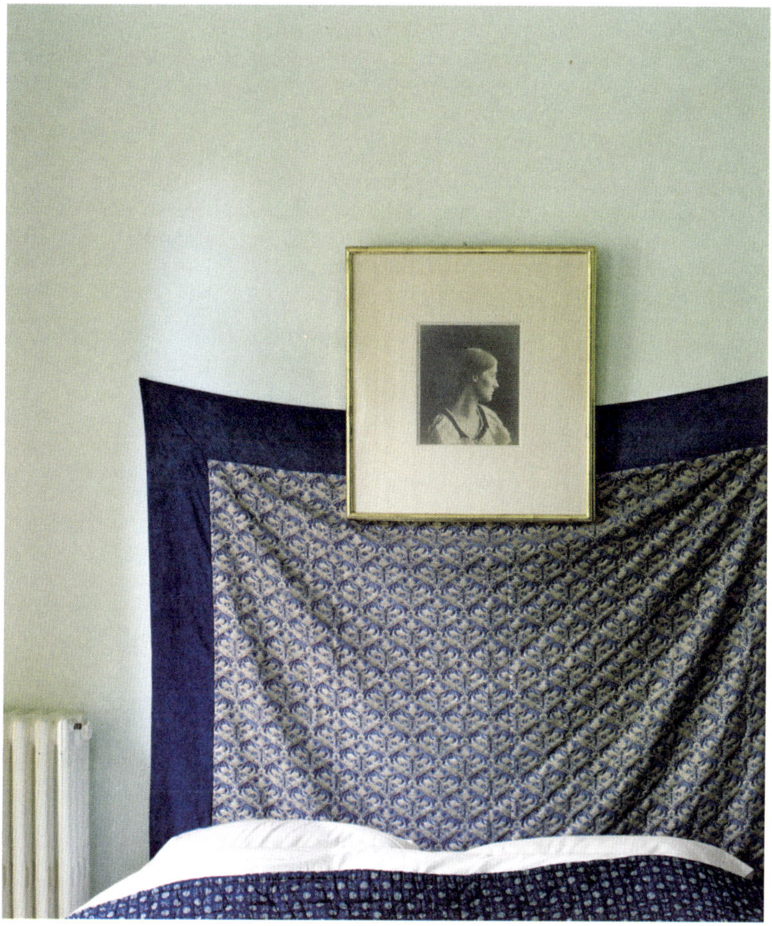

Louise Lawler, *WAR IS TERROR*, 2001/2003, silver dye bleach print on museum box, 30 x 25 ¾ in. (76.2 x 65.4 cm)

Lawler is acknowledging the limitations of critical discourse and art making in effecting substantive political change. However, conversely, the more layered and emotionally complex images require new interpretive modes. We can borrow the previous ones as much as we want, too wasted or tired or strung out on failure to write our own, but in the end there will be no drinks for those who don't support the antiwar demonstration, no confident pictures in such terrible times, no sense that the facts ever speak for themselves.

In her searching essay "Why War?" psychoanalyst Jacqueline Rose makes some modest suggestions about the character of war. War, she writes, "neither simply threatens nor simply advances the cause of civilization," rather "it mimics or participates in the fundamental ambivalence of civilization itself."[14] War's fundamental ambivalence is also expressed in its relationship to knowledge. Rose argues that war is the limit of absolute or total knowledge, that it produces uncertainty even though it is usually fought in the name of absolute truth. (This helps us to understand the simultaneous dissemination of lies by the Bush administration while maintaining its moral certitude in its Christian worldview.) For Rose, war and the unconscious share an ability to trouble "the clear distinction between reality and fantasy" and in doing so both also wreak havoc on the "category of cause."[15] The problem of the truth and its relationship to absolute knowledge and the kind of intellectual or ideological confidence game that produces narratives of causality is that which enables war and that which war destroys. Such logic is insidious, and damning, and the rejoinder that Rose offers is what she calls an "ethics of failure," war breaks out, uncontrollably so, because we are not willing to fail *enough*.

Narratives of failure can have their own brand of romance. Bob Dylan reminds us that "there's no success like failure and failure's no success at all." And yet Lawler's recent pictures sometimes put forward a mixture of vulnerability and obliqueness that complicates the seeming straightforward confidence of her earlier work. Lawler's photographs—of paintings lying on their sides; art handlers straining to install a heavy object; sculptures in pieces on the ground, their status as art not yet clear; paintings reflected in the floor instead of seen head-on; objects languishing in storage, living lives of quiet desperation; a figurine trapped in a bell jar on a mantel; halos of light illuminating empty museum walls—are distinct from their earlier, more confident counterparts, images of art on view, properly authored and installed. Pictures like *Grieving Mothers (Attachment)* convey a mixture of vulnerability and obliqueness that gets at the poignancy of our current failure and complicity. In the images in which we are no longer exactly sure of what we are looking at or where we are, when the arrangements of pictures are no longer authored or when their critical context is not offered as demonstrably as it once was, and when such images bear titles that make direct reference to the war, I think Lawler comes whisperingly close to practicing what Rose calls an ethic of failure, in which we hope that borrowed tunes might matter, even when we have our doubts.

Postscript

It's hard to remember the numb, dead fear that overcame most of us in the wake of the terrorist attacks of September 11. It's harder still to remember the rage and disgust that accompanied the early months of the Iraq War. At the time, the level of mendacity at the highest levels of government felt unparalleled. (In the wake of the Trump administration, all is relative.) But the facts remain. The United States waged an unprovoked war in Iraq, courtesy of the so-called Bush Doctrine, which retooled the long-standing ethical agreement between nations that one "strike only after ye has been struck."

The war made me miserable, and more than that, it also challenged my faith in art and the entire critical enterprise. Could art and writing about art really help us to see the world differently? Was culture going to be the engine that helped humans engage with one another more ethically and thoughtfully?

I was fortunate enough to be working on a Louise Lawler exhibition during this period. Her subtlety, her brand of low-key feminism, and her attention to the everyday details of which a life is made, kept me deeply grounded. As a result, I worked through my feelings of despair and rage using her method, which was to never let the war out of my sight, though also, to never deal with it head-on. One evening, at a dinner hosted by our beloved mutual friends, artists Jason Simon and Moyra Davey, the activist and poet Gregg Bordowitz told me that anytime he was given the opportunity to speak publicly, or was offered access to print, he had decided to give an antiwar talk. It wasn't the first time Gregg said something that changed my view of things—I'd been following his writing and work for years, and his impact on my thinking has frequently been transformative.

I proceeded to take a page from his playbook. I commenced mentioning the war in my writing whenever I had the privilege of an audience. I was still governed by melancholy. I was still grappling with a reduced amount of faith in the whole endeavor, but I tried to keep my head in the clouds, and to hold on to the idea that it mattered—even as I had my doubts.

Klara Lidén: In Memory of Static

Originally published in *Artforum*, March 2011, 214–23.

In early June 2000, I visited Art Basel for the first time. I was naive, which meant that I was subsequently shocked and dismayed. The convention hall was filled with stalls, many of which were displaying objects I knew and loved (works by Piero Manzoni, Marcel Broodthaers), pieces made by people I admired from afar (Jeff Wall, Rodney Graham) or by artists of great historical merit (Piet Mondrian, Ed Ruscha). Then there were pieces by artists I knew personally. All of this gave me a charge of recognition mixed with a creeping sense of sadness; by the time I reached my hotel, unironically called the Hotel du Commerce, I realized I was suffering from a kind of equally unironic, decidedly old-fashioned heartbreak. For, more than being an assortment of proper names, the objects themselves had, up until that point, represented constellations of ideas to me, their primary form of exchange taking place in books and in journals, in buzzed late-night conversations in bars, and, increasingly (in ways that were deeply exciting), in the space of exhibitions. To see all those ideas hung up on the trade-show walls ready for sale was just short of crushing. The next day, as I made my way back to the Messeplatz to take another stab at this new form of art viewing, I ran into an artist I knew. She was one of the very few artists there, and on hearing that she had just arrived, I cautioned her not to go in. This was no place for artists.

Needless to say, a lot has changed in the past ten years. Art fairs have had their apotheosis. They rival, and often exceed in prestige, large-scale group exhibitions; and, in a perverse reciprocity, many exhibitions now replicate the look and feel of the fairs—rabbit-warren arenas in which art is densely installed, where the thrill and velocity of the search for the next new thing is privileged over the slower temporality of the forming of consensus. One of the biggest changes has been the role that artists have been asked to play in this new formation. They are no longer expected (or allowed?) to stay away. Rather, these trade shows increasingly thrive on the presence of artists, who are routinely asked to make "special projects" specifically for the fair and to perform their ideas in the guise of lectures and panels. For many artists, the fairs are as viable and legitimate a form of exhibition as a museum show. While this makes me uncomfortable, I can't pass judgment. Artists are workers too, and the state of employment has changed dramatically, across the board. My father has a pension; I don't. Shit happens. Capitalism rules.

* * *

Several years later, while attending a fair, I scrawled "Klara Lidén/Reena Spaulings" in a small notebook. But because I am a bad archivist, I didn't write down the name of the fair where I saw the work, nor did I write down the name of the piece. Recently, thumbing through that book, I found Lidén's name in smudged graphite, and it was mnemonic enough for me to be able to summon my first impression of the piece—"cute baby butch, wielding a steel pipe, smashing up her bicycle good." This short, low-tech video, *Bodies of Society* (2006) seemed like the perfect early-twenty-first-century riposte to Pipilotti Rist's joyful girl-smashing-cars video *Ever Is Over All* (1997). *Bodies of Society* is affectless, rather than delightful; it is situated in a shabby domestic interior, rather than outside; and, counter to the random destruction on display in Rist's video, the way Lidén stalks the bicycle is very precise and controlled. She toys with it at first, stroking it almost lovingly with the steel pipe, and then slowly she comes down hard, picking the bike apart bit by bit. In some ways the video is an erotic masterpiece—an S&M scene of inference, delay, and slow gratification. Another salient difference between Lidén's and Rist's destruction is that we assume Lidén is doing damage to her own property, rather than to other people's, and that in doing so she is doubtless making her daily life just ever so slightly more difficult.

Watching Lidén pulverize her bicycle in the middle of an art fair was pretty great. Clearly indebted to the punk ethos of destroying your instruments, the video suggests a deeply ambivalent relationship to possession and use-value. If Rist's video celebrates the 1990s riot grrrl's ascendancy, and can retrospectively be seen as part of the latter's ultimate commodification, then Lidén's video heralds the muted, nearly autistic sensibility of the post-gender, post-critique artist that may be the mien of our moment. The romance of crime (or guitar smashing) is not what is on offer, nor is the fantasy of rage turned to glee; no such redemption is imagined. Rather, the artist at work is imaged as silent, sullen, solitary, and quite possibly self-defeating.

The more I encountered Lidén's work, the more I was intrigued by it and the quality of the affect it exhibits. In *Paralyzed* (2003), Lidén does a wild, uninhibited dance on a train in Sweden, mildly terrifying her fellow passengers as she tries to squeeze into the overhead luggage rack and hurls herself into and out of seats. At the Museum of Modern Art in New York in 2009, she built an enormous white cube and placed it in the center of a small room so that it occupied the majority of the floor space, leaving only a narrow passageway around its perimeter. Carefully placed on top of the cube were scaffolding, tar paper, and large bundles of cardboard for recycling, instantly transforming the useless cube into a humongous plinth. It was hilarious: a white cube in the ultimate white cube, used as a base for a "sculpture" composed entirely of trash. Take that, MoMA! And yet it's clear that Lidén understood that the work was still bounded, even precisely delimited, by the gallery. She didn't break huge holes in the wall à la Urs Fischer or Kate

Gilmore; she just riffed on pedestals and garbage—Manzoni and Arman—in the White House of modernism.

Things are bound, folded, and tied up, or they are propulsive and borderline violent —they shift between the restraint and immobility connoted by the title of *Paralyzed* and the wild behavior that ensues. The difference between Lidén's work and a temper tantrum, though, is the former's knowing allusion to the history of modern sculpture and dance, early cinema, and the practices that compose site-specificity. The rage is so tightly controlled, so precisely sublimated, that instead of evoking exasperation (the parent in the face of the small child), it provokes a kind of empathy ("Dude, I know how you feel, but you know how it is, you've just got to keep it together").

These pieces led me to recommend Lidén for an Artpace residency in San Antonio last year. There, she presented two works. One was a short video in which we see the artist at a spare desk, her back to the camera, in what we assume is her studio. Nothing much happens until she gets up and, very deliberately, begins to fold herself up into the adjacent garbage bin, as if her body were no more than a crumpled piece of paper. The work is laugh-out-loud funny, and as if to counteract its outsize emotiveness, Lidén showed it on what was certainly the most modest television monitor available at the local Best Buy. Meanwhile, upstairs, she had constructed an elaborate installation out of tar paper, within which were projected three videos, each of Lidén performing a completely futile but nonetheless arduous physical activity. In one wall projection, she climbs down a concrete column outside. All we can see are her legs and arms gripping the pole, her head a good twenty feet above the ground. On the other wall, we see her on top of what looks like an abandoned parking lot. It is the dead of night, and she is rocking slowly back and forth on her feet until she hurls herself into an athletic somersault, hits the asphalt hard, and bounces back up. The ensemble, from 2010, was given the title *Corps de ballet,* the term for the dancers in a ballet company who, despite their inestimable skills, are not the stars of the show—the dancers whose role it is to remain in the background, filling the stage with plenitude, thereby allowing the soloist's star to shine ever more brightly.

* * *

While the first three pieces I had seen by Lidén had traces of humor in them, the San Antonio works amplified her slapstick sensibilities in ways that brought to mind the silent performances of Buster Keaton and that still indispensable text by Henri Bergson, *Laughter*. Keaton's work is frequently seen as emblematic of a crisis of masculinity in early-twentieth-century representation. His persona developed around his physical diminutiveness and the fact that he never smiled on camera. His films repeatedly trap him in bodily dilemmas in which the classic Hollywood use of suspended time not only creates a kind of physical tension in the viewer but also brackets the codes of masculinity as such. Long before Judith Butler's *Gender Trouble*, there was Keaton's exposure of masculinity as a set of conventionalized responses to stimuli, responses that could be performed either well or badly. The badly part is where Bergson comes in. In *Laughter*, Bergson observes that things are funny when they break down or don't work properly. This is the language of slapstick, and the malfunction of either a device or the body is the basis for much of Keaton's mournful form of humor. But I would add to the list of "malfunctions" here Keaton's failure to properly inhabit the conventions of masculinity, indeed of agency itself; in this failure, he shows us masculinity's very constructedness.

It's interesting to try to think about Lidén as operating in the "tradition" of Keaton.[1] For what failures or breakdowns are on offer here? Lidén's work is so resolutely low-tech that mechanical failure itself isn't the engine for laughs as it is in traditional slapstick. While it's true that her spasms of performance are interpellated by the mechanical and technological (the train, industrial products, the structure of cinematic and video-based motion) and are in dialogue with them, failure as a specific term, a designation for screw-ups and mishaps, is only part of the issue. Futility, here articulated as a pervasive condition of contemporary life in general and of cultural production in particular, is what's really at the heart of the matter. It's not that the bicycle doesn't work, but the very idea that it should have a sole efficient function at all is what appears to be on the chopping block.

This failure/futility nexus is seen again in Lidén's video *Kasta Macka* (2009) (Swedish for "throwing a sandwich," idiomatically translated as "skipping stones"), in which we watch her on three different screens, at the banks of three different rivers, skipping stones. But the childhood pleasure of this activity soon changes tenor, as Lidén begins to throw increasingly large objects into each river in an almost desperate, and resoundingly futile, attempt to return all of the materials washed ashore to an ultimate resting place in the water. In *Ohyra* (2007) we see her in a cramped, dingy kitchen, facing the camera as she berates herself for things not done (seeing her grandmother) and for things not done well (doing the dishes, keeping her mind off girls). Wearing an old-fashioned leather helmet, she punctuates this litany of negative self-assessment with punches to her head. She has failed at some of life's most rudimentary tasks, but watching the video, I can't help wondering: Even if she succeeded . . . what would it matter? What would "success" in these arenas mean? For Lidén, the futile action and the productive action are essentially one and the same. The cumulative effect of these petty failures is the staging of what may be the central dilemma of today's emerging artist: the futility of being one in the first place.

The other breakdown that Lidén's work flirts with is her own failure to occupy any kind of conventional gender assignation. Writing this piece, I feel hemmed in by the pronouns she and her, as Lidén never appears to perform any characteristic typically associated with either women or the feminine. At the same time, as her diminutive butch body moves through cities draped in the everyday camouflage of jeans, tank tops, and hoodies, she hardly appears masculine, either. But the ruthless binary of gender still haunts the work. This intractability is apparent in a photograph taken on International Women's Day in 2008 that shows two people wrestling on the ground in what looks like a street fight. The caption in the exhibition catalogue explains that one of the figures is Lidén, but there's no way to prove it, and neither person's gender can be ascertained from the picture. Because Lidén makes an issue out of the bodily effort and expenditure involved in the work's own production, I feel tongue-tied as I try to sidestep the grammar of gender in describing it. This jamming of language isn't limited to my own critical efforts; the work's concentrated, brute physicality makes it seem deeply mute. Indeed, muteness operates on several levels here, both as tactic and as affect. There is the pronounced lack of spoken language, which when combined with the droning noise of the post-punk soundtracks indicates a mandated or enforced silence. And there is the foiling of gender's linguistic imperative, which seems, in turn, to squeeze out the differences between bodies and between actions. Just as the voice is mute, the body, despite its aggressive force, is routinely denied the agency we typically afford artistic presence—which is to say, there is no physical action that is unmediated (by either video or photograph). The conflation of mediation and muteness is not an attempt to stay outside of language or of representation (the work is far too canny to imagine an "outside" of anything); it is only maybe, and just maybe, a way of staying one step ahead.

For Lidén, staying a step ahead has, up until now, meant one of two things: ducking out of view or controlling the space in which her videos are displayed. In *Untitled (Back Room)* (2007), she built a room in an art fair booth (later replicated in a gallery) where only a handful of people could be at a time. The door to this hideaway was occluded behind a "painting" composed of an approximately ten-inch-thick layer of old billboards, which Lidén had cut out of their street frames, topped with a snow-white layer of paint (leaving only the borders of the posters showing), and hung on the wall. Or there was *Hus AB* (*House Inc.*) (2003), a small subterranean shelter built along the banks of the river Spree in Germany. Unmarked on the outside, the space was only large enough to accommodate two people and was invisible to passersby. These structures, along with other provisional interventions into gallery spaces, usually composed of fitted pipes and rudimentary drywall, have led many to write about Lidén within the framework of architecture (she studied as an architect before going to art school). While it would be silly to refute the architectural impulse in her work, I don't find myself particularly engaged in the idea of Lidén as a maker—or attacker—of space. Her blocked and stuffed rooms and secret passages are more interesting to me as morphological analogues to her obstruction of the grammar of gender than they are as a critique of architecture and its institutions. Are Lidén's hidden rooms and curious constructions a proposition about what a room of one's own might look and feel like today, eighty-two years after the need for one was first made public?

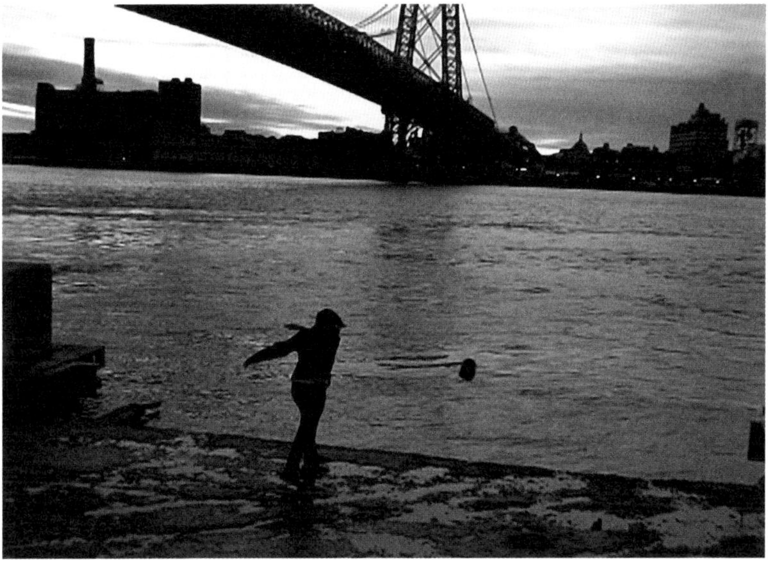

Klara Lidén, *Kasta Macka*, 2009 (still), video, color, sound, 3:45 min.

If they are, then it would seem Lidén is suggesting that it might not be a discrete place complete with a steady source of income. In Virginia Woolf's day, the maintenance of gender and class distinctions was transparent and unabashedly top-down. We, on the other hand, operate within a society in which the policing of these categories is typically invisible but always nimble. To stay one step ahead of this game, the artist needs to be nimble, too.

* * *

Lidén never stops moving; she continually reuses and reformulates her own work, for example by creating new contexts for screening her videos. In *Unheimlich Manöver* (*Uncanny Maneuver*) (2007), she studiously packed the entire contents of her Stockholm apartment into a dense sculptural form in the center of the room, within or around which a video was displayed. She has repeated this installation, as well as others, elsewhere and frequently changes the videos she shows inside them.

At her recent solo exhibition at the Serpentine Gallery in London, which travels to the Moderna Museet in Stockholm this May, she drastically reconfigured the videos originally made as part of the environment at Artpace. The footage of her clinging to the concrete pole and inserting herself into the studio garbage pail were folded into a new work, *Toujours être ailleurs* (*Always Be Elsewhere*) (2010), which comprised two parts (and which was first shown at the Jeu de Paume in Paris). First, there was a room completely filled—floor to ceiling—with folded billboards, which made entering the space impossible. These obstructions were echoed by billboard "paintings" also arrayed throughout the show. In an adjacent room, three slide projectors shuttered away, each projecting large-scale, degraded black-and-white images so rasterized that they were almost illegible. Slowly, as you got used to the pace and the atomization of the images, you could begin to glean Lidén—or, rather, you could discern a figure in relation to a ground, a slightly denser accumulation of black dots of ink (and, let's face it, it's particularly perverse to go about ascribing gender to ink spots)—in stop-motion, folding herself into the garbage pail, climbing the pole, and, in the third projection, riding her bicycle into the Seine. In order to achieve the pixelated effect of the images, Lidén took photographs of frame grabs of each video, greatly enlarged them, and had the images printed onto clear acetate, which she subsequently fashioned into homemade slides. The click-clacking of the slides added a metronomic dimension of time to the videos, thereby neutralizing their original belly-laugh comedic pacing. Sure, they were still funny, but in that "I'm laughing on the inside" kind of way. This feeling of suppression was exacerbated by the works' inhabitation of a medium that no longer exists—Kodak stopped producing its legendary Kodachrome slide film in 2009. It's one thing to be low-tech, but another to have to reinvent a once low-tech technology via DIY means, the effect of which was to render the work a kind of slapstick for the digital age.

The temporality of *Toujours être ailleurs* points everywhere to what has been—the disused billboards, the documentation of performances past, the ghostly summoning of the slide projection, and the previous iterations of Lidén's own work. In other words, while the title implies a constant dislocation of place (the global nomadic art worker, forever on the road), the piece is also incapable of being fully present in either a temporal or a spatial way. (So much for the "You had to be there" immediacy of performance or reperformance). Once again, Lidén degraded the frames of art's production and distribution, building into its network such a vexed relationship to functionality that I wouldn't be surprised if the next iteration of this work were invisible.

I approached Lidén's Serpentine exhibition already intrigued by the quality of embodied silence in her work. Discussing it with a friend, I was steered toward Roland Barthes's penultimate lecture, *The Neutral*, in which he meditates on the neutral as the third term that disrupts the binary logic underwriting Western civilization. "As everyone knows, speech, the exercise of speech, is tied to the problem of power,"[2] writes Barthes, and hence "Neutral = postulates a right to be silent—a possibility of keeping silent."[3] I read this with delight. I should just stop talking forever, I thought. It's the only way "out" of the unbearable way in which we have all been turned into consumers, "voting" with our dollars, most of us unable to live according to our own internal code of ethics (all those unavoidable Chinese imports, frequent-flyer miles, cell-phone batteries, and casual drugs). And yet any reliance on silence as a "position" would become unbearable. Such silence, as Barthes argues, "congeals itself into a sign (which is to say, is caught up in a paradigm): thus the Neutral, meant to parry paradigms, will—paradoxically—end up trying to outplay silence."[4] And therein lies the rub: to transform silence into a strategy is to risk turning it into doxa. This helped me think through the ways in which Lidén is always morphing her work into something else. Her restlessness is not in the service of producing novelty but is yet another (futile?) attempt to avoid congealing into an image, to avoid successful deployment in art's current modes of circulation: the art fair, the survey show for an artist in her thirties, the endless residency programs . . . all of which appear on her résumé as markers of her increasing success and legitimation. By never settling into any one of these channels of distribution, she tries (and fails?) to outrun the congealment system itself.

* * *

The two mental pictures I carried away with me from the Serpentine exhibition were of blankness and of static. The beauty of the billboard "paintings" is undeniable; I felt immediately covetous. I wanted to own one. To make plain, to erase, to white out all the noise of the spectacle culture's mind-numbing address in a mixture of petty vandalism (is it a crime to steal out-of-date ads?) and artistic autonomy (ah, the monochrome), was to condense punk and modernism in a way that thrilled a girl like me, who came of age in the 1980s believing that art and criticism were still arenas in which change could happen. But Lidén went to art school in the years after 9/11. And spending time with her work, one realizes that the twentieth-century paradigm of art's utopian aspirations is not what's at stake. Lidén offers blankness—and its aural handmaiden, muteness—less as a critique or a way out than as a condition, less as a program than as a given (reduce, reuse, recycle). In her work, I sense a tacit acknowledgment that the jig is up, that being an artist is just another way of getting by, a coping strategy for living under late capitalism.

Lidén's reinvention of static, on the other hand, may function slightly differently. Her projected "slides" look remarkably like the kind of snow that used to appear on analog television. Seeing the slides made me realize that one of the things missing from the digital age is this kind of static. Without question, interrupted signals and interference happen all the time today: we need only think of the degradation of the image and sound on cell phones, slow bandwidth, and watching YouTube videos amid stuttered buffering. But there is something different between watching the download circle spin around indefinitely on your handheld and being immersed in the archaic, televisual version of downtime: an allover composition of moving lights, complete with accompanying white noise. For me, there is something about that experience that is tied to the time when I fully believed in art's redemptive potential—not as transcendence but as the possibility of alternate paths, other worlds. Lidén's makeshift static foiled my laughter and gave me a glimmer of (something less than) hope; it slowed me down—visually and cognitively—so that rather than being frustrated by technological delay, I had to adjust my internal temporality of perception. I had to wait for myself to catch up to the image, rather than wait for the image, its concentrated transmission, to catch up to me. Lidén's static offered a dispersed energy that was far from unmoving or unchangeable. It was trying, modestly and continuously, to outplay (*déjouer*, a favorite word of Barthes's) art's contemporary conditions of speed and density. However somber, then, her exhibition managed to be my primary antidote to the art fairs of fall 2010.

Postscript

I've long been interested in idleness and failure. Or perhaps I should say I've long been made anxious by my contradictory response to idleness. On the one hand, I see it as a form of failure, born out of an inability to work. Like a car that idles, I imagine it to be a state in which one spews dank exhaust, wasting energy and resources. On the other hand, idleness is a utopic anti-capitalist state. What is idleness if not the only legitimate resistance to a system that literally forces you to sell your time? In the latter scenario it is I who fail. I cannot muster the radicality necessary to sit around and do nothing. My ego just can't handle it. My ambivalence about labor in general, and my inability to know how much work is enough work specifically, has continually propelled my attraction to artists who flirt with the possibility of using art as a form of truancy. I haven't heard much about Lidén's work in quite some time. My hope is that she's gone underground—like Duchamp working on *Étant donnés* in secret.

Jim Hodges: The Whole World Is Watching

Originally published in *Jim Hodges: Give More Than You Take*, ed. Jeffrey Grove and Olga Viso (Dallas: Dallas Museum of Art; Minneapolis: Walker Art Center, 2013), 170–85.

It is now an art world commonplace to encounter talk of AIDS and loss, grief and mourning, when reading about the work of the artists, and friends, Jim Hodges and Felix Gonzalez-Torres. Both came of age artistically, and as gay men, during the plague years of the AIDS/HIV epidemic (and Gonzalez-Torres lost his life to the disease in 1996), yet their work eschewed any direct reference to the disease and/or its effects. Nevertheless, the work of both artists seemed to function as elegiac meditations on the structures of feeling and the overwhelming affective sensibility that governed the staggeringly pervasive amount of death in the New York art world and gay male communities of the 1980s and 1990s. Hodges's work—curtains made out of artificial flowers, newspapers covered in gold leaf, delicate snapshots of tender landscapes, large-scale photographs of trees with each individual leaf cut out, drawings of flowers on paper napkins—trafficked in the physically delicate and the physiologically melancholic. This combination has sometimes led to a hum of anxiety about the work's relation to sentimentality. Even among Hodges's stalwart supporters, one can detect a slightly defensive tone, as when curator Susan Cahan said of his work, "[It's] very provocative because it's beautiful, very emotionally expressive, and it comes this close to being sentimental but it never crosses the line."[1]

But what if the work does "cross the line"? What if it *is* sentimental? What is it about sentimentality—both as an emotional state and an aesthetic manifestation—that causes Cahan (and me, to be completely honest) to want to hold it at bay? After all, the delicate nature of the materials—their porosity to the quotidian stuff of the world, their very tenuousness as "high art"—seemed to offer a response to the crisis that was as suffused with tenderness as the contemporaneous activist interventions of ACT UP were structured by rage. And it's not as if activists had an exclusive relation to rage. Artists and collectives such as Donald Moffett, General Idea, Group Material (of which Gonzalez-Torres was a member), Marlon Riggs, and David Wojnarowicz all made deeply acerbic works regarding the AIDS crisis. These tended to be

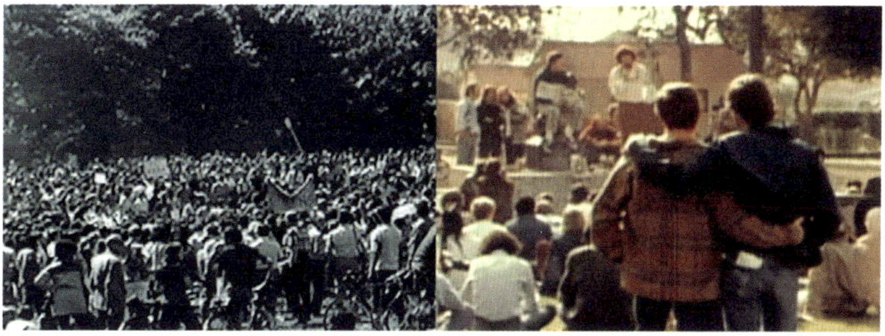

Jim Hodges, Encke King, and Carlos Marques da Cruz, *Untitled*, 2010 (still), video, color, sound, 60 min. Left: *After Stonewall* (dir. John Scagliotti, 1999). Right: *One Nation under God* (dir. Teodoro Maniaci and Francine Rzeznik, 1993)

strongly didactic, as they typically deployed a mixture of text and image to address the misinformation and prejudice that dominated coverage of the epidemic by the mass media. Hodges and Gonzalez-Torres (along with Ross Bleckner and Robert Gober) took a different tack. Certainly their work may have been related to the anger being expressed on the streets, but Hodges and Gonzalez-Torres each produced a body of work that registered the surrealistic dimensions of the crisis, work haunted by loss and love and fear.

These antinomies—art and activism, delicacy and rage—are at the heart of a recent work by Hodges, *Untitled* (2010),[2] which resulted from an invitation he received to talk at Artpace in San Antonio about Gonzalez-Torres's work.[3] Rather than deliver a lecture, Hodges found himself assembling a sixty-minute video montage. *Untitled* is a bit surprising, for the sentimentality one typically associates with Hodges's (and Gonzalez-Torres's) work is here held in a tense network of relations that, in addition to recalling Hodges's early spiderwebs, complete with their menacing referent (for what is a spiderweb after all but a trap intended to kill?), helped illuminate for me what is indeed so very powerful about his overall project. In other words, *Untitled* feels simultaneously out of step with the rest of Hodges's oeuvre (it is not at all sentimental) and like a Baedeker to understanding it better (for it is a meditation on why the sentimental is necessary).

Untitled is pieced together from a variety of sources—including television news footage, AIDS activist documentation, and 1950s film reels—that are meticulously spliced together. The imagery is accompanied at times by a lush soundtrack, ranging from opera to the Smiths, and at other times by real-time sound. There is no voice-over narration to suture the disparate images and sounds; instead, the heterogeneous images and voices alternate between moments of contingency, contradiction, and complementarity. Viewers, left to their own narrativizing tendencies, may either fashion a story out of the clips or simply ride in the slipstream of the sometimes random, sometimes pointed juxtapositions. Furthering this splitting—between image and soundtrack, between narrative and chance—is an intermittent use of a bifurcated screen, whereby occasionally an image fills the entire field of vision, edge to edge, like a landscape, or two images run parallel to each other, with the pictures being either radically different or twin-like in their similarity. Hodges's deft use of these editing strategies means that *Untitled* harks back to the heyday of experimental cinema, and, in fact, the film feels a bit like a work from the late 1960s or early 1970s, one that might have been shown in a double feature with a work by Jean-Luc Godard or Stan Brakhage. This is another way of saying that the handmade quality of *Untitled* has no clear relation to the kind of sumptuous, Hollywoodesque, gallery-based video that has become a mainstay of contemporary art, and indeed it is commensurate with the cut-and-paste quality of works by Hodges such as *As close as I can get* (1998), a mosaic-like collage fashioned out of Pantone chips, and *Untitled (Love)* (2000–2001), a brilliant collage of cut-up sheet music that isolates the word "love" over and over again.

In addition to summoning the handmade logic of both collage and experimental film, *Untitled* echoes Gonzalez-Torres's "portraits," works in which descriptions of seminal events in a person's private life, along with events that happened before the person was born, or that happened in world history to everyone, are painted in nonchronological order around the perimeter of a room, at the edge where wall and ceiling meet. The words, like crown molding, delicately ride the line between art and décor. Gonzalez-Torres's portraits intimate that there is no such thing as an individual identity, no selfhood separate from the events that shape us all, and, likewise, the portraits suggest that there is no idea of the social or the public that isn't imbricated in the interior or the private.

As an elegiac portrait of Gonzalez-Torres, *Untitled* is a compilation of the historical world events that shaped his life and death—primarily the homophobia of pre-Stonewall American culture, the emergence of a gay liberation movement, and the political mendacity that fueled the AIDS crisis—combined with the events his premature death caused him to miss, notably the 2001 terrorist attacks on the World Trade Center in New York and the decade-long, unprovoked wars waged by the United States on Iraq and Afghanistan that followed. As a stand-alone film, *Untitled* tumbles historical events, like so many semiprecious stones in a polishing machine, and functions as a collective portrait of the end of the twentieth century. By virtue of this toggling between the highly individual and the generically public, *Untitled* allows for a rigorous meditation on the complex role that sentimentality plays in Hodges's oeuvre.

In her short but deeply informative essay "What Is Sentimentality?," June Howard argues that this particular quality is linked with emotions that are characterized as affected, shallow, and excessive. Sentimentality, she says, is "haunted by its vulnerability to accusations of banality and inauthenticity," and though it is "not always stigmatized, [it] is always suspect; the appearance of the term marks a site where values are contested."[4] Why should the representation of emotions provoke such a stigmatizing logic, especially when the history of emotions can be seen to be bound up with the articulation of our moral lives, such that, for instance, benevolence is viewed "as a defining human virtue"?[5] Howard's answer is bracing: "'sentiment' and its derivatives indicate a moment when emotion is *recognized* as socially constructed," and the "packaged" quality of emotion "is a distasteful reminder that the partition of the public and private" is indeed impossible.[6] In other words, sentimentality galls us because it makes us aware that we feel as others feel, and that our emotional lives are neither unique nor proof of our exceptionalness. Rather, the sentimental registers our emotions as socially produced and shared. Given the outrageously persuasive and coercive function of mass culture, sentimentality is frequently used to create feelings of consensus when perhaps there is not one, and many have, rightly so, resisted being addressed as an undifferentiated mass in this manipulative manner. Yet the sense that sentimentality, and the anxiety that attends it, flares up at the borders between social values is a compelling matrix through which to examine its role in Hodges's oeuvre, and is something I want to pursue further in discussing *Untitled* and its relation to his earlier work.

Looking back at some of Hodges's earliest (and most sentimental) works, we can track a consistent working method across a seemingly diverse range of objects, beginning with the coffee-shop and diner napkins he used as a ground for his drawings, the store-bought fabric flowers and metal chains that were the material for his curtains and webs respectively, and the camouflage pattern that recurs in both wall drawings and mirror mosaics. All these examples point to his playful use of the readymade, harking back to Duchamp's original use of objects culled from the domestic world (hat racks, combs, bottle dryers, and the like). For his part, Hodges amplifies the domesticity of his choices through the acts of doodling, sewing, and fastening, compounding the quotidian nature of his choices even as these activities transform everydayness into the register of the special or the poetic. And yet, Hodges's work was never positioned within the tradition of the avant-garde or neo-avant-garde register of appropriation that governed the critical discourse of the 1980s; instead, it was discussed as part of the return of "beauty" in the 1990s. Even when he made "paintings" out of shattered and mosaic pieces of mirror—works such as *On Earth* (1998) that explicitly borrowed the disco ball as their starting point—he still was not seen as an appropriationist.

This is ironic, considering that American gay culture has been involved in the occupation of readymade forms and the appropriation of dominant mass culture to its own ends for most of the last century, whether it is the androgyny of the lesbian scene of the interwar years, the role of camp in the closeted days of the 1950s and 1960s, or the heady days of disco in the late 1970s.[7] With the AIDS crisis, the two most dominant of these formations (the humor of camp and the liberatory excess of disco) withered in the face of the need for an activist, highly mobilized intervention in the absence of medical and governmental response. (Sometimes the humor and pleasure of both camp and disco were utilized to feed the activist movement, but they tended not to appear in the high-art culture of the late 1980s and early 1990s.)

Hodges crossed the wires of the readymade activities of Duchamp and the neo-avant-garde with a set of activities and practices gleaned from queer subculture, resulting in materials saturated with allusions to other cultural formations, exponentially rich in affect. For instance, his utilization of fabric flowers summons the realms of adornment, costume, and interior décor, provoking associations with artifice, permanence, domesticity, and mourning as readily as they evoke painterly strategies of allover composition (a thing without an end, apocalyptic wallpaper) and the Rauschenbergian desire "to act in the gap between art and life." This mélange of allusions suggested the commonality (as well as the specifically queer or art world meanings) of these ideas across the culture as a whole.

This desire to be legible to both of these precisely rendered publics (gay, art world) as well as to more generally conceived publics (the consumers of fabric flowers, for example) can perhaps be seen most clearly in a particularly skillful and surprising segue in *Untitled* between footage of a 1992 ACT UP action in which people threw the ashes of their deceased comrades and lovers over the wrought iron gate and onto the lawn of the White House and the display of the AIDS quilt in Washington, DC, in 1989. The dispersal of cremated remains on the White House lawn was one of the most emotionally gut-wrenching of ACT UP's actions, and it engendered a brutal response as mounted police officers used their horses to quell, thwart, crush, and intimidate the rush of activists descending upon the White House gates. In *Untitled*, the video footage of the demonstration is haunted by the ongoing piercing scream of one of the activists. It is the unadulterated sound of human anguish. The protesters' rallying cries alternate between the admonishment "Shame! Shame! Shame!" and the declaration "The whole world is watching," in essence toggling between invectives based, respectively, in private conscience and media publicity. This scene cuts directly to an image of the AIDS quilt unfurled over the National Mall; a solemn voice intones as it reads off the names of the dead while the image depicts individuals in stunned silence moving around the edges of the quilt, at times kneeling down and weeping. I found this juxtaposition to be simultaneously emotionally unbearable and revelatory.

Back in the day, the quilt was seen by many activists to be an overly sentimental rendering of the crisis, meant to appeal to mothers and aunties struggling to accept their gay children. Its handmade quality and patchwork reality seemed an anodyne mode of dramatizing individual losses, when what was needed was a way to galvanize a public toward more generalized political action capable of disrupting and disabling the homophobia and racism at the root of the crisis. The activism of ACT UP was designed precisely to strike deep into the muscle of those agencies—governmental, medical, and mass media—whose inaction in the face of a major national health emergency was responsible for the epidemic. The quilt seemed to say that the losses were private rather than public (each rectangle is dedicated to one person, made by that person's friends and/or relatives). And because one effect of the AIDS crisis had been to demonstrate that the "conditions in which sexuality seems like a property of subjectivity rather than a publicly or counter publicly accessible culture"[8] was no longer tenable, this meant the "privacy" of the quilt felt out of step with an emergent politics of queerness that was to demand not only *access* to public space, but the *queering* of public space.[9] But *Untitled* refuses the division between private and public, or between acts of personal commemoration and mourning and public and communal activism.

Untitled offers the quilt as a brilliant spatialization of the loss, a literal queering of public space—the National Mall—marked by previous historical assemblies for civil rights that took place there. So too does the film demonstrate the shared communal logic of historical quilt-making circles and the action groups of ACT UP. And the handmade lettering and reparative act of sewing—tactics frequently deployed by Hodges—are seen to straddle amateur and high-art practices. In other words, *Untitled* shows us that both the rage of ACT UP and the sentimentality of the AIDS quilt were doing the work of imagining queer public space—and with twenty-five years of history between then and now, Hodges's film tells us that we don't have to make a choice along an aesthetic axis of agitprop versus sentimentality, for, as his film goes on to argue, we have more pressing problems to face.

In a tour de force of cutting and collaging, *Untitled* takes us from the appropriation inherent in the AIDS quilt, complete with its striking and effective deployment of sentimentality, to an activist use of camp, as we watch AIDS activist and artist Ray Navarro, dressed as Jesus, speak to a fake news camera about the 1989 ACT UP "Stop the Church" protest at St. Patrick's Cathedral in New York. This segue makes clear the sympathetic relation between camp and sentimentality: both are invested in excess; both are a function of taste; and both use what Susan Sontag called "artifice and exaggeration."[10] That each should be an aesthetic associated with queerness perhaps goes without saying (though I don't want to argue that queerness offers any exceptionality on this front, just a historical propensity). In addition to being historically queer, sentimentality and camp also share the logic of appropriation—and as such, both work to create a "counterpublic" of viewers, adept at reading a popular culture that refuses their existence by reading it against the grain. This idea is amplified in *Untitled* through a clip of French philosopher Jacques Derrida's discussion of the story of Echo and Narcissus. Echo, Derrida says, takes the words of another in repetition and through her appropriation makes them her own, such that "she speaks in her own name by just repeating his words."[11]

By establishing an implicit recognition of gay culture's history of appropriation, *Untitled* explicitly refuses to fashion a hierarchy of "correct" or "better" aesthetic responses to the AIDS crisis. Instead, the film proceeds to collage clips of the first Gulf War conducted under the first President Bush in 1990–91 with those of the Iraq War waged under President George W. Bush, including clips that allude to extradition and acts of torture perpetrated by the US military. Most of these events transpired after Gonzalez-Torres's death, and it is here where *Untitled* makes some of its largest claims. When *Untitled* intercuts images of 9/11, and the United States' warring and vengeful response to it, with those of the AIDS crisis, it does so with utter parity, underscoring that the victims in both cases are equally innocent. The lack of government response to the AIDS crisis and the vindictive response of the same government to the terrorist attacks are both posited as indiscriminate abuses of state power, in which innocent lives have been sacrificed in the name of profit.[12] The pairing is an object lesson in what happens when we exhibit an ethical disregard for others, particularly when we refuse to see others as constituting a public. This juxtaposition insists upon the trauma of both events; indeed, it requires us to think of these events concurrently, seeing in them the same structural logic of state violence and the same inability to properly mourn the dead.[13]

If, as so many have felt before me, Hodges's work of the late 1980s and early 1990s can be seen as a response to the devastation and trauma of the AIDS crisis, then what might those objects and gestures have to tell us now about our country's deleterious response to the trauma of 9/11? In using the sentimental as a way to foreground the socially constructed nature of our emotional lives, or in using mirrors to intervene into the space of the museum whereby his work gathers up the reflections of other artists' works and makes them contemporaneous with and co-equivalent to our own reflections and images,[14] Hodges has offered us opportunities to engage in moments of intimacy in public. The same is true of *Untitled*. Its recurrent images of the abuse of power are relentless (although it does possess one bright spot as we witness two older lesbians being married in San Francisco, and hence watch the state act, in an uncharacteristic manner, to affirm love and intimacy rather than to destroy souls). One could be forgiven for quickly brushing away the tears and walking away from the film, eager to return to the banality of the everyday. And yet the film suggests that nothing is more everyday than asking how and whom do we mourn? Is there a way to learn from the dead in addition to mourning them? How does a nation come to terms with itself and its violence? How do citizens come to terms with the violence done against them?

Judith Butler has written of the "precariousness" of the body in relation to the violence of the state, asking if we can imagine a way to mourn and grieve that does not include the fantasies of retribution that have come to dominate the post-9/11 landscape of the United States. She asks: "Is there something to be gained from grieving, from tarrying with grief, from remaining exposed to its unbearability and not endeavoring to seek a resolution for grief through violence?"[15] And commensurate with this probing emotional and ethical question is her rumination on how we might ensure that grief does not lead to violence, namely, by not doing what we currently have done, which is to establish groups of people who cannot be grieved, constituencies

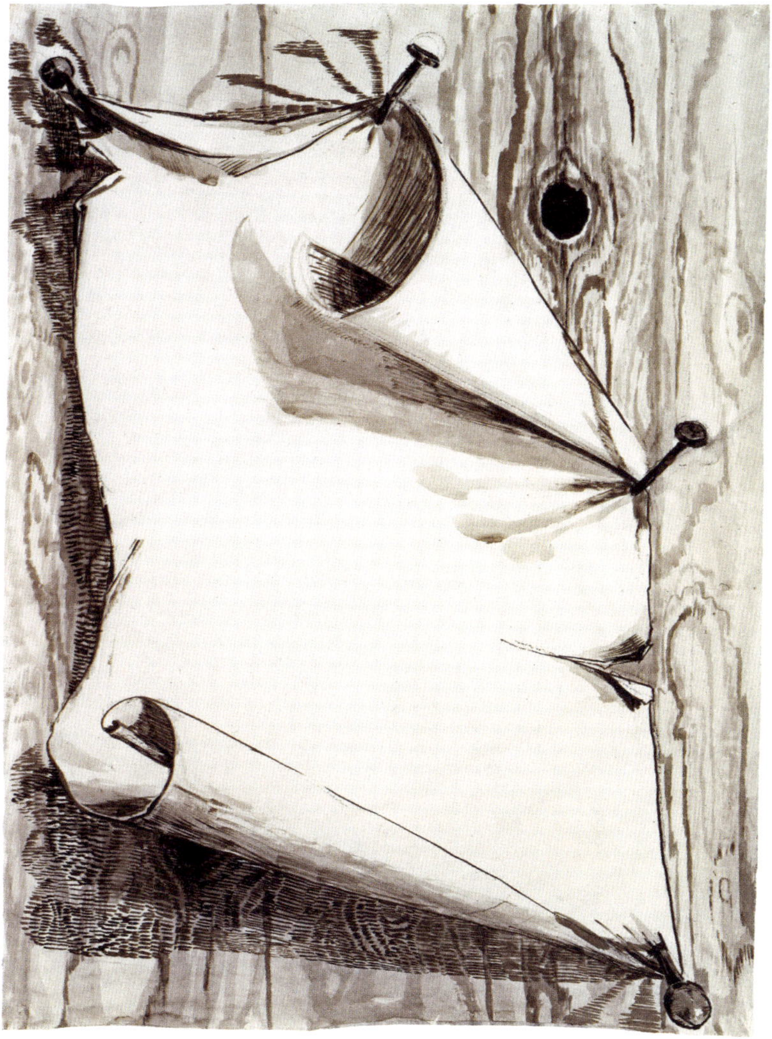

Jim Hodges, *Wanted Poster 3*, 1991, ink on paper, 24 ½ x 18 ½ in. (60.9 x 45.7 cm)

who are ungrievable publicly: Palestinians murdered by Israeli troops; Afghan citizens killed by US drones; or the more than six hundred thousand who have died of AIDS in the United States and the millions who continue to die in Africa. *Untitled* establishes the shared trauma of AIDS, terrorism, and war, and shows us that part of the trauma of these events is not simply the extraordinary loss of life that attends each of them, but the state's inability or refusal to allow these human losses to be named, to be grievable.

Even as *Untitled* stages this dilemma, it also shows me that Hodges's oeuvre is littered with models of how to grieve for and mourn the dead as well as how to learn from them. *Untitled* is a portrait of Gonzalez-Torres that never announces itself as such. It refuses the contemporary art world's increasingly hagiographic relation to "Felix" as an exceptional individual; instead, Hodges allows his subject's absence to permeate our current understanding of the violence under which we live. Similarly, Hodges's objects do not affirm our radical separateness from one another, but, instead, through the language of sentimentality, they demonstrate the ways in which our emotional lives are constructed and shared, how they are mutually imbricating. The flower curtains are provisional walls, demarcating spaces for intimacy—for sadness and joy. The napkins with flowers drawn on them flutter slightly, altered by the energy of passing bodies. The disco mirrors remind us of the ecstatic utopian nights of sweaty dancing and the preposterous way youth can postpone time, just as the mirrors' fractured surfaces disallow any fantasy of wholeness, leaving our image shattered along a thousand fault lines—fault lines of shame, pain, excess, gravity, love, passion, touch, and taste. When I see myself in one of these mirrors, I hear the old ACT UP refrain "The whole world is watching," and I realize that the desire to be seen and to see is potentially as sentimental as it is political.

After watching *Untitled*, I went back to look at the artist's 1991 *Wanted Poster 1*, a work that slyly references Duchamp's self-portrait "Wanted" poster of 1923. Hodges's work is a trompe l'oeil drawing of a wanted poster nailed to the wall. Its style evokes the old American West, a kind of Spaghetti Western version of criminality, and belongs to an image tradition haunted by the posters used to track down escaped slaves. But Hodges's poster is blank—there is no face, no name. The empty sheet curls and strains away from both the nail and the wood. Here the logic of retribution is substituted for one of coming undone, of unfurling and revealing. Exposed is a knot in the wood—which is simultaneously an imperfection in the material and its linguistic counterpart—a problem to be untangled. The knot is offered as an opening, a void, a site of physical and metaphysical desire. And what is "wanted" in the drawing is neither vengeful nor memorial. There is no proper name, no picture of an individual; instead, all we see is a blank space, one haunted by the vestiges of past wrongs, but open for a new beginning.

Doris Salcedo: Readymade Time

Originally published in *Doris Salcedo*, ed. Julie Rodrigues Widholm and Madeleine Grynsztejn (Chicago: Museum of Contemporary Art Chicago and University of Chicago Press, 2015), 201–7.

Sometime in the early winter of 2007, a friend and I routed our travel through London so we could see Doris Salcedo's work in Tate Modern's monumental Turbine Hall. A case of fortunate happenstance had befallen me, although I did not yet know it, in that I had heard nothing about the work: I possessed a kind of blankness that protected me from the critic's tendency to prejudge. Walking down into the hall, I saw at once that it was not filled with objects, light, or media of any kind; rather, a crack had been made in the floor, a crack that meandered and traversed its way across the entire long hall. It was cold and damp—in that up-through-your-shoes-and-into-your-bones way that I associate with London—and the effect of tracing the crack, eyes down, hands buried in pockets, was exaggerated by the hard coldness of my leather-soled shoes against the polished, poured-concrete floor. The crack seemed simple enough—it shifted in depth and width, shrinking and expanding. At one moment I looked up, and a group of small schoolchildren, attended by two women in full burkas, made hay of it all, jumping and skipping over the crack, prattling on as they transformed what for me was a solemn "intervention into the space" into an ersatz playground.

This seemingly apocryphal encounter reminded me of Marcel Duchamp's *Mile of String*, an early iteration of the twinning of site-specificity and institutional critique. Duchamp's 1942 contribution to the *First Papers of Surrealism* exhibition in New York was a maze of string, suspended from the ceiling and attached to the floor and walls, making the exhibition impenetrable to conventional viewing. On opening night, when asked by a small group of children if they could run and play in the show, Duchamp, apparently pleased by the prospect, said yes. Not surprising, really; Duchamp was a funny man who trafficked in the ludic, the slapstick, and the puns and jokes of the schoolyard. And while playfulness is not an affect we typically associate with Salcedo—her work has consistently offered a meditation on play's dialectical other: mourning—the ease with which the children's game brought Duchamp to mind led me to think anew about Salcedo's oeuvre as sustaining a rather high-level conversation with various permutations of the Duchampian readymade.

In *Shibboleth* (2007), as Salcedo's work in Turbine Hall is bracingly titled, the poured-concrete floor is taken as a readymade. Preexisting, industrially produced, conventional beyond measure (what says "twenty-first-century art space" more clearly than a poured-concrete floor?) and just below the threshold of aesthetic visibility, the floor had been emphatically chosen by Salcedo to serve as both the site and the medium of the work. Salcedo's early work has a long history of engagement with the readymade. Her sculptures using domestic wooden furniture—beds, drawers, chairs—speak to her interest in deploying things that were already made, rather than fashioning them anew. The typical understanding of the Duchampian readymade is that an industrially produced object is chosen by the artist and re-presented as a work of art. However, Salcedo, like many artists of her generation (such as Robert Gober and Rachel Whiteread), made incursions into the mass-produced commodity form, insisting upon her own handwork, and as such created the philosophical conundrum of the "handmade readymade." This can be seen most clearly in Salcedo's filling of pieces of old wooden furniture with wet concrete, the result of which was a body of leaden, lugubrious, and labored sculptures. Rendered useless, these formerly banal objects of everyday life—of sleeping and physical comportment—took on new lives as art objects. They stood upright, or on their sides, the wood aching under the weight of the concrete. The dominant reception of this work, and indeed of Salcedo's oeuvre as a whole, has been to see it as performing mute witness to the state-sponsored violence of her native Colombia; as Monica Amor wrote, Salcedo's works are "poignant readymades pierced by the violent narratives of her local context."[1]

There can be no argument with this approach: Salcedo's art is a profound reworking of the historical trajectory of sculpture's relationship to the monument, to memorializing, and to the explicitly public dimension of those activities. But as is true with much writing about "political art" or, to be more precise, writing about art that is explicit in its relationship to political content, there has not been a full accounting of Salcedo's work on the readymade. Perhaps everyone thinks the readymade is too simple a form, perhaps discussions of form are seen to be naive in the face of the torture of innocent civilians by the state, perhaps the handmade nature of Salcedo's works, the clear investment of time and labor that goes into their making, has obscured their dialogue with the logic of industrial production that has governed so much twentieth-century sculpture. Whatever the reasons, critics of Salcedo's work have not fully heard her when she said, "From very early on, I paid special attention to Duchamp and Beuys."[2]

It's well known that instead of going to the studio to make things, Duchamp went shopping in the first two decades of the twentieth century, and when he did so, he attempted to choose objects that were devoid of his personal taste. The objects he chose—a hat rack, a comb, a urinal—were meant to be impersonal, leading Duchamp to write: "The choice of these 'readymades' was never dictated by esthetic delectation. This choice was based on a reaction of visual indifference with at the same time a total absence of good or bad taste."[3] Elsewhere he would claim that the objects

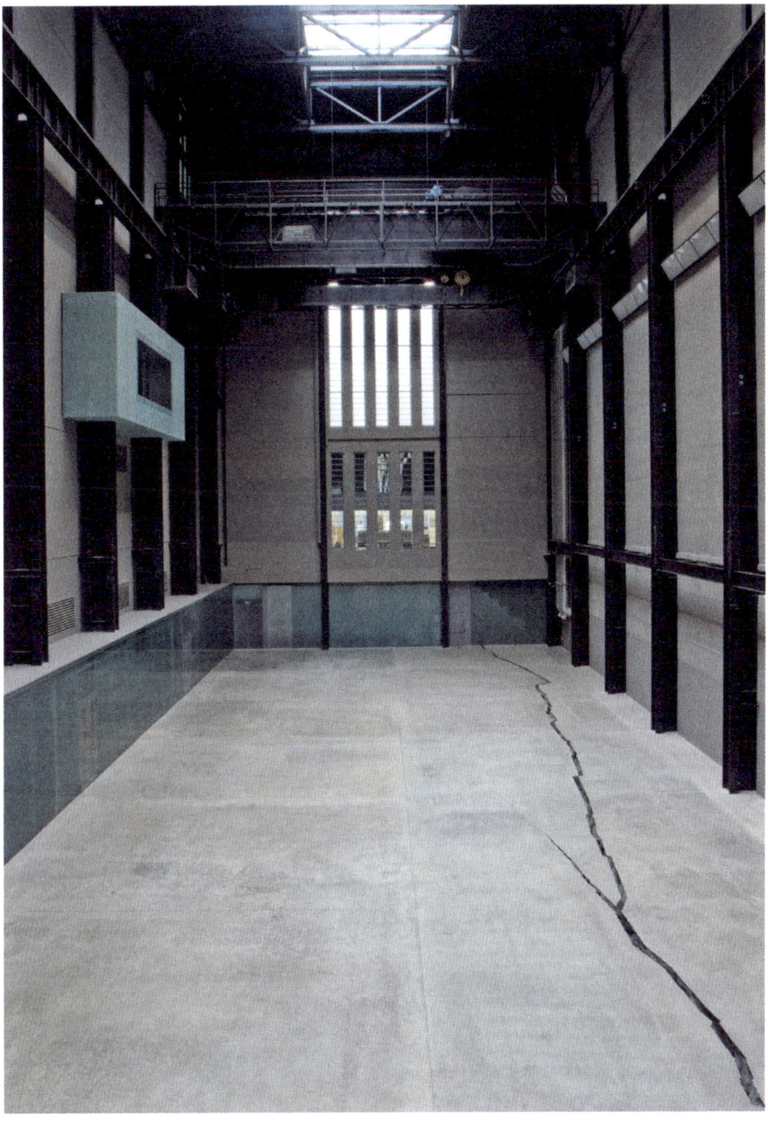

Doris Salcedo, *Shibboleth*, 2007, concrete and steel, length: 548 ft. (167 m)
Installation view: Turbine Hall, Tate Modern, London, 2007

"choose him," a further abdication of his authorial role, as well as an early acknowledgment of the animistic power of commodities to speak to us, to call out to us. In addition to challenging the idea that the artist must physically make his or her work, Duchamp's readymades were a subtle critique of what he called "the demand of the shop window"—the call to consume as a way of articulating our taste, of shoring up our identities. Similarly, Salcedo's works consist of featureless furniture—simple, wooden, without decorative flourish or embellishment. And she echoes Duchamp's ambivalence about choosing as an aesthetic act when she says, "Everything precedes me, everything makes its presence felt with such urgency that I am not the one who chooses; my themes are given to me, reality is given to me, the presence of each victim imposes itself."[4]

If Duchamp's early-twentieth-century readymades were a challenge to the then-nascent logic of the commodity to capture and calcify our identities, Salcedo's late-twentieth- and early-twenty-first-century readymades investigate the fate of those for whom such luxuries of the self are denied by the ruthless imbalance of world power. Hence, Salcedo's choice of domestic artifacts can be seen less as a Duchampian experiment with the elimination of taste (as a way of trying to circumvent commodity culture's hold on the self) than as the result of a political system that denies the very selfhood Duchamp seeks to critique. Salcedo's "furniture has been forced into a state of anonymity, as the individual elements have lost their identities and, through an act of subtle but vigorous distortion, been obliged to abandon their role as symbols of the self and repositories of personal history."[5] This reworking of the readymade's critique is structural to Salcedo's work, appearing again and again as an anchoring formal logic that propels her work and expands upon the fecundity of Duchamp's project of working through the relationship between art and life and, furthermore, navigating the different temporalities that structure those negotiations.

Duchamp's readymades were, for the most part, commonplace household objects, and Salcedo's choice of simple furniture extends this decidedly domestic tradition of the readymade. This overt concern with the quotidian in Salcedo's work harks back to the feminist art movement of the 1970s, which frequently politicized Duchamp's readymades by using everyday objects to examine the gendered quality of space (such as the site-specific rooms in *Womanhouse*, organized by Judy Chicago and Miriam Schapiro) and labor (the diapers and baby clothes in Mary Kelly's *Post-Partum Document* [1973–79]). Salcedo's use of furniture and clothing evoked the bodies of those disappeared by the government, guerrillas, and paramilitaries, and did so in part via a feminist impulse to bestow value on the overlooked and the unseen and to resist the historical marginalization of the everyday. Salcedo's work also emerged in the wake of the appropriation artists of the 1980s. Here the commodity was plucked out of circulation to be reframed as an explicit object of desire (I am thinking of Jeff Koons's vacuum cleaners and Haim Steinbach's arrangements of objects on shelves) and to make clear the parallels between the art object and the commodity, indeed to insist upon their utter commensurateness. Salcedo (and her fellow travelers Robert Gober, Fischli and Weiss, and Rachel Whiteread) countered by offering the handmade readymade as a retort to the smoothness of commodity exchange, slowing it down with the discernible tactility of the handmade.

In doing so, their work made an issue of the body—the absent body, the body of the artist-laborer, the body of the viewer—extending Duchamp's early play with the commodity into the realm of late capitalism, a period that had forgotten the time before the commodity form ruled with such precision and efficacy.

Shibboleth begins with a crack in the floor, just like any one might regularly see in a museum or art gallery: concrete slowly opening up, giving way to gravity, to entropy; concrete acting as a kind of palimpsest; concrete as man-made sedimentary rock; concrete as the stuff below our feet. But this kind of everyday fissure grows into a full-blown crevice, several inches wide and three feet deep, a split that makes one aware of a hazard: don't trip, don't fall, don't drop your glasses, don't get your heel caught. As the children skipped and played, I realized that the crack itself was a readymade; the crack is endemic to concrete as a material, to the structure of the floor itself: the crack was what was going to happen—with or without the artist's intervention. Just as Duchamp plucked one commodity out of the seemingly endless stream of industrially produced commodity goods and brought all of art's institutional and aesthetic powers of scrutiny to bear upon it, transforming it from something overlooked and unseen into an object of philosophical debate, Salcedo has taken that which was already there, the floor, and subjected it to what was already going to happen to it, its fissure, and gave it a name that already existed in the culture: *Shibboleth*.

A shibboleth is a linguistic effect of profound belonging and has historically been used to ascertain the true identity of a speaker. In the Bible or in times of war, certain pronunciations of words or cultural meanings are used to suss out imposters or spies. A shibboleth is language used as exclusion, an indicator of "true" belonging, a gauge of the degree to which language precedes us, a marker of how much we enter into it, how much it shapes what we can think and how we can think it. A shibboleth shows us that language—despite its extraordinary plasticity—also functions as a readymade. The words exist before us, and we merely choose from what is already there. For Salcedo to call her intervention, her riveting crack in the foundation of the museum, *Shibboleth* is a way of rendering the children's easy schoolyard game of jumping over cracks rife with global meanings. While a little girl might lightly hop over the crack in the floor, will she be able to navigate the borders of nation-states? Will she be able to shift class? Will her native tongue lock her in place or bestow upon her the unthinking framework of the hegemonic? Will she be inside or outside the culture of her birth, the culture she migrates to, the culture she will, in some way, help to create?

But Salcedo's crack in the floor is deceptive. She didn't merely open the floor; she filled it as well. Looking down into the crack one could see more concrete, plaster, and embedded chain-link mesh, the internal guts of the building. All of this was made by hand and laboriously "inserted" into the riven gap, continuing Salcedo's exploration of the handmade readymade. Such labor-intensive work is typical of Salcedo's oeuvre, and whereas "in other art works surface may be nothing but superficial beauty, in Salcedo's work, it is the unexpected site of homage, labour, and care."[6] But because we are inured to respecting the labor of others, this facet of her work sometimes goes unremarked upon. Yet the handmade quality of Salcedo's exploration of the readymade is central. When Duchamp first started buying everyday objects like kitchen stools and bottle-drying racks as readymades, he did so in part to "expose" the time of the commodity. By arresting the commodity, he obliterated its utility value, and when they were ultimately placed in the museum, they entered the putative realm of timelessness. However, for Duchamp, none of this was immediate. Indeed, he talked of the delay inherent in the activity of choosing and presenting everyday objects as art. In his essay "The Creative Act," he acknowledged that the artist alone could not determine what was and was not art; he or she would have to "wait for the verdict of the spectator in order that his declarations take a social value and that, finally, posterity includes him in the primers of Art History."[7] He understood that it would take time for the viewer to complete the work,[8] and he knew that history would produce the narratives that helped to transform the lowly commodity into a work of art.

This delay, this waiting, was part of Duchamp's sly critique of a new world governed by the logic of speed that is the time of the commodity—the time of ready-to-wear, the already made, the shop window calling out with its siren promise of instant gratification. Duchamp was attempting to counter this speed. In an early note from *The Bride Stripped Bare by Her Bachelors, Even (The Green Box)* (1934), he muses about trying to incorporate delay into the work itself: "Use delay instead of picture or painting," he writes. "Not so much in the different meanings in which delay can be taken, but rather in their indecisive reunion."[9] Then, in the 1960s, when it became clear that the original readymades were lost, or misplaced, or discarded, Duchamp authorized his Italian dealer, Arturo Schwartz, to remake them, according to blueprints okayed in Duchamp's own hand. The twelve versions of *Fountain* (1917) that currently exist, scattered across museum collections, were made in an Italian factory.[10] If only for a day, the production schedule designed to meet the demand for bathroom fixtures was slowed and, instead, the philosophy of art was teased into a new way of being. The handmade readymade, established in the 1960s, was Duchamp's updating of the readymade's critique from the teens. To go out shopping for everyday objects in 1917 was to do so at the moment when domestic space was being transformed by new commodities, it was to do so at a time when women were being asked to change their habits of shopping, housewifery, and self-presentation to accommodate the new mass-produced goods.[11] To *not* shop for readymades in the 1960s, but rather to authorize them to be made by hand, was an attempt at radically altering the late-capitalist nexus of factory time and consumer time. To make readymades by hand is to fold a wrinkle into the time of making, choosing, and presenting. It slows time down (factories delayed and artisans employed) while also freezing time: it permitted a bottle rack when they were no longer in fashion; it meant a relatively "faithful" recording of the objects from the teens, objects that if simply repurchased in the 1960s would have smacked of the new, and hence would have deployed a different temporality than the so-called original readymades. The handmade readymade not only offers the artisan as the critic of the factory, it also insists upon the persistence of the old as a means of resisting capitalism's drive toward the ever-new.

If Duchamp's readymades were a foiling of commodity time, then Salcedo's handmade readymades reframe the problem of postcolonial time. Her stacks of starched white shirts, saturated with white plaster, arranged in a pile and brutally pierced by a steel rod, act as monuments and memorials to the unnamed victims of the dictatorship and paramilitary violence. By asking everyday objects to stand in for persons (something she did as well in *Atrabiliarios* [1992–2004], in which discarded shoes were delicately placed into cubbyholes cut into the museum wall), Salcedo rubbed the anonymity of Duchamp's readymades against the grain. It's not that Salcedo's work ever pretended to be able to account for specific individuals as such; instead, the work makes an issue of the erasure of the very idea of the individual. In this way Salcedo's handmade readymades feel haunted, not by the impersonality of commodity time, but by the violence of postcolonial time, in which the legacy of conquest and domination form a *longue durée* in which the ideology and freedoms of democracy come at the profound expense of those who do not possess it. Perhaps no work concisely condenses this concern with time more than *Plegaria Muda* (2008–10): a grouping of wooden tables, upon each of which is stacked another wooden table (quantities of tables vary, depending on venue), separated by a thick layer of soil. The doubled tables require vast expanses of exhibition space—the scale of a warehouse—and when exhibited, the rooms they occupy feel muffled, as if the wood and dirt conspire to absorb almost all sound. The space between them—which for some has been a philosophical quandary—is a space of improbable life: as the viewer approaches, the more she begins to see blades of grass pushing upward through the dirt, struggling to reach light. The work has a temporality outside of the frame of the museum or gallery, distinct from the time that an "average" viewer is likely to spend with it. This is one of the striking effects of postcolonial time, and how greatly it differs, for those who are crossing borders and for those who are watching them.

The critical reception of Salcedo's work has circled largely around the problem of memorialization, and particularly of sculpture's traditional role in the transformation of memory into monuments. We know all too well the role sculpture has played in Western culture's fetishism of the monument: upright, erect, anthropomorphic, phallic, patriarchal, figurative. The list of petty crimes is long. Duchamp's readymades were, in part, an attack on this version of sculpture. His choice of everyday objects refused the monumental, and his idiosyncratic placement of them—nailed to the floor, suspended from the ceiling—worked against any kind of portentousness or commemorative function. Salcedo's everyday objects, however, are suffused with the problem of memory and commemoration. One can narrate her project as an attempt to recuperate the monument in the name of the memorial, to supplant hubris with modesty; to counter forgetting with the vagaries of memory; to resist denial with knowledge. This concern with memory and the memorial amplifies the structural role temporality plays in the logic of the readymade. Indeed, time is such an enormous part of Salcedo's project that Mieke Bal has argued that Salcedo attempts nothing less than to "incorporate the temporal dimension of history" into the spatial strategies of art.[12]

The inextricability of space and time (a noteworthy given in contemporary physics) can be seen particularly clearly in *Neither* (2004), a site-specific installation created for White Cube in London and now housed at Inhotim in Belo Horizonte, Brazil. Similar to *Shibboleth, Neither* is a sculpture that flirts with emptiness, as the viewer walks into a white room that appears, at first glance, to be bare. However, close looking reveals that the soft white plaster walls give way to a delicate web of steel fencing that pushes out and sinks into the surface of the wall, an exercise in haptic subtlety that evokes feelings of enclosure and death, of simultaneously being buried alive or being excavated from a delicate archeological dig. As in *Shibboleth*, in *Neither* Salcedo has taken the architectural conventions of the art world—the white walls that form the so-called autonomous white cube—and exposed the readymade nature of its conventions, and in doing so she intimates that there is nothing more violent than the fantasy of neutrality.[13] In *Neither* the white wall is ruptured by expanded mesh (the same material used by the United States in the military prison at Guantánamo Bay), forming an almost subconscious appearance of the violent logic of private property—complete with barriers to entry—resulting in a topographical caesura that means the walls are no longer available for "business as usual." Similarly, the "neither" of the title is redolent with the force of negation, which is further articulated by the web of interlocking *x*'s that make up the expanded mesh. Once again Salcedo uses the logic of the readymade to draw attention to the frameworks of art (concrete floors, white walls) while also silently negotiating the ongoing implicit violence that shores up such seemingly neutral values.

Given that Salcedo herself has said that her work takes on "with full responsibility the theme of violence and war,"[14] it is perhaps no surprise that the temporality of her work is typically framed as an encounter with the past in the present. Many critics have assessed the work with terms such as "suspension" and "delay." Olga Viso writes: "The notion of delay is indeed central to her art, and one of the intriguing characteristics of her sculptures is the manner in which they record a rupture in time. Registering suspended moments, time is simultaneously arrested and accelerated as the past and the present violently collide."[15] And Mieke Bal argues: "Salcedo's answer to monumentality, then, is to bring in time by suspending it; the suspension of time that counters time's erasure into eternity."[16] This sense of time's delay or suspension resonates with Duchamp's play with time in *The Large Glass* (1915–23), a painting that he saw, formally, as a "delay in glass."[17]

Suspension is germane to the subject matter of *The Large Glass* as well, since the painting depicts the act of lovemaking permanently stalled—the bride forever suspended in glass above her bachelors, who in turn are trapped below, resigned to an eternity of unfulfilled desire. Salcedo's work does seem to suspend time, largely through its production of silence, its dramatic quieting of experience, its hushing of language. A pronounced sense of muteness accompanies the experience of looking at Salcedo's work, whether it involves walking around her concrete stuffed furniture, whose wooden joints can no longer creak or scrape, or perambulating down the long line of *Shibboleth*, taking in its metaphor of uncrossable boundaries and borders, or standing before the haunted shirts and shoes of those who have been forcibly and permanently silenced, or taking in the oddly reverential hush that accompanies the putative void of *Neither*.

But Salcedo's suspension of time firmly resists any notion of timelessness. One of feminism's most trenchant critiques was against ideas of timelessness, for embedded in such ideas is the naturalization of the way things are (women tend the home, men go to work, etc.). Indeed, whenever Anglo-American feminism tilted toward a universal idea of "woman," it veered into the realm of the timeless and in doing so lost much of its critical acumen.[18] When Salcedo's work delays or suspends time, it neither freezes nor jettisons it, but rather builds time into the structure of the work itself. In other words, I don't think Salecdo is interested only in the time of the past or in the past as a metaphor. Rather, I think *Shibboleth* anticipates what is to come: for itself, for the Tate, for London, and, ultimately, for the very idea of the museum. The crack in the floor operates in the realm of the imminent: it is an inevitable point in the future—the crack shows us the moment in time when all of this twenty-first-century extravagance is but a sliver in the fossil record. So while the discourse around Salcedo's work tends to focus on her marriage of past and present, on her insistence that traces of the past persist in the present, I have come to see her work as anticipating its own future as a trace, a shard, or a fragment. The concrete-filled pieces of furniture are not only memorials to lives lost, but they also exist as fossils in potentia. This quality of unearthing or fossilization in the work is a way of seeing Salcedo's affective commandeering of spaces as not only about space, per se, but also about the inextricability of space and time. It suggests, as Salcedo herself recently stated, that however commemorative her work might be, however evocative of the past, however invested in pulling the threads of the past through the weave of the present, each pausing of time dedicated to remembrance, each anniversary, is also an announcement of "its return, it is also a date to come."[19]

CODA

We have grown too accustomed to weak interpretations of Duchamp, in which the readymade is art because that artist said so, or a version of political art that is imagined to be all content and no form. This is partly due to the inherent deficit of language, partly due to the easy reduction of complicated ideas into truisms that become the lingua franca of an art world perpetually on the move. One of the most trenchant aspects of Salcedo's practice has been to complicate such anodyne formulations. Her oeuvre's engagement with the Duchampian readymade complicates our understanding of it. Salcedo's work's anticipation of a time yet to come, her work's understanding of itself as both art for our time and an artifact for the future is a potent release from the stranglehold commodity time has on our culture, on our ideas about art, on our very sense of self.

Preoccupied with mourning the deaths of those who go uncounted, unnamed, and unrecognized, Salcedo's work offers us a vision of our own futurity and implicitly asks us to think about the long judgment of time. Refusing immediacy is brave, for it implies that not all meaning is available in the moment, or to each of us. To refuse the contemporaneity of art is to make us aware, as viewers, that perhaps not everything is for us. Salcedo herself has written: "Art speaks to the other; it addresses an other altogether other, even if it does not reach the person it is addressing."[20] Reading this reminded me of a quote by art historian and anthropologist George Kubler: "Astronomers and historians have this in common: both are concerned with appearances noted in the present but occurring in the past."[21] Salcedo says: "The past is the only place where we can find both our origins and our destiny."[22] This is true. And now, as we sit surrounded by the all-encompassing present, we can possess only curiosity—curiosity tinged with hope—about how Salcedo's handmade readymades will pass through time, messages buried deep within the concrete, for those whom we will never know.

Postscript

Which came first, my interest in Duchamp's readymades and the problem of labor, or my interest in artists who use everyday things as their primary medium? I don't have an answer to this question. What strikes me most is the thoroughness with which the structure of the readymade infiltrated art after World War II, and how little we talk of the readymade as a set of formal operations, as we do, say, with painting. It strikes me that the default critical position in relation to the readymade is to read it primarily as a conveyance for subject matter. I think this essay elaborates how the readymade—which means the acts of choosing, acquiring, presenting, and reframing a commodity object—is in fact a set of operations, every aspect of which is available to be torqued and manipulated. The readymade object is very similar to paint in this way: it's a medium, a tool, with a one-hundred-year tradition of use. In other words, it's a gold mine.

Simone Leigh: Art Is Medicine

Originally published in *Artforum*, March 2018, 164–73.

Before my encounter with Simone Leigh's work, I had never heard of the United Order of Tents. Founded in 1867 by former slaves Annetta Lane and Harriet Taylor, the Tents is a secret society of Black women whose focus was nursing, and they are the oldest continually existing sorority of Black women in the United States. Today, the organization continues to pursue its mission of nursing and healing members of the Black community by providing a variety of additional services, from aid in securing mortgages to assistance for building housing for the elderly to ensuring proper burial services for the dead. We know that members of the Tents are called Sisters and that those who have performed exemplary service are referred to as Queens, but beyond that, very little is known about the society's inner workings. Leigh has cited the Tents as an inspiration for her own work, and it's easy to see the parallel, not only because Leigh, too, has focused on practices of care, but also because much of her art is, if not exactly secret, not exactly public, either.

This was very much the case with Leigh's installation/social-practice project *The Waiting Room* (2016), presented at the New Museum in New York. The title of the work alludes to the real-life, not-at-all-fake-news account of Esmin Elizabeth Green, a Black woman who, in 2008, sat in the emergency-room waiting area at Kings County Hospital Center in Brooklyn for twenty-four hours and died on the floor, of a blood clot that had worked its way up from her legs to her lungs. She was never seen by a doctor. Green's case is unusually appalling, but structurally it is decidedly not an isolated event, given the invisibility of Black pain in our medical system. The statistics on Black women's health issues are harrowing in their starkness. According to the CDC, Black women die in childbirth at three to four times the rate of white women. Black women are 35 percent more likely to develop heart disease than white or Hispanic women and are almost twice as likely as white women to be diagnosed with diabetes. The litany of disparities could continue for pages. Suffice it to say, Leigh's interest in the historical denial of Black women's bodies—their experience, their suffering, their pleasure, their knowledge—galvanized her to create *The Waiting Room*.

It was not a particularly visual event. Mostly what I recall is a gallery whose focal point was a large cabinet lined with glass jars luxuriously filled with herbs and dried flowers. This relatively empty room suggested that the real work lay elsewhere, namely, in the workshops on such topics as complementary medicine, folk-healing traditions, acupuncture, and meditation. Many of these events occurred while the museum was closed to the public, notably *Home Economics*, a program designed specifically for fifteen Black schoolgirls that investigated ways to address the holistic needs of Black women in relation to wellness and the medical establishment. However, you will not find a plethora of photos of happy museum visitors attending the workshops and events she organized. The scarcity of documentation is a choice, and a pointed one. Leigh's programming was neither an offering to the archive nor a feel-good tonic for the general public; her concerns were exclusively directed toward her work's primary audience, Black women.

The Waiting Room built on, and in some respects continued, Leigh's 2014 Creative Time project *Free People's Medical Clinic*, curated by Rashida Bumbray. Located in the historical Weeksville neighborhood of Brooklyn, a settlement founded by free Blacks in 1838, the *Free People's Medical Clinic* offered HIV and blood-pressure screenings, modern dance, lessons in Caribbean herbalism, and more. In each of her forays into wellness, Leigh subtly demands that the field of medicine, as currently constructed by the white, colonialist West, broaden to address the specific concerns and health issues of Black women (an expansion mandated by the exclusion of Black women from being the subjects of medicine as it has been traditionally conceived). Both *The Waiting Room* and *Free People's Medical Clinic* identified wellness as encompassing practices habitually not considered under the rubric of medicine, such as the knowledges that emanate from sources as disparate as folk songs and the philosophical work of Black feminist theorists like Hortense Spillers and Saidiya Hartman (to name only two). *Free People's Medical Clinic* was also a direct nod to the legacy of the Black Panther Party's neighborhood activism and to Dr. Josephine English, one of the first African American ob-gyns in New York, whose home served as the project's base. This complex layering of historical allusions and contemporary events is a hallmark of Leigh's work.

The Waiting Room was on view at the New Museum during the fateful summer week when Philando Castile and Alton Sterling were murdered by police. Leigh's response, inspired by the ethos and tactics of the Tents (recall that they were established both to heal and to bury the dead respectfully), was to mobilize and quickly convene a group of Black women artists, who would ultimately become Black Women Artists for Black Lives Matter. Upward of one hundred members met privately for weeks, without the museum's staff, to plan a day of activities to take place at the New Museum on September 1, 2016. This time and space were to be primarily for the people that occupy the center of Leigh's practice—Black women. What was on the table was a takeover, a claiming of the space of the museum, with no sense of apprehension or apology, for a group of people it has historically barely registered—whether as subjects, artists, visitors, or employees.

To be honest, there was a time I would have felt Leigh's call for exclusively Black women to organize this event "problematic" (I suppose I would have argued that it was "essentialist," while sidestepping my feelings of being left out), but I no longer do. This is partly because of Leigh's forthright insistence that Black female subjectivity is the historical framework of her practice, that Black women are its subject matter, and that Black women are the work's privileged audience. Given the lack of any such systematic inclusion of Black women in the fields of Western culture prior to this moment, this recalibration seems both deeply necessary and positively exhilarating. Indeed, the assertion of this entitlement seems like an extension of Rosa Parks's fundamental act of resistance: space claiming. Considering it as such, I began to recalibrate my own "feelings" about pointedly being left out of an organizing meeting. Why? Because I understand Leigh's need for exclusion as bound to the Tents' use of secrecy—it's part of the strategy that enables her to do the work of placing Black women at the center of her practice. Surely the Tents would not have survived had white women been invited to attend, and surely the Tents have produced a body of knowledge that owes its very longevity to its exclusive privileging of Black female subjectivity. To be situated outside of the main event, to be refused entry, to be placed in a position of radical unknowing—these are deeply interesting aspects of Leigh's work for me as a white woman. And perhaps more to the point, this is the position from which I must engage with the work, and it is demonstrably different from the place I typically occupy, marked as it is by my status as insider, learned, knowledgeable, comfortable. For centuries, all of culture's agents—its makers, benefactors, and audiences—have been presumed to be white men, and for centuries, Leigh's primary audience, Black women, were denied a place in this hegemonic structure. This was not a victimless crime. There are ramifications. And one of them, Leigh suggests, is a profound need for intimacy and privacy, for secrecy, for going underground. In an era of selfies and social media, the same era that witnessed 53 percent of white women voting for Donald Trump, looking back at the logic of privacy that protected the Tents offers very particular possibilities. Similarly, in an era when Harriet Tubman is denied her place on our most public currency, the power of underground networks might be conducive to the difficult and iterative work of decolonizing one's mind.

And yet, some of Leigh's work is decidedly aboveground, marking space and taking up room, fully participating in the symbolic cultural value of Art. Her discrete sculptural art objects operate in tandem with her social-practice work, a call-and-response that engages a dynamic of hiding in plain sight, of being in public while managing privacy. These objects fall loosely, but not exclusively, into three categories: ceramic-rosette-festooned heads of Black women; large ceramic forms in the shape of cowrie shells; and large-scale architectural domes. The portrait busts are as anonymous as they are sensuous. The ceramic rosettes that form their hair are as nonnaturalistic as the palette of Rihanna's Fenty Beauty lipsticks: a dry cobalt blue, a shiny and seductive oyster pink, etc. This stylized hair is gloriously coiffed, and one imagines every rosette's meticulous and repetitive placement on each figure's head. These silent figures are similar without being generic, and the proliferation of style within a constrained set of forms is offered with all the complexity of a Sol LeWitt wall drawing. The figures don't have eyes per se; instead the forms register the eyes as a depression, each eye about the size of the thumb that made it. The texture of these gentle depressions, the smoothness caused by a thumb rubbing their surfaces over and over again, makes them a ravishing combination of the iconic and the indexical. Their lack of eyes might seem to invite viewers to regard them in a classically colonializing manner: you can look and they cannot look back. But this is not the sensation I have when looking at them. I feel as if it is I who cannot "see" them. They do not, importantly, "refuse" my gaze (because that dynamic would still place me at the center of the event). Rather, their lack of eyes counterintuitively means they are "unseeable," and hence unknowable, to me. They remain self-possessed, looking inward, contemplating and thinking things that I cannot fathom. Here, too, I'm reminded of the logic of the secret as an age-old strategy for contesting being named and controlled by a hostile other. I suppose it should go without saying that this claiming of the right to privacy feels deeply germane to our current moment.

Interiority is also at play in Leigh's ceramic sculptures of oversize cowrie shells, each the scale and shape of the watermelons Leigh uses as a mold to generate them. Salt-fired to produce an array of extraordinarily haptic glazes that are a perfect marriage of color and texture, they evoke scarification, ritual, and exchange. Their shape is open to extreme slippage—eyes, vaginas, bellies, shells, sculpture, objets d'art. They lay claim to craft, technical sophistication, and tradition. The gestalt of these pieces is fast and rich, and I sense the feel, the weight, the process all at once. The cowrie sculptures are deeply truthful to their source. Like shells found on a beach, they feel like a gift from the world. And, as with real shells, their interiors are unavailable to vision, and your pinky will get stuck for sure as you run your fingers surreptitiously along their toothed edges.

Commensurate with the repetition found in her ceramics and her social-practice work, Leigh's oeuvre is punctuated by an architectural form that is an ineffable mixture of the infamous "decorated shed" (to cite Denise Scott Brown and Robert Venturi's favorite type of vernacular architecture); the 1940s-era restaurant Mammy's Cupboard in Natchez, Mississippi; and the dwellings of the Musgum people of Cameroon. These bell-shaped volumes, which are echoed in the rounded torsos of Leigh's portrait heads, are frequently life-size and adorned with concentric layers of raffia suggestive of women's clothing—whether Victorian crinoline hoop skirts, the flapper garb of Josephine Baker, or a nurse or cook's apron. Leigh's room-scale, dome-shaped sculptures produce a twinned sensation of limit and possibility. In her 2016 exhibition at the Hammer Museum in Los Angeles, a monitor inside the dome was showing *Aluminum* (2016), in which Bumbray (who is a dancer and choreographer as well as a curator) appears in a floor-length gown, wearing anklets adorned with the tops of cans—jewelry Leigh purchased at the *muthi* (traditional medicine) market in Durban, South Africa. Bumbray dances gloriously, furiously, religiously. She dances as if her life depends on it. She dances her energy into the space of a future we can't see, disturbing and animating particles from atoms to muons. On entering these sensuously surfaced huts, I always feel like I missed whatever it was that happened there. The video is a residue of what occurred before I arrived. The video is a promise of something that will transpire after I've left. For me, these mild acts of aesthetic refusal start to engage the limits of empathy: I can't have it all. I can't know it all. Not everything is available to everyone, not even to a privileged gatekeeper of culture such as myself. Such are the ongoing fantasies of the colonialist mind-set. The museum, the Western institution I have dedicated my life to, with its familiar humanist offerings of knowledge and patrimony in the name of empathy and education, is one of the greatest holdouts of the colonialist enterprise. Its fantasies of possession and edification grow more and more wearisome as the years go by. Leigh's work intimates the increasingly discomforting possibility that an overconfidence in the power of critique might itself be a vestige of privilege. I confess that more days than not I find myself wondering whether the whole damn project of collecting, displaying, and interpreting culture might just be unredeemable.

Leigh's work makes it plain that I can't enter into its field of knowledge, when it suggests that my very capacity for sight and empathy and knowledge is bounded and limited. Such acts of aesthetic refusal are not new. Hilma af Klint mandated in her will that her abstract work not be exhibited publicly until at least twenty years after her death. Marcel Duchamp worked on *Étant donnés* in secret for twenty years (1946–66), letting no one but his wife Teeny open the secret door in his studio. It was during these two decades that he opined that the artist of the future would do well to go underground. But going underground doesn't mean decamping. Even as Leigh refuses certain aspects of visibility and publicity, and insists on the right to private assembly, her work also lays claim to space. Her work's occupation of spaces both literal (taking over the museum) and metaphorical (the synthesis of body and architecture) is not a possessive "claiming" of space. Rather, her work—in both its sculptural and social-practice formations—is bound up with new ways of thinking about things, new ways of claiming or holding space.

For the past few years I've heard people use the phrase "holding space," and I confess I've chalked it up to a general decline in grammatically correct English. That changed when I heard Patrisse Cullors talk about "holding space" in the context of a Black Lives Matter event. When Cullors used the phrase, it seemed clear she was pointedly avoiding the semantic trap of asserting power through spatial dominance. She was offering something much gentler, and something much more powerful in its gentleness. Holding is an act that implies weight and assistance, an act of touching and proximity, a gesture of binding rather than division. Holding is also temporary. No one holds forever. Holding is tiring. Holding is provisional. One of the most famous acts of resistance in the history of the civil rights movement, Parks's refusal to give up her seat to a white person on a segregated bus, was an act

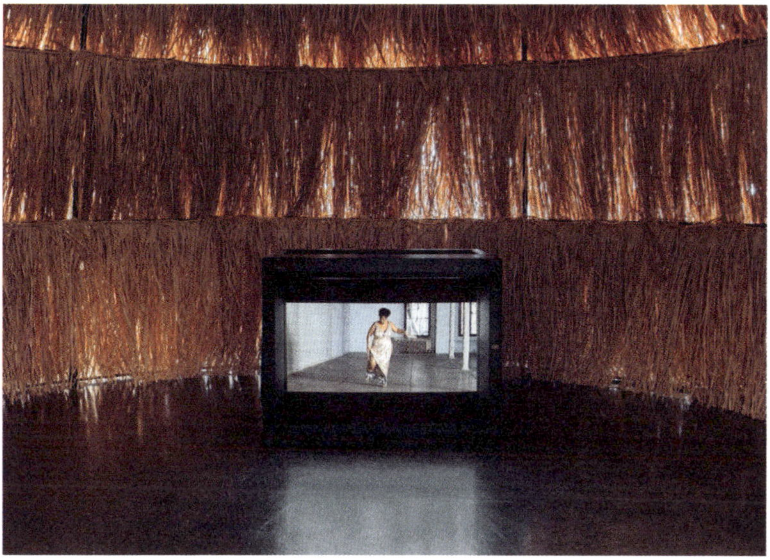

Exhibition view: *Hammer Projects: Simone Leigh*, Hammer Museum, Los Angeles, 2016–17. Background: *Cupboard VI*, 2016. Center: *Aluminum*, 2016. Rashida Bumbray

of holding in this sense. Generations of schoolchildren, myself included, were taught that the reason Parks wouldn't give up her seat was that she was tired. And that is doubtless true. But, of course, her not getting up was also a form of displacement. When Parks wouldn't give up her seat she was refusing to make room for whiteness. She was holding the space for Black subjectivity. Her action reimagined space; she was reshaping rather than territorializing.

Leigh's work helps me to see that the logic of the secret has that force. Part of the predicament of whiteness is its constant demand that everyone "else" legitimate themselves in the face of it. One of the (many) implicit effects of Leigh's oeuvre is to intimate that there may be much to learn from listening to silence, for in that quietude is the profound realization that the dream of equality mandates a set of massive adjustments to some of our mostly deeply held beliefs. I've come to see her mute ceramic female figures as sentinels holding space for a culture that is very much in the making, a culture in which whiteness is neither the center nor the frame. Her sculptures figures are not giving up their secrets. They are not there for the taking. They cannot be occupied, colonized, co-opted, or subjugated. Their existence indicates a set of possibilities and limitations—of empathy, of knowledge, of rationality. The rosettes that adorn their heads speak to the repetition of handwork, to the eons of women who have sat at tables rolling and pinching clay, bread, vegetables, hair; they situate themselves in the *longue durée* of craft; they evince the meditative state that may have accompanied their making. (Was their laughter at that table? Were there tears? Undoubtedly there were deep exhalations of breath. When will we see these activities and gatherings as a form of medicine?)

The ceramic heads, the architectural sculptures, and the social-practice work all partake of the ongoing transmission of knowledge—oral and aural—between generations of Black women. There may come a time when the strategy of the secret is no longer needed, but clearly that future has not yet landed on our shores. Now, it seems, there is a need for Black women to ensure that the knowledges they carried over the ocean, protected in the hulls of ships, guarded in fields, and nurtured in city apartments remain secret. For to be secret, to be underground, is one strategy against the constant colonialist imperative to name, and the longer one can stave off the naming, the better a shot one has at not being subject to the subjection, the co-optation, and the control that are the hallmarks of the colonialist mindset. Leigh's workshops for Black women and her sculptural sentinels leave me to do my own homework (to learn, for instance, as much about the United Order of Tents as I know about Jonas Salk, to understand that Musgum architectural feats are as world-transforming as flying buttresses, to see the knowledge produced by Black feminism as a form of medicine as well as a form of philosophy). And while I learn these things as a counterbalance to the colonialist Western history I carry in the very structure of my thought, I know that deep down I also find myself wistful, wishful, hoping that one day the silent sentinels will speak, and that I might be ready to listen.

Postscript

This essay appeared in print just one week before I was very publicly fired from a job I'd long coveted and was dedicated to for approximately four years. Timing is everything.

The following sentence was often quoted in media accounts of my dismissal: "I confess that more days than not I find myself wondering whether the whole damn project of collecting, displaying, and interpreting culture might just be unredeemable." For some, it was evidence that I had spoken ill of the museum and should be terminated. For others, it was evidence of my martyrdom to the cause of museum reform. When I originally wrote that freighted sentence, I meant to convey the depth of my melancholy. I was struggling with my role as "gatekeeper," the caustic recasting of the curator as someone who selfishly controls access to the playing fields of art rather than the more benign version of the curator as the caretaker of works of art.

What was written in the language and affect of feeling had become critique. When I read it now, I am more stumped by the word redeemed than anything else. The word has two meanings: the action of saving or being saved from sin, error, or evil and the act of regaining or gaining possession of something in exchange for payment, or clearing a debt. These definitions engender my curiosity about whether or not we can invent models of display and interpretation that enumerate the transactional quality of the museum experience with more transparency and nuance, and I find it ironic/useful/complicated to have such thoughts in the face of Simone Leigh's practice that, at the time, was extolling the virtues of secrecy and privacy—long-standing concerns of mine that you can see in multiple ways in the section on Duchamp.

Deana Lawson: *Nation*

Originally published in *Artforum*, December 2018, 150–53.

It's been quite a year—talk about the personal being political—and I'll be as glad to see the back of 2018 as anyone. But there were some good moments, and one of them has been haunting me: *Nation*, an image from Deana Lawson's exhibition at Sikkema Jenkins & Co. in New York.

I was introduced to Lawson's work by the late artist Noah Davis. Davis hung Lawson's *Dirty South* (2010), a moody photograph of an old car in a pitch-black nocturnal landscape, in the back room of the Underground Museum, the exhibition space he cofounded in Los Angeles. (It remains there today.) Later, Lawson's work was included in Davis's now legendary *NonFiction*, an exhibition I installed after he died in 2015. In the wake of that show, I acquired two photographs for the Los Angeles Museum of Contemporary Art, where they were quickly included in two separate collection installations. All this familiarity, and still I was not prepared for the intensity of my response to *Nation*.

The picture bears all the hallmarks of what is quickly becoming a "classic" Lawson image. Its subjects are Black people, two of whom gaze directly toward the viewer. Access is granted to a domestic interior as marked by class as any photograph by Tina Barney. As is the case with almost all of Lawson's images, despite the feeling of "authenticity" and "truth" connoted through its direct address, the picture is heavily stage-directed. Lawson frequently works with subjects she encounters as strangers and asks to take their picture. She often brings accoutrements to the shoot—clothing, accessories, decorative objects—to shape the image to her liking. In the case of *Nation*, she arrived with a bag of bling and some orthodontic headgear that she had spray-painted gold. The man on the right volunteered to put on the mouth guard. He had also chosen, much to Lawson's surprise, to get his hair done that morning in an almost pompadour that anachronistically evoked the early days of rock and roll. Everything else about this sinewy guy, with his chains and tattoos, reads as heterosexual, and the same is true of his two friends. But here he is, holding either a blunt or a cigarette in one hand (a bright green lighter is lying on the sofa next to him), his other arm resting effortlessly across his own body, with hair that incongruously evokes the whacked-out polymorphous sexuality of Little Richard. As his eyes roll perilously close to the tops of their sockets, his mouth is held open by a contraption that manages to be as futuristic as it is medieval. The parquet floor, so common to post-World War II apartments, tilts up toward the back of the picture, while the arm of the man on the left

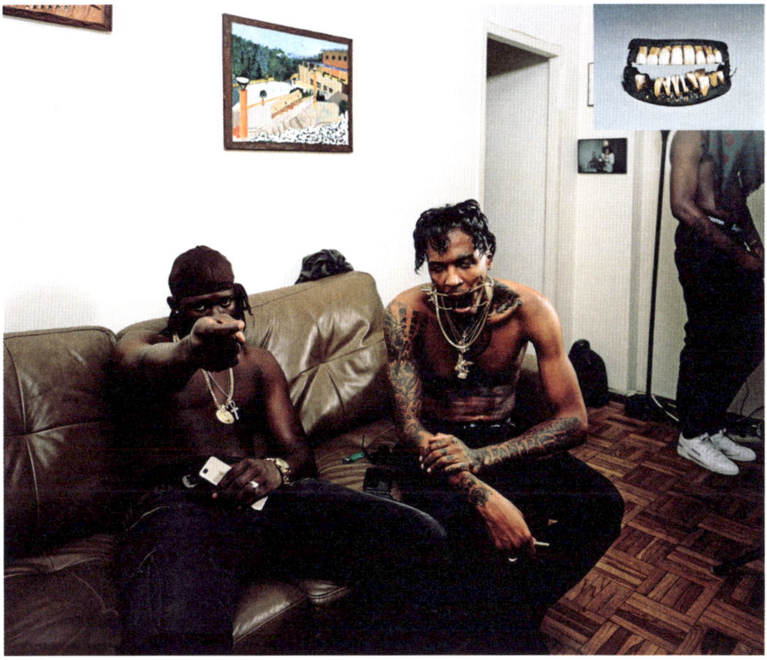

Deana Lawson, *Nation*, 2018, pigment print, collaged photograph, 55 ½ x 67 ¼ in. (141 x 170.8 cm)

breaks the plane of the figures and propels the tension of the picture out into the space of the viewer. This spatial wobble is steadied by Lawson's inclusion of a postcard-like digital print, tucked into the upper right-hand corner of the frame. The postcard quickly performs the work of reminding us that this is "art," and, as such, it's flat and not "real." On the other hand, a postcard tucked into the edge of a frame is a display rarely, if ever, found in art galleries and museums. This gesture is the province of domestic mementos—school photos, prayer cards, pictures of departed loved ones. In a way, the faux post-card falls into the last of these categories, but it also serves as the clue that unravels this mysterious picture. It is an image of President George Washington's dentures, the last surviving complete set, which, I learned as a result of my encounter with *Nation,* is on permanent view, and one of the most popular tourist attractions, at Mount Vernon.

It turns out that Washington suffered from terrible dental problems for his entire adult life and by the time of his inauguration as our nation's first president possessed only one remaining original tooth. As a result, he had many sets of dentures, and the ones shown here are fabricated from human teeth. The purchasing of human teeth for dental use was relatively common among the European aristocracy (a class, it should be noted, that Washington had just led a revolution to overthrow). A quick Google search for "Washington false teeth" will lead one to a slew of articles, including a *New York Times* piece by Michael Beschloss, the presidential historian familiar to all Rachel Maddow addicts. Written six years into the Obama presidency, it is, to my ear, a breath-taking account, or should I say a breath-sucking-in account, that includes a devastating parenthesis: "Folklore notwithstanding, Washington's false teeth were not wooden. He obtained them instead from horses, donkeys, cows—and human beings. (According to his account books, in 1784, emulating some of his affluent friends, he bought nine teeth from unidentified 'Negroes'—perhaps enslaved African Americans at his beloved Mount Vernon; the price was 122 shillings.)"[1]

Did he say *Beloved*?

I can't.

To be clear, I only read that after my haunting had begun. What had been dogging me since I first saw the picture was a lie I was taught in elementary school. You know, the one about how George Washington could not tell a lie, and how he chopped down a cherry tree, and how he was such a fucking Goody Two-shoes that he told somebody he'd done it, and that's why he was able to lead our great nation into being, because he was a man among men, not a king. And the story didn't stop there. No doubt some nice teacher lady went on to say "any of us" (as she swings her arm wide toward a class of kids circa 1972 at P.S. 219 in Flushing, Queens) could be president too, because Washington's inherited wealth and status aren't what made him special; instead, he signaled the beginning of a meritocracy, in which hard work and speaking the truth and being on the right side of history were the things that made you—one, me, us—American. It hadn't occurred to me in the intervening forty-some years that Washington had spoken any and all truths he ever uttered by placing his tongue up against the teeth of slaves, persons barred from the new experiment in meritocracy by virtue of their having been born with melanated skin.

And what of these three possible progeny of ancestors who once resided at Mount Vernon? What to make of a man who chooses to hold his mouth open with the most fantastical grill? To render himself both speechless and vulnerable? To drape himself in gold, a standard of currency long since abandoned? What to make of a Nation whose exceptionalism was made possible through slaves? What to make of a Nation whose version of the truth had at its center, at its origin, in the very mouth of its founding father, the unspeakable? I can't answer any of those questions head-on and still keep my wits about me. So instead I think about Deana Lawson, a photographer who carries props around in her purse, looking for people to make pictures with, pictures that condense these contradictions with the pressure it takes to turn coal into diamonds.

Ruth Asawa: "San Francisco Housewife and Mother"

Originally published in *Ruth Asawa: Life's Work*, ed. Tamara H. Schenkenberg (St. Louis: Pulitzer Arts Foundation; New Haven, CT: Yale University Press, 2019), 35–43.

Doing is living. That is all that matters.
—Ruth Asawa

For quite some time the story of art in the post-World War II period has been told beginning with either Arnold Newman's or Hans Namuth's iconic photographs of Jackson Pollock. These images, meant to herald a new era in the history of art, proclaimed the selfevident truths that Pollock, particularly his swaggering masculine identity, connoted American art's radical break with European easel painting, and art as it was understood up until the advent of World War II. And yet for a while now feminists—myself included—have been telling other stories, with other beginnings. Indeed, it seems that one of feminism's hallmarks as a hermeneutic is its endless propositional mode, one in which the writer or the artist basically says: "I wonder what happens if we start this another way?" This is one of those stories.

Several years after Newman's photos of Pollock appeared in *Life* magazine, the photographer Imogen Cunningham made *Ruth Asawa and her children at home on Saturn Street, San Francisco* (1957), a ravishing, complicated, and subtly indelible black-and-white image depicting exactly what its title describes. In the background, we see the picture's ostensible subject, Asawa, working on the floor, bent over an in-progress sculpture, both hands tending to the wire that was her most essential material. Her face is doubly occluded; for not only does she look down at her hands and her work, but we see her through the semi-transparent looped wire mesh that forms the bottom edge of the lower section of one of her large hanging sculptures. We are afforded a partial view of two sculptures as well as four of Asawa's children, each of whom is as absorbed in their own activities as their mother is in hers. One child squats and looks intently at images on a table; another gazes off as if in a daydream; her eldest daughter is caught mid-motion, waving a long wooden dowel—the tool Asawa used to loop her wire—and, like a conductor's baton, the stick is blurred at its tip. All the while her baby sits naked on the floor jauntily sucking down the contents of his bottle. In addition to the suspended sculptures and drawings laid out on the table, we see a toy banjo; dead center on the floor, a spool of wire.

Cunningham regularly photographed Asawa in her home, and the strong friendship they enjoyed transcended their age difference (Cunningham was forty-three years older than Asawa), their ethnicity (Asawa was Japanese American and Cunningham was what we still call white), and their vastly different circumstances: Asawa had a husband and six young children, and Cunningham, after her divorce and raising three children of her own, lived a fiercely solitary life. However, both were artists and mothers, and their shared attributes enabled an intimacy to which Cunningham's photographs of Asawa clearly attest.

To hold Cunningham's image of Asawa in relation to Namuth's and Newman's equally engaging images of Pollock is almost laughable in its simplistic reliance on art history's favorite method of analysis, "compare and contrast," though in this case, it bears consideration: Pollock, newly branded as the "action painter," stands, stalks, and moves energetically, Asawa is seated and focused; Pollock is alone, Asawa is surrounded by her children; Pollock is portrayed as a master, mid-masterpiece, Asawa is engrossed in making what, at the time, was routinely perceived to be a craft object or an objet d'art; and finally, Pollock is male and Asawa female, which means that all of the other antinomies at play here end up being ruthlessly marshaled along the binary axis of gender.

And yet, perhaps feminism's rhetorical alignment of differences along gender lines, while meant to elucidate how the structural dimension of patriarchy functions to exclude women artists from the canon, also tends toward a reinscription of those gendered divisions—of labor, ideas, and methods. One of the effects of this is that any recovery of the attributes which are gendered female typically means a rewriting of those modalities as possessing the same value as things gendered male, hence leaving in place the structures of value that have historically precluded women and artists of color from the annals of Western art history in the first place. Not surprisingly, part of the reception of Cunningham's photo has been to see it as confirming Asawa's status as a "San Francisco housewife," a phrase used by a contemporaneous critic's assessment of her work. Decades later, writer and curator Sarah Archer neatly summed up Asawa's early reception:

> The reviews of Asawa's 1956 solo exhibition at the Peridot Gallery were generally complimentary of her skill and aesthetic sense, but dismissive of her work with regard to the larger context of contemporary art practice. The review in *ArtNews* left little room for interpretation: "These are 'domestic' sculptures in a feminine handiwork mode." The

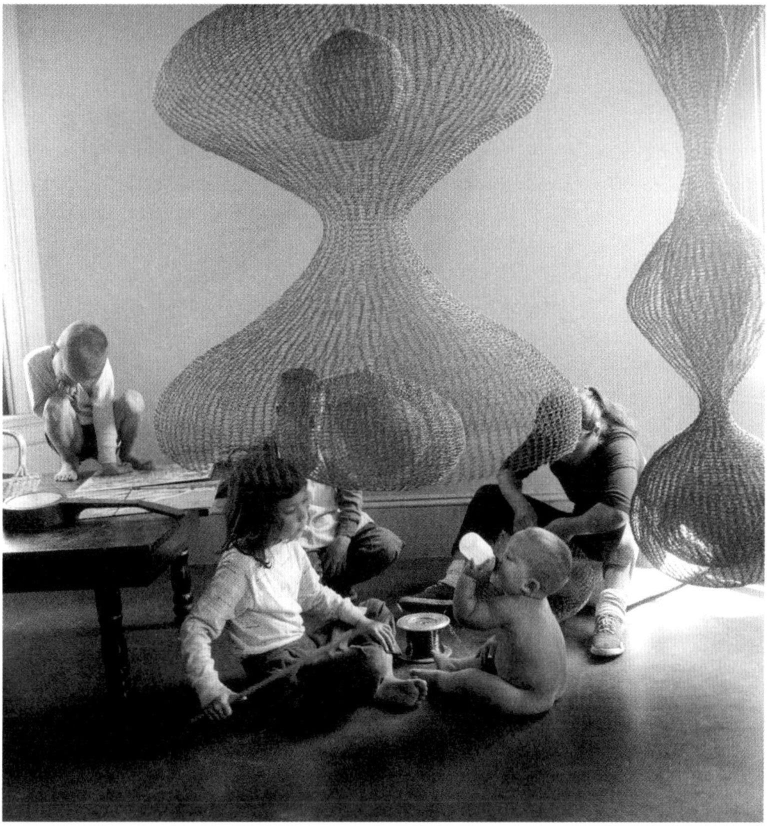

Imogen Cunningham, *Ruth Asawa and her children at home on Saturn Street, San Francisco*, 1957

New York Times review described her work as "beautiful, if primarily only decorative objects in space."[1]

The reasonable desire to "combat" the images of Asawa as a wife and mother of Japanese origin first, and as a mere craft hobbyist second, has tended toward readings of her work that assert the formal attributes of her work as divorced from any of her identities. This has produced critical assessments such as, "nor does her work directly correspond to her Japanese heritage or her role as a mother and wife."[2] I certainly don't want to see those identities as overriding any and all of her innovative formal concerns with the putative subject matter that emanates from such categories, but I don't entirely want to take "wife," "mother," and "Japanese" off the table either. My hope is that feminist art history can begin to work toward a more sensitive hermeneutic, one striated with degrees of complexity about these matters.

I crave a discipline capable of negotiating the formal and the biographical, one skillful at navigating systems of value that are cognizant of their sexist formation but not beholden to reiterating that sexism at every turn. My proposition is as follows: if we compare these images of Pollock and Asawa at work, can we see Asawa's resolve in having fully embraced being a mother (hardly a detriment, or something that needs to be negated) so that she might fully possess the identity artist? Might Cunningham's image potentially offer an altogether different model of who and what an artist is?[3] For instance, Cunningham's photograph of Ruth Asawa and her children depicts art making as an inherently social activity rather than a solitary one. And within this space of sociality, society, and family, we see that the field of play in which Asawa operates is filled with—and energized by—other forms of creativity. Not only is Asawa one person among others, but her creative work is but one example of art in the picture. I view the drawings on the table and the musical instrument laid next to them as harkening back to European allegorical paintings depicting the creative arts, even the gently gathered arrangement of the figures in the picture seems to ride slipstream on the history of such pictorial compositions. In Cunningham's picture, however, the central female figure is neither allegorical, nor is she a "typical" mother. She is neither exclusively concerned with her children, nor is her identity as an artist in any way at risk. Rather, what the picture makes abundantly clear is that Asawa fully inhabits the role of artist and mother with seeming ease, without sacrificing one modality to the other. This interests me deeply, for it seems to offer a way out of the impasse of thinking that motherhood (and by extension other forms of labor historically gendered female) is either antithetical to being an artist, or is not a form of labor equal to the labor of being an artist.[4] What can such a reframing of Asawa's practice—and art making in general—afford us? While my focus here is primarily on Asawa's early sculptures, my hope is that some of the interpretive strategies I'm thinking about might be equally applicable to her later tied and bundled wire sculptures, her lifelong practice of making casts of the faces of her friends and family, and her extraordinary drawings.

Cunningham's photograph shows Asawa at work on the type of artworks she would ultimately become best known for—albeit belatedly. Ranging in size from handheld to over twenty-one feet long, these airy sculptures hang suspended from the ceiling, literally upending the problem of the base or pedestal that has plagued sculpture from its inception. If the twentieth century's radical answer to the problem of the base was to place the work directly on the floor (e.g., Constantin Brancusi), Asawa took the less traveled path of suspension (established by Alexander Calder) and studied the forces of gravity through an exploration of weightlessness. The lightness came from her extraordinary technique of looping thin pliable wire into basketlike forms that are both nested within one another as well as extending vertically to achieve the length and the effect of the human form.

The genesis of this shape was a set of drawings, made while Asawa was a student at Black Mountain College, where she and her peers danced under the tutelage of Merce Cunningham. In these student drawings, beautifully colored blue, green, and purplish, biomorphic shapes and double-lobed forms float on a series of grounds. Their motif repeats both on the page itself and across many drawings, lending the works a provisional attitude somewhere between doodling and practicing. That she would have seen some bodies as awkward and others as graceful, though all engaged in acts of repetition in space, seems to me germane to how we might begin to talk about the sculptures as well.

Many of Asawa's sculptures are permanently on view at the de Young museum in San Francisco, in an installation that the artist participated in, and one that mirrors the arrangements in the family home she shared with her husband, the architect Albert Lanier (whom she met when they were both students at Black Mountain College). Photographs of the sculptures in the Asawa-Lanier home reveal dynamic groupings, in which heights of the artworks vary, sunlight streams through and around them, and their repetitive internal forms are amplified by the repetition of the forms as a whole. This installation set the template for how these works would be displayed moving forward. (Recent exhibitions of Asawa's work at Hauser & Wirth in Los Angeles and at David Zwirner in New York signal the persistence of her vision.)

More than merely looking stylish in the aggregate, which they undeniably do, when installed in groupings such as these the sculptures double down on the work's formal attributes. As already noted, Asawa's use of wire displays a play and tension with weight: the sculptures simultaneously deny and acknowledge gravity. This doubleness is further compounded by her extraordinary facility with positive and negative space. The exploitation of negative space comes through several avenues: each of her works plays with one of sculpture's primary binary oppositions—solid and void—recasting it as a meditation on empty and full, in which "empty" reads as negative space, and the very distinction between empty and full is attenuated by the continuous inside/outside movement of the looped wire. When the works are suspended in close proximity to one another, the undulating negative spaces in between the individual sculptures are almost as dynamic as the actual objects, and viewers can simultaneously take in the negative spaces internal to each object along with the sculptures themselves. Finally, the works' transparency creates beautiful shadows that feel so intentional as to be part of the work itself, and this shadow play both alludes to and functions as a kind of meta-commentary on negative space as one of sculpture's formal attributes.

While Asawa is undoubtedly mining the formal properties of sculpture, she is doing so by linking sculpture back to the medium of drawing. Not a purist when it comes to matters of medium, Asawa's use of wire allows a visual morphology to occur between the looping wire of her sculptures and the undulating line of her drawings. A heterogenous modernist, we find her everywhere paying attention to the specific formal concerns of a given medium while at the same time allowing subtle overlaps and contingencies to develop between them.

Asawa's preferred method of installing her sculptures demonstrates her engagement with that most enduring of modernist tropes—repetition and difference. She aligns repetition and difference alongside negative and positive space, allowing us to see these binaries in parallel relation, which in turn presents the interpretive possibility that Asawa's sculptures might be proposing a structural framework that governs relations between things. For instance, Asawa's manipulation of negative and positive space makes clear her sculptures complete and utter inextricability as a dialectical image. Cunningham's photographs of the individual artworks readily convey that within each object there is no hierarchical distinction between the empty and full forms, that distinction is suggested through the linguistic apparatus that cleaves these two types of space in half, designating one as "positive" and the other as "negative." At times even making both positive and negative prints of her photographs, Cunningham interprets the "problem" of negative and positive in sculptural space as being analogous to the specific visual operations inherent to photography.

What might it mean to think about these formal attributes—all of which are performed with an undeniably sophisticated sense of aesthetics—through the lens of motherhood? Might we begin to consider allusions to cells, embryos, fetuses, and whole human bodies in these forms? And can we see these things without overstating them? I don't mean to say that Asawa's work is "about" the generative power of the female body, but I do want to talk about how her particular set of formal problems is not exclusively formal, for Cunningham's image and the narrative of Asawa's life seem to suggest something other. This might be one way of looking at the Cunningham image, in which Asawa is working on a sculpture while appearing to be inside of it; it's a kind of uncanny conflation of maternal and fetal development with artistic production. And might Cunningham herself have been interested in extending this quality of Asawa's works when she printed them as negative images, in which they appear downright cellular in structure? I am intrigued by how these plays with inside and outside, empty and full, negative and positive, and their possible allusions to biology might be part of the wordless dialogue transpiring between Asawa and Cunningham in their dual roles as artists and mothers.

Similarly, if we think about Asawa's early sculptures in concert with her history of making casts of her friends' and family's faces and we combine that with her work to bring artists into the San Francisco public schools, can we connect the dots of her concerns as being deeply immersed in the idea that art and life are deeply intertwined, which would in turn allow us to see her as interested in repetition and difference both as a modernist trope and as a structuring feature of being the mother of six children, who by their very existence and actuality are a living embodiment of the repetition and difference enabled by DNA?[5] In this regard might we read her castings project as a literalization of the formal attributes of her abstract sculptures (especially as casting is one of the most indelible modes of playing with negative

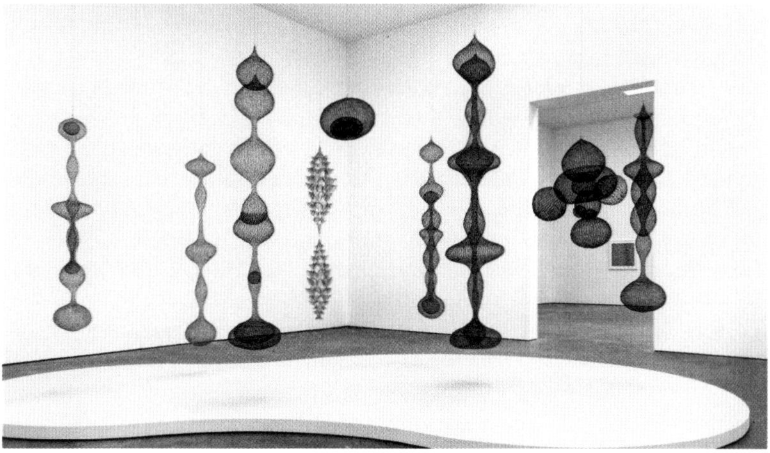

Exhibition view: *Ruth Asawa: All Is Possible*, David Zwirner, New York, 2021

and positive space, solid and void, repetition and difference)? Can we see in Asawa's intensely social activities—her belief in public education and art in public spaces—a commitment to art not as a solitary endeavor but as part of a profoundly social network? And might these questions help us to see the later tied-wire sculptures, whose tree- and branch-like forms are bound together with a repetitive coiling of wire, as a kind of bundling, a keeping together of disparate energies that branch out into the world even as they remain connected to others? And given how the previous description of the work could also be read as a depiction of family life in general, could we then jump to a discussion of how all of the sculptures might articulate something of the great mystery of siblings? For what are siblings if not the elucidation of parity and difference, interrelatedness and autonomy, being bound together by a common thread, and so on?[6]

Given that Asawa's time at Black Mountain College was so crucial to the development of her personal artistic idiom, I think a brief exegesis on her influential teacher Josef Albers's attitudes toward form makes sense. For Albers, form was not separate from the problem of content. Rather, his writing, teaching, and art practice all seem to indicate that in his mind, there was no content without form. Albers taught that form was a "never-ending performance," as his longest project, *Homage to the Square* (1950–76), clearly demonstrates. Albers's decades-long formal play with color relations was a continual testing of perception in the name of ethics.[7] For it was through his explorations of one individual color's relationship to another color that he could articulate that there was indeed no qualitative difference between colors. What a viewer felt about color was different from how they perceived it, and the task of both the artist and the viewer is to negotiate that gap between perception and feeling with critical awareness. These were the rich and clearly rewarding lessons on tap for Asawa and her peers at Black Mountain College.

I think Asawa's work in general, and her suspended sculptures in particular, are deeply indebted to this "Albersian" idea about what an artwork does. If one of the tasks of the artist is to work on problems of form through acts of repetition, in a manner that permits an actual and theoretical engagement with the issues of making and perception, such that those activities can be used to help gain a greater understanding of the world we inhabit and create, then can we think of Asawa as doing this work from the ethical position of the mother within the framework of the family?

And since Asawa did not produce sentimental images that extolled the nuclear family above all other social formations, and instead sought to engage deeply with her community, through her children, and even more specifically through the apparatus that creates society—the public school[8]—can we open up a discursive field around her work that links her interests in wire and sculpture, in negative and positive space, in repetition and difference, in the social, to her dynamic position as an artist and a mother, as a Japanese American, as a product of progressive education, and as a believer in arts education? To put this another way, were Asawa's family, their home, and these activities her art world?

These questions and the field of inquiry they map out suggest to me that the proper name Ruth Asawa, and the remarkable oeuvre attached to that name, can now open the story another way and stand in for the mid-twentieth century's early efforts at rethinking the definition of artist. So I'd like to end with a bit of a provocation: it seems difficult—but readily available—to recoup the maternal or the position of the mother in relation to the identity "artist." Less so is any possibility of rethinking "housewife." One effect of art history's reclamation of female artists has been to argue that critics have historically missed the formal integrity and sophistication of women's work because the overriding framework of identity was allowed to obliterate the "true" or "real" concerns and/or intentions of the artist. But what if the denigrated terms hold knowledge that we need? What if instead of insisting that women artists be judged by the same formal parameters as their male counterparts we instead ask what the terms *mother*—or even the more scandalous, and typically pejorative *housewife*—might have to teach us about being an artist? What does a housewife-artist look like? Late in life, Asawa offered a small clue in an interview contained in a volume titled *On Women Turning 70*: "Something very important I want to tell women is that it's never too late but don't wait until it's too late, because you won't have the energy. You should do a little bit at a time. It's important to learn how to use your small bits of time. All those begin to count up. It's not the long amounts of time you have that are important. You should learn how to use your snatches of time when they are given to you."[9]

Lee Lozano: Drawings

Originally published in *Lee Lozano: Drawings 1958–64* (New York: Karma Books, 2020), 25–41.

She is sitting behind a table covered with metal parts: dies, bits, screws, pipes, and bolts arranged in a totemic line as they edge out the books to the right and the stack of papers to the left. Every word for these industrial things is a homophone, each object is a part of something else. The blacks and whites and grays and silvers of the photograph are rendered as both depth and clarity. The left-hand corner sits in darkness; the right-hand corner hosts a blank screen in the background. A gamine face sits like the moon above a landscape, a short mop of bangs cut straight across her forehead, with, no joke, a small curl in the middle. Her coal-black eyes—eyes the color of fuel, round as polished stones—look out, level, steady, penetrating. Our eyes meet hers. Look at me. Look at this.

My wife peers over my shoulder. "That's an amazing photograph," she says. "Hollis Frampton took it," I say. "Oh," she replies, with an inflection that registers both confirmation (that's why it's so good) and a trace of disappointment (it'd be nice to learn a new name). It turns out Lee Lozano knew exactly what she looked like. Her self-portraits from the 1950s depict her with the same intensity—a set of eyes whose energy radiates from the sockets in her skull. I have been flipping through the drawings in this book in the same order that you have or are about to. I'm as moved by their pacing and development as I am by the individual drawings themselves. I cannot divorce the drawings from the order of their appearance, one after another. Some arrest me. Others flow over me like a current. This means I don't find it accidental when Lozano's drawings of skulls follow her self-portraits, as if she were straining to see underneath the flesh and the veins, the blood and the viscera. As if she were trying to gather information about the structural housing of the human body's first, and most difficult, registration of difference—the eye. The eye, like nothing else on the body, a set of cones and rods, a viscous floating orb with a dilating and contracting center, in a constant state of judgment about the quality and amount of light in any given situation. No other texture on the body approaches it. Its precarities are legion. The eye itself is not Lozano's forte. Her pencil tends toward renditions of its lodging. Her skulls are all apertures, all nooks and crevices for the shelter of soft things. Because Lozano is restless, the drawings crackle with the energy of kindling a fire, and as such her skulls and skeletons quickly combust as they give way to cross sections of the body. Truncated limbs belie their messy interiors, and, in Lozano's hands, the human form begins to feel like a farcical lie—a cover up, a scam, all those soft bits on the outside and the hard stuff in the middle. Lozano would later call it out as bad design:

> THE HUMAN FIGURE IS IMPOSSIBLE TO DRAW!
> PROLOGUE
> WHOEVER OR WHATEVER DESIGNED HUMAN BEINGS & ALL EVOLUTIONARY FORMS THAT LED UP TO THEM WAS A BAD ARTIST WHO TOOK THE IDEA OF FORM FOLLOWS FUNCTION TO ITS ULTIMATE DISASTER. ANY RUMINATION ABOUT MANKIND'S SHAPE WILL DISCLOSE HOW EXCEEDINGLY UGLY HE OR SHE IS. THE SILLY LITTLE HEAD SITTING ON THE GOLF-TEE NECK SITTING ON THE GREAT GAWKY BODY, THE SEPARATENESS OF FRONT & BACK, THE SUDDEN PROTRUBERENCES UNRELATED TO THE MAIN SEQUENCE, THE MESS OF MOUNDS, ANGLES & HOLLOWS, THE EMBARRASING VULNERABILITY OF THE EYES AND GENITALS, THE DEAD & STUPID BLANKNESS OF THE BACK OF THE HEAD, THE PISSHOLE COYLY HIDDEN IN THE SEX ORGAN, THE ASSHOLE NOT SO COYLY SHOVED UP BETWEEN THE CHEEKS IN BACK . . . OUTASIGHT (DESIGNER LUMPS SEX & ELIMINATION TOGETHER!) . . . THE CORNY S-CURVES, THE RUBBERINESS, THE INELEGANT MOVEMENT.[1]

For Lozano, the socket comes before the tools. See it there, lurking in the background of the drawing. Innocuous, inert, waiting. To be sure, I was looking for it. I wanted to find it. After falling down the rabbit hole of the skull as a housing for the eyes, knowing her love of homophones, it was inevitable that she'd end up thinking about the sockets in every room she'd ever been in. Those two dumb holes, silent, everywhere. Those two holes called a word with two meanings, here courtesy of the Google Dictionary: (1) a natural or artificial hollow into which something fits or in which something revolves; "the eye socket"; (2) an electrical device receiving a plug or lightbulb to make a connection.

And isn't that what Lozano wanted to do, make a connection? Isn't that what *Dialogue Piece* (1969), her magnum opus, is all about, an attempt to use art as a way to connect with people? Isn't that why, even in her Private Books she never tells us what she talked about, only that she met with people under its umbrella? What I love about Lozano—besides the crazy, ham-fisted quality of her drawn line, pictures made with pencils that appear to have been held with a fist—is how her demonstration of the word *connection* is not bound to any of the anodyne ways we currently use it. There's nothing about "listening" or "building community" or "empathy" in any of these drawings. For Lozano, connection is fraught and hairy. Connection is dangerous. Connection is static. Connection is the coming together of two states,

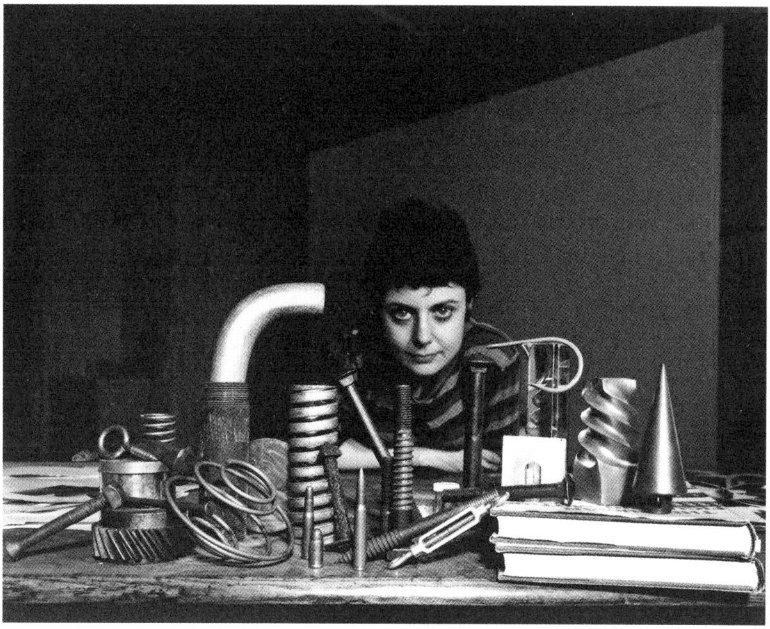

Hollis Frampton, *Lee Lozano*, 1963, gelatin silver print, 8 x 10 in. (20.3 x 25.4 cm)

objects, or planes of existence. This is not *Sesame Street*. This is not Marlo Thomas singing "Free to Be . . .You and Me." This is sparks flying out of two holes in the wall.

By the time the second socket appears, it's cloistered in a junction box, a housing that acknowledges the danger inherent in the situation. And on the very next page is her somewhat infamous graphite and crayon drawing of a floating toothbrush and a knife slicing through what might be sausage, or maybe it's a loaf of bread—in either scenario, the phallus has made its appearance. Below is written, in now nearly obsolete cursive, an instruction: "Eat cunt for mental health." I don't need to look up *cunt* in the dictionary to know that it's putatively the worst word you can call a woman. That our epithets and our genitals are one and the same is not so surprising. What's surprising is that "dick" is so available and "cunt" so scandalous. I don't think this is due to any particular sympathetic geniality when it comes to the category "woman"; after all, according to Edison Research exit polls from the 2016 presidential election, 53 percent of white women voted for Trump. What was a cunt for Lozano? A hole you could eat from? A hole that could guarantee your mental health? A hole that made things? A hole in the wall that you could insert all of those dumb tools into? A slot that allowed for connection? If a cunt was a woman, was a woman just a set of holes? Was a woman not whole?

Tools and connectors, just like human bodies, are gendered male and female. The Wikipedia page on "Gender of connectors and fasteners" is a hilarious read. I recommend it for studio rats, rage-filled feminists, and gender theorists alike. For Lozano, the Canal Street of hardware, plumbing supply, and electrical parts stores must have been on par with the old days of Forty-Second Street, a veritable porno of protrusions and holes, screaming with the electric energy of screwing, boring, plugging, and drilling.

For Lozano, dicks are tools: like thumbs, they are set apart from the body (another example of the faulty design logic of the human form). Alone, it seems, they need somewhere to go—a mouth, a socket, any hole will do in order to make them whole. A "tool" is also slang for a stupid bro-ish dude who thinks much of himself—good for only one thing (and maybe not even that). Pages and pages of this book are filled with dicks, dicks as noses, as thumbs, as cigars, as tools. They are as dumb as the sockets that enliven them. Dicks are like Frankenstein, jerkily animate, teetering on consciousness. Inelegant and clumsy, fleshy and elephantine, in Lozano's world they migrate everywhere. You can't flip a light switch, or brush your teeth, or thumb your nose, or screw in a lightbulb without encountering the terrible reality of dick logic: they have to be needed all the time. And, as if she can sense the embarrassment all these dicks might cause, she scrawls "FUCK TACT" on a drawing where a drill bit emanates from the center of an ungendered face. A few drawings later and some dude has a dick poking out of his ear. "Is that a dick in your ear or are you just too full of yourself to hear me?" skitters through my Trump-addled and fury-filled brain. Much has been made of the fact that Lozano stopped talking to women; very little has been mentioned about what she might have said to men.

Then there are the soft holes filled with hard parts. Teeth. Bone that tears through flesh (gum, another homophone), tools for eating. Vagina dentata. Sheela na gig. Cunts are soft holes that squeeze out hard screaming baby humans. More design flaws in the prototype (explained to me succinctly by a mother of two, "it's the shoulder following the skull that's the real problem"). A dick gets hard, although surely, it's called a boner precisely because that is what it is not. (I dread the algorithm Google will produce for me as a result of this essay. My internet fate currently resides somewhere between Old Skool red-and-white checkered Vans and some porno situation I'm too vanilla to fathom.) Teeth are the tools that permit speech, pushing your tongue up against them allows you to make sounds that cohere into something more than guttural. Teeth are the enablers of the language that spills out of that soft, wet hole in your face. All that talking, all those opinions, everywhere, all the time, the ego in search of its match; the ego always boring, in service to itself.

Dicks and more dicks. Dicks that become planes, planes that look like cigars, cigars that look like cigars—things to be sliced, lit on fire, and gnashed between teeth. Each drawing is as propulsive, rich in velocity, and hyped up on adrenaline and hormones, as the next. The plane drawings (my favorites

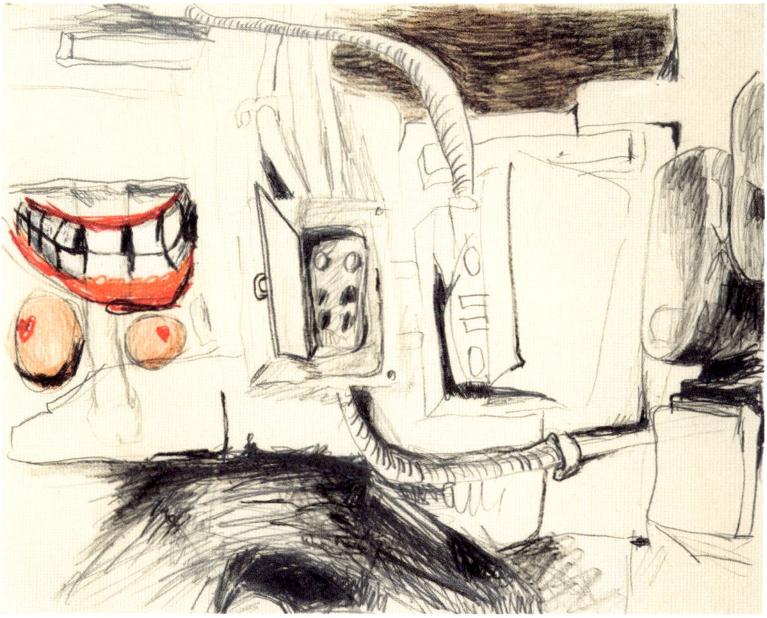

Lee Lozano, *No title*, 1961, graphite and crayon on paper,
17½ x 22½ in. (44.5 x 57 cm)

are the ones that fly in and out of the ear, an underused orifice if ever there was one) are followed by *A Boring Drawing* (1963), a cross section of an electric drill, unique in that it is drawn with the precision of Albrecht Dürer. Sliced in half we see its bloodless interior, a compact arrangement of negative space, gears and screws, housings and cavities. All the words have two meanings. Boring a hole. Bored to death. *A Boring Drawing* reminds me of how arrested I was by her earlier drawing of a walnut, tightly encased in its uncracked shell, the severity of its closed seam, the implicit cracking to come. I think I understand why *A Boring Drawing* is boring, drawn as if an exercise in a mechanical engineering class. Only Lozano's cursive handwriting betrays her more typically spastic energy. It is cramped in the small hollow on the bottom right-hand side of the paper, which puckers around the *b* and *d* and the two *g*'s. The title makes it clear that this "realism" is something she won't repeat. Instead, the claw of a hammer lifts up a penis. And a three-headed hammer has a slot in it, a little cunt for the day laborer, another hole for the artist's studio. Flathead screwdrivers thrum with the energy of erect dicks. Blood-red wrenches, drawn with an aggressive crayon, grip straight-edge blades with fury. Canal (anal) Street will be pronounced the asshole of New York. In a graphic parade of "slam-bam-thank-you-ma'am," the drawings careen toward the end of the volume, the last pages a welter of threaded screws, bolts, and nuts: the agents of structural connection, the parts that

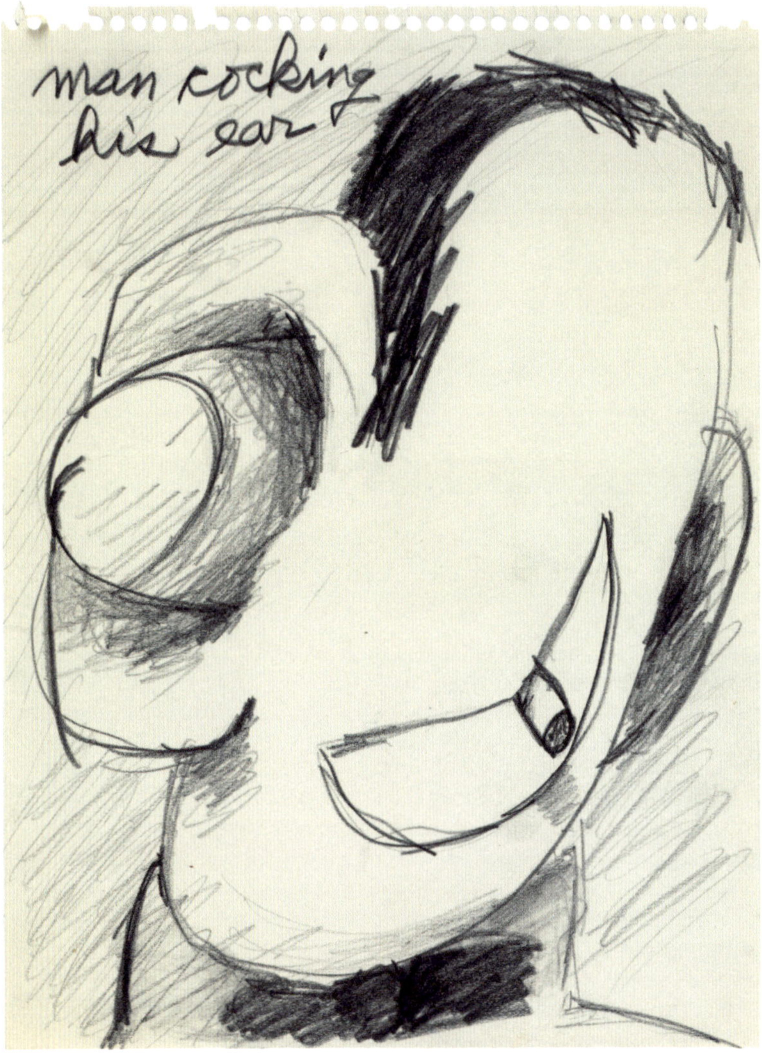

Lee Lozano, *No title*, 1962, graphite on paper, 12 x 9 in. (30.5 x 23 cm)

make wholes. Now that all the tools and the connectors are gendered, what's a girl to do? What do you do when every hole is a cunt and every cunt is a woman? The only answer I can summon bubbles up from the Borscht Belt of my unconscious: hold your nuts, screw, and bolt.

Postscript

I'm certain that I'm drawn to Lee Lozano, Marcel Duchamp, and others like them because they possess a state of fearlessness to which I aspire. Like Duchamp, Lozano, too, abandoned the art world in favor of something more private. This is the second essay I wrote about her remarkable life and oeuvre.

Art propels one—propels us—into public life. That's part of its aim and pleasure. It has propelled me into a public life. And yet I can't help but valorize the artists who make art without regard for an audience. These are the folks for whom art and life are truly merged to such an extent that there is no daylight between them. For Lozano, art appears to be the way one lives one's life: not as lifestyle, but as necessity. Out of the deepest respect, I tried to write about her drawings with the same sense of urgency and inevitability with which I think she made them.

Catherine Opie: Politics

Originally published in *Catherine Opie* (London and New York: Phaidon Press, 2021), 215–22.

1.
As artworks move through time, they have been known to shed. Throughout millennia, we find objects that have lost the names of their makers, their sites of origin, the original contexts of their production. Bureaucracy's constant is its fallibility. Papers go missing. War and famine mean things are stolen and left behind. What seems terribly important to one generation is inconsequential to the next. Color fades, limbs are broken off, paper tears, wood is eaten by insects. Triptychs lose panels. Conservators paint over figures. One response to this aspect of the living and breathing—by which I mean the ever-changing—quality of art was the drive toward a certain kind of expertise once called connoisseurship. *Connoisseurs* were not simply the people who could identify the finer things in life (this is today's weaker version of the word), they were people who knew enough to say, "I think that might be a Caravaggio," and possessed the skills to back up that sort of claim. One thing typically left implicit about the traditional work of the connoisseur (and I am not talking about the jivers and hucksters who can "feel" the truth of a "real" Rembrandt) is that they are individuals capable of diagnosing a work of art in the wake of its massive time travel. They can look at something and see the things about it that connote its pastness through the kaleidoscopic effects of its appearance in an unfolding present.

I'd like to think that if I lived in the future, I could be a connoisseur of a Catherine Opie photograph. I've been looking at her pictures since the early 1990s, marveling at the desolate Los Angeles freeways, the blank stillness of the domestic exteriors of Southern California, the spooky emptiness of corporate America's downtowns. Then came the infinite landscapes, reaching edge to edge in every photo, the ocean, the football field, the great lakes, each dotted with individuals, almost always rendered anonymous, in pursuit of a perfect wave, a touchdown, a fish. There was, in other words, the figure and the ground, the cosmic and the molecular, the empty and the full.

2.
I don't know when you will read this. I only know that I am writing it in the midst (I'd love to say middle, but that implies a time frame that has currently been obliterated) of a global pandemic. COVID-19—a virus that jumped from

animals to humans, a virus that no human being has any defense against. Billions of the earth's inhabitants are under orders to stay inside, to remain six feet apart, to wear masks and gloves, to wash our hands more regularly and with more efficacy, and to learn the nearly impossible task of not touching our faces—something humans do instinctually and unconsciously upward of fifteen times an hour. I am writing, in other words, within the context of a plague.

The irony is not lost on me that my first encounters with Opie's work, sometime between 1990 and 1992, were also within the context of a plague. That plague, HIV, was only acknowledged by a few—mostly faggots and dykes—screaming in the streets, "The whole world is watching" (they weren't) and "Shame, shame, shame" (it turns out the powers that be felt none). Opie was part of a wickedly brave cohort of artists whose emergence as sexual beings and as aesthetic practitioners were indelibly fused. She was part of the generation that came of age in the wake of the first openly gay person elected to public office in California, Harvey Milk, who famously said:

> Gay brothers and sisters. . . . You must come out. Come out to your parents, your relatives. I know that it is hard and will hurt them, but think of how they will hurt you in the voting booth! Come out to your friends, if indeed they are your friends. Come out to your neighbors, to your coworkers, to the people who work where you eat and shop. Come out only to the people you know and who know you. Not to anyone else. But once and for all, break down the myths, destroy the lies and distortions. For your own sake. For their sake.[1]

In 1978 Milk was assassinated in broad daylight, at City Hall, in the gay mecca of San Francisco. There isn't a queer person alive today who doesn't understand the seriousness of the phrase "the personal is political."

Opie's generation took Milk's call to come out one step further. They (she) didn't only come out to their parents and their friends, they (I) came out to the world; they decided that to be out was a matter of ethics. They didn't so much come out as be constitutively "out." They (we) were available to be seen and heard in every tranche of life as gay, homosexual, queer. This was the framework within which Opie made portraits of her San Francisco queer scene—a bohemian scrum of artists, vagabonds, leather dykes, performance artists, drag queens, stone butches, high fags. She made alarming self-portraits: her face covered by a dastardly comprehensive black-vinyl hood; running up both arms, like an exoskeleton, were two perfectly placed lines of symmetrical needles puncturing her skin. The finishing flourish, the word *pervert* floridly cut into her décolletage—her skin red and inflamed, the blood still bright red. The picture scared the shit out of me. If I'm honest, it still does. But past the fear was something else, a profound stillness. Opie's immobility, her hands folded, resting in her lap, suggest the tranquility of the Buddha. Here, all the lessons learned behind the camera—to be patient, to wait, to compose, to look, to identify—are woven into the picture itself, as dense and lush as the sumptuous brocade fabric used as its backdrop.

3.
Photography apprehends, freezes, and skins time. This is its superpower. This is its cliché. And yet, Opie never captures a dramatic moment. No one is ever jumping over a puddle, caught midair, defying gravity. The drama, if that's even the word for it, in Opie's work comes from its stillness. In a series of photos of lesbians in their domestic environments, nothing happens. Women sit around; sometimes they look at the camera, sometimes they don't. Images of South Central Los Angeles streets show us bland news reporters, their gazes locked in the middle distance while stuck on location in between takes.

It's not lost on me that a photo taken of me *right now* would show a fairly nondescript lesbian in front of her laptop at a kitchen table. The streets outside my house are as devoid of people as Opie's pictures of the gated communities of affluent Beverly Hills. My Instagram feed is peppered with apocalyptic images of a desolate New York and aerial shots of LA's abandoned freeways. More hopeful are hilltop photos of LA's downtown skyline, visibly etched into the sky due to the lack of smog. No one is moving around. We have been asked to be inside, to work from home, to be still. The sound of airplanes above is nearly nonexistent. One hears sirens in the distance. Once again, the people in charge decided not to listen to the medical professionals. Once again, the only way to stop the virus is to radically change our behavior. Once again, the disenfranchised—the poor, the imprisoned, Black people, brown people, immigrants—bear the brunt of the virus. Once again, no matter how many marches, no matter how many protests, no matter how many dead, the richest country in the world lacks an ethical and effective health-care system. Once again, the government has failed its citizens.

4.
All my adult life I have heard the following two sentiments repeated so often that I confess they blur together into something almost completely inconsequential, like a penny on the street I've decided is not worth the effort of picking up: "I don't like art that's political." "All art is political."

5.
From the closet to coming out, to queer liberation, to gay marriage, to Pete Buttigieg running for president—does being a Gen X queer in 2020 mean we understand the unfolding of time as an evanescent slow bloom of increasing freedom? I have liberties that my great uncle Ed, a confirmed bachelor, would never have dreamed of. He pursued his desires under cover of night, rough trade, dangerous shit. I marched in the streets. I stood on the sidelines and cheered as others marched.

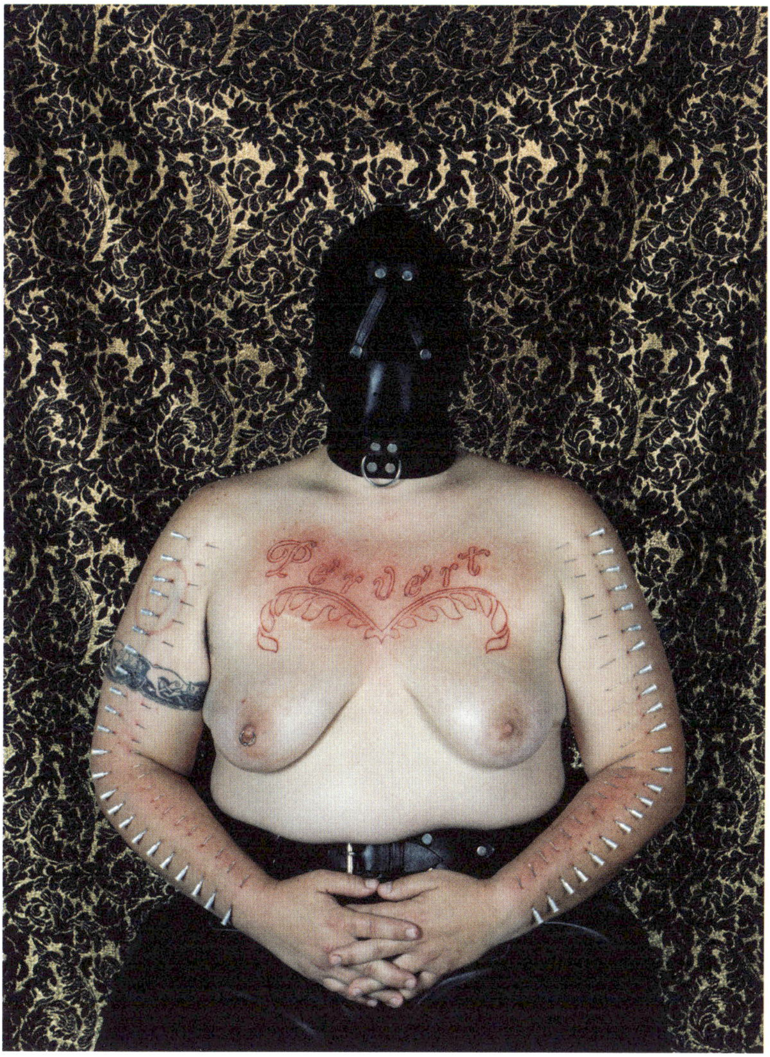

Catherine Opie, *Self-Portrait/Pervert*, 1994, chromogenic print, 40 x 30 in. (101.6 x 76.2 cm)

Opie went out into the streets as well. In a flat, affectless style reminiscent of her undergrad photography teacher Henry Wessel, she took pictures of members of the Tea Party and immigrants fighting for their rights. She took pictures of the millions of people who flooded the Mall for President Obama's first inauguration. She took pictures of downtown LA engulfed by women carrying sardonic signs in the wake of Donald Trump's election.

There is nothing "arty," or even artful, about Opie's images of citizens making their demands known in city streets. There is something so workaday about these pictures, something so deeply quotidian—everyday people engaged in acts of banal bravery—that it seems as if Opie is eyeing the line between art photography and photojournalism with benign neglect. No matter her subject, Opie maintains a cool distance. Wholes are privileged over parts. Extreme cropping is avoided. Context is given. The ethics is one of placement: I want to show you what I am seeing.

6.
In 2017 Opie made her first film, an almost entirely silent, black-and-white picture composed of still images, called *The Modernist*. We watch as a solitary genderqueer makes collages from the local newspaper coverage of an arsonist burning down famous modernist houses in LA. As their dreams turn into reality, we watch our criminally minded protagonist slither their way onto the grounds of the A. Quincy Jones–designed home currently owned by art-world dealer Larry Gagosian. One can of gasoline, one match. The only moment of sound, the only moment of drama, the only moment of live action, is the swiping of the match head, the burst of flame. This homage to Chris Marker's seminal futuristic masterpiece, *La Jetée* (1962), was made in the delicate two years after Trump's election and before COVID-19. The silence of *The Modernist* was deafening. As I sat and watched Opie imagine the burning down of one utopian dream space after another, a nearly two-centuries-old sentiment uttered by Jean-Jacques Rousseau, the philosopher-architect of the Enlightenment, drifted through my mind's ear: "When the poor have nothing more to eat, they will eat the rich."

7.
In the spring days of 2020, amid a global pandemic, we can't march. We can't gather. We can't lock arms and sing, "Keep your laws off my body" or "This is what democracy looks like." We cannot hold our government responsible for its gross mismanagement of this crisis. Now, we must imagine what a politics of stillness looks like. In an ironic twist of fate, just weeks before the global pandemic shut down the world, Opie debuted two new bodies of work. A set of freestanding monitors resembling smartphones displayed collages of explicitly political imagery drawn from the newspapers—images of Trump and his evil cohorts tumbled like so many pieces of confetti from the top of the screen to the bottom. The monitors were arranged in a circle, a kind of apocalyptic twenty-first-century Stonehenge. Around the perimeter of the gallery were ravishing landscapes of Louisiana swamps. Trees, their trunks and roots submerged in water, reach out with their fertile leafy filigree and touch every edge of the composition. Verdant, dank, mysterious, impenetrable; at first these landscapes recalled the sumptuous and pristine nature photography of Eliot Porter. But, ultimately, I found the allusion to Porter was mostly one of a shared sense of wonder

(in the face of natural beauty) and a commitment to the extreme technical sophistication required to produce images with such extraordinary detail.

The artist and, more specifically, the image that came to mind was even more counterintuitive: Vermeer's *View of Delft* (ca. 1660–61). The famous street scene is one of only two painted by this most elusive and enigmatic of painters. In it we see a city from across a riverbank. The buildings are both impressed upon the skyline and reflected in the water; rain clouds give way to bluer skies in the far distance. There are church spires, docked boats, while some buildings catch the setting sun and others fall into shadow. A small group of people cling to the river's edge in the foreground. There is nothing in the image that would lead us to believe that a year before it was painted, Delft was ravaged by a fire set off by an ammunitions explosion that killed hundreds. Or that from 1652 to 1674, the Netherlands had been involved in three deadly wars. There is nothing, in other words, to direct a contemporary viewer to look for the political implications of Vermeer's preternatural picture of stillness. And yet, as the writer Lawrence Weschler has pointed out, what is a Vermeer painting without a map hanging innocently on the wall in the background? And how such maps represented the ever-changing borders of nation states due to war. And just who was writing all of those letters that women read in solitude, if not men away at the front? What are we to make of the silent appearance of soldiers in the domestic spaces, tenderly painted in all of their exactitude?

To be honest, before the global pandemic of 2020 I never considered that there might be a deeply submerged sense of politics in Vermeer. But in trying to make sense of Opie's most recent body of so-called nature photography, I found myself making recourse to other artists who had trafficked in stillness. It turns out Opie's politics, so often described as "radical" or "in your face," was only a half-truth. For every image of a queer in leather gear, for every picture that intimated the rituals of BDSM sex, for every heavily tattooed, scarred, or pierced body, there were many more photographs of stilled oceans, placid lakes, football fields ringed by distant mountains, unoccupied front yards, empty chairs at an inauguration, tents dotting a forest, and empty freeways.

This eerie stillness had been there all along, waiting for the rest of us to catch up, waiting for the rest of us to see how what we don't do and don't say is as political as what we do. And that perhaps silence didn't only, or even mostly, connote acquiescence (at best) or death (at worst) but that quiet and stillness connoted above all else observation: the deeply cultivated skill of careful and considered looking and listening. Had Opie been trusting that if, in the fading twilight of 2019 in the United States, one produced a suite of ravishing images of swamps and called them *Rhetorical Landscapes* (*rhetoric*: the art of effective or persuasive speaking or writing, especially the use of figures of speech and other compositional techniques), one's viewers might find themselves equally still and attentive?

Over the course of the upcoming century, these images will invariably be separated from their more explicitly "political" siblings, the animated collages

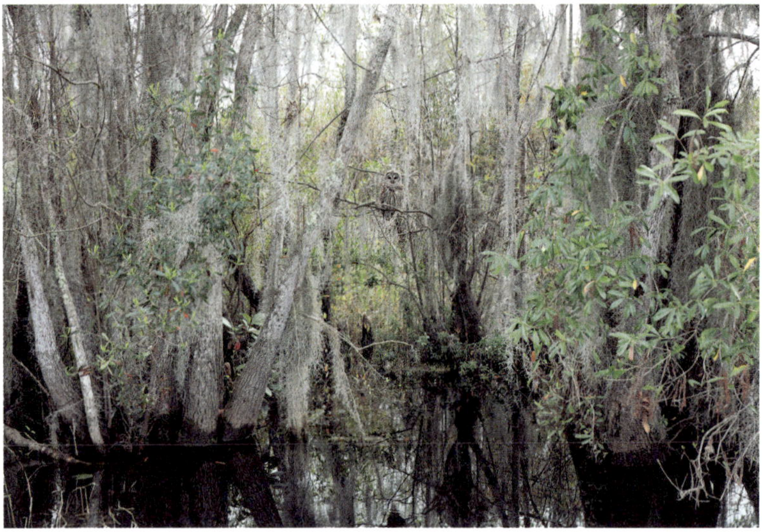

Catherine Opie, *Untitled #1 (Swamps)*, 2019, pigment print,
40 x 60 in. (101.6 x 152.4 cm)

displayed on large-scale monitors. Indeed, I suspect the photographs will travel through time more effectively. They will be stored flat or framed, while the digital videos will change storage formats several times over. The photograph's beauty means they will have adorned the walls of affluent homes, and all the while their ostensible subject matter will provide them with the deep cover of "universality." Will the viewers of the future understand them to be as political as I comprehend them to be now? In one hundred years will the bogs of Louisiana even exist? In a century's time, will there be a new plague? And will that new plague be analogized to COVID-19, just as now we are inundated with tales of the Spanish flu of 1918? It is worth noting that in the course of my studies, an education that ultimately garnered me a PhD in twentieth-century art history, I never once heard about the 1918 pandemic, although a simple Wikipedia check informs me that it was responsible for between twenty and forty million deaths.

8.
During the first two months of the 2020 quarantine, Opie left Los Angeles to be with her family in their country home in Three Rivers, California. On the phone one day, we ruminated on when she should return to LA, a move that didn't make much sense to her, since, as she aptly observed, no one was going to be coming to the studio to sit for a portrait. "So what are you doing up there?" I asked. Well, she said, "I'm teaching myself how to fish." I had to laugh, since her pictures have been teaching us how to do just that for several decades now, even though it took me not one but two plagues

to realize it. It comes as no particular surprise then to find in one of her swampscapes, deeply camouflaged in broad daylight, an owl sitting in a tree. If Hegel is right and "the owl of Minerva spreads its wings only with the falling of dusk"—his metaphorical suggestion that the work of the historian can only be done at day's end—then it appears we will have to keep waiting and keep watching to see how exactly this story we are in the midst of ends, only to then notice how the next one begins.

9.
The silence and the stillness broke open. The streets filled, first in the cities, then in the suburbs and small towns; all over the world people marched. They marched in solidarity with Black people in America. And every night we watched on television as young people, and then old people too, marched. They sang. They shouted. They built memorials with flowers and candles. They danced. They carried homemade signs. They were teargassed and arrested and shot at with rubber bullets. They protected themselves with umbrellas and garbage-can lids. They demanded justice for Breonna Taylor and Elijah McClain. They demanded an end to policing. They demanded the abolition of prisoners. They said no more snuff films on the nightly news. It went on like this for two months. We all know the protesters will be back. We all know the work to be done. And if you are unsure, join hands and kneel down, and hold silent space for eight minutes and forty-six seconds.

Dedicated to the memory of George Floyd.

AFTER ALL THIS, IT TURNS OUT I REALLY LOVE PAINTING

Anyone interested in art from about the 1970s forward has had to negotiate the recurrent, apocryphal statements regarding the death of painting. Despite the valiant attempts of critics, Conceptualists, Minimalists, and art historians, reports of its death were greatly exaggerated: it turns out too many artists wanted to keep doing it.

There's no need to argue against the arguments for the death of painting. They all make sense: Our lives are saturated by the televisual, the projected image, animation, screen culture, all things digital, not to mention AI and NFTs—what could a six-hundred-year-old image-making system rooted in capitalism, patriarchy, white supremacy, and Christianity have to tell us about our contemporary moment?

And yet, it turns out that the last six hundred years of painting (be it representational or abstract, painted on an easel or the floor, featuring invented imagery or transcribed from photographic source material) have produced an extraordinary dialogue between and among painters that ranges across time, geography, gender, sexuality, ethnicity, and nationality. This intramural event has been commented upon by critics since its inception—from Giorgio Vasari to Erwin Panofsky, from Linda Nochlin to Rosalind Krauss, all the legendary art historians of the Western tradition have taken a crack at coming to terms with the very tricky affair that is the representation of the three-dimensional world on a two-dimensional plane.

For sure, my interest was there from the start, and the essays that follow show me dipping my toe in the water of this discourse. Even though I wrote my dissertation on Duchamp's readymades, I was trying to figure out Kerry James Marshall's work as early as the late 1990s. But, if I'm truthful, when I read the essays on painting as a group, what I hear and feel in the texts is the undertow of my adolescent self's love of looking at paintings in museums. I love the stories, the public address, the scale, the sumptuousness, the voyeurism, the uncanny magic of an alternate universe. What I hear in all of the texts is my admiration for the logic of painting—which I see as one of accrual: a painting is when an artist adds color, to paint, to composition, to scale, to texture, to history, to feeling, to gesture, to sensuality, to gestalt, to hierarchy, to abstraction, to monochrome, to the decorative, to genre, to iconography, and lays all of that down (and then some), on a canvas/hard surface/wall. And when it's finished, it joins a conversation that is six centuries long.

Painting is the place I go to find a degree of complexity about the present, held in a constant tensile relationship with the *longue durée* of the past. Painting is the place where I have to struggle the hardest as a writer to stay close to the work, to find the right words, the best words. When I write about painting, I feel my task is more akin to being a translator than anything else. When I write about painting, I am trying to figure out what is happening in the image and what the painting of that image tells us about both painting and the image. I'm trying to reckon with what looking at and thinking about the painting tells me about the time and place it was produced. What does my experience of the painting tell me about my understanding of myself in relation to the painting? And how do all of these vectors of intention and possibility cohere and/or dissolve into some kind of meaning? I think I have gotten better at this activity over time. It's that last sentence though, that smuggles in a different kind of truth about painting. I think painting (maybe I should say “good painting”?) is about the complexity of adult things.

Perhaps this is one of the reasons I was so mute in front of it when I was younger? I knew it exceeded me in some way. I was waiting to catch up to it. Good painting might just be one of life’s rewards for hanging in there, for still being curious and hopeful in the face of all of the reasonable and well-argued opposition to both of those sentiments.

Luc Tuymans: Painting the Banality of Evil

Originally published in *Luc Tuymans*, ed. Madeleine Grynsztejn and Helen Molesworth (San Francisco: Museum of Modern Art; Columbus, OH: Wexner Center for the Arts; New York: Distributed Art Publishers, 2009), 15–29.

The "state of emergency" in which we live is not the exception but the rule.
—Walter Benjamin[1]

Luc Tuymans was nearly two years old on May 11, 1960, the day Adolf Eichmann, a member of the Nazi party responsible for the implementation of the Final Solution, was captured in a suburb of Buenos Aires. Hannah Arendt covered the trial, held in Jerusalem, for the *New Yorker*, in a suite of serially published articles that were uniformly structured by her shrewd juridical observations and her subtle sense of suppressed horror. When Eichmann was charged with "crimes against the Jewish people," he pleaded "not guilty in the sense of the indictment." In contrast to the judges and the prosecution, who continually attributed Eichmann's inability to admit his guilt to his character as either a liar or a monster, Arendt insisted upon Eichmann's "normalcy," a claim she initiated by quoting a psychiatrist who had interviewed him for the prosecution and proclaimed Eichmann to be "more normal, at any rate, than I am after examining him."[2] It was Eichmann's inability to distinguish right from wrong, his refusal of remorse, his profound lack of any particularly anti-Semitic or ideological fervor, the absence in him of sadism or any discernible perversion, that led Arendt to make her final and lasting claim about the bureaucratic nature not only of Eichmann specifically but also of the vast number of people implicated in the Holocaust: "It was as though in those last minutes he was summing up the lessons that this long course in human wickedness had taught us—the lesson of the fearsome, word-and-thought-defying *banality of evil*."[3]

In 1979, Tuymans was twenty-one and studying painting in Brussels. This was the year of Francis Ford Coppola's *Apocalypse Now*, in which Martin Sheen's Captain Willard replaces Arendt in the position of participant-observer. Sent upriver in Vietnam to find, capture, and kill an officer gone AWOL, Sheen's character experiences the banality of evil against a decidedly spectacularized backdrop, as drugged-out soldiers openly resist authority (very few people in the film appear to be "just following orders"—save, that is, Willard himself), a rebellion that nonetheless does not do much to stop the free-for-all of mindless death and destruction. About two-thirds of the way through the film, we encounter the inimitable Dennis Hopper as a strung-out photojournalist. Cameras strapped around his neck like so many rounds of spectacle-fueled ammunition, he circles a caged Martin Sheen. Delirious from the stench of death, drunk on the secret powers of Marlon Brando's Kurtz, and high on a psychedelic cocktail of unknown ingredients, Hopper's character says of Kurtz, his eyes lit up like the night sky: "What are you going to say? That he was a wise man, a kind man? That when this dies he dies, when he dies it dies—NO." Unlike the restrained Arendt or the monosyllabic Willard, Hopper's character responds to the incomprehensibility of Kurtz's capacity for evil with an outpouring of language dedicated to describing language's failure to account for him. Coppola's masterpiece is an adaptation of Joseph Conrad's canonical novella *Heart of Darkness*, the tale of an English sailor's excursion deep into the Congo to find and repatriate the original Kurtz, an evil ivory trader, to "save" him from the sin of "going native." In sharp contrast to Hopper's strung-out deluge of language, the enigmatic and phlegmatic Kurtz's last words in both the novel and the film are merely: "The horror, the horror." The novel forms an unwitting but excruciating critique of Belgian colonialism—a critique Tuymans was to make hauntingly explicit years later in one of his most powerful bodies of work, *Mwana Kitoko: Beautiful White Man* (2000–2001).

If for Arendt the evil of Eichmann was, in its banality, "thought-and-word-defying," an evil that could be rendered only in a tightly controlled discourse of muted horror, then for Coppola the failure of language in the face of Kurtz's embodied evil produces in Hopper's character the affect of unmitigated hysteria. It is in the crosshairs of these two responses—affectlessness and a kind of linguistic frenzy—and these two characterizations of the mordant nature of the West in the twentieth century—the banality of evil and the heart of darkness—that I want to situate the oeuvre of Belgian artist Luc Tuymans.

Like Arendt and Coppola, Tuymans has consistently taken on the world-defining and life-shattering events of the last century: the Holocaust, colonialism, nationalism, and most recently, the events and aftermath of 9/11. For Tuymans some of the most salient questions are: What do we remember and how? What do we do with the things we remember and those we forget? Once this project might have warranted calling him a history painter, but the battered nature of painting is such that the designation feels too antiquated to be useful.[4] Nonetheless, Tuymans's métier is the venerable and outmoded medium of painting, and his subject matter is the possibility and limitations of representing history at the end of the twentieth century. And like both

Arendt and Coppola, Tuymans is often concerned with the becoming historical of the present; his paintings question how one narrates cataclysmic or catastrophic events and how we constitute our relationship to such events of the relatively recent past.

Despite these theoretical or philosophical parameters, Tuymans's work tends to be discussed—with a regularity that assumes that it could not be otherwise—exclusively within the discourse of painting.[5] What happens if we perform a semantic shift and replace the word *painter* (with all its equally magnanimous and defiled connotations) with our century's most expensive nomenclature—*artist*? Doing so allows a discussion of Tuymans's work in the context of other artists working with what Hal Foster recently called "the archival impulse." For Foster the archival impulse is associated with artistic practices that assume the "anomic fragmentation" of history and representation "as a condition not only to represent but to work through" and, in doing so, propose "new orders of affective association, however partial and provisional."[6] This essay's opening gambit alludes to the kind of affective associations Tuymans's work creates in its attempt to represent historical atrocities that are putatively unrepresentable. And as with many artists of his generation, the old antinomies between painting and photography, modernism and the avant-garde, or abstraction and figuration simply don't stand as the structuring intellectual and psychic frameworks within which his work is produced. Calling Tuymans an artist permits a reconsideration of his work, in the tradition not only of painting but also of photography, film, television, and the internet—in other words, it allows us to situate his work within the largest archival network possible.

THE TASK OF PAINTING

Tuymans's paintings are shot through with the kind of subtle beauty one finds in seashells when the glow of the sun has diminished and the sheen of the water has dried. Their faded sumptuousness nonetheless elicits a kind of consummate chill. Sometimes called the "Tuymans effect," this affect of beauty mixed with difficulty, coldness, restraint, and distance has several sources.[7] Tuymans's palette is muted beyond measure. His paintings are studies in a kind of monochrome in which colors are subjected to an excess of light, fading whatever intense hue might have once been present, leaving behind an indeterminate gray-blue-green-brown, the color of institutional hallways and old newspapers. Then there is the famed brushstroke—no matter how the image is oriented, the strokes run horizontal to the picture plane, creating a planar barrier that prohibits any sense of projective depth.[8] This stroke, designed to keep the viewer at bay, creates a state of disinterest, distance, and indifference. These dampening attributes compound the already flattened dimension of the paintings' compositions, most of which are based on photographs. The photographs are sometimes culled from existing sources—such as *Signal* magazine, a Nazi wartime propaganda publication—that result in a patina of age and decay. Alternately, Tuymans frequently uses Polaroids that he takes himself of highly cropped objects and places from contemporary life. This device lends a sick, chemically saturated quality to the palette. He borrows the very viscous nature of the Polaroid, and ironically, this means that his paintings reproduce poorly. In "real life" they possess a unique temporality: often appearing muddy and monochromatic at first glance, they come into an uncanny focus after a few minutes, as if they were photographs developing in a darkroom tray. *Diorama* (2001) and *Demolition* (2005) are particularly strong examples of this phenomenon. Tuymans also takes pictures of the television, but instead of focusing on the medium's fictitious spatial scenarios, he has a tendency to reiterate the flatness and artificiality of the screen. The use of television as source material has led to a unique deployment of light. He borrows the television (and increasingly the computer screen) as a source of light itself, creating paintings in which the light seems to emanate from within the picture out toward the space of the viewer rather than appearing to come from a direction exterior to the image, in a mimicry of window or stage lighting.

Tuymans combines all these painterly strategies—each designed to promote a cool, almost uncomfortable distance between the viewer and the painting—with an array of subject matter that presents the viewer with a fairly high degree of psychic difficulty; indeed his oeuvre can be read as an atrocity exhibition of the twentieth century. The formal devices of distanciation and his subject matter would seemingly place him in a dialogue with Andy Warhol's Disaster paintings, but Tuymans does not seem particularly enamored of Warhol's mechanically auratic version of death and disaster. Although his use of photographic source material initiates comparisons with the work of Gerhard Richter and Sigmar Polke, Tuymans's paintings are very handmade in appearance and, for the first two decades of his career, were consistently modest in scale. In their painterly intensity they eschew, for example, the desultory quality of Polke's early Pop work and the dramatic production values and melancholic sensibility of Richter's. In other words, Tuymans broke from his postmodern predecessors' engagement with representational painting, a body of work characterized by the powerful neo-Kantian conception that the primary task of modernist painting was "precisely the working through the end of painting."[9] These artists (such as Richter, Polke, Anselm Kiefer, Peter Halley, David Salle, or Ross Bleckner) typically produced paintings with the affective registers of irony, sentimentality, belatedness, or mourning. But according to critic and curator Ulrich Loock, "Tuymans apparently frees his work from any modernist commitment to the category of the new and the problem of the medium itself."[10] Tuymans's subject matter, combined with his paintings' characteristic chilly distance, disallowed either irony or melancholy. True to Foster's sense of the archival impulse, Tuymans was to see the history of painting not as "excavation site" but as "construction site," a productive position that disallowed the 1980s affect of mourning for painting's death and the attendant postmodern formulation of history as a kind of impossible trauma. Forfeiting the logic of painting's death (and if nothing has died, then it appears nothing need be mourned) permitted Tuymans's divestment from the medium's slow and seemingly inexorable turn toward abstraction and instead activated its specifically *narrative* possibilities. Yet lest this feel like a *rappel à l'ordre* or a humanist enterprise soaked in nostalgia, Tuymans was to push the historical narrative function of painting through the sieve of the twentieth century's dominant image and narrative machines—photography, film, and most importantly, television.[11]

This celluloid matrix disallowed any mythic totality of painting (in opposition, for instance, to painters like Kiefer) and operated instead with a strong sense of reciprocity between past and present forms of image making. In a dual acknowledgment and refusal of painting's imagined totality, Tuymans turned to the logic of the fragment—literally, small canvases made up of partial glimpses of objects and spaces or isolated objects that occupy the entire frame, divorced from any contextualizing whatsoever. This strategy resulted in an oeuvre that consistently evokes the flickering, disembodied images encountered while surfing a muted television. And like a muted television, Tuymans's paintings both possess and produce a kind of silence, a demonstrable lack of legibility even, a difficulty that outstrips their subject matter per se.[12] That this recalcitrant aesthetic and emotional impenetrability somehow would be bound up with the problem of what it might mean to make contemporary history painting reminds me of art historian Hubert Damisch's description of his ideal art history. Art history—after it has accounted for the troika of form, the unconscious, and history—should be able to articulate the following problematic: "It was the idea that in the midst of a history that was narrative, discursive, something suddenly occurred in the work . . . a kind of silence." He continues: "That's what absorbed me: How is it that history can pose questions that it nonetheless cannot answer?"[13]

Just as a photograph is too little in a mass society, a painting is too much.
—Susan Sontag, *On Photography*[14]

The mounting interdependency of photography and painting is a well-rehearsed story, and thus Tuymans's hybridization of the two mediums comes as no revelation in and of itself. What is unique to Tuymans, however, is his concern for the very different *spatial* and *psychic* apparatuses of painting and photography. He does not merely paint from photographs or in relation to them (he does not, for instance, project photographs onto the canvas like either Warhol or Richter); instead his paintings work against the spatial logics of both systems of representation. They do so through a curious temporal dance of historical "understanding" (as witnessed through an erudite appropriation) and contemporaneous negation. Given abstraction's assault on representational painting, and the naturalization of the mechanically reproduced space of photography, for Tuymans to reinvest in the sphere of representational painting, he needed, in part, to "return" to the fundamental structure of visual representation itself: perspective. Single-point perspective in painting emphatically articulates the place of the viewer: the canvas enacts a spatial interpolation in which the viewer is deemed to be "there" looking through the picture plane into a space. This "you are there" effect is due to the creation of a single vanishing point, establishing an ideal and immobile placement of the viewer outside the picture looking in. But the presumed fixity of the viewer is only one spatial dimension of perspective. According to Erwin Panofsky, it was Jan van Eyck (a great idol of Tuymans) who invented the idea "that the picture has become a mere 'slice' of reality, to the extent and in the sense that imagined space now reaches out in all directions beyond represented space." This inherently expansive and possessive sense of space was mathematical as well as psychological, "for the discovery of the vanishing point, as the 'infinitely distant point of all orthogonals,' is, in a sense, the concrete symbol for the discovery of the infinite itself." So the magic of perspective occurs because of, or at the expense of, the "translations of psychophysiological space into mathematical space; in other words an objectification of the subjective."[15]

Tuymans's paintings revel in this network of spatial manipulations and their subjective implications. This gamesmanship usually comes about through his refusal to let perspective "work." (In this he too is a child of Cézanne.) In *Blacklight* (1994), we see a darkened domestic interior, a television, a couch, a lamp; only slowly do we realize that a prone, we assume dead, body is draped on the sofa. What appears to be a genre scene borrowed from TV crime serials melts into an infeasible arrangement of space. The chair of the foreground blurs into the sofa, and what you first read as dark, receding space behind the sofa suddenly seems like nothing more than blackish paint on canvas. Slowly any gestalt of foreground and background slips away. As with Cézanne, when Tuymans interferes with the smooth workings of perspective, his paintings unsettle the presumption of a secure and confident beholder, properly positioned to receive the painting's message. *Die Blaue Eiche* (*The Blue Oak*) (1998) engages in a similar fort-da game of depth and flatness, representation and its disappearance. Based on Caspar David Friedrich's compositions, the painting feels like an accumulation of abstract marks that struggle to cohere into an image. Softly painted and luxurious, the canvas is an exercise in the rudimentary strategies of painting. The vaguest hint of a window frame is suggested by its dark edges, the tree in the "foreground" is given a perfunctory set of brush marks to designate shadow, a horizon line is halfheartedly drawn across two-thirds of the canvas. But the longer one looks at it, the less the composition hangs together. After a while, like the character in Jean-Paul Sartre's *Nausea*, you hardly even have faith in the tree itself, as it too results quickly in a series of painterly gestures. Even though the painting refuses to cohere in actual time, however, it has coalesced—through the combination of its title and its strong evocation of Friedrich's oeuvre—in your mind's eye. Counterintuitively, Marcel Duchamp's dictum "the viewer completes the work" hovers in the air. Tuymans imagines the viewer awash in a phantasmagoric mélange of references and allusions, ranging from the linguistic effect of the title to the cultural history of images. The viewer, far from a coherent beholder, is imagined as a supplement, or complement, to the image; to be a viewer of a Tuymans painting is to be interpolated as a walking caption.

The logic of the caption is one that we are familiar with from photography, and its deployment is partly how Tuymans achieves his melding of painting and photography. But before we address his reworking of photography's linguistic turn, I want to attend to its spatial relations. If painting works to secure the position of the viewer in relation to a seemingly infinite space, then the photograph's indexicality establishes the exclusive reality of the photographer. As opposed to painting's "you are there," the photograph offers, "I was there." This is why we attribute to the photographic a forensic degree of spatial veracity. We steadfastly ignore the translation of embodied binocular vision into mechanical monocular vision and fetishize instead the plays of light and shadow that cohere into "truth." As such, the psychic dimension of the photograph resides not in the submission of the world to the objectifying rigors of math, but more in its ability to signify time. Roland Barthes's now-indispensable little volume on photography, *Camera Lucida*, transformed the spatial indexicality of "I was *there*" into a temporal condition: "I *was* there."[16] Barthes described the relay between the historical reality of the photographer in a particular place and time and the inevitability of the photograph's freezing of human life into a slice of time as the dialectical tension between the *studium*—photography's evidential domain—and the *punctum*—the realm of details that prick our affective states into a meditation on the inevitability of loss. In both registers the psychic realm of the photograph is death, an infinity of time, signified by an endless past and a yawning futurity, in which the present is turned into the past by the click of the shutter. Given that so much of Tuymans's work is based on photographs, his paintings often promise the photograph's claim to veracity. This is perhaps seen most clearly in his ongoing obsession with shadows, the most iconic instantiation of photography's indexicality. *Lamproom* (1992), a virtuosic white-on-white composition, depicts an antiseptic interior with three suspended lights and a door. The seeming simplicity of the space feels photographic, rendered in gray and white and compressed such that the three-dimensionality of space is easily apprehended on a two-dimensional plane. But upon closer inspection all the markers of photographic indexicality are scrambled. The shadows and the placement of the door do not add up to any "real space": the lamps are too close to the wall, and the door is at an unlikely angle to the adjacent wall. The painting promises a spatial authenticity through the signifying function of shadows only to deny our naturalized desire for photography's veracity.

Tuymans's mutual negations of the spatial operations of painting and photography occur largely because of the way he borrows their compositional logic only to refuse it, resulting in paintings that articulate a liminal nonspace within the confines of the canvas. This liminality is extended as his work electrifies the space between the canvas and its title, the space occupied by the viewer. Indeed a Tuymans image is often so fragmentary or murky, its spatial sensibility so confounding, that the title serves as an interpretive lifeline of sorts. Consider how initially grounding the title *Lamproom* is, for instance—offering a tenuous first step toward legibility and potential interpretability.

Sometimes, however, even the titles are not enough. If images like *Chalk* (2000) or *Pillows* (1994) remain obscure, a picture like *Insomnia* (1988) is inscrutable. Most of what I know about Tuymans's subject matter I do not glean from his titles alone. I continually have recourse to the numerous interviews with the artist, as well as to the essays that frequently accompany each exhibition and that are almost always written in a manner that betrays the author's extensive talks with the artist about individual paintings.[17] Ulrich Loock was sensitive to this phenomenon: "Tuymans' supplementary discourse, which adds otherwise inaccessible information to the pictures and which traces a complicated sequence of ideas, is a sign of the shortcomings of indexical and iconic representation, an indication of the symbolic incompleteness of Tuymans' works, and is structurally necessary for them to be completed."[18] In a telling footnote he continues: "It is interesting to note that in numerous interviews over the years, Tuymans has repeated certain statements almost word for word. Some reflections and formulations appear 'petrified'—as if to protect against random interpretability of a weakly codified work."[19] This outpouring of language (shades of Dennis Hopper) and this making of a carapace of language (shades of the calcification of Arendt's phrase "the banality of evil" or Kurtz's "the horror") are another instance of the work's archival impulse.

This imagined viewer-as-caption rhymes with Jacques Derrida's argument in *Archive Fever*. For Derrida the logic of the archive is everywhere. Describing the archive as spectral, he claims that there is nothing outside it: the archive is as much a machine of forgetting as it is a manic engine for remembering.[20] Tuymans's oeuvre suggests that he, like Derrida, believes that there is nothing outside the archive and that the totality we once fantastically called history is now an ever-shifting compendium of fragments at the mercy of the radical contingencies of the viewer. For both Derrida and Tuymans, the archive is not the problem of the past, or even of history as such, rather: "It is a question of the future, the question of the future itself, the question of a response, of a promise and of a responsibility for tomorrow."[21] This philosophical and psychic sense of responsibility puts an enormous amount of pressure on what Derrida calls "intergenerational memory." What becomes important and/or necessary from the lived experience of one generation to the next? Which memories of the Holocaust, memories that properly belong to Tuymans's parents' generation, are legible and important? Which shall be remembered

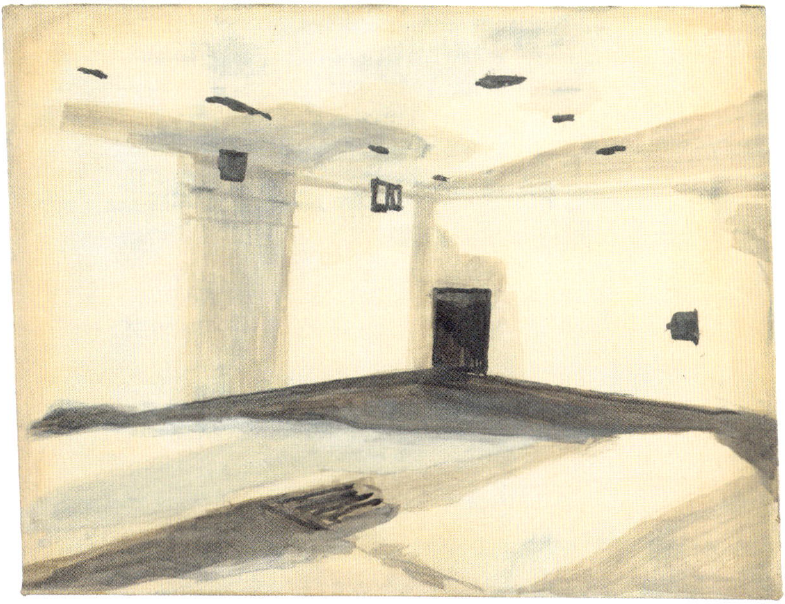

Luc Tuymans, *Gaskamer* (*Gas Chamber*), 1986, oil on canvas, 24 x 32½ in. (61 x 82.5 cm)

in our present? Which images will be plucked from the steady stream of film and television, or chosen from the infinite number of photographs, or siphoned out of the vast repository of painting? The archival impulse at play in Tuymans's work means that each painting wobbles from the struggle between the artist and the viewer over who will play the role of archivist—who, in other words, has forgotten or remembered what?

No painting exemplifies the result of Tuymans's enterprise of combining the spatial logic and implications of painting and photography with the linguistic and affective challenges of the archive more than his early and excruciating *Gaskamer* (*Gas Chamber*) (1986). A modestly scaled painting (only 24 by 32 ½ inches), it is a chromatic study in dishwater gray, muddy browns, and shit-stained yellows. The vaguely fecal quality of the palette makes the painting's hue intensely bodily, an attribute amplified by the fleshy peach color that washes along the left side of the image. In many ways the painting is like a bad joke about perspectival painting. The rendering of space is so diagrammatic as to be crude, its five lines (four horizontal bars that create the ceiling and floor plus the one vertical line that creates the corner) a kind of childlike doodling exercise in the creation of the illusion of depth on the flat surface of the page or canvas. The "single point" of the perspectival arrangement is painfully obvious. Placed slightly off center, it is figured simultaneously as a gaping brownish-black mark of paint, a void, a monochrome, a rectangle, a door. At first the work appears to be a rough draft, a sketch of a room, just an idea of a space. It exemplifies Panofsky's argument that perspective insists that "place exists prior to the bodies brought to the place and therefore must first be defined linearly."[22]

In its nondescript quality the painting bears a haunting similarity to the photographs of the remaining gas chambers at Auschwitz and Dachau.[23] And just as a picture of a gas chamber is just a picture of a room until one reads the caption, so too *Gaskamer* is merely a depiction of a room until one reads the title of the work. It is only then that one feels the reverb, the physical sense of recoiling from the image. It is only then that the dots on the ceiling are no longer blobs of paint meant to indicate receding space, but showerheads. Only then do the washy smears of brown paint read as blood and shit as opposed to inexpertly rendered shadows. It is only then that one sees the grate on the floor, and only then does the grate—with all its implications of cleanliness, efficiency, and planning—become utterly and completely nauseating.

The more I have looked at this work the more I have come to feel that the picture is shocking not because of its subject matter, but, rather, due to its rendering: no histrionics, no hyperrealism, no painterly mastery of craft, no narrative specificity. What's shocking is the parsimoniousness of the representational means, the pared-down logic of the articulation of space and its lack of distinction before naming. What is shocking is not an aesthetic image of the putatively unrepresentable, but rather the *simplicity* with which the idea and the space *can* be imaged. *Gaskamer* sits pitched between the expectations of painting and photography, mining the fault lines of each in a game of mutual negation. As a painting it is an exercise in dirty, clumsy doodling; as a photograph it is a filthy fantasy of indexicality (the shadow as stain); as an image and an object, as a picture and its caption, it finds itself poised between two modalities of horror: Arendt's banality of evil (the nondescript quality of the image) and Coppola's baroque outpouring of hysteria (one's reaction to its naming).

THE PAUSE AND THE STILL LIFE

Unlike most artists, Tuymans did not start his career in a haphazard manner, episodically exhibiting paintings in large group shows. He understood, surely as a result of the critique of art brought to bear by Conceptualism and institutional critique, that the logic of an artistic career is embedded in distribution and reception: a career is built upon the convention of the one-person exhibition. Enterprising, audacious, and ultimately foolhardy, Tuymans organized his first one-person show in 1985 in the empty swimming pool of a once-glamorous, then-defunct seaside resort, the Palais des Thermes, in the Belgian seaside town of Ostend. Nothing could have been more evocative of Walter Benjamin or W. G. Sebald than a painting show installed at a defunct luxury hotel that was tacitly and stubbornly refusing to disappear, sitting crumbling at the edge of the sea, its empty pool now filled with fragments from the archive, monuments to the tenacity of memory. And as if to augment the ultimate fallibility of memory, the exhibition was a consummate failure. Tuymans mailed out more than a thousand invitations, and not a single person showed up. It is hard not to recall the image of Duchamp, sitting in a booth at a science and technology fair with his Rotorelief optical machines. No one was interested, to which his response was rumored to be "100 percent failure, total success."

The lack of attendance did not stop Tuymans from developing his idea of the exhibition as such. Each subsequent exhibition was to have a title—*Embitterment, Suspicion, At Random, The Heritage, Proper*—and each was to make a similar series of moves or gestures. Series of paintings (usually eight or ten), however different one from the other, shared a cohesive element, all borrowing heavily from the compositional language of cinema: paintings were broken down into long shots, establishing shots, and extreme close-ups. These frozen fragments are not the Hollywood publicity department's carefully composed film stills; they are the pause of television. The images in Tuymans's paintings feel as if they have been plucked from the seemingly infinite stream of moving images on television—encountered whether randomly surfing or pausing via VHS or DVD. They are notable not for their polish, but for their utter randomness, for their very chance sense of composition. (Think of the open mouths and closed eyes, the inarticulate and awkward way persons occupy space in the paused image on television.)

Collectively a suite of Tuymans's paintings produces an extremely high intimation of narrative without actually providing film's traditional narrative arc (development, continuity, and closure).[24] This refusal of the narrative arc also mimics the deeply chance-based and nonnarrative logic of channel surfing. Tuymans's paintings consistently impart much of the effect of TV to the language of painting. Like a stilled TV image, a Tuymans painting often feels as if it is not so much the frozen slice of time offered by the photograph, but rather suspended time, poised for movement either backward or forward. So too the liquid, developing-before-your-eyes quality of his paintings intimates the not-quite-still nature of the paused televisual image, an image that still possesses the fluid transmission of electric currents despite the pausing of the narrative action.[25] Eschewing the sharp compositional elements of the photograph (or their blurred effect in a Richter painting), Tuymans's paintings revel in the suspended nature of the paused image.[26] This silent stillness finds an analog in the intense non narrative of the painterly genre of still life.

According to Norman Bryson, in still life painting the banishment of the human form is an omission that assaults "the centrality, value, and prestige of the human subject." The figure's profound absence is part and parcel of how still life refuses narrative, for "to narrate is to name what is unique: the singular actions of individual persons."[27] Still lifes in Tuymans's oeuvre are an aporia: on the one hand, they function like forensic details in a fragmented narrative; on the other hand, they signal the banishment of the unique individual, the agent and subject of history. The tension of this contradiction produces the third term, the silence evoked at the beginning of this essay—here most radically configured as an inability to know properly what is happening in the painting. Despite the more conventional historical paintings of proper names—*Albert Speer* in the series *Der Architekt* (1997) or *Patrice Lumumba* in *Mwana Kitoko* (2000)—the images that twist in the wind are the inscrutable and hauntingly silent still lifes: *Recherches* (*Investigations*) (1990), a vitrine exhibiting Holocaust remains; *Peter* (1994), the stove top in a serial killer's apartment; *Leopard* (2000), an animal pelt laid out for the Belgian King to walk over; *The Perfect Table Setting* (2005), a table set in advance of a bourgeois dinner. These works are analogous to paintings that depict fragments lifted from films watched on television, such as *Reconstruction* (2000), based on a TV dramatization of Lumumba's murder.

The silence of these works is complicated by Tuymans's orchestration of what he exhibits where: *Der Architekt* (a series examining Speer) was his first show in Berlin, *Mwana Kitoko* (a series dedicated to the history of the Belgian colonization of the Congo) was placed in the Belgian Pavilion at the Venice Biennale, and *Proper* (which explores US politics after 9/11) opened in Chelsea after the unprovoked US invasion of Iraq. This version of site specificity returns us to our function as walking caption. This self-conscious engagement of the exhibition as a public-sphere institution and titles as the framing device for the work speaks to the kind of linguistic excess provoked by the obscurity of the works themselves. Suddenly everything means something: the host city, the exhibition venue, the title of the show, the gallery press release, the ubiquitous artist interviews—all are equivalent in their status as clues, as information. This heterogeneity of types of information belies the fact that all the data is treated as relatively homogeneous (a trait consistent with the casual flattening and leveling of visual information on television). The lack of a properly coherent narrative produces a kind of conspiracy theory (in which everything means something), itself a form of linguistic panic or hysteria. This hysteria produced by the effect of everything meaning something is countered by the spectral nature of the archive; Tuymans's oeuvre shows us the effects of the new digital archive, in which visual fragments and morsels of information orbit around frozen images whose flickering emanates light but not necessarily meaning.

All these contradictory moves consistently work toward the seemingly bottomless amounts of distance that Tuymans is able to place between the viewer and the painting, the painting and its referent, the fragment and its relation to the whole. If this is the new possibility of history painting—if, as Tuymans's oeuvre suggests, the Enlightenment project of history itself has been replaced by the logic of the archive—then the paintings perhaps answer the nagging historical question "what is to be done?" with a quiet, horrible "nothing." Then again, in the distance and the silence, in the muted disdain, there is sometimes an electric current of horror, in the manic and repetitive outpouring of language, a glimmer of a barely suppressed rage.

In closing, I want to return to Arendt and heed her words as she tries to comprehend the causes of rage and violence, as a way of understanding not what is exceptional about them, but rather what is normal and human about them. In *On Violence*, she writes, "Only when there is a reason to suspect that conditions could be changed and are not does rage arise."[28] In its rocking movement between silence and linguistic excess, between the paused TV image and the still life, between the scene through the window and the fantasy of presence, in its insistence upon memory as the road to history and the presentation of its fragmentary impossibility, Tuymans's oeuvre suggests that the heart of darkness within which we currently find ourselves, our present conditions of possibility, means that some days we are consumed with the news of the day, shattered by the unstoppable flickering light of the television—some days, that is, we are possessed by rage. On other days, however, and perhaps even on most days, silence prevails, and we are not. What this says about the archive's "promise" and its "responsibility for tomorrow" is perhaps the ultimate Tuymans effect.

This essay benefited greatly from numerous public audiences, particularly those at Cooper Union, the Humanities Center at Harvard University, and Northwestern University.

Dike Blair: Hook and Eye

Originally published in *Dike Blair* (New York: Karma Books, 2018), 4–9.

Apart from the details, everything is always the same.
—Karl Ove Knausgaard

During the early '90s, I used to drink in a bar called the Chanticleer. Located on a prominent corner on the main drag in Ithaca, New York, it had a fantastic neon sign of a rooster with a cockscomb. Because the bar was on a corner, there were actually two neon roosters on a semicircular marquee, facing each other as if in a mirror or fight. I googled it recently and found it on Yelp's list of the ten best dive bars. My relief was palpable. Not only was it still there, but its status as a louche hangout could remain solidly unchanged in my mind.

There was another bar down the block from the Chanticleer, whose name I have since forgotten, where most of the humanities and MFA writing grad students hung out. In the days before cell phones, one could simply show up and invariably there would be a table of folks discussing this, that, or another text, as well as a thorough critique of whichever guest speaker had just rolled through town. At the Chanticleer there was very little, if any, parsing of the day's reading. The Chanticleer was for serious drinking and playing pool and having encounters with real drunks—the ones farther along than we were: the folks who were from Ithaca, the folks who were gonna stay in Ithaca. Not everyone from the other bar came to the Chanticleer. There was a fair amount of gumption one had to muster in order to walk through its door. This all worked for me since, at the time, I wore motorcycle boots and chain-smoked cigarettes and was using bravado as a tool to negotiate just exactly who I wanted to be.

One night, after God knows how many shots of Wild Turkey (washed down with just as many Yuengling ales), I found myself wending my way to the bathroom. The wooden door had a hook-and-eye closure and as I slipped the smooth metal hook into the perfectly positioned eye, I became entranced with the groove in the wood created by the history of this motion. The circle was worn into the door's surface as if it had been drawn with a compass, and part of its tactile satisfaction came from the fact that, in my sloshed state, this indentation appeared a perfect marriage of line and texture. As my pants fell down around my knees, I found myself in a reverie about all of the people it took to make such a mark.

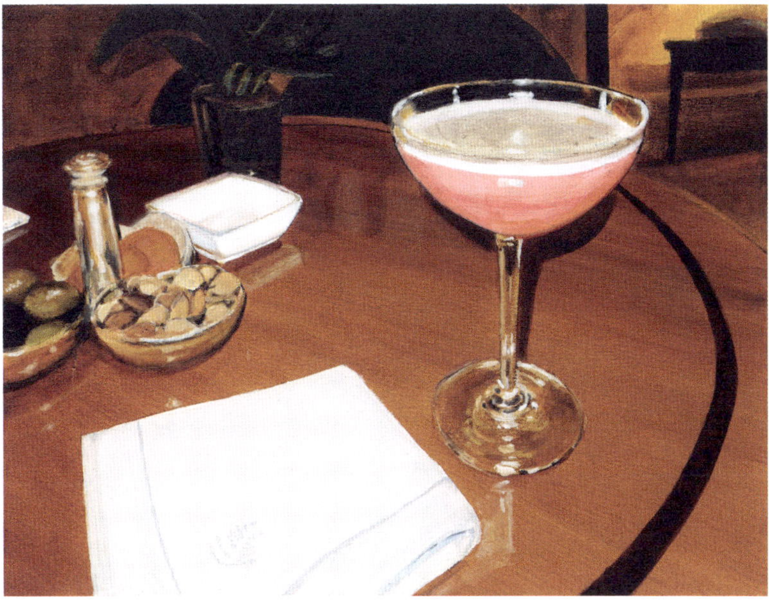

Dike Blair, *Untitled*, 2018, oil on aluminum, 10 ½ x 14 in. (26.7 x 35.6 cm)

Because I was in the throes of getting my PhD in art history, in my inebriated state I marveled at the power of the indexical, the art historical term for mark making that has a one-to-one correlation from maker to mark (think a handprint in the sand, or a photographic negative on a piece of paper). Here, in the bathroom at the Chanticleer, was a complication: this indexical mark had been made by many rather than one. We had all played our part, each of us alone, to be sure, but the sum of the whole was indeed larger than its parts.

Time and again Dike Blair's pictures provoke this kind of memory in me. Over the years, his closely observed and oftentimes delicate gouaches of cocktails on bars, ashtrays on countertops, and cropped images of airplane windows that look out onto fields of sky-blue paint have caused my knees to go a bit weak. The texture of the paper, the way the pigment grabs at the fibers, the way the water has caused them to both swell and dry, have all conspired to bring on feelings of intense covetousness. I can't tell you how often I have wondered, "How difficult would it be to slip this under my coat or into my bag?"

The most recent image of Blair's that shot through the haze and activated my memory banks, making me think of the Chanticleer for the first time since I left Ithaca in the mid-'90s, is a straightforward oil painting of a door with three locks: a knob lock, a jimmy-proof deadbolt, and a security door chain. Anyone who has ever lived in New York City will immediately recognize the situation. The door speaks to the time when New York was dangerous, and apartment dwellers stacked locks one on top of another, as if that would help. The door in Blair's painting was installed before the digital world gave us Nest Cams to watch our pets when we aren't at home. What I love about the painting, though, is not its provocation of my analogue-based childhood nostalgia, but rather the way in which the painting registers, as so many of Blair's images do, the intensity of human habit. How many times have each of us confronted the interior of a friend's locked apartment and fumbled around with how to open the door only to step aside and mumble with a half laugh, "Why don't you do this?" and then watch our friend speedily move through all three locks, none of which you could figure out mere seconds beforehand? This is the space of bodily habit, the realm of the quotidian, the jurisdiction of the banal; and yet it's the only way out of the apartment, which I mean both literally and metaphorically, for habit is the only way we can go out into the world. Without the matrix of habit, how exactly would we even cohere into a self? The details of how one takes one's coffee (in Blair it's almost invariably in the thick old-fashioned pottery of a diner mug or the cheap takeout cup of Dunkin' Donuts) is as stabilizing as a marriage. These small moments of personal preference and bodily knowledge behave similarly to how the fascia of the body connects muscle to bone, girding us from the ongoing effects of gravity. We step away from someone else's door because it's *their* door. We open our door effortlessly because it's *our* door.

This toggling between oneself and others is, for me, the hallmark of Blair's work. Both the psychic heft and the existential truth of his pictures' loneliness—their production and registration of this most human of affects—emanates from his unsentimental depiction of how habit allows us to navigate the ongoing logic of the generic and the specific. Every scene he paints—the waiting areas of airports, bars, the too-harsh incandescent light on the outdoor plants at night, the blue sky out of a plane window, the seams of windows that frame the view from the bed, leaving us just a glimpse of the treetops, the bare fluorescent bulbs on the ceiling—is generic. There is nothing here we haven't already seen. Novelty is not what is at stake; familiarity is. And yet each image is rendered with a degree of specificity that is undeniable: *that* door, *that* hotel bar, *that* flight. In Blair's hands, life is as much in the details as it is in the main event. And in Blair's world of images there is no main event other than a detail. (This is why his pictures are so modest in scale and why the "action" is pretty much always placed at the center of the composition; Blair is not one to work the edges.) This is why I think his unpretentious pictures trigger such vivid memories for me. It's a bit of a bait and switch. I am seduced by the existential loneliness and the generic banality of the red bucket on the studio table, and the snowy white of the hydrangeas against the velvety black of a country sky. Just as I am equally cast back into the most particular of memories when I look at his suite of paintings of dingy ceilings and fluorescent lights. (I'm lying on the shrink's couch, staring at the ceiling, a play of white on white that always reminded me of a cross between a Joseph Cornell construction and a Robert Ryman painting. I recall now how, even then, I knew I would remember that corner of the ceiling for a long time.)

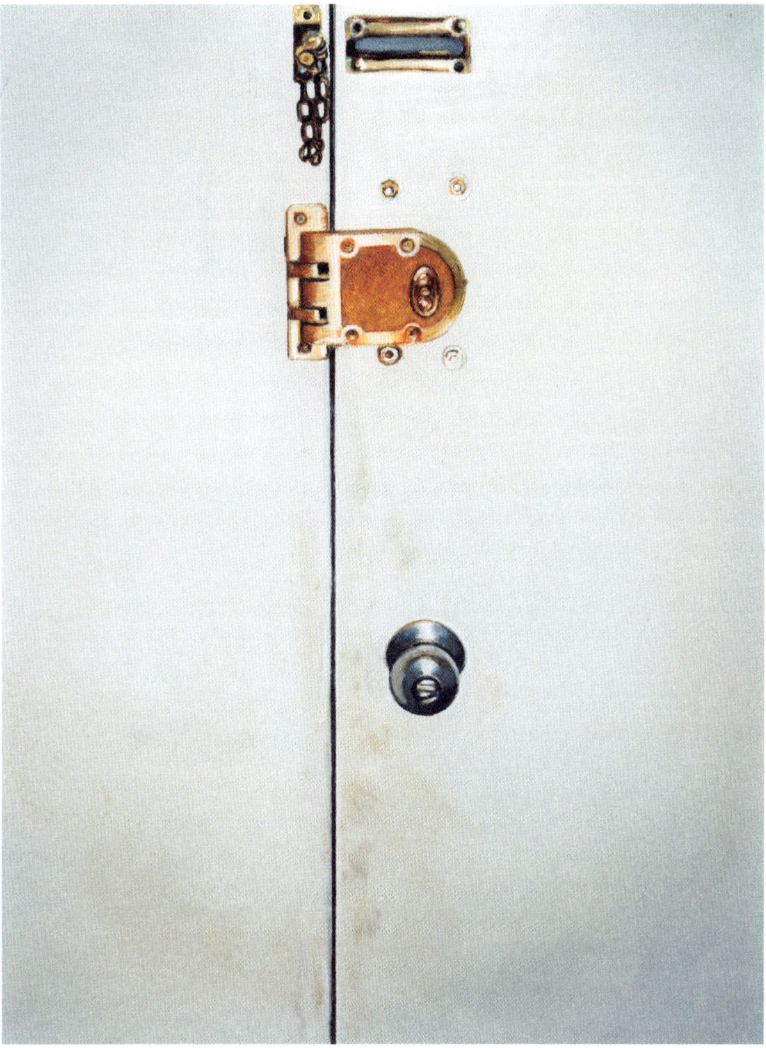

Dike Blair, *Untitled*, 2018, oil on aluminum, 24 x 18 in. (61 x 45.7 cm)

This is the double gift (generic/specific) of a Dike Blair painting: first there is the exquisite image, the ethical offering of the everyday, and the space of habit as absolutely bound up with our very possibility of being, and then there are the memories such rendering of habits induce; memories frequently folded away, not due to trauma or displeasure, but an overinflated sense of our specificity. Isn't it a marvel to encounter an image where there is so much room to move in a space so precisely contained?

Manny Farber: One Day at a Time

Originally published in *One Day at a Time: Manny Farber and Termite Art*, ed. Helen Molesworth (Los Angeles: Museum of Contemporary Art; New York: DelMonico Books/Prestel, 2018), 16–34

The ego—what a racket.
—Hilton Als, *White Girls*

Oedipa wondered, whether, at the end of this (if it were supposed to end), she too might not be left with only compiled memories of clues, announcements, intimations, but never the central truth itself, which must somehow each time be too bright for her memory to hold; which must always blaze out, destroying its own message irreversibly, leaving an overexposed blank when the ordinary world came back.
—Thomas Pynchon, *The Crying of Lot 49*

MANNY FARBER

Our leading man was born in 1917, the same year Marcel Duchamp entered *Fountain* in the Society of Independent Artists exhibition under the pseudonym R. Mutt. This might not be the best way to begin the story, but it's a coincidental fact nonetheless. Duchamp and our protagonist's stories intertwine in the negative, inasmuch as Duchamp, through his introduction of an everyday store-bought object into the field of art—an item called the readymade—profoundly changed the category of art. Duchamp's iconoclastic gesture has been used, for over a century, to shore up the perpetual death notice of painting. Our leading man took notice, but ended up a painter nonetheless. After decades of carpentry, writing film criticism, and teaching, it was studio life that caught him in the end.

He showed up in youthful Southern California in 1970, already fifty-three years old, having driven cross-country from New York in an old taxicab with his girlfriend Patricia Patterson, a fellow artist, sometime-collaborator, and his soon-to-be wife. That summer "Close to You" by the Carpenters and "Ball of Confusion" by the Temptations were topping the charts. The couple spent their nights in national parks, and they rolled into La Jolla, California with almost no possessions and even less cash. He was there to teach painting at the University of California, San Diego, but it turned out that the UCSD professor and poet David Antin, who gave him twenty dollars to tide him over, knew who he was and said, "Why don't you teach the history of film as well?" And just like that, he was given a painting studio on the then decade-old UCSD campus and started to teach what would become his legendary VA84: History of Film course. Farber then began to stock the newly formed art department with contrarians: filmmaker Jean-Pierre (J-P) Gorin, camerawoman and photographer Babette Mangolte, artist Ree Morton—folks who were rubbing up against the boundaries of ideas about narrative and medium. Patterson started to teach as well, first painting and then classes on utopian communities, art, and artists: William Morris, the Shakers, De Stijl, the Russian Constructivists—all of whom or which, it should be noted, trafficked in the revolutionary potential of the decorative.

I arrived much later. Sometime early in the summer of 1987 I flew from New York to San Diego at the invitation of a friend who offered free lodging (aka the sofa) in an apartment her boyfriend had already paid the rent on through September. She was the first artist I knew who was my age. In other words, she was the first artist I knew who wasn't dead. I had been studying art history—David, Goya, Géricault. She had been reading Gertrude Stein and Roland Barthes. I worked a temp office job in Manhattan, answering phones at the front desk of a public relations firm. Once I had made enough money for the one-way ticket, I quit and flew west. San Diego was about as exotic a locale as a girl from Flushing, Queens, could imagine. Birds-of-paradise grew like dandelions in front of two-story apartment buildings—back home they were five dollars a stem, sold in buckets outside of corner delis. My new friends all listened to punk, read theory, and had a slightly hostile relationship to the overwhelming beauty of the coastline, which they displayed by dyeing their hair black and generally staying indoors. I drove to the beach every day after work to gawk at the Pacific and upped my intellectual game by reading Leo Steinberg essays and Marcel Proust. By the end of the summer I had resolved to finish my last year of college at UCSD. I was in the thrall of my peers, some of whom were, in turn, in the thrall of our protagonist.

To be honest, I'm not sure I was ever "officially" enrolled in Manny Farber's lecture class in the fall/winter quarter of 1988. (I was a bit of an academic grifter with a fairly attenuated relationship to university protocols such as attendance and registering.) The buzz around my circle of friends about how it was going to be Manny's last class, combined with the fact that my boyfriend and roommates were TAs for the course, conspired to place me in the auditorium on any given evening slack-jawed, with my mind reeling, as I watched Jean-Luc Godard's *Les carabiniers* (1963) (that scene with those two dopey cops and all of their postcards), and Preston Sturges's slapstick Hollywood picture *The Palm Beach Story* (1942) (with Claudette Colbert appearing thriftily glamorous in men's pajamas), and Rainer Werner Fassbinder's *Katzelmacher* (1969) (with the totally beguiling Hanna Schygulla dancing in the shortest miniskirt ever). So far so good, but he really got me to sit up straight in my seat during his screening of Martin Scorsese's *Mean Streets* (1973). He showed the opening scene several times—once straight through, once without sound, and once while he spoke (or something like that, it's unclear to me how much of my memory I can trust). When Farber talked, he talked about how Robert De Niro moved like a dancer, and he asked us to watch carefully as De Niro moved his body through the streets, to see how the character seemed to inhabit his physical frame, how a low hum of criminality was embodied in those lilting footsteps—the compactness of his hips over his knees—all this, just before he put a cherry bomb in a mailbox on a street corner in downtown New York and scampered away, his entire body looking like a shit-eating grin. Even as the early-1970s palette of the film made me long for home, I knew I would never watch a movie in the same way again. Farber had destroyed my suspension of disbelief, replacing it with a keen attention to detail—indeed, he taught me in that instant to let myself be distracted by the minutiae that were operating on a different level from the master plot. It was a total inversion of everything I had understood about interpretation up until that moment.

And then: that was that. He retired. I went on to take more classes, watch more films, meet more artists, and write my first pieces of "criticism" for the local San Diego arts paper. The path that led me to the life I lead today—in which my work as a curator occupies the central axis of my identity—had unfurled, and I was on it, although I didn't know it at the time. Certainly, when I sat in Manny's lecture hall, I had no inkling of what a curator even did, this being the time before the profession had achieved its bizarre cult status. And my current understanding of its operations, demanding a constant oscillation between the big picture and the details—the big picture being the institution of the museum and its central role in the creation of value, the formation of canons, and the presentation of private artistic acts for public experience; the details involving the development of intimacies with both objects and their makers, the why and how of choosing specific objects, the why and how of installing them, and what each act of adjacency in an installation might connote—was still a decade away.

During those heady college days, I, like so many others, developed a crush on the twentieth century's call for art to broker an arrangement with life. My cohort and I existed in the slipstream of the teachings by those who had lived through and believed in the revolutionary potential of 1968. We combined that with the punk and hip-hop leanings of our own generation. And I, like so many others, was more than happy to reject high culture for its own sake, more than happy to reject contemplation as the primary form of viewership, connoisseurship as the framing device for taste. Feminism blossomed in me and, in the closing years of the 1980s, having not yet learned the ills of essentialism, I found myself interested in the labor, thoughts, practices, ideas, and stories of the half of the world's population that had been systematically overlooked and undervalued. In other words, I was interested in women. This meant I was interested in décor and the decorative and decorum, and, by extension, housework, interior decorating, and style. I was compelled to reclaim underrecognized women artists. I was turned on by the proposition that the canon could be refashioned to make their concerns central rather than peripheral. Then I learned that there was no center or periphery. That's when things started to get really interesting.

Everyone (by which I mean the art students hanging around UCSD's original Mandeville studios building) knew that Manny and Patricia were painters, and the gossip about them—their love, her fabled garden, and their magical life—hung in the air. It would be decades before I looked at their work seriously, even as my interest in the everyday grew more acute and poignant over time. Back then, I couldn't have seen their work for what it was: I was too much in the grips of what I thought were the (exclusively) serious concerns of critical theory. Now, I find my attraction to the everyday to be a form of defense against what I perceive to be the near total eclipse of criticism by the market values of art as an asset class, the demand for museums to produce blockbuster shows, and the apotheosis of profit as the primary marker of cultural value that I see embodied in the frictionless finish fetish of Jeff Koons, the narcissistic grandiosity of Damien Hirst, or the production of charm without affect by Takashi Murakami. Harsh judgments for sure, and I don't mean to suggest that I don't find any of those artists interesting—it's just that the ideas and affects that their works promulgate are commensurate with the neoliberal values of "pure" market exchange, hedge funds, and financial instruments. I find myself longing for the days when art and culture were considered spaces where the human characteristics of curiosity, empathy, and critique held stronger sway. I think that my belated interest in Farber's and Patterson's work means that I need their version of the everyday now. I need to think about what people actually do with their time, how they come together at table, how we create spaces for fellowship and exchange that are not measured by metrics borrowed from the for-profit world. Perhaps this is why I am I brought to my knees by Moyra Davey's photographs of empty booze bottles on a still-dirty kitchen counter. Maybe this is why the well-ordered and closely observed interiors of Becky Suss's paintings—with their flat planes of pastel colors and their well-placed vases and pillows—produce such strong feelings of kinship in me.

Still life, nature morte, trompe l'oeil, vanitas . . . these kinds of images are as old as representation itself. The myths of Zeuxis established the game of representation to be one of illusion and the everyday: grapes painted with such tenderness that they fool the birds. It appears as if the twentieth century's profound questioning of art—what it is, what it can be, what it is good for, what it does—has not yet produced any scorched earth around the filiation we have for still lifes' uncanny ability to represent the world as it exists, complete with its ever-transitory dailiness and its messy conditions. It turns out the official culture of monuments to white men on horseback who won wars (or perversely, in the context of the United States, statues of those who lost a war) placed in the public square feels as antiquated as having a man deliver milk to the house each morning. (It's a distant memory: cold air, the texture of the bottles' thick glass rims, the sound the empty bottles made in their metal carrier when it was placed on the rough concrete of the stoop.) Nevertheless, Wolfgang Tillmans's still life photographs of food remnants eaten out of hand persist in capturing my imagination. Part of this epochal attraction must surely be the eternal return of the same, the *plus ça change* quality of it all: no matter how much we love our iPhones, we all must eat, and eating, being at table, with all its implied necessity and conviviality, remains a constant—a truth, even. (And yet [the cranky feminist in me resents having to feel so cranky], the recent foodie revolution hasn't produced a society committed to the migrant workers who pick our food. Just as the new love of craft in the art world has yet to produce a canon of anonymous practitioners, and the intimacy between the art world and gentrification [i.e., the creation of increasing amounts of wealth held in the name of real estate] has not enabled much dignity to be bestowed upon the folks—primarily brown, predominantly women—who keep all those new homes clean. I digress.)

In 1978 Patricia Patterson wrote an essay for *Heresies*,[1] a journal born of feminism's dramatic eruption in the art world. In it she writes gently of the everyday aesthetic practices of women in Ireland's Aran Islands, which Patterson had visited and which had a transformative effect on her. She wondered if perhaps the women themselves did not conceive of their domestic labors of arranging and repairing and knitting as "aesthetic acts." But she noted them duly nonetheless. And then she tried to paint them: shallow domestic interiors where women spoke to one another of the things that structured their lives. In her essay, she takes note of the ceramic roosters that dotted the windowsills of Aran. Reading it I recalled the quixotic collection of ceramic roosters that punctuated the margins of Patterson and Farber's home in Leucadia. "She must have brought them back with her from her trips," I thought, remembering how all of the window sashes and jambs in their home were painted bright, flat shades of lemon yellow, robin's-egg blue, or a milky verdant green, a palette that lives on in the furniture and sculptures of Roy McMakin, a student of Manny and Patricia's at UCSD.

Their house began its life as a modest beach bungalow, probably no larger than seven hundred square feet, with a beautiful row of four-over-four paned windows that lined the bedroom. When Patterson realized Manny would lose his studio upon retiring from USCD, she set about redesigning their home. "I got busy," she said. She added two new wings, making it into a U-shaped structure, each addition acting as a studio: one for Manny and one for her. Both studios connected to the original house, and both opened out onto the garden via the French doors so typical of the indoor-outdoor architecture of Southern California. The garden was, and remains, a gentleman's agreement between the planned and neglected, filled with old-growth roses that climb to the roof, pomegranate trees, artichokes allowed to go to flower along with their sibling thistles, apple and lemon trees, parsley and mint, bougainvillea, rosemary, a fig tree, and a host of flowering plants that, as an Easterner, I sheepishly still don't know the names of.

During one of my visits Patricia described how Manny worked. She started at the beginning, when they were living in a loft in New York in the 1960s. Farber painted large abstract paintings on brown craft paper that he layered with wet paint and muslin. He would wake up in the middle of the night to go to the studio to turn them so they would dry properly. After he removed the muslin he used a chalk-encrusted thread to snap drawn lines on their mottled and variegated surfaces. All of this took place on the floor. Sometime in the mid- to late 1970s he began making modest square-format oil paintings on paper; images of stationery supplies and candy littered the pictorial field in an allover composition lifted directly from the Abstract Expressionism playbook. When it came to depicting the stuff of the world, he didn't take his cues from Pop; he preferred to miniaturize rather than to blow up. And despite the precise rendering of bottles of Wite-Out and Hershey's candy bars, the fetishism of the brand was not at play. What was at stake was the ubiquitous nature of the things themselves; their commonness and their appearance in the spaces of work. The labor of representation was very specifically acknowledged in the ground of the composition, for Farber painted, in an almost trompe l'oeil spirit, the craft paper etched by the lines of an X-Acto knife. The grounds of these small paintings counterintuitively offered the residue of a process via the logic of representation. The painted paper background acted as segue between abstraction and representation, and its resolute flatness was simultaneously offered as a plane of color and a surface troubled by the painted renditions of the cut lines. Some of these drawings bore titles that hooked them up to Farber's other great passion, the cinema, as in the painting of an open box of Red Hots and a broken Hershey bar titled *McCabe and Mrs. Miller* (1971). (Remember the scene where Warren Beatty chases the elusive Julie Christie in the winter forest, and how director Robert Altman perfectly captured the muffled quality of sound in the snow?)

These workplace tableaux ultimately gave way to large, slightly unwieldy, canvases that because of conventions we can call still lifes. Although, truth be told, they are anything but still. Rather, they appear to race and pulse with an energy that might be called cinematic, as they jog along establishing both the connections and breaks between the things they represent: handwritten notes, open books of Japanese shunga (erotic prints), flowers, gardening and painting tools, books, toy figurines, miniature train tracks, plates of fruit, notepads, rulers, strips of film leader, matches, razor blades, glasses of water, seed pods, detritus from the neighboring Batiquitos Lagoon, rebar, and vegetables from the nearby Chino Farm. Farber's still life paintings were also conceived horizontally. First he laid the canvas or board flat on a table and prepared a colored ground. These typically planar and rectangular grounds were frequently divided: black and white or contrasting colors, as in *Untitled Red/Green Diamond* (1988–89). This seemingly simple act of dividing the canvas into bands of color destabilizes both the visual and conceptual aspects of the ground as fundamental to the figure-ground dyad so essential to representational painting. Upon this "compromised" ground, Farber placed the actual objects of his everyday life—plates of half-eaten food, scrawled notes, open books—before climbing a ladder to look down at the composition forming before him. Then, with a pencil taped to a long piece of rebar, he proceeded to trace the outlines of the forms. He would remove and replace objects at will, and would commence new traces. Patricia would bring flowers from the garden into Manny's studio, and he would say, "Put them there," gesturing with the rebar to where he wanted them to go. It was, she recalled, their way of communicating without interrupting the work of the day. What she didn't say was that they were gifts, tokens of affection, love letters.

TERMITE ART

In 1962 *Film Culture* published Farber's now-legendary essay "White Elephant Art vs. Termite Art."[2] A mere nine years later the article was included in an anthology of Farber's writings titled *Negative Space*. The essay is a screed against the idea of the masterpiece, a diatribe against monumentality, a manifesto against the narcissism of the artistic ego, replete with lines such as: "The painting, sculpture, assemblage becomes a yawning production of overripe technique shrieking with preciosity, fame, ambition; far inside are tiny pillows holding up the artist's signature, now turned into mannerism by the padding, lechery, faking required to combine today's esthetics with the components of traditional Great Art."[3] Let's keep going: "The three sins of white elephant art (1) frame the action with an all-over pattern, (2) install every event, character, situation in a frieze of continuities, and (3) treat every inch of the screen and film as a potential area for prizeworthy creativity."[4] Both quotes refer as much to the sins of Hollywood cinema as they do to New York School painting. Farber's ire regarding a lack of commitment to detail ("frame the action with an all-over pattern"), his disdain for an evinced preference for the smooth and sinuous rather than the tactile and the disjointed ("a frieze of continuities"), and his deep suspicion of the tyranny of the first person pronoun ("prizeworthy creativity") all speak to an on-time arrival of Farber and what would become the dominant hallmarks of postmodernism, particularly the postmodernism of the Deleuzean strain—a rhizomatic form of thinking, in which horizontality trumps verticality, where all ideas are capable of hooking up with other ideas, and where the "I" is merely a transitory position occupied provisionally and awkwardly. For French philosopher Gilles Deleuze (and Farber), desire did not come in the form of an aching absence (to be framed, enacted, and disguised by fame in an all over composition) but instead came from the contingency of ideas and bodies grasping and releasing one another. But I've rushed ahead a bit here, because the previous

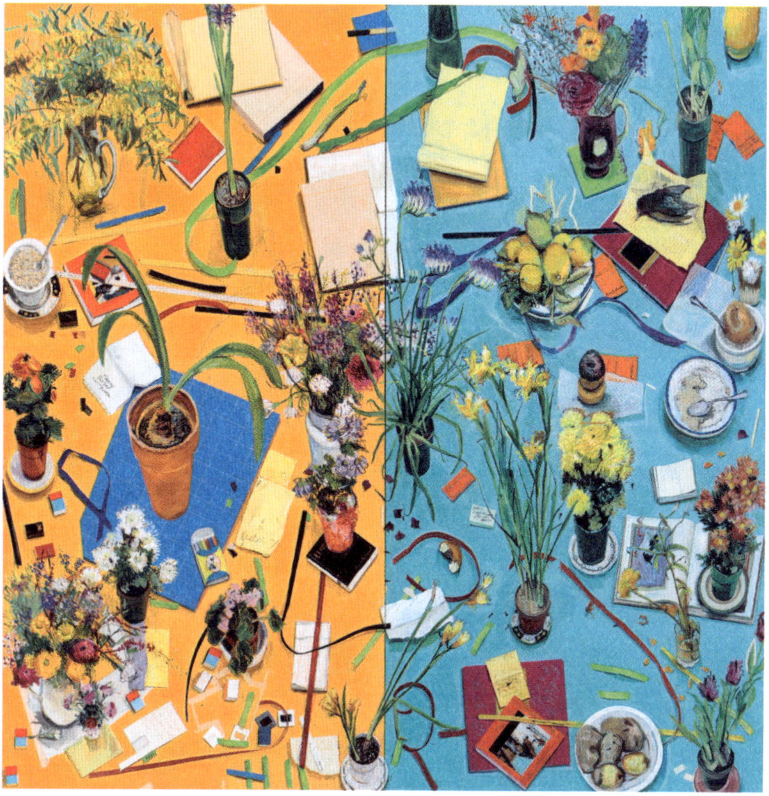

Manny Farber, *Domestic Movies*, 1985, oil on board, 96 x 96 in. (243.8 x 243.8 cm)

sentence is a better description of a Manny Farber still life painting than it is of his termite essay.

I think it's fair to say that in 1962 Farber was struggling to articulate and validate his neologistic phrase "termite art." Castigating white elephant art was the much more effortless task. Statements of negation are easy; affirmation—really and truly getting at why something is good (or why one values it or finds it beautiful)—is a much harder proposition. And termite art, even in the hands of a writer as tenacious and innovative as Farber, was no exception. He spends most of his time dissecting the performances of John Wayne to get at the small gestures and details that constitute the "termite tendency." He's at his most explicit when he says that termitism "feels its way through walls of particularization, with no sign that the artist has any object in mind other than eating away the immediate boundaries of his art, and turning those boundaries into conditions of the next achievement."[5] This commitment to process, to the artist's own working-through of their medium was not, however, the only characteristic of "termite art." Lest the whole project devolve into a kind of studio navel-gazing, Farber clarifies in his introduction to the 1971 anthology: "The important trait of termite-fungus-centipede art is an ambulatory creation which is an act *both of observing and being in the world*, a journeying in which the artist seems to be ingesting both the material of his art and the outside world through horizontal coverage."[6]

In my copy of *Negative Space* the sentence above is heavily underlined; it's what allows me to hang on. Traditional representation seems to rely on the idea that the artist is somehow separate from the space of the world, sitting at her easel, peering out at her subject. For me, this omnipotent fantasy of objectivity sits at the core of Western civilization, and is one of the roots of its ills. Farber calls instead for an artist who can navigate the complexities of being in the scene and describing the scene, who can occupy an ethical position of enormous nuance. No pretending objectivity, no pretense toward a state of pure being, but instead a situation in which observation and action, if not exactly simultaneous ("ingesting"), are equally valued ("horizontal coverage"). Farber would do this in his criticism by breaking with standard grammar, meaning that he never let the form of representation obscure the act of thinking—with all its ellipses, doubling back, stammers, and revisions. The filmmaker Kahlil Joseph (himself deeply gifted at the filmic capturing of the details he calls "black gesture") once told me that the best part of reading a piece of criticism by Manny is that you get to the end of the essay and wonder, "Did he like the movie?" Because the liking, of course, isn't the point. The liking or disliking is the intrusion of the hyper-personal ego into the situation of trying to be with and observe the film. Farber's great friend, the filmmaker J-P Gorin, understood the termite part of Farber's essay as a repudiation of the omnipotent "I": "The advantage of bringing the Farber quote into the debate is that it takes the I out of the equation and aggressively replaces it with the instinctual energy of a bug that prompts generally more a call to the nearest exterminator than the celebration of an aesthetic."[7]

J-P Gorin: former collaborator of Jean-Luc Godard, shows up in California, meets Farber, and falls for him hard. The feeling is mutual and Farber gets Gorin a teaching position at UCSD, where Gorin goes on to make a trilogy of essay films dedicated to mapping the bizarre suburbia that is Southern California. The second film in the trilogy *Routine Pleasures* (1986) is half about Manny and half about a group of model-train enthusiasts and their storefront hobby space in the beach town of Del Mar. It's a buddy movie about termite art where most of the action comes via Gorin's befuddled, bemused, and bewildered voice-over. Never explaining nor teaching, the film is essayistic in its observation of the intensity with which a group of grown men attempts to enact rituals designed to impose order on the entropic state of things in their Lilliputian world. Their efforts are as poignant and humorous as Gorin's attempts at dissecting the American psyche. The film's sculptural analogue is Fischli and Weiss's masterpiece in miniature, *Suddenly This Overview* (1981–2012), a suite of tabletop unfired clay sculptures that typologizes the foibles and successes of Western man, making no discernible distinction between the two. The failure of the enterprise is built into the work, much like the futile endeavor of trying to exterminate the termites in Southern California that gnaw away at single-story houses without foundations while the exterminators who tent those very same houses watch as they fly through the open French doors the day after the tent is removed.

Gorin's first film in the trilogy, *Poto and Cabengo* (1980), was the stuff of legend during my senior year at UCSD. The film followed the local development of a pair of twin sisters who linguists believed had created their own language. To hear Gorin recount the origin of the project is to get a glimpse into the film's ultimate game plan:

> I got hold of the event through the press. It was the middle of the summer and news was sparse. The Loch Ness monster had been nowhere in sight that year, and I suspect the journalists felt the twins would be a good substitute. They built up a case, which reeked of Wild Child mystique. The very day I saw the first article on the twins, Eckart Stein from ZDF was passing through town and I sold him the idea of a film. I lied through my teeth, told him that I had seen the twins, seen the therapists who took care of them at Children's Hospital, secured the rights to the story. I assured Stein that they spoke a "private language." He agreed to do the film. But when I saw the twins for the first time I immediately realized that the story as the press—and by then, myself—had cast it was not there. There was no private language and never had been. All along the twins had spoken a Creolized language, some densely unintelligible American/English, a patchwork of southern lingo spoken by their father and of the deformations imposed on the English language by their German-born mother.[8]

How to make a film about a nonevent? How to make a film about a failure of the discourse of discovery and objectivity so crucial to the narratives of science? How to make an anthropological film that neither elevated nor pathologized its subjects? How to make a film about a pair of twin girls communicating in secret that is also a film about the displacement of a French artist in the dry, overdeveloped canyons of San Diego County? The film was mythical amongst us students because its very existence was proof of a category we might call "interesting failures," proof that there was a virtue inherent in chipping away at a project, doing the work, proceeding against the obstacles. There was a virtue in not knowing what you were doing. The unintelligibility of *Poto and Cabengo* recalled every punk show you'd ever seen: a bunch of guys who barely knew how to play their instruments, shouting the words to a song you didn't understand, and, if you were a girl, trying to make sure you didn't get hurt in the pit. The scene I remember most vividly is one in which Gorin is preparing a meal for the twins in his kitchen. While slicing a cucumber, he holds a thin celadon sliver up to the light and says to the girls, "Look, isn't that beautiful?"

STILL LIFE

While I was cutting my teeth on the history of cinema according to Farber, and its current vicissitudes according to Gorin, I was not capable of looking at, much less "getting," Farber's paintings. Nor was I particularly adept at reading Farber's criticism. Like so many of my generation, I was finding my way, through the byways of Continental theory, to feminism: feminism as a means to critique patriarchy, and by extension the very concept of the West; feminism as a way to rethink the primacy of gender as a tool to structure the world; feminism as a way to query power, its effects, and one's relationship to it. The idiosyncratic struggles of a couple of white dudes in Southern California wasn't exactly where I was at. So the irony of finding myself, now a woman of a certain age, obsessed with both the termite essay and Farber's still life paintings, to the point of thinking they might be an interesting set of coordinates around which to build an exhibition, is not lost on me. When I first started explaining the project to people, almost every encounter devolved into playful banter dominated by the question "Is (fill-in-the-blank) a termite artist?" Surely this game had losing as its only outcome. Clearly the task of the exhibition was not to produce a category, although of course I was narcissistically interested in valorizing my curatorial choices. The problem was that the damn essay doesn't make a strong enough case for what termitism is, and it could only partially describe what termitism looked like in action. Termite art was like pornography: you knew it when you saw it. I felt my enterprise to be as flawed as Gorin's pursuit in *Poto and Cabengo*. People looked at me blankly and I would just mumble, defeated, "The show is basically about still life," which mollified most of my interlocutors and left me in a pit of self-doubt. Until, that is, I found myself sitting in Gorin's San Diego apartment, surrounded by his Jurassic-era DVD library (my laptop doesn't even have a DVD/CD drive). The apartment had one of those classic pink-and-black-tiled bathrooms from the 1940s, a Proustian madeleine for anyone who has ever lived in Southern California. It also appeared to be dangerously close to the airport. Even though I grew up in the shadow of both LaGuardia and JFK, I flinched with every takeoff and landing. Gorin's face remained implacable, reminding me of a phenomenon I remembered from my childhood, when my parents' friends from out of town would be surprised by the cacophony above us that no one in my neighborhood even heard.

"It's the 'versus,'" he said. Of course! The essay is structurally flawed by a false antinomy, an either/or scenario doomed to generate opinions rather than dialogue. Anyway, who wants to have an argument that only has two sides? The paintings, on the other hand, operated with the logic of "and, and, and. . . ." The paintings were the enactment of termite art twenty years after the idea had first occurred to him. Farber had somewhat famously given up writing in the late 1970s. His last essay, cowritten with Patterson in 1977, "Kitchen without Kitsch," was on Chantal Akerman's *Jeanne Dielman, 23 quai du Commerce, 1080 Bruxelles* (1975), perhaps the most perfect film ever made. Considered by many to be a feminist masterpiece (an oxymoronic phrase if there ever was one), *Jeanne Dielman* was the ultimate suturing of art and life, one that was shot with structuralist rigor by director of photography Babette Mangolte. The impeccable and implacable Delphine Seyrig plays a housewife who turns tricks in the afternoon for a living. But the tricks play second fiddle to the real labor of housework: cleaning the bath, making the bed, shopping for dinner, making a meat loaf—all represented with quiet dignity, in near real time. In *Jeanne Dielman* the everyday is about repetition and duration. Farber and Patterson described it as a "still life film"—a genre painting by a '70s Chardin (to quote Babette Mangolte: "a Forties story shot by a Seventies camera").[9] Farber said that he abandoned writing so he could devote himself entirely to painting. "The writing was very difficult," Patterson told me while we sat together in weathered leather club chairs in Farber's former studio. "The paintings don't seem exactly easy," I thought, knowing that wasn't the point.

What was clear was that, in Farber's hands, painting's complexity—its ability to compress and condense meanings, its capacity to traffic in aporias—simultaneously competing realities—and its adeptness at registering its process as part and parcel of its final product—rendered it an essayistic medium without the inherent limitations of writing as such. Writing has no choice but to be consumed in a linear fashion: the mere incident of one word having to follow another, all of which must, in turn, cohere into sentences with proper syntax that are further obliged to coalesce into paragraphs with topic sentences, obliged to have a beginning, a middle, and an end. From left to right, we read one word after another, encountering one idea after another; thus it is difficult not to presume that one idea comes before another, to put them in an order, to imagine the cause and effect implicit in such an ordering, to start the unconscious production of hierarchies for which the human mind has such a profound facility. Unlike writing, painting has the gift of gestalt: an immediate apprehension of a situation composed of both a whole and its parts, or parts that exceed the whole, or a whole comprised of parts both present and absent. This is the force of visual information and intelligence. This is what pictures do before, during, and after our attempts to discuss what it is that we see when we look at them.

Farber was one of the first critics to take this capacity of painting and use it as a hermeneutic for how to look at film. This is why the details of an actor's performance, or the choice of chairs and tables on a set, or the way the camera is moving, or the way light is imagined are so crucial in Farber's criticism. He is trying to look at a film "all at once," rather than allowing himself to be sidelined by linear narrative. Each shot is a composition. Each edit offers a new one. Farber's criticism was a way of articulating the "and, and, and" of all the particularities that give the film its totality, and Farber's willful breaking of language was his way of forestalling the film's linearity for as long as possible. One of the best descriptions of the sympathetic relationship between Farber's writing and his picture making comes from Kevin Parker, who wrote: "Synecdoche expands space by enabling a small part to stand for the whole; asynedeton, on the other hand, cuts space back. It is the suppression of linking words, conjunctions, adverbs, or even conventional punctuation between sentences. . . . In Farber's painting these two rhetorical moves are simultaneously at work anywhere you look."[10] And just as Farber's criticism used painting as a lens to look at film, his paintings took up the logic of the essay as a form.

I first encountered the writer Elizabeth Hardwick in a text by Gorin written to accompany a selection of films in the termite tendency. A quick Google search established her provenance: she was a pedigreed writer, cofounder of *The New York Review of Books*, and tumultuously married to poet Robert Lowell. Her *New York Times* obituary reads like a screenplay about a New York intellectual whose life was undeniably caught in the undertow of feminism, but who swam parallel to the shore so steadily that she may not have admitted it. The last two paragraphs read:

> In a 1984 interview in *The Paris Review*, the writer Darryl Pinckney asked her about her feelings about getting older. "You can always ask," Ms. Hardwick responded. "It's only value is that it spares you the opposite, not growing older. People do cling to consciousness, and under the most dreadful circumstances. It shows you that it is all we have, doesn't it? Waking up, the first and the last privilege, waking up once more."
>
> When Mr. Pinckney asked her, "Do you think it is more painful for women than for men?" she replied: "More about women and men? About something so burdensome it doesn't seem valuable to make distinctions. Oh, the dear grave. I like what Gottfried Benn wrote, something like, 'May I die in the spring when the ground is soft and easy to plough.'"[11]

Tracking down Gorin's citation and reading Hardwick's obituary made me think of Moyra Davey's writings and her video essays, treasure maps composed of footnotes. Whenever I think of Moyra, I imagine her notebooks filled with other people's words. Davey was in the MFA program at USCD, and was one of the TAs for Manny's famous last class. She didn't start making her own video essays until much later, when her son was old enough to fend for himself, and after a long period working as an editor for a small publisher. Clearly, she had been influenced by Gorin's essay films,

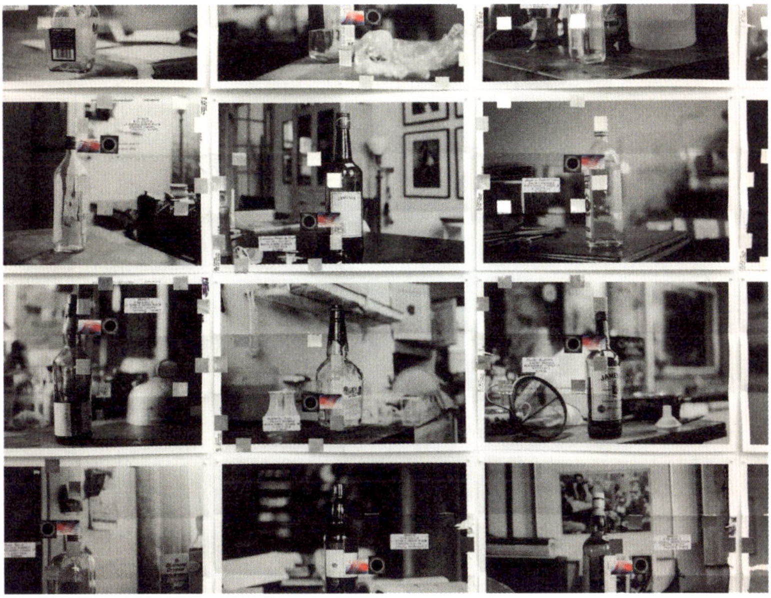

Moyra Davey, *Empties* (detail), 2017, C-print, tape, postage, ink,
56 parts: 12 x 18 in. (30.5 x 45.7 cm) each, overall dimensions variable

but in the best way, long after her exposure to them, so that the influence is more of a faded trace than a strongly drawn line.

For Hardwick, the "aggressiveness of the essay is the assumption of the authority to speak in one's own voice," and her essays "are addressed to a public in which some degree of equity exists between the writer and the reader."[12] I think Farber was ambivalent and suspicious of the authority of the first-person pronoun, and reading Hardwick's account of the essay helped me understand why Farber had tacked toward the seemingly timeless terrain of still life and landscape—genres whose purchase on the everyday remain unrivaled. Who hasn't made an ersatz still life arrangement? And everyone lives in a landscape. By this I mean to suggest that it is not only the "accessibility" of the imagery as such that matters. It is also the structural connections of that kind of imagery to people's lived daily lives that takes on a special role in Farber's slightly ham-fisted American populist hands. And yet for Farber, ever the contrarian, populism only went so far, for any viewer of a Farber painting knows that his work assumes your familiarity with the flowers of late Manet, the apples of Cézanne, the spatial flights of fancy of early Picasso, single-point perspective, the dragon of the conventional composition, and its St. George, the expansive fields of Abstract Expressionism. To look at a Farber painting is to be aware of late modernism's fetish for flatness and anti-illusionism: it is to recognize Ellsworth

Kelly's recuperation of color, to see the ukiyo-e print's confirmation of the influence of Japan, and to see in Farber's use of stencils a nod to Jasper Johns. It is, in other words, to see a field littered with objects and images laden with referential meaning. Their organization, however, breaks from any modernist pretense to order. The words "centrifugal" and "meandering" appear again and again in the writing about Farber's pictures. Jonathan Crary keenly observes the "willfully unreconciled spatial systems at work."[13]

As it did for countless numbers of still life painters before him, the terrain of the everyday, as mapped by Farber, exists on a tabletop. But whereas previous painters used the tabletop as a site of relative stability (discounting the history of perilously placed knives that rest at the threshold of gravity's intervention), Farber's pictures start out on the horizontal plane of the table and then tilt violently, elastically, euphorically to embrace the verticality of the wall. The extreme literalness of Farber's move from horizontal making to vertical presentation always summons, for me, the work of that other great gymnast of the everyday, Robert Rauschenberg. Farber's practice evokes Leo Steinberg's still-trenchant essay from 1972, "Other Criteria," in which the deeply insightful critic comes to terms with the radical implications of Rauschenberg's work by coining the term "flatbed picture plane." For Steinberg, the work of art made on the tabletop was produced in the space of work—it was about the language of the printing press, kitchen counters, and the draftsman's table. Steinberg saw this as a profound shift in worldview: from a painting that imagined itself as a window offering a view out onto the world, to an artwork that behaved as if it was at work in the world. The change in pictorial orientation was analogous to a larger societal shift in the wake of World War II from the modern to the postmodern, from a belief in rational order to a belief in entropy, from art as illusion to the art of the actual, from the idealized to the pedestrian. Farber's work is sensitive to these arguments, and the deliberate heterogeneity of the objects in his paintings, his confounding of the spatial relations between individual details, and his proliferation of ways in and out of the picture, means that his paintings enact the postmodern sensibility that revels in "the hopelessness of all systems of organization, of storage, of categorizing."[14]

One of the defining features of the postmodern era is that knowledge became more horizontal and networked, and less vertical and hierarchical. We might even say that Farber, Steinberg, and Rauschenberg were all at work on this considerably profound paradigm shift. Rather than the old Enlightenment conception of knowledge as functioning like a tree, with its central trunk and many branches, and its intense verticality ever lifting and craning up toward the sun, Deleuze offered us the metaphor of the rhizome, an image of knowledge, culture, and human organization that escaped categorization, that ran horizontally along the ground, splitting into networks that break off from one another like errant rivulets, only to find a confluence with ideas that had germinated elsewhere. Farber's pictures visually play out the rhizomatic impulse and they behave like essays as described by Hardwick, in which an "essay is nothing less than the reflection of all there is: art, personal experience, places, literature, portraiture, politics, science, music, education—and just thought itself in orbit."[15]

This is where Farber's canvases move the needle for me. His still life paintings avoid the genre's historical pitfalls: no *vanitas* moralizing, no staging of objects as a form of psychological displacement. The everyday objects strewn about Farber's canvases are not placed there in a pretense at formal exploration. To see him as updating Cézanne's play with apples—if what you see in Cézanne's apples is the use of an everyday, negligible thing, so that the artist could better concentrate on the formal and spatial problems of painting as such—is to miss the point of Farber's termitism. Farber wasn't trying to reinvent the language of painting, because he didn't seem to treat it as a grandiose act. (In *Routine Pleasures*, Gorin quotes him as saying, "Life isn't too big a deal and shouldn't be painted as such.") He painted Deleuzean pictures from the position of the carpenter he had once been. He painted them to figure out how to make a picture not of how the world looked but of how it functioned. In this regard, he may have shared the poet Charles Olson's understanding of metaphor: "Metaphor is not what a thing is like: it's how it behaves."[16] In Farber's termite essay it becomes clear that the details of an actor's performance, or the particularities of the mise-en-scène, are what make the enterprise real for him; they are what grounds it and bestows upon it legitimacy. It's not the devil but reality that lives in the details. And without the details all you have is a white elephant story. This is why one of my favorite scenes in Kahlil Joseph's *Fly Paper* (2017) is one in which a young woman sits with a child underneath an open window. Their physical intimacy leads us to believe they are mother and son, and as they sit, close and still, they watch, with evident pleasure, a diaphanous curtain blow in the breeze. The vignette is an offering of time slowed, time suspended, of air defying gravity ever so provisionally. It's why I find Dike Blair's gouache of an empty chair in an airport so devastating: the relief of it, to know that one's loneliness has already been accounted for. It's why seeing myself reflected in extreme miniature in the chrome of Josiah McElheny's *An End to Modernity* (2005) always feels so pleasurable; finally, I am depicted at a scale that feels appropriate to my place in the multiverse.

THE EVERYDAY

I have long wondered exactly what it is we're talking about when we talk about the everyday. Since I am not interested in masterpieces—to the point of being allergic—or war, or a theory of everything, or people who insist upon their rightness, I tend to stick pretty close to the quotidian. But still, just where and what is that? Is it the sound of mourning doves at dawn? The laundry? The dust under the bed? The picked-at cuticle? Is it how you arrange your desk, or how you like your breakfast? Is it the photographs we

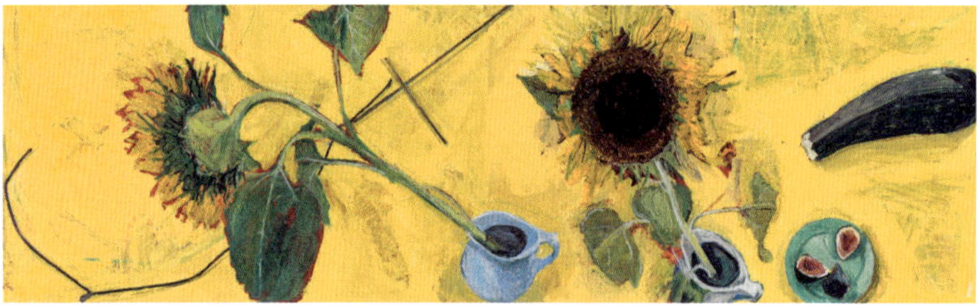

Manny Farber, *About Face*, 1990, oil on board, 21 x 72 in. (53.3 x 182.9 cm)

remember so well we think they are our memories? Is it the microaggressions of everyday racism? The casual sexism of the office? Is it the way we idly scroll past the parts of the newspaper that don't speak to us, as in that staggering scene in *Jeanne Dielman* where Delphine Seyrig spreads the newspaper out on the immaculate dining room table and turns page after page but reads nothing? Is it the contents of the junk drawer? Is it the oil stains in the driveway? Is it the water bill? In the words of Georges Perec, "It matters little to me that these questions should be fragmentary, barely indicative of a method, at most of a project. It matters a lot to me that they should seem trivial and futile: that's exactly what makes them just as essential, if not more so, as all the other questions by which we've tried in vain to lay hold on our truth."[17]

The everyday implies an endlessly horizontal proliferation of concerns, each with its own specific tonality, each with its own tributaries. To be truly curious about the water bill is to open out onto the systems of the state and its putative concern for the common good of its citizens; it is to encounter the phenomenon of money, power, and the discourse of resources. It is to attend to the monthly time of the billing cycle, and the daily time of the drip irrigation system. It could become a conversation on the relative merits and pleasures of showers and baths, the effectiveness of dishwashers, and the women's work that is never done. It is a way of thinking about all the flowers in Farber's paintings. The ones laid flat on the canvas. The vegetables with dirt still attached to their roots. It is to speak of the vases filled with flowers arranged by Patricia. It is to understand the repeated nature of the activity of making. It is to see it as an endless performance: the sowing and weeding, the selecting and arranging, the trimming-down and the discarding, the washing of slime out of the vase, the starting over again. It is to think in the realm of the verb, of the gerund and the infinitive. It is to be invested in the process of things. It is to know the pleasure of process resolving itself into a noun. It is to loosen one's dependence on one's proper name, a name, after all bestowed on you by others who did not yet know you at the time of their Adamic act.

And to paint that gift economy over and over? To double down on the sunflower in the blue vase: to paint it twice from two different angles in the same painting? To do this is to recall the opening line of Olson's poem "The Kingfishers": "What does not change / is the will to change."[18] Farber's pictures are about the timelessness of change, the beautiful banality of a lifelong love, the small pleasures of a job done well. To make work of this kind is to see that space and time are indeed inextricable; it is to know that everything happens one day at a time.

Lari Pittman: Décor, the Decorative, Decorum

Originally published in *Lari Pittman: Declaration of Independence*, ed. Connie Butler (Los Angeles: Hammer Museum; New York: DelMonico Books/Prestel, 2019), 59–75.

Décor (noun): 1. The furnishing and decoration of a room. 2. Stage setting. Emerges in France in the nineteenth century, first known usage 1897. Derived from the Latin decorare, *"to embellish" or "to decorate."*

Within the framework of American mid-century modern and the hegemony of Minimalism and Conceptual art, what could be more of a quandary, or present more of an aesthetic problem, than *décor*? What self-respecting member of the white art world's avant-garde could profess an interest in the display of interiority through objects, the creation of the domestic interior as a stage set for the self? *Décor*—both the concept and the set of objects it describes—remains a word too close to *objet d'art*; a notion too close to desire, to covetousness; a situation too easily exchangeable with the problem of commodity fetishism, that magical moment in Marx's *Capital* when he describes how an object takes on its own animistic life. *Décor,* a word whose French pronunciation speaks of a monied interior. After all, nobody says *tchotchke* with a French accent.

Instead of décor, the architects and interior designers of mid-twentieth century America offered floor-to-ceiling windows, glass planes upon which no pictures could be hung, complemented by white laminate surfaces devoid of clutter. Décor, when it was allowed, was stripped down to one or two well-placed craft or design objects. Certainly, these domestic interiors were also imagined as a stage set for the self—a self autonomously in charge of its desires and its surroundings, a self that needed no exteriorizing through things. If the mid-century modern interior offered an image of transparent self-sufficiency, then mid-century abstraction was its faithful companion. Minimalist painting and sculpture distilled the aesthetic impulse to a set of building blocks: color, texture, form. Anti-figurative, anti-expressive, anti-affect, works by artists such as Jo Baer and Donald Judd (to name but two, albeit two of my favorites) deployed stripped down materials such as unprimed canvas and brushed aluminum in order to underscore the cultural logic of repetition, particularly the kind generalized by industrial production and the seriality of the photograph, as a value unto itself. The kind of repetition that creates a self in need of a stage set—the habits and daily performance that structure our experience of the everyday—was, generally speaking, elided.

Such was the backdrop against which Lari Pittman attended CalArts in Los Angeles in the 1970s. Luckily for us, his arrival coincided with nascent feminist rustlings against such restrictive orthodoxies. To be fair, there were rebellious whispers even during the heyday of mid-century modernism. In Los Angeles, one could look close to home, to the counterintuitive example of Charles and Ray Eames, about whom, even though they were in the pantheon of mid-century designers, Robert Venturi could nevertheless claim that "they had reintroduced 'good old Victorian clutter' to interiors."[1] Photographs of the now-famous living room of their Pacific Palisades home show an interior arranged around the modular seriality of the bookshelves and the requisite plate-glass windows that create the ineffable interior-exterior mix of so much mid-century modern housing, but the interior is also chockablock with stuff: rugs, lamps, objets d'art. In short, it is a space defined by décor, a stage set for a new way of living. Pittman surely knew of this interior, just as he was well aware of another famous Los Angeles domestic space, *Womanhouse*, created in 1972 when students in the CalArts Feminist Art Program turned an abandoned house into a multimedia, interdisciplinary, site-specific art project. Like the Eames living room, *Womanhouse* eschewed any version of a Minimalist aesthetic drained of subjectivity. Instead, it delved deeply into the psychic effects of domestic space and domestic labor on the people who were considered responsible for it—women. One key implication of *Womanhouse* was its suggestion that domestic space helps to produce the effects of private and public, and it articulated, alongside much contemporaneous feminist scholarship, how space—both public and private—and the labor needed to maintain it were (and remain) profoundly gendered. In the context of feminist art writ large, and with *Womanhouse* specifically, décor could be understood as a way of navigating the myriad effects of gendered spaces, a low-level tactic for blurring the problems of public and private. Décor contributes a set of objects that help to create private space that is inevitably shot through with the problems of public space.

Lari Pittman understood this highly charged version of décor when he made, early in his artistic life, a group of deceptively simple painted gourds collectively titled *Memento Mori* (1985). Literally biomorphic, round and bulbous, phallic and breastlike, as fecund as ovaries and testicles, each gourd carries a word painted in an ornate white cursive script: *Charity, Compassion, Faith, Forgiveness, Hope, Kindness*. At first it seems these objects are trafficking in the resolutely sentimental. Indeed, given the words' somewhat New Testament connotations, one might expect to find them for sale at a holiday market. And yet they are guileless in their presentation of these essential human characteristics: after all, who can say they are above (or below) wanting such attributes? If décor is bound up with a presentation of self, then these objects offer that operation literally, using the linguistic as a form of condensed aesthetics where both the cursive script and the sentiment it conveys operate in the spirit of desire and self-presentation (and not, pointedly, as a Conceptualist form of anti-aesthetics).

These objects tend to take me down a bit of an interpretative rabbit hole. What would it mean to choose one over another, *Faith* over *Forgiveness*? Would you choose the virtue you think best describes your strengths or the one you are most deficient in? What would it mean to be given one as a gift—how would one rend the intention of the giver? Then again, what if one were to be given one or acquire one by chance; what if fate brought you *Faith* rather than *Kindness*? In all of these scenarios, the layers of overdetermined meaning seem almost too much to navigate, for each of these words is as individual (some folks are way more compassionate than others) as it is universal (we all possess some degree of each of these qualities).

And it's not only the words, it's the objects themselves. Frequently used as decorative objects, gourds have been dried and embellished for millennia. So, too, they have been used by nearly all cultures as containers for food and water, as burial vessels, and as musical instruments. What can one make of all of this affective signification? And I haven't even mentioned the intensity of the black paint that covers the gourds and their stems, or the delicate 1940s-esque landscapes that float in pictorial cells on their surfaces. Nor have I focused on the light-blue shading of the white lettering, a kind of script achingly familiar from hand-painted store windows found all over Los Angeles, a form of mark making brought to the United States by a generation of immigrants from Mexico. All this is a way of saying that these painted objects, these early works of Pittman's, have all of the complexity we associated with Art, yet their scale and their resolute objecthood lands them squarely in the realm of décor. These are objects destined for domestic space, for private space. They lack the "power" we traditionally expect from a museum-sanctioned object, and tellingly, none of them reside in museums as public objects.[2] I'm fairly certain their intimacy and domestic scale are why they were not repeated. Pittman was on his way to becoming an Artist; he was interested in the public space that art lays claim to. The painted gourds would ultimately cross the threshold from actual object into the field of representation. Images of gourds entered his paintings and would become one of his most abiding and recurrent motifs. Décor would ultimately be submitted into the picture plane so that it could perform the work of the decorative.

Decorative (adjective): 1. Serving to make something look more attractive. Synonyms: ornamental, embellishing, garnishing. 2. Relating to decoration; "a decorative artist."

I want to return to those two iconic Los Angeles domestic spaces: the living room of the Eameses' home in Pacific Palisades, with all of its tactile and material pleasures, and *Womanhouse*, with its funhouse displays of white feminine hysteria. Looking at the famous photo of the Eameses' living room, I feel like I can see the deep structure of a Pittman painting. One can begin with the underlying grid structure of the Eames interior—seen in the floor tiles, the bookshelves, and the panes of the floor-to-ceiling windows. Looking closely at *Ennobled and Needy* (1992), one can imagine the deeply sublimated grid that allows the cacophony of images that rests on the surface of the painting to click into place. Pittman works the edges of the canvas as sharply as the Eameses work the frame of the photograph, both of them using the great gift of Abstract Expressionism's abandonment of centered composition in favor of allover composition and the effect of infinity it produces. I hear the cheery *hello!* that adorns the vase in the upper right-hand corner of the painting as if it were an echo in the Eameses' convivial living space. And just as the Eameses' interior is filled with moments of décor, so too Pittman's printing gives us an object lesson in, well, objects: six pitchers, each meticulously decorated and embellished with a variety of precise marks that speak equally to craft's traditional love of adornment and industrialization's demand for efficiency. As each pitcher lets loose some of its contents in an orgiastic display of fluid release, vignettes of properly attired rooms, replete with vases, mirrors, chandeliers, wainscoting, and wallpaper, cling to the edge of the picture like barnacles. Public space is also accounted for; witness the three campaniles that embellish and articulate a well-protected green space. Lampposts stand at the ready for evening. Everywhere one looks, abstract, biomorphic, and crystalline shapes undergird this otherwise disparate array, generating a confounding question, literally unanswerable, as to whether this is a "representational" or "abstract" picture. The only answer to which is "neither," or "both," or "yes." In the center of the picture, just like the money shot in a porno, is an orifice. Its labial openings are vaginal, and yet this beguiling opening sits (or rises, or opens) at the bottom of a phallus: it's one of the funniest visual expressions of the logic of both/and (as opposed to either/or) I have ever seen, To compound the hilarity, this impossibly erotic stela is adorned as if a Christmas tree with what appear to be a bevy of decorated gourds. "Hello!" indeed.

The stylized orifice, this site of pleasure, self-regulation, and shame, recalls for me the funhouse quality of *Womanhouse*. Installed in a dilapidated mansion on Mariposa Street in a rundown part of Hollywood by artists involved in the Feminist Art Program led by Judy Chicago and Miriam Schapiro, *Womanhouse* explored the dark and bawdy underbelly of white American housewifery—suburban, constructing—and as such formed a carnivalesque send-up of all the platitudes and regressions that accompanied being a woman, a mother, and a wife during the period when Americans were debating the merits of the Equal Rights Amendment. The kitchen in *Womanhouse* was a space where the cooking of eggs had gone terribly awry, with sunny-side up ventures peppering every surface from floor to ceiling. The bathroom was filled with dirty tampons, and a nude female mannequin emerged from the linen closet in a scene that feels like a cross between a Vuillard painting and *The Stepford Wives*. The messy humor of the enterprise had a profound impact on a generation of artists—notable among them Pittman and his peers Mike Kelley and Paul McCarthy.[3] Despite their similar circumstances, however, Pittman would stake out entirely different terrain than Kelley and McCarthy. If their rebellion against the rigid social conventions of gender on the one hand and New York-style Minimalism on the other took place primarily through the psychic force of abjection, then Pittman would disable these social and aesthetic norms through the language of the decorative.

Within the advanced artistic circles Pittman found himself, nothing could have been more denigrated, more gendered, more seemingly unredeemable than the logic of the decorative. Long the subject of twentieth-century moralizing on the part of architects, designers, art schools (the Bauhaus), and art critics, the decorative was seen as a scourge: an impulse to be purged, an affair to be terminated. Perhaps no one summed up the anxiety and antipathy toward it better than Adolf Loos in his infamous "Ornament and Crime," in which he argued that "the evolution of culture is synonymous with the removal of ornamentation from objects of everyday use," and that "anyone who goes to . . . [Beethoven's] *Ninth* and then sits down to design a wallpaper pattern is either a fraud or a degenerate."[4] As ludicrous as these statements seem today, one can still summon with extraordinary ease a whole host of people in positions of cultural power who likely believe such things but lack the temerity to say so. After all, how many people do you know with a wallpapered living room?

Pittman was to have an entirely different relation to the decorative. Instead of seeing it as a historical problem to be outgrown, or its suppression as an affirmation of one's vanguardism, Pittman viewed the decorative as a strategy—historically deployed by women and gay people—to ward off the extraordinary violence of the world at large. In a cogent analysis of his own motivations, Pittman has said: "The way I navigate the world personally, which is also how I make my paintings, is to try and initiate a set of aesthetic decisions that can push my perception of violence as far from me as I can, so that philosophically, and as a citizen, I feel safe. I'm not interested in resolution or enlightenment: I won't go that far. Aesthetics for me are just a temporary but aggressive maneuver to push that wall of violence away from me. So in that sense, the making of the paintings comes out of the long historical tradition of making the home a safe place."[5]

Somewhere between the Eameses' careful and carefree orchestration of décor as a presentation of self and *Womanhouse*'s ludicrous elaboration

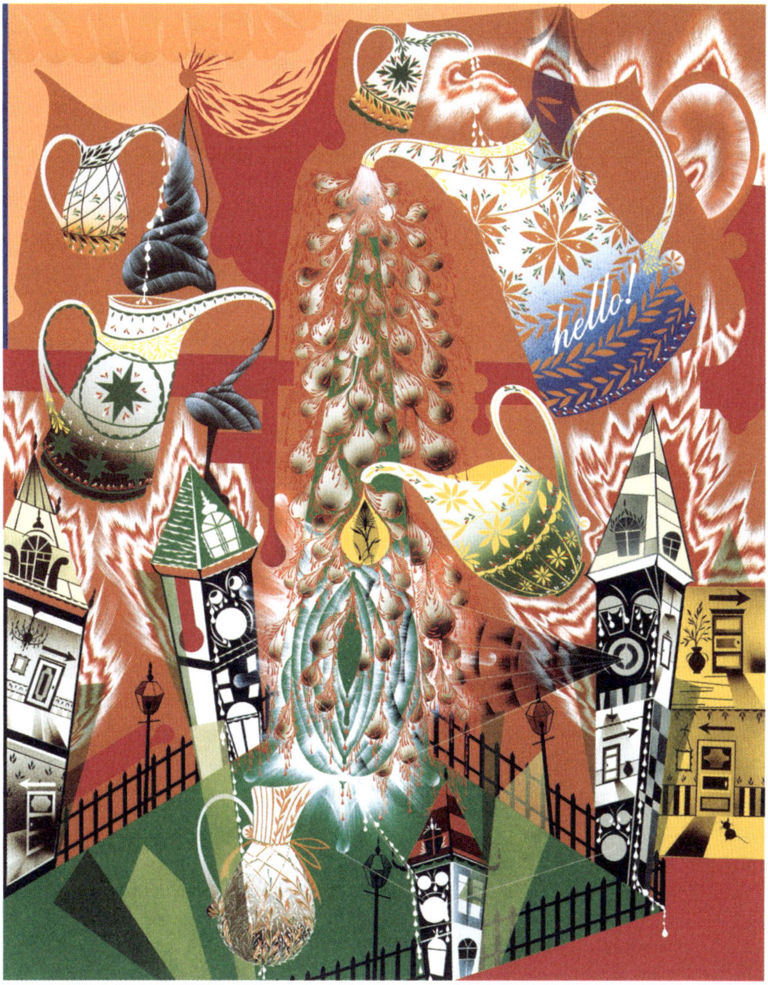

Lari Pittman, *Ennobled and Needy*, 1992, acrylic and enamel on panel, 82 x 66 in. (208.3 x 167.6 cm)

of society's repressive terrors within the home, we find Pittman's extraordinary canvases, replete with their glossary of decorative marks and decorative moves. Vessels and orifices converge, each equal to the other, each with a role to play in the constant negotiation of the violence that is constitutive of civilization itself. But as any viewer of a Pittman painting knows, these images neither resolve one to the violence of the world nor alleviate that violence via a tasteful composition. Instead, the canvases both display and deploy the aesthetic as a form of passionate and furious energy. In some ways they are homeopathic: they resist the violence of the world with the violence of aesthetics. I think this is what Pittman means when he says, "I'm not interested in brute force. I'm interested in the brute force of high tea."[6]

Decorum (noun): 1. Behavior in keeping with good taste and propriety (seemliness, decency, correctness, politeness, courtesy) 2. Etiquette (protocol, good form, custom, convention).

What could be more emblematic of decorum than high tea?[7] Every world has its own etiquette, established over time and enacted through a set of agreed-upon rules and regulations. The world of paintings is no exception. Pittman's work has been tendentious in relation to "good taste" and the proper conventions of how to put together a painting, inasmuch as his work does not follow the typical decorum of placing the needs of the viewer at the center of its compositional strategy. Indeed, it seems as if even Pittman's own needs are not addressed in the final composition. Listen as he breaks it down: "I think the work takes on a form of drag and there is drag that passes and drag that doesn't pass. Drag that doesn't pass is a provocation. I think when you stand in front of the paintings you're aware of an artificially accelerated experience, more than anything you know it has been constructed and assembled. . . . I'm outside of those aesthetics. The aesthetics and taste of the way the work looks is made by the work. . . . The way the work looks—its physical appearance, its effects—is not a reflection of my personal taste."[8] A little further on he continues: "I'm excited by my work. But that doesn't mean I have to like it. I'm intellectually excited by it. But viscerally I don't like it sometimes."[9] In other words, these paintings are not here to please you. They are not here to reaffirm your sense of yourself.

This is not to suggest that Pittman's paintings are unruly—precisely not. Like high tea, a Pittman painting is a carefully orchestrated aesthetic event. This event bears strong formal similarities to Abstract Expressionism: the paintings work the edge, they are explicitly public in their address, they engage the problem of the difference between the wall and the canvas, and they do almost all of this via notions of the decorative. They also, for me, form a visual commentary on art historian T. J. Clark's searching essay on Abstract Expressionist painting. In one of the more bracing accounts of these pictures, Clark argues as follows: "Abstract Expressionism . . . is the style of a certain petty bourgeoisie's aspiration to aristocracy, to a totalizing cultural power. It is the art of that moment when the petty bourgeoisie thinks it can speak (and its masters allow it to speak) the aristocrat's claim to individuality. Vulgarity is the form of that aspiration."[10] The vulgarity comes in large measure from the effusive expressiveness of the canvases—paint applied coarsely with palette knives and dripped with sticks—and the belief on the part of artists, critics, and collectors that such images of putative interior states were tantamount to the victory of the individual, each artist in pursuit of his own signature move. For Clark, such aspirations, both political and aesthetic, constitute a trafficking in the vulgar.

I think Pittman's paintings are a late-twentieth-century investigation of the persistence of petit bourgeois aspirations for "totalizing cultural power." If Pittman borrows some of Ab Ex's formal strategies, he does so to display a kind of vulgarity different from the one articulated by Clark. Pittman's canvases, produced in the wake of the feminist rebellion (among others) against the humanistic values typified by Ab Ex and its critics, are not concerned with the problem of cultural dominance via the logic of the individual per se but are instead deeply invested in the problem of equality, and its putative guarantees, through the mechanisms of citizenship and democracy. When I stand in front of Pittman's work, I often find myself aware of the difficulty of squaring individuality and equality. And I wonder even more about the spatialization of these ideas: In a Pittman painting, is individuality "'private" and equality "public"?

Certainly, his pictures are explicitly public. Hence, they do not have to conform to his own (or anyone else's) personal sense of taste; they have to go out and do their work of signification in the public space of the world. And public space demands decorum—society depends on a set of frameworks that allows us to behave in public in ways that accommodate the needs of others. We learn etiquette so that we can have public life. Humans establish the terms of engagement—variously called customs or manners or culture—and for centuries these arrangements were largely governed by the dictates of organized religion and class hierarchies. Democracy turned out to be a profound monkey wrench in this scenario. If, as our "Founding Fathers" declared, "all men are created equal" and we share the right to "the pursuit of happiness," then how can citizens, constitutively equal to one another, negotiate and manage all our inherent diversity and competing interests and ideas? Pittman's paintings consistently infer that the marriage of decorum and democracy is an uneasy one. Made in the post-civil rights, post-Stonewall era, the pictures have to operate in a world grown weary and suspicious of the traditional class and ethnic connotations of decorum and good behavior. One of the reasons I think these paintings are so resistant and intractable, so difficult and complex, is that they are negotiating the problem of decorum in a society that is slowly abandoning it. This is another way of looking at the pairing of the Eameses' living room and *Womanhouse*. The Eameses' space uses the deep logic of the grid to align a set of disparate objects to offer the rebellion of being simultaneously cosmopolitan (décor from around the world!) and iconoclastic (the persistence of décor in a field trying to banish it), while *Womanhouse* breaks with all sorts of good manners in order to destroy the stranglehold those manners exerted over the lives of women. In other words, these two Los Angeles spaces together articulate not only the formal logic of Pittman's paintings but their deep affective structure of rebellion and inquiry as well.

I've come to understand Pittman's oeuvre as a lifelong exploration of the difficulties inherent to democracy. His paintings from the late 1980s indicate an interest in the history of America, or more precisely a reckoning with some of its mythologies, through the painted black silhouettes of American colonial-era figures—always white, predominantly male—that heavily populate the canvases. In *This Discussion, Beloved and Despised, Continues Regardless* (1989), we see the ruthless gendering of the world. Women occupy the upper half of the painting, with images of full-grown men ensconced in medallions decorating their hoop skirts. The women read and listen, their backs as straight as ladders, while below them (there are directional arrows in the painting, literally guiding your gaze) men play chess—a game of sublimated war and distant aristocracies. The patriarchal logic of domination and separate but equal is in full effect, and the fault line of democracy American-style runs through the canvas. The promise of equality was problematic and driven from the beginning, promised to all and guaranteed to only a few.

Democracy and citizenship are represented not only through colonial imagery; the dilemma of parity is built into the formal construction of the compositions themselves. Such is one way to wrangle with the profundity of the slippage between foreground and background in a Pittman painting, not to mention the near-constant trickery with transparency and opacity. Look at one of Pittman's works long enough and its vertiginous quality will emerge.... You think you've located a gourd, or a vase, or some lettering on the surface of an object, only to realize that you are looking *through* one object and/or plane and *at* another. Objects in the mirror may be closer than they appear. This is a warning. This is also an image world born of driving in Los Angeles, where every car stuck in traffic—Range Rover or Kia—is equally stuck in traffic, and the local rules of engagement (the most famous being two cars turning left on a red light) must apply equally to all. If not, the whole system stops working. Just like LA traffic, in a Pittman painting everything is equal; everything comes at you all at once. The level of labor this condition implies for the viewer is enormous, analogous to the daily labor of citizenship in which democratic subjects must remain vigilant to the parity of all humans, a vigilance that we know ebbs and flows. A vigilance we know we must maintain structurally; a vigilance we know we have yet to achieve. The difficulty of looking at, and making sense of, a Pittman painting correlates to the difficulty of democracy's promises of, and failure to achieve, true equality for its citizens. I think this is where Pittman picks up T. J. Clark's sense of the vulgar. If for Clark Ab Ex paintings were about the desire for totalizing power invested in the body of the petit bourgeois individual, then for Pittman the issue is the impossibility and violence of that desire. The pictures are a means to help figure out how one can be a citizen and an artist in a society that promises democracy while being unable to deliver it. What is the role of decorum in such a world?

Enter queerness, as more than a mere set of sexual choices and, more importantly, for its deep and submerged history of aesthetics and performance—cultural conventions that have permitted an extraordinary play with the logic of decorum. Queerness writ large, particularly the fierce queerness embodied by Pittman (both in his person and in his work), is the wild permission that the world and its inhabitants need not all abide by the established conventions of heteronormativity established by the institutions of the family and the church. Queerness is the pursuit of happiness embodied. Queerness is the pursuit of happiness registered as both a necessity and a virtue. Queerness is the statement—sexual, aesthetic, intellectual, and affective—that one's happiness belongs to oneself and must be pursued as such. But queers know all too well that historically, and presently, their pursuit of happiness has often had lethal results. Thus rules of decorum were established (one of which was the tea dance, a late-afternoon party that skirted the prohibitions against same-sex dancing in nightclubs) that permitted queers to thrive in private, closeted enclaves, and to exist publicly as open secrets. With this lens, we gain another way of reading the difficulty of a Pittman painting: everything is absolutely all there for you, but your antennae must be alert, your eyes well trained, your ability to decode honed from years of experience. This is my own way of saying that I have gotten better at looking at Pittman's work. It took me time to allow them their difficulty. It took me time to understand their formal logic, both at the level of aesthetics and at the level of decorum. It took me time to understand that the rigor of Pittman's mark making, the precision of his edges, the complete occupation of the canvas with imagery, the self-consciousness of the arrangement of things on the picture plane, the use of a color palette that reeks of retail, the legibility and cohesion of individual forms, the consummate skill and craft of the production, and the uniformity of energy across the entire canvas collectively form a way of insisting that decorum is a means toward ensuring equality. Decorum is a way to enact parity. Decorum is the brute force of high tea that allows those outside hegemony's conventions to comport themselves. If, as Bob Dylan once sang, "to live outside the law you must be honest," then Pittman's paintings suggest that in order to really have equality everyone must behave. They suggest that citizenship doesn't only mean the pursuit of one's individual happiness; it also means making accommodations for others. It might even mean making and doing work you don't particularly "like."

When I think about Pittman's work, I think about how putative equality offered by the invention of the internet engendered a profound lack of decorum that has enabled extraordinarily vulgar human behavior (bullying, mindless rants, lying, the endless proliferation of opinions without facts, etc., etc.). In contradistinction, Pittman's insistence on consummate parity within each and every picture—on every mark on the canvas being equal to every other mark—leads me to a consideration of the vulgar as both an aesthetic problem and an ethical one. For to abandon the braided logic of décor, the decorative, and decorum is to deny strategies that enable democracy, that offer us a way to be in and of and with the heterogeneity of the world's peoples, things, and customs.

The Eameses' iconoclastic living room and the ribald, rage-fueled rooms of *Womanhouse* challenged the stultification of a certain kind of taste and manners as a way of forging new identities via new aesthetic paths. Their aims were democratic. Operating in alliance with these predecessors, Pittman's paintings perform the vulgarity inherent in our near-incessant need for "individuality." In so doing, they suspend taste (or good taste) to expose the most difficult underpinning of democracy—the structural equivalence of all citizens, an equivalence we claim at the level of the ideological but rarely enact in daily life. In the world presented by a Pittman painting, the only way to negotiate this chasm is through rigorously polite manners—even or especially when the demand for that happiness, that pleasure we have been promised is paramount. (How else to explain the proliferation in Pittman's universe of the number sixty-nine?) The paintings offer the radical and difficult proposition that the violence of the world can be countered by the violence of aesthetics; to remove the decorum even from aesthetics is to be in a space of noncohesion and violence. If the promise of democracy is its guarantee of the equality of all its citizens, then Pittman's paintings suggest it cannot exclusively be legislated or determined by the courts; all citizens must treat each other as equal, and this daily ethical labor is profoundly difficult. Democracy is dissonance. And so decorum is a necessity. The realm of the aesthetic is a realm of tools designed to navigate and manage the violence that parasitically accompanies all acts of civilization. Aesthetics are violent for they entail constant choice (this and not that), and those choices can be made through the apparatuses of class, gender, ethnicity, habit, history, and culture. But all those choices depend ultimately on the decorum through which they are enacted. For without decorum, we are left with merely the stage set and no script for how to inhabit it.

Decorum—like all forms of aesthetics—can be ruthless, and Pittman's paintings imply that decorum might mean being quiet and levelheaded when one feels instead like screaming and throwing things around the room in a rage. One finds that explosive energy in Pittman's work, and yet it is never succumbed to; hot emotions are painted with a cool hand. After all, there are rewards for good behavior, and one of them is the fierce, rigorous, and ruthless pleasure of a Lari Pittman painting.

Lisa Yuskavage: Meissen v. Hummel

Originally published in *Lisa Yuskavage: Wilderness* (New York: Gregory R. Miller, 2020), 125–35.

Sometime early in the twenty-first century I saw an exhibition of Lisa Yuskavage's paintings at the ICA Philadelphia. I had just given up my tenure-track academic job for a museum position, and for the first time in my life the paycheck was real. The money and the title "curator" made me feel an enormous responsibility to see as many exhibitions as I could, and because I had enough cash to buy exhibition catalogues, I had the lofty idea of building a library. One of the first things I bought under this new regime was the modest, saddle bound book from Yuskavage's exhibition.

When I arrived home, I placed the catalogue on the coffee table of my girlfriend's house. Even though I had purchased it, I had no idea what to make of the pictures it contained. Girlish figures with impossibly huge tits, perfect nipples (erect, pink, practically leaning forward, arching toward your mouth), pubic hair that looked like it had been backlit by a golden setting sun, juicy asses (round, smooth, dimpled), thighs that spread easily, small waists, rounded bellies, lips parted, lips puckered, mouths open, veritable tendrils of hair. These were pictures about perpetual availability. Time stilled. Time infinite. Paint become flesh in domestic interiors and landscapes rendered in a foam of sea green, sunrise periwinkle, and lemon cream. The figures were girls with women's bodies. They were women with girl's faces. They were a teenage dream: posters on a bedroom wall. They possessed a slight charge of adrenaline, as if part of their thrill emanated from memories of shoplifting scented lip gloss at the mall. They were the shock of the first time I saw pubic hair, on my older friend in the locker room at camp in Maine.

I'm not sure I'd ever been so embarrassed in my life—embarrassed by a picture. Embarrassed by the feeling between my legs when I looked at these pictures. Pictures that any reasonable post-ACT UP, abortion rights-supporting, self-regarding feminist with a PhD in art history and a decent job should rightly dismiss out of hand. This parade of sex dolls, an endless supply of white women, each with three holes, open and wet. "It's like Kara Walker for white girls" drifted through my cerebral cortex, after which I could not find it in myself to "critique" the work. I could not bring my inherited baby-boomer feminism about body positivity and self-actualization down upon these pictures. Nor could I muster the "proper" Marxist antagonism to images that were clearly meant to be bought and sold on the open market, pictures meant to be hung, winkingly, above the bed in master bedrooms with en suite bathrooms, where the his-and-her closets were larger than the childhood bedroom I shared with my brother.

I knew enough to know that my embarrassment in the face of this work was worth holding on to. Indeed, I wondered if my aversion to it might be structurally similar to the denunciations of Walker's images made in the mid-1990s by numerous African American artists and scholars. Looking at Yuskavage's work, I started to understand the mortification Walker's antebellum psychosexual tableaux may have caused them. I now had a bird's-eye view of the rage they may have felt, an insight into their fears about how pernicious and uncontrollable such images might be in the "wrong" hands. I intuited how troubling it may have been to be implicated in someone else's twisted fantasy. I confess that at the time I found their protestations problematic. But I strongly suspect that if a white man of a certain age had been the first to show me Yuskavage's work, I would have rejected it immediately.

If Walker mined the violent, traumatic tragedy of slavery and found in the deepest reaches of her mind a montage of sexualized fantasies that she could no longer repress while retaining her sanity, then Yuskavage's bravery came from her refusal to clean up the nettlesome Venn diagram comprising sexuality, the act of looking, and the act of being an artist. Her soft-core paintings were an exegesis of white American lower-middle-class girlhood. My discomfort was profound. My feelings of exposure were real. Nevertheless, I hadn't yet discovered just how deep my embarrassment actually ran. My girlfriend's house was extremely tidy, and the house was kept clean by a white lesbian housekeeper named Barb. I didn't know Barb well, but I knew she was working-class. She had a Baltimore accent and bad teeth (I have a New York accent and bad teeth). Hiring her felt like keeping money in the family, so to speak. The mornings when she was scheduled to come and clean, once every fortnight, I took the Yuskavage catalogue off the coffee table and put it on a bookshelf. When I returned from work to find the house dusted and polished to a shine, I took the book off the shelf and put it back on the coffee table.

I found that I couldn't laugh off my behavior as a form of residual prudery. Given that Barb was a dyke, I was hard-pressed to see my behavior as a vestige of the closet. I felt too much solidarity with Barb, in terms of our shared sexuality, for that. And laughter, the mechanism that attends embarrassment, like batteries with a new toy, was not really forthcoming. It wasn't an "accident" that I had this book filled with lurid pictures. And I had too much pride about having bought the damn thing for this to be guilt. Now that I was someone who did research on artists, having the catalogue was protected under the wheelhouse of "work." Ruling out embarrassment, guilt, and accident, all of which I could have apologized for, I was left with shame. I had to admit that I was worried what Barb would think of me, that she would judge me not for my lesbian desire—I assumed she had plenty of that herself—but for my taste. This put her, for the first and only time, in the

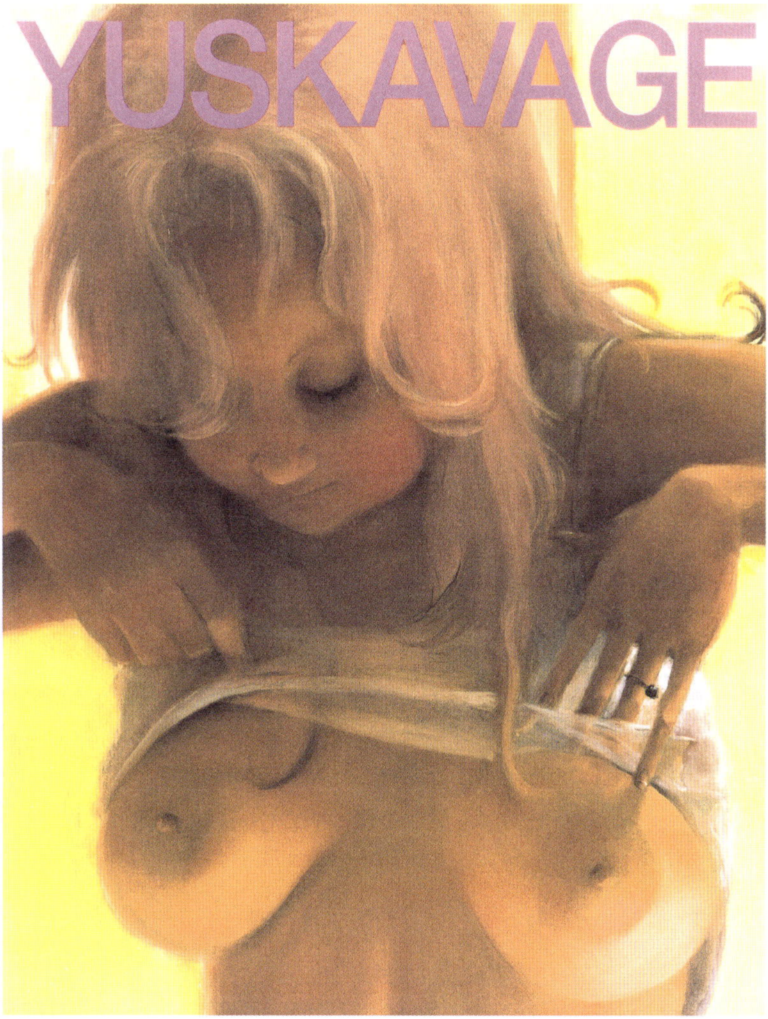

Cover of exhibition catalogue for *Lisa Yuskavage*, Institute of Contemporary Art, Philadelphia, December 2, 2000–February 9, 2001

same mental pantheon as my dissertation advisors. I couldn't imagine admitting to them, either, how much I liked Yuskavage's work. At least with them I could have martialed an argument about how Yuskavage's paintings "stage the problem of female desire." I could have manufactured some connective tissue between Cindy Sherman and the image as the "site of sexuality." I could have spun theoretical tales and sidestepped the problem of "taste" with the putatively "objective" language of theory. But in the face of Barb

I was silent, wordless. I turned away from the encounter. I couldn't even face the idea that she would see the thing in my absence.

For years I narrated my shame to myself as being "something about class." But, to be honest, I couldn't drill down and figure it all out. I never attempted to buy one of Yuskavage's paintings for a museum. Nor could I imagine proposing a show of her work. Both felt tantamount to announcing in a staff meeting that my father had had a stash of *Playboy* magazines in his study and that I would sneak in when he was away and look at all those dreamy pictures and rub my prepubescent vulva on one of my dolls because it felt really, really good to do *that*. And even if I had had the temerity to say that, it still wouldn't have gotten to the heart of the matter. I knew tons of dykes who'd had their first sexual awakening in the midst of their father's soft-core porn. Yuskavage talks about her dad's pile of 1970s *Penthouses* in almost every published interview. She's not hiding that; with pictures like hers, how could she?

No, what I was worried about with Barb was the problem of class taste. I thought Barb would think I was crazy for needing/wanting my porn to be all fancy. I imagined her saying something akin to "Dude, you know you can just get that in a porno mag, right?" Basically, I couldn't leave the catalogue out because I didn't want the housekeeper to think I was some kind of snob who likes/needs her porn to be a *painting*. When the fact was that was exactly who I was: I was someone who liked my porn in painted form. I was like one of those stupid yuppies who enjoys high-end comfort food. Sweet Jesus. My shame seemed to emanate not from my sexuality as such but from the fact that in this context I could accurately be perceived as a snob. And to complicate matters, my very same attraction to the very same paintings could, if made public, lead me to be seen by my grad-school cohort of teachers and friends, by some amorphous thing called "the critically inflected art world," as a feminist with suspect politics, a lesbian who had lost her stripes. At either end of the class/taste spectrum I realized that to be forthcoming about my fascination with Yuskavage's paintings was to incur judgment about my capacity for judgment.

You'd think that after claiming my desire in terms of living out my sexuality—as complicated as both the claiming and the sexuality itself had been—saying what pictures I liked would have been easy. This is one of the vagaries of life in the art world. Each participant—from curator to dealer to collector to art historian—stakes a claim based on the work they support or critique. Your public approbation becomes a marker of what you stand for, of who you are. Liking everything is too pluralistic; the art world demands partisanship. The walls of the museum are not infinite. The high temples of art are arenas of competition, and who gets in, how they get in, and where they are installed all matter. The art world is a residual form of court culture in which your taste is not benign. Your taste is all you've got. And if you don't have money, your taste is *really* all you've got. It's ride or die. Saying what you *like*—always so much harder than saying what you don't like—runs the risk of exposure, of vulnerability, of ridicule, suspicion, of being whatever fill-in-the-blank thing you don't want to be seen as, which, in this specific instance, would be a bourgeois snob, a bad feminist, or worse: a snobby bourgeois bad feminist. Hiding the book from Barb made me realize that what I was most ashamed of was my own fear in the face of how compelling I found Yuskavage's work to be. To advocate for it publicly would have been to make plain the carnal nature of my queerness. My interest in women was not political. My interest in women wasn't avant-garde. My interest in women wasn't theoretically rigorous. Exposure as a libertine pleasure seeker rather than a tough-as-nails super-smart curator—apparently that was more risk than I was up for.

Years later I went to work at a museum that owned a terrific Yuskavage painting called *Northview* (2000). Under the deep cover of a reinstallation of the permanent collection dedicated to upending the old-master narratives of post-1945 art, I decided to put the painting on view. It was one picture among hundreds. I was going to have my cake and eat it, too. In *Northview*, a young blonde woman appears in profile, backlit by a window, a voluminous drape pulled aside to let in the golden light. Next to the curtain is an imposing floor-to-ceiling bookshelf, and just to the right of the books we see the corner of a gilded picture frame. Of all the improbable soap-opera scenarios, we find ourselves in the library. The figure, sandwiched between a desk and a chair, places her long, thin fingers, one of which is graced with a wedding band, ever so gently on the desk. A red shawl falls off her body, exposing one perfect breast and her gravity-defying ass, both of which are housed in her flawless, golden-sun-kissed skin, with its perfect undertones of pink. A long strand of pearls falls behind her from her elegant neck. Compositionally, it forms a plumb line that heightens the impossibly exaggerated curve of the small of her back.

She is there for us to look at. Her gaze is occupied by a small statuette of a monkey. For sure it's an inside joke, a moment for rueful self-awareness built into the picture. Such a clever little monkey. Is it Meissen? Is it Hummel? What does it mean that I'm the kind of person who not only knows the difference but thinks the difference matters? That's the part of the picture that makes me laugh the hardest—the part that makes an issue of my taste. In this confectioners'-sugar sea of sexual desire, Yuskavage opens the trapdoor of class. All this talk of drapes and libraries and *statuettes* is the talk that attends a very particular kind of monied interior. The clever monkey registers that this space is fancy. And the fancy figurine is a classic site of displacement, a useful diversion from the T&A; thinking about the monkey is like buying *Playboy* for the articles. The monkey is a foil. It can act as a marker of my taste in the way the woman cannot, because my "taste" in women is not the soft-core fantasies designed by men for men. I had no interest in the copious bullshit that came with the fantasies of my parents' generation (all that dross about bringing home the bacon and never letting you forget you're a man). My queerness "freed" me from such banalities. But in the face of these pictures I had to admit that what my queerness *didn't* liberate me from was the template for desire established when I was a child. If Freud was right and the logic of the unconscious is "and," never "either/or," then Yuskavage's paintings showed me what it feels like when you admit that your field of desire is riddled with things you don't think are cool, acceptable, or politically correct. Her paintings pulled back the curtain on my earliest yearnings, the ones formed in the back seat of someone's car listening to love songs on AM radio, desires formed in the wake of someone's older brother, or your dad's best friend's foxy new girlfriend. Yuskavage's work opens up the rich minefield of desires formed when you didn't have much agency over your life, when you weren't in control of your own visual field, desires formed long before you had any language capable of describing them. And it's not just that she showed them, like some kind of bloodless illustration—her work let me know, in no uncertain terms, that those desires were all still operative. They were all still online, so to speak. They were all still at play in the complexity of my current desiring self. I'd wager that Yuskavage is hard for feminists because her paintings make it clear that while politics is the sphere of "either/or," desire is the realm of "and," and in her case, in my case, that meant there was simply no getting rid of the sexual aesthetics of the 1970s.

What's great about the category "queer" is that it's like a grab bag; it can handle all the surprise, all the ambiguity, all the embarrassment, that attends sex and sexuality, and it does so, in part, by flipping all that awkwardness the bird. Queer says there's no reason why a straight woman can't make pictures of nubile girls in physical proximity to one another, who look at one another and themselves with awe and assurance, whom a bunch of women who are not heterosexual could find so devastatingly sexy that they might just wanna put their hands down their pants. Is this what Susan Sontag meant when she said that instead of a "hermeneutics of art" she wanted an "erotics of art"? Somehow I don't think so, and yet . . . True to Sontag's call, I have no desire to *interpret* Yuskavage's painting. Instead, I want to revel in its rococo excess. I want to play out an erotics that is utterly nonmimetic, nondidactic, and nonradical. I want the space of fantasy to be just that—a dreamy, hazy space lit by magical light that I enter with all the ease of a finger sliding into a wet pussy. I want an open field that is made specifically for me. I want a picture that sees that a huge part of the specificity of "me" is the part of "me" that is a historical subject. I enjoy the feeling of having my specifically Gen-X subjectivity fed back to me in the form of an oil painting that hangs in a museum. (For those of you interested in continuity, I placed the Yuskavage painting in a room with an Andrea Fraser video called *Little Frank and His Carp* [2001], in which Fraser humps the walls of Frank Gehry's Bilbao; Robert Gober's outsized sculpture of a cigar; some pictures by Matthew Barney of hunky guys in kilts; and an obscene Kaari Upson wall relief that resembles a huge vagina but is really a pink-rubber cast of a wall in her house.) I want to be in a public space and feel able, encouraged, even, to recall my 1970s haptic sexual awakening. I like remembering the velour, the corduroy, the velvet, the terry cloth,

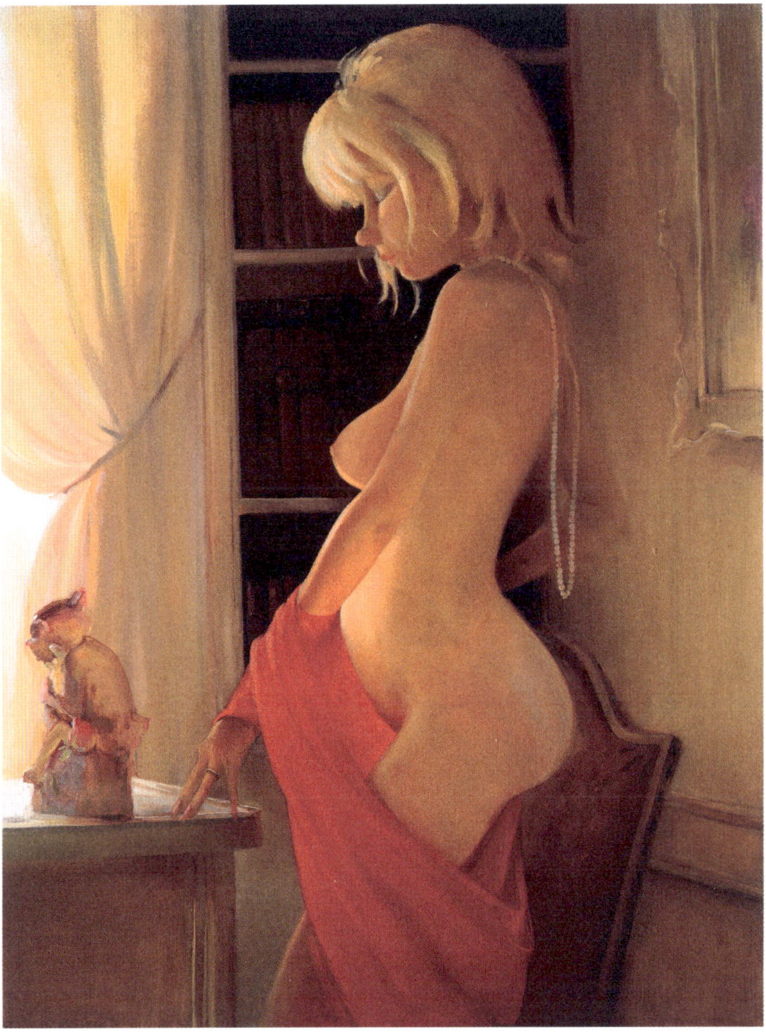

Lisa Yuskavage, *Northview*, 2000, oil on linen, 70 x 54 in. (177.8 x 137.2 cm)

and the chenille. I like the complicated time warp *Northview* establishes: It is a painting of an adult memory of childhood sexuality. It's an image of nascent desire remembered in such a way that the "turn-on" is not recalled ironically but happens in real time. It's not a picture of what it felt like to be turned on in the past; it's a picture about how all the desire we had in us before we had words for that desire is still flowing in the veins between our legs and our ears. That's why Yuskavage had to make a painting. Because it's not really about *Playboy* and *Penthouse*—it's about the fantasy life of young girls as imagined by an adult woman who is taking the fantasy life of prepubescent white girls *very* seriously. And Yuskavage takes the fantasy life of such girls, and its troubling and joyous, giggle- and wet-pussy-inducing persistence in adult women, so seriously that she makes paintings designed to hang in museums, paintings designed to hold their own against all those pictures made by men for men about *their* sexual fantasies.

And what do we find in this idyllic space of soft light and soft women? Yuskavage gives us a space where tactility reigns, both in the creaminess of her paint and the sumptuousness of her surfaces. The distinction between the skin of bodies and the skin of paint rides along a knife's edge. Her universe is a continuation of the Rococo, a made-up world of adornment, flirtation, and play. Penetration is not the point. Her pictures aren't the straightforward heterosexual fantasy of fucking as a form of conquest. I think her pictures are about the time between your first fuck and the next one—the warm space when anticipation has stalled and assured flirtation reigns. Yuskavage is keenly attuned to the fact that, for women, flirting is impossible without self-regard. Her pictures are filled with women who look at themselves. They gaze down on their bellies, they glance across their hairless legs and arms, they behold their own nipples. They do so with pleasure. They do so with shame. They know the two things are intertwined. I always get the feeling, looking at a Yuskavage painting, that the figures in the picture look at themselves gently. I feel that Yuskavage looks at them gently, too. But she is no sentimentalist; her empathetic eye has no mercy in it. Because she is an adult in an adult woman's body, she knows exactly what will happen to the bodies of her fictional characters when the harsh reality of life inevitably befalls them. She knows that the breasts will droop, the bellies will spread, the asses will sag. Her pictures forestall entropy and gravity with great tenderness. In a Yuskavage painting, a passing sensation is rendered as infinite. She knows that some of her viewers still know all the words to songs by Bread and Hall & Oates. She knows they can remember sitting in the back of the camp bus singing along to Jackson Browne, and she knows they're going to give all that up for Black Flag and the Wu-Tang Clan. But if Bob Dylan is right and "inside the museums, infinity goes up on trial," then a Yuskavage painting asks: Can you hang with this? Can you stay in this space? Can you observe all its coordinates? Can you, as women have always been asked to do under the hegemony of patriarchy, engage in an ongoing act of self-regard? Can you look at yourself? Can you look at an image that exaggerates what your desire feels like?

Part of what I find so amazing about Yuskavage's project is the way it allows me the difficult privilege of seeing my sexuality, to the extent that it's mine, as part of something larger than I am. Another thing that's shameful in "liking" this work is the way it suggests that neither she nor we, her viewers, can outrun the ways in which we are indelibly shaped by the world, even those of us who discovered the loophole called "queer" (maybe especially those of us who live in that loophole).

But I've skirted the problem of the monkey. I've avoided the problem of the monkey with an exegesis of Yuskavage's paintings that squares my once-nascent sexuality with my adult one. And while I'm generally OK with that, what Yuskavage's work really makes me wonder is whether there is a class corollary to "queer." Which is a way of asking if it matters if the monkey is Meissen or Hummel. Which is a way for me *not* to say that the Hummel part of Yuskavage is more embarrassing than the *Playboy* part. I won't judge your or my sexual desires. I won't play cop to anyone's fantasy, and I bar cops from my own fantasy life. But when it comes to matters of décor, the decorative, and decorum, I am ruthless. And just as I'm not interested in mimetic porn, I'm not interested in any "ironic" assessment of taste. I have no way out of the monkey cul-de-sac. Camp and irony—the tools of the generation antecedent to mine—aren't going to do it. I'm gonna have to own up to my resistance, my snobbery, my complicated class formation. I'm just not going to have to do it around, over, and against the body of a woman. I'm going to have to do it in the space of taste. I'm determined to ride the meniscus of Yuskavage's twisted oeuvre without recourse to kitsch, sentimentality, or irony, without, that is, the loopholes that let people out of the profundity of their class markers, without reveling in her painterly virtuosity (though Lord knows it's there), without making recourse to art historical erudition (neither mine nor hers). Instead, I'm going to continue to be troubled and elated by her color palette. Almost all of me loathes it, as in I can't imagine those colors in my home or on my person. As much as I'm interested in the continuity of my preadolescent desire into the space of my adulthood, it turns out I cannot abide these creamy pastels with an edge of acid to them used in what I find to be an overly sentimental and saccharine way. How crazy is *that*? That's what I mean about how clever the monkey is; it's as if Yuskavage is determined to flirt with every possible way to make her expertly painted paintings into some form of a bad object.

If I'm drawn in by the imagery, seduced by the expert facture, and humorously bewildered by the palette, then I'm leveled by Yuskavage's commitment to painting different versions of the same painting over and over again. It's clear that she has made an issue of painting the same type of body, and often within individual series of works she deploys the same composition numerous times. This practice is clearly intentional, as on her website each picture is cross-referenced with all the other pictures like it. When we look at *Northview*, for instance, we see that she has made seven other pictures with the same composition, which share the same model, in the same pose, with different degrees of finish, one with flowers, one without, and so on. This iterative staging and restaging is part of the game of viewership; the works are similar enough that it shouldn't "matter," and yet I can't help but choose the "best" one. In one single lapsarian gesture Yuskavage has collapsed my two registers of looking at her work: first, there is the libidinal, which image is sexier, more voluptuous, which one offers the fantasy that best secures pleasure. That this is basically a description of masturbating is not lost on me—which of the generally repetitive fantasies will get you off today?

And the second register is taste: Which image—with its ever so slight adjustments of lighting, color scheme, decorative arrangement in the mise-en-scène—is the "best"? Which picture offers the satisfactory "click" of all the elements falling into their ineffable places? Here is where Yuskavage the painter shows us her hand as Yuskavage the conceptual artist. She could decide only to release the "best" picture. But instead she's committed to the complexity of the situation. The run of pictures shows us how we come to understand our taste through negation—not this one but that one. Both sexual fantasy and taste require temporary resolution: you orgasm, and you decide where the picture looks best, and you don't do either of those things just once. You do them both again and again.

Repetition in Yuskavage's work is a simple statement of fact. She is an artist who works in series. She is an artist who has committed to a certain palette, paint application, and type of figure. But because she traffics in deeply embodied memory, I think she needs the repetition to get it "right." I also think she needs to let us see how hard she's worked to get it right. Because that's what working-class white girls from Philly are asked to do—prove themselves over and over again. And that's what feminism has to do—insist over and over again that the concerns and fantasies, ideas and pleasures of women are worth pursuing. I mean, how could you make just one picture of the feedback loop that "explains" how it came to be that there was a time when young working-class girls, girls from whom nothing special was expected, found the porn that liberated their fathers and experienced its igniting of their sense of themselves as both desirable and desiring?

And because this particular girl grew up in an era dominated by pictures, she found herself wanting to be an artist. And because that girl grew up in Philly, she found herself, in addition to pawing through stacks of someone else's porn mags, roaming the halls of the Philadelphia Museum of Art (where maybe, just maybe, she saw *Étant donnés*). And then that girl conjured a fantastical world populated almost exclusively by women. She made pictures about women looking at themselves, of women looking at other women. And all these images had the DNA of six centuries' worth of paintings made by men for men of means that were about looking at women, that were designed to be looked at in well-appointed rooms like libraries and museum galleries. DNA's a bitch—there are only forty-six chromosomes, after all. There are only so many combinations.

So, when our girl grew up and became a painter, she made her pictures over and over and over again. Because she knew her viewers were going to need more than one shot at quieting the white male dude in their heads who tells them that pictures like these aren't serious. And after she labored intensely, learning painterly techniques from the Renaissance, and made sumptuous, creamy paintings that simulate the warmth of apricot-hued bodies and the honeyed aura of intimacy, after she made those pictures in the sanctity of her private studio, where she decided she could act in the name of freedom rather than politics, she thought it best to let them out into the world to be seen in public. She sent them to the galleries and museums, to the spaces that cater to the visual fetishists among us, but especially to those of us who like our porn in a painting. These paintings are for those of us who are entranced by the intricate ways our fantasies, desires, and memories are both personal and public. And hence we marvel at how Yuskavage's paintings possess the capacity for transmitting the feelings that course in the veins between our ears and our legs, allowing us to understand, more beautifully, the connection between the two.

Postscript

This essay was written during my transition from being a full-time member of the institutional/museum affiliated art world to someone who functioned "independently." Writing it reignited my lifelong dream of identifying myself as a writer first, and as someone who arranges pictures second. It is telling that it is one of the most explicitly queer texts I've ever written. In addition to being about queerness in general, it is written from a specifically lesbian point of view. It is no small irony that writing about Lisa Yuskavage's work engendered my first explicitly lesbian text. I am keenly aware that I was only able to write this text, which is marbled with terrifying vulnerability, because I had lost my job. In this new space of economic and professional precarity, I no longer represented anything other than myself. And since being a lesbian was part of why I was fired (never underestimate the implicit hostility of heterosexual patriarchy toward the women who are structurally uninterested in its privileged subjects, either libidinally or intellectually), it seemed all the more important to write explicitly as a lesbian.

There was no better subject on which to do this than Yuskavage's remarkable oeuvre. In taking it up, I tried to write a text that met her work head-on, by which I mean I wanted to write with the same amount of bravery she paints with. I know it's wrong to play favorites, but this essay is one of my favorites, as it signifies the beginning of a different way of thinking and writing about art. It is both a culmination of all I knew up to that point—about paintings, Yuskavage, and lesbian desire—and a new beginning, marked by a dawning pleasure and expansiveness of how to write about the feelings and ideas that reside closest to the bone.

Noah Davis: The Forest and the Trees

Originally published in *Noah Davis: In Detail* (New York: David Zwirner Books, 2023), 7–11.

Sometimes the only way I can start writing is to look something up. In the old days, my first port of call was the *Oxford English Dictionary*, the olde *OED*. The apartment I grew up in had the boxed-set version with a magnifying glass in a sliding tray that was nestled above the two volumes of the dictionary. It's a writerly tic designed to get the juices flowing—a way of cutting off the ring, as they say in boxing. Start with a definition and you have immediately narrowed the playing field. Now, like most folks, I look shit up on the internet.

I've known for a while that I wanted to write about Noah Davis's paintings. I've also known how difficult it would be for me to do so. Silly me, I thought it would get easier with time. In the wake of the Underground Museum closing, truth be told, it just got harder.[1] But I'm pulling my version of a Bill Clinton here: it's the paintings, stupid. My focus newly established, I found myself marveling at how expansive and complex Davis's paintings are. They are the kind of paintings you don't really understand all at once. They are paintings that reveal themselves over time. This is partly because of the complexity of his compositions, partly because his palette is so unusual, and mostly because they are so packed with details that each time I see a painting, I typically see something I hadn't seen before. So I looked up "Where does the phrase 'the devil is in the details' come from?" It seemed an innocent enough question, until the internet spit out the answer. The origin of the phrase is disputed. One thing that's clear is that it started out, in both French and German, as "God is in the details." Somewhere along the line, God exited stage left and in walked the devil. Ain't that always the way? I had to laugh. I had to laugh because I could immediately summon the sound of Noah's laughter—big, from the belly—the sound of a man accustomed to laughing in the face of life's foibles. One of the painful realities about those who die young is that they are often sainted; all the devilish details of their lives are tidied up. Sadness is a broom.

It's hard for me to be formal when I talk about Davis's paintings. It's hard not to call him Noah and resort to anecdote. The hard truth is I've been avoiding writing about his paintings because I was afraid to pin them down with interpretation. I didn't want to suture them into an art historical lineage. To do so felt heavy, taxonomic, objectifying. To do so ran the risk (for me) of turning academic, bringing the whole critical apparatus to bear, and that felt like too much to bear. The details gave me an out.

It was Daniel DeSure's idea to go hard on the details. Daniel was Noah's best friend, and Daniel's crew—they roll under the name Commonwealth Projects—are the folks who designed this book. It was their idea to break the convention of art publishing and structure the book around the details. Typically, we foreground the whole painting first and the detail is an afterthought. They flipped the script. What happens if you just get right down to it—with both God and the devil—and let yourself fall into the portal offered by the details? What if you hold off the forest for as long as possible? What if there are only trees?

Detail (noun): an individual feature, fact, or item.

Paintings are nouns, items, things. They are also philosophical treatises in the minor key. They are pictures that suggest ways of organizing material into a world. They are a worldview; a worldview produced by an individual who has gathered some facts. But the facts are always just that, facts. The story we make of them is where the truth resides.

There's *Mary Jane* (2008), with her small face peeking out from under a bonnet, surrounded by a camouflage pattern of interlocking black, green, and white biomorphic shapes constructed out of heavily built-up paint that coheres into an image of a hedge. Her lips are parted. She has the face of a child but the eyes of an adult—limpid, wet, highlighted by the contrast between her ebony iris and the brightest of bright whites that accentuates the eye's white part, the inelegantly named "sclera." And, true to the magic of painting, the white paint that creates the whites of her eyes migrates. Flecks of white paint sit precariously on top of the pupil. Flecks of white paint become the pupil. We accept this transubstantiation even though the order of the world has been reversed in a singularly small gesture. There are facts and there is the truth. They are often confused with one another. The fact is this painting shows us a small child with a white pupil. The truth of the world is that human pupils are black. After Noah died, Daniel got a tattoo on his arm, in an excruciatingly delicate script, that reads "a Noah Davis kind of truth."

Zoom out from the eyes of Mary Jane to take in the whole picture. Then we see a young girl neatly dressed, posing with her hands docilely gathered at her midsection. She stands against the hedge dutifully, as if for a family photo, the kind you send to grandma at Christmas. Her pinafore has vertical stripes while her tube socks have horizontal stripes—a little decorative game that highlights the already outrageous contrast of figure and ground.

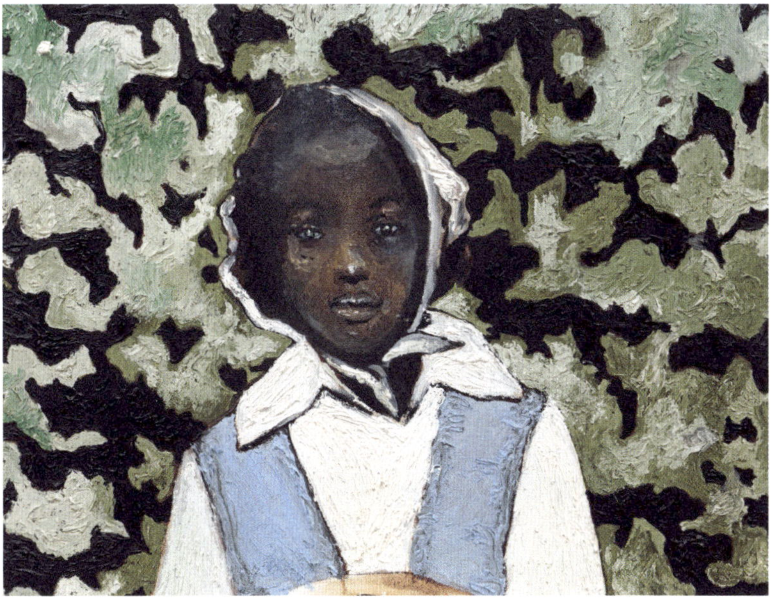

Noah Davis, *Mary Jane* (detail), 2008, oil and acrylic on canvas, 60 x 52 ¼ in. (152.4 x 132.7 cm)

Her feet, shod in the titular Mary Janes, bump up against, or sit on top of, a casually drawn horizontal line that runs from edge to edge at the bottom of the canvas. In a painting where there is a lot to marvel at, I often get hung up on this line. All the magic of representation in a simple line—a line that creates depth where, in truth, there is only flatness. A line that creates recessive space on a flat plane. A line that summons the omnipresent law of gravity. A line that tethers the figure to the ground. A line made by a hand dragging a loaded paintbrush across a canvas from left to right with the analog efficiency of the writer who once advanced her manuscript with a flick of the left hand on the carriage return of a typewriter. The line says, "This is how you build a picture." The white painted pupils say, "This is how you perceive a picture." The painter and the viewer, together and apart.

If you come at *Spoonfed* (2010) head on, you might get blinded by the klieg lights spelling out "Picasso." The guitar, the face that sits on the figure's shoulders like a sculpture, the elongated distortions of the limbs—all the moves Picasso stole from Ingres. Then there's the inscrutable nature of the Surrealist object lurking at the left edge of the canvas and the moody vibe established by the Rothkoesque color field of blue. It wouldn't be the only time Davis let you see that he was digging in the proverbial art historical crates. I don't think we can underestimate the degree to which Davis is a member of the hip-hop generation—the first generation of artists born into a world in which hip-hop already existed, a world in which the logic of Black excellence would pervade nearly every aspect of contemporary life, from music to sports, from fashion to branding, to the election of Forty-Four, which happened the year Davis turned twenty-five. Hip-hop made appropriation into a high art form. Hip-hop is archive fever, a continual pillaging of the vast repositories of the past, a pulling through of history into the present, a virtuosic display of the knowledge and history of a craft. Kerry James Marshall would call it "Mastry."

When Davis was an art student at Cooper Union in New York, he fell in with the crew that would become Bruce High Quality Foundation. What kind of nerdy kid gets all involved in a restaging of Géricault's *The Raft of the Medusa* (1818–19)? A kid with a head filled with pictures. Davis carried a world of pictures in his head. No matter how much appropriating and borrowing and stealing (all forms of honoring and excellence within the framework of hip-hop) one does, a hip-hop track is great as much because of its archivally sample-driven hook as its emcee-driven lyrical flow. While the archive is public, the flow is as personal as it gets. The flow is your tempo, your heartbeat, the length of your breath, your mind-tongue coordination. Your flow is as personal as your DNA. In a Davis painting, the flow is in the detail.

In *Spoonfed* he shows you how the detail and the flow are one and the same. Look at the broken elliptical brushstroke that loops from shoulder to hand, making a bull's-eye out of the sound hole of the guitar. That black hole becomes the sun, the energy of the player's body orbits around it like a planet. The brushstroke sits on top of the canvas showing us the real deal: the artist is someone who makes something out of nothing, or, to put a beat on it, some thing out of no thing. And that thing? That brushstroke, which started by the shoulder with a phat brush laden with paint, watch how, when it crosses over the body and onto the guitar, that's where Davis puts some pressure in it, laying into the wet paint, laying it down all juicy and thick. Once the stroke or the flow passes the struts and the strings, the paint starts to break up. The smooth unity won't hold. The paint atomizes into a Milky Way galaxy, a constellation of stars rounding its way back to the musician's hand. Facts. Truths. Because it's also just the paint running out, the texture getting drier, sparser, increasingly ethereal, until it's almost not there. It ends up where it started. Like a note running its course. Like a note blending with other notes to make a chord. Like a clock's hands marking time. As individual as a thumbprint, as universal as music.

Art criticism is filled with a lot of hype. I mean, how else can you describe a genre that talks about "the death of painting"? Or how so-and-so is "the best painter of his generation" (almost always a "his")? Or triumphant talk about the "return" of figuration? I mean, who talks like this? What kind of crystal balls are people stockpiling? No matter. We all do it. Me too. Davis once wrote in a notebook that he was the greatest painter alive. I've been known to say that Davis was at the forefront of our current vogue for figuration. The details don't lend themselves to such apocryphal talk. The details keep

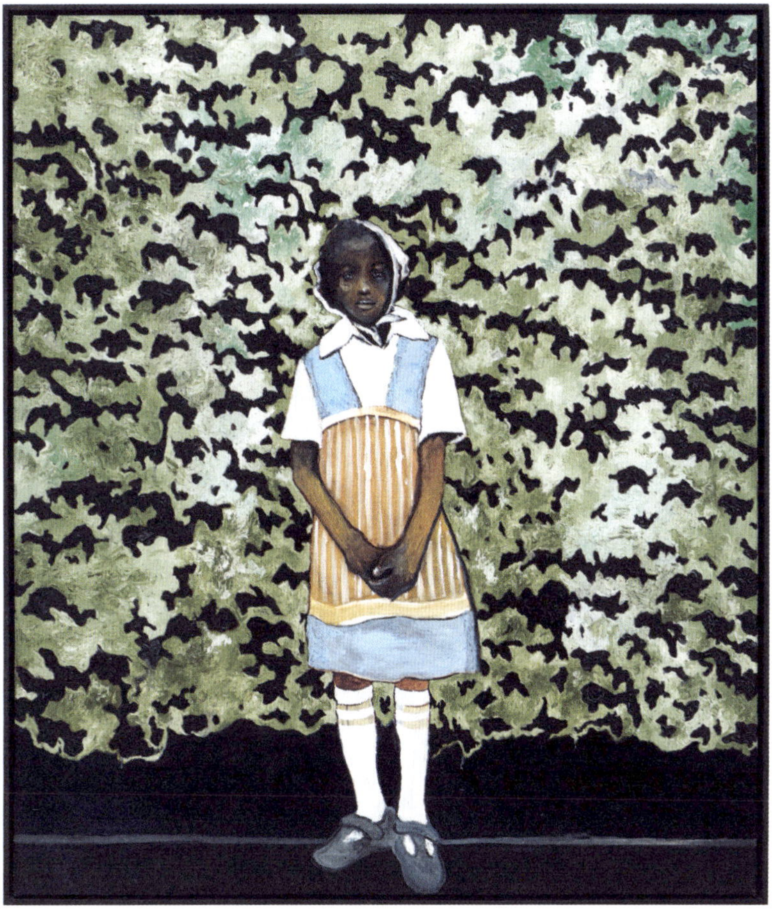

Noah Davis, *Mary Jane*, 2008, oil and acrylic on canvas, 60 x 52¼ in. (152.4 x 132.7 cm)

you grounded. The details keep you looking. Look at *Golden Boy* (2010) from across a room and you'll see the long arm of Manet. The moody way the boy occupies the frame, you might even recall Manet's fascination with Goya, whose lurking dissatisfaction with royal privilege produced some of the most harrowing pictures of the Enlightenment. *Golden Boy* is a twenty-first-century infanta—a child poised for greatness, a golden rod in his hand. A pink suit that's part school uniform, part aristocratic church attire. When else does a child wear a tie? The golden color migrates from the figure's staff to his skin. Race is rendered almost permanently ambiguous. Look closely at the face. (Is the face a detail?) Here paint just barely coheres into features. A yellowish ground acts as a foil for the circular daubs of blue-gray paint. The gestures feel fast, vaguely aggressive, as if the artist needs to dispose of this face with alacrity. The flow is fierce. The paint is moving. From tube to palette to brush to canvas, Davis is working with the speed and efficiency of a line cook at a diner. Black circles underneath a smashed semicircle of paint equals an eye. A rapidly placed vertical daub of paint gets you a nose. A diagonal slice of electric blue becomes the plane of a cheek. You almost have to squint to make it all fall into place. The vibe is more gestural abstraction than figuration. Shades of Willem de Kooning and Joan Mitchell—what kind of face is that? An abstract face, that's what. And truly what could be more abstract than a face? All those wet holes—eyes, nostrils, mouth—framed by protruding cartilage holes—ears. Think about it too long, look at it too long, and it can all start to come undone in your head. Like when you look at a word you know on a page and it momentarily doesn't make sense. The abstraction of making sense. The abstraction of the painterly idea of figuration. The gamesmanship of rendering the three-dimensional world on a two-dimensional plane. Truth, facts, and all the mess in the middle. When I look at the rough abstraction of the face in *Golden Boy*, I recall a long-ago teacher's admonition that any argument with only two sides isn't worth having. And here's Davis having his cake and eating it, too—the big picture is figuration and all the details are abstract.

It was none other than the master of "less is more," Mies van der Rohe, who was famous for saying, "God is in the details." And it's true, if less is more then the less has got to be perfect—because it's the details that transform the ordinary into the extraordinary. Every sneakerhead knows this. The less there is the more it counts. In the world of Davis's painting, in the worlds created in his canvases, he offers us detail on detail. The devil is in the details because the details are what makes something difficult. God is in the details because the details are where perfection enters the picture. But Davis's version of the perfect veers away from the hyperstylization of the detail. In *Sugartown* (2011), a man lies smoking in a bed framed by extravagant vermillion velvet curtains and a French window that depicts the blinding white light of midday Los Angeles. His face is an elliptical plane of brown; a dark line connotes the chin. Two brushstrokes—one for a slightly arched eyebrow, the other a closed eye. With an extraordinary economy of means, these two lines of paint portray both individual feature and gesture. For those who knew Davis, it's a self-portrait. The hand that holds the cigarette is like a sketch of an idea, almost clumsy in its lack of anatomical articulation. The magic (the detail) is the exhaled smoke. It emerges from a mouth that is nowhere present. It drifts up to form a nimbus that occludes the eye he hasn't painted. It's a whole vibe. *Luxe, calme et volupté*. Davis has even painted some Matissean stripes behind the hand that just barely grazes his chin. The exhaled smoke is also exhaled air. Breathe in, breathe out. Here the cigarette is a measure of time, a metronome of breath, each exhalation a downbeat.

Some folks become mythic. Noah Davis seems destined to be one of those people. Myth is all big picture. Myth lacks texture, and instead hangs its drama over us like a veil, encompassing us in a kind of delicious passivity. Myth confirms our smallness. Myth lets us have awe, mouth agape, limbs loose. Myth does not traffic in details. When folks say, "The hat makes the man," what they are saying is the detail is what makes us human, all too human. Subjectivity comes about from the way you wear your hat, the way you sip your tea. Gesture is how we know the body of the other. Detail is where we feel our specificity as separate and distinct from someone else's subjectivity. It's why that line of paint that makes an ever so slightly arched eyebrow lets us know the picture is a self-portrait. The languorous gesture of the hand behind the head, the crossing of the ankles: it's all Davis to a tee. Davis the specific. Davis as a detail. Is it too obvious to say that the logic of racism is literally obliterated by the realm of the detail?

Time is a thief. My memory of Noah is faded and blurred. The more time passes, the more the details fall away, the more myth grows. In the end that's what the paintings are for. The paintings both make the myth and dispel it. They don't fade. They keep offering their worldview, their accumulation of facts. It's always up to the viewer to make up the story. When I look at the details in Davis's work, I see the way he took people as they were. One at a time. Each one of us a walking and talking compendium of details. Each one of us part of the swarm called humanity. Each one of us a detail—always worth a second look. Each of us a key to unlocking a larger composition. Each of us only and always an entanglement of specificities. Details on details, for only trees can make a forest. And only forests can clean the air, the stuff we breathe, the stuff we see through, the stuff that surrounds us, the stuff of life, the crucial details. A Noah Davis kind of truth.

NOTES

Robert Rauschenberg: Before *Bed*
pages 16–27

1 John Cage, *Silence* (Middletown, CT: Wesleyan University Press, 1973), 108.
2 Calvin Tomkins, *Off the Wall: Robert Rauschenberg and the Art World of Our Time* (Garden City, NY: Doubleday, 1980), 71. Tomkins claims that Rauschenberg would randomly drop glue-soaked newspaper onto the canvas, implying that the canvas was horizontal, but no other scholarship makes that assertion.
3 Rauschenberg made at least nine black paintings during 1952 while at Black Mountain and at least seven at his Fulton Street studio in New York during the spring and summer of 1953.
4 Walter Hopps, *Robert Rauschenberg: The Early 1950s* (Houston: Houston Fine Arts Press, 1991), 62.
5 Ernest Jones, "Anal-Erotic Character Traits," in *Papers on Psycho-Analysis* (New York: William Wood and Company, 1918), 676.
6 Two examples are: Roni Feinstein's "Random Order: The First Fifteen Years of Robert Rauschenberg's Art, 1949–1964" (PhD diss., New York University, 1990), as primarily descriptive; and Mary Lynn Kotz's monograph *Rauschenberg: Art and Life* (New York: Harry N. Abrams, 1990), as biographical.
7 The importance of the desire to mark bodily form in 1950s art practice is an idea that had its genesis in the context of Rosalind Krauss's seminar "The Transgressive '50s" at the CUNY Graduate Center. Krauss's work on Jackson Pollock and Pamela Lee's work on Cy Twombly created the space out of which this article grew.
8 The exception is Jonathan Weinberg's "It's in the Can: Jasper Johns and the Anal Society," *Genders* 1 (Spring 1988): 40–56.
9 The relationship between Rauschenberg and John Cage has been well documented. See Calvin Tomkins, *The Bride and the Bachelors* (London: Penguin, 1976). The relationship between Rauschenberg and Olson is much less clear. They were both, however, part of *Theater Piece No. 1* (1952), a multimedia event that is often referred to as the first performance art piece. Among many other activities, Olson read poetry, and Rauschenberg's *White Painting* was included.
10 Cage, *Silence*, 98.
11 Ibid., 8.
12 I must thank Charles Molesworth, who brought this text to my attention and who initially suggested the link between the concerns of Olson and Rauschenberg.
13 Charles Olson, *Additional Prose*, ed. George F. Butterick (Bolinas, CA: Four Seasons Foundation, 1974), 17.
14 Dore Ashton, "Robert Rauschenberg," *Art Digest*, September 1953, 20, 25.
15 Alan Solomon, *Robert Rauschenberg* (New York: Jewish Museum, 1963), n.p.
16 Barbara Rose, *Robert Rauschenberg* (New York: Vintage Books, 1987), 23.
17 Ellen Johnson, ed., *American Artists on Art from 1940 to 1980* (New York: Harper & Row, 1982), 4.
18 Dennis Cooper, *Frisk* (New York: Grove Weidenfeld, 1991), 69.
19 Ibid., 78.
20 See Sigmund Freud, *Leonardo da Vinci and a Memory of His Childhood*, trans. Alan Tyson (New York: Norton, 1989), and "On the Sexual Theories of Children," in *The Standard Edition of the Complete Psychological Works of Sigmund Freud*, ed. and trans. James Strachey, vol. 9, *1906–1908* (London: Hogarth Press, 1959), 205–26.
21 See Jean Laplanche, "To Situate Sublimation," trans. Richard Miller, *October* 28 (Spring 1984): 7–26.
22 Melanie Klein, *The Psycho-Analysis of Children* (London: Hogarth Press, 1963), 208.
23 Sigmund Freud, *Civilization and Its Discontents*, trans. James Strachey (New York: W. W. Norton, 1961), 54. In the same passage, Freud notes that despite sublimation we are rarely repulsed by our own excrement.
24 Roland Barthes, *The Responsibility of Forms*, trans. Richard Howard (Berkeley: University of California Press, 1985), 207. Barthes establishes this idea of turning oneself inside out to discuss the work of the French painter Bernard Requichot.
25 Ibid., 210–11.
26 Jones, "Anal-Erotic Character Traits," 683.
27 Georges Didi-Huberman, "The Index of the Absent Wound (Monograph on a Stain)," trans. Thomas Repensek, *October* 29 (Summer 1984): 68.
28 Rose, *Robert Rauschenberg*, 52.
29 Andrew Forge, *Robert Rauschenberg* (Amsterdam: Stedelijk Museum, 1968), 65.
30 Norman O. Brown, *Life against Death* (Middletown, CT: Wesleyan University Press, 1959). Brown makes a distinction between the neo-Freudian definition of anality as "an attitude in interpersonal relationships" and orthodox Freudians who relate it directly to toilet training. He argues that anality is a function of fantasy life connected to the anal zone, of fantasies that are subsequently projected onto the world.
31 Forge, *Robert Rauschenberg*, 64.
32 Brown, *Life against Death*, 289.

33 See Sándor Ferenczi, *Further Contributions to the Theory and Technique of Psycho-Analysis*, ed. John Rickman, trans. Jane Isabel Suttie (New York: Basic Books, 1952), especially "Composite Formations of Erotic and Character Traits" (1916/17), 257–58.
34 Brown, *Life against Death*, 293.
35 Barthes, *The Responsibility of Forms*, 211.

Kerry James Marshall: Project America
pages 33–39

1 Clement Greenberg, "'American-Type' Painting," *Partisan Review* 22, no. 2 (Spring 1955): 188.
2 See Dave Hickey, "The Delicacy of Rock-and-Roll," in *Air Guitar: Essays on Art and Democracy* (Los Angeles: Art Issues Press, 1997), 96–101.

Work Ethic
pages 43–60

1 Leo Steinberg, *Other Criteria: Confrontations with Twentieth-Century Art* (London: Oxford University Press, 1972), 60.
2 This essay argues that art practices and labor practices are inextricably linked. Although the transformation of the American economy has had global ramifications, this essay deals primarily with the ways in which American artists negotiated the changing definitions of labor. The intricate relations of labor practices, ideologies, and their impact on art making in other parts of the world are beyond the scope of this essay.
3 See Mark Seltzer's *Bodies and Machines* (New York: Routledge, 1992). Writing about the phenomenon of Taylorization and the rise of scientific management, Seltzer observes: "The real innovation of Taylorization becomes visible in the incorporation of the representation of the work process into the work process itself—or, better, the incorporation of the representation of the work process as the work process itself" (159).
4 Paul Osterman et al., *Working in America: A Blueprint for the New Labor Market* (Cambridge, MA: MIT Press, 2001), 33.
5 B. Joseph Pine II and James H. Gilmore, *The Experience Economy* (Boston: Harvard Business School Press, 1999), 8.
6 For the shift from a goods-based to a service-based economy and the definitions of each, see ibid., 8–9. This work also claims that we are currently in the midst of a shift from a service-based economy to an experience-based economy, with experiences described as "events that engage individuals in a personal way" (12).
7 On the importance of Duchamp's reception in America, particularly its deferred nature, see Hal Foster's "What's Neo about the Neo-Avant-Garde?," *October* 70 (Fall 1994): 5–32.
8 The rejection of the museum means that while much advanced art from the 1960s and 1970s now forms the canon of art history within the academy, its entrance into the narrative of art history offered by the museum has been infinitely slower. This has changed in recent years with the advent of important exhibitions. See, for instance, Ann Goldstein and Anne Rorimer, *Reconsidering the Object of Art: 1965–1975* (Los Angeles: Museum of Contemporary Art; Cambridge, MA: MIT Press, 1995); Paul Schimmel, *Out of Actions: Between Performance and the Object, 1949–1979* (Los Angeles: Museum of Contemporary Art; New York: Thames & Hudson, 1998); and Luis Camnitzer et al., *Global Conceptualism: Points of Origin, 1950s–1980s* (New York: Queens Museum of Art, 1999).
9 Marcel Duchamp, "The Creative Act," in *The Writings of Marcel Duchamp*, ed. Michel Sanouillet and Elmer Peterson (New York: Da Capo Press, 1973), 140.
10 Roland Barthes, "The Death of the Author," in *Image Music Text*, trans. Stephen Heath (New York: Hill & Wang, 1977), 143, 148.
11 For more on the relations between these two texts, see Benjamin H. D. Buchloh, "Readymade, Objet Trouvé, Idée Reçue," in *Dissent: The Issue of Modern Art in Boston* (Boston: Institute of Contemporary Art, 1985), 106–22.
12 Sol LeWitt, "Serial Project #1, 1966," *Aspen*, no. 5–6 (Fall/Winter 1967): n.p.
13 Howard Singerman, *Art Subjects: Making Artists in the American University* (Berkeley: University of California Press, 1999), 144. When Rauschenberg was a student at the Art Students' League in New York, he rebelliously turned his back on the live nude model and made a white painting with numbers instead.
14 Harold Rosenberg, "Everyman a Professional," in *The Tradition of the New* (New York: Horizon Press, 1959), 63.
15 Caroline Jones's *Machine in the Studio: Constructing the Postwar American Artist* (Chicago: University of Chicago Press, 1996) argues that a veritable industry of documenting artists at work in their studios accompanies the rise of Abstract Expressionism. I would like to suggest that a certain anxiety may have been at work regarding whether abstraction was legitimate artistic labor; the inordinate amount

of documentation might seem to make it so. For a discussion of Pollock's and Newman's self-presentation, see chapter 3 in particular.

16 As quoted in ibid., 121.

17 Allan Kaprow, "Should the Artist Become a Man of the World?" (1964), in *Essays on the Blurring of Art and Life*, ed. Jeff Kelley (Berkeley: University of California Press, 1996), 35.

18 Sharon Zukin, *Loft Living: Culture and Capital in Urban Change* (Baltimore: Johns Hopkins University Press, 1982), 5. Zukin argues that in a concerted effort to create high-end office space and equally luxurious residential spaces, city and bank investments consistently foreclosed manufacturing options in Manhattan. She contends that "the residential conversion of a manufacturing space provides a substantial part of the infrastructure for a supposedly post-industrial economy," adding that "this infrastructure fulfills the physical needs of the service-sector and white collar employees" (19).

19 Ibid., 50.

20 Ernest Mandel, *Late Capitalism*, trans. Joris De Bres (London: Verso, 1978), 387.

21 According to Harvard School of Business professors Pine and Gilmore, authors of *The Experience Economy*, the service industry is in the process of being eclipsed by the "experience economy." Here, services are tailored to clients in ways that increase their experiential quotient. A cup of coffee is no longer served to you by a counter person but by a "barista," and the event takes place in an environment dedicated to the experience of coffee as opposed to a "mixed-use" environment (like a lunch counter or deli). This shift is what enables a three-dollar cup of coffee. Such micromanaged and highly orchestrated services become "experiences" whose driving motive is the creation of profit.

22 As quoted in Tony Godfrey, *Conceptual Art* (London: Phaidon Press, 1998), 127.

23 See Darsie Alexander's "Reluctant Witness: Photography and the Documentation of 1960s and 1970s Art," in *Work Ethic*, ed. Helen Molesworth (Baltimore: Baltimore Museum of Art; University Park: Pennsylvania State University Press, 2003), 53–65.

24 Sol LeWitt, "Paragraphs on Conceptual Art" (1967), in *Conceptual Art: A Critical Anthology*, ed. Alexander Alberro and Blake Stimson (Cambridge, MA: MIT Press, 1999), 12.

25 Benjamin H. D. Buchloh, "Conceptual Art 1962–1969: From the Aesthetic of Administration to the Critique of Institutions," *October* 55 (Winter 1990): 128.

26 Quoted in Marcia Tucker and Robert Pincus-Witten, *John Baldessari* (Dayton, OH: University Art Galleries; New York: New Museum, 1981), 15.

27 See Helen Molesworth, "House Work and Art Work," *October* 92 (Winter 2000): 71–97.

28 Allan Kaprow, telephone conversation with the author, November 2002. Kaprow's work was never designed to be exhibited in museums, and he continues to resist the kind of historicization that such exhibiting entails.

29 The work was entitled *Disappearing Music for Face* (ca. 1965), and the participant was Yoko Ono.

30 Fellow traveler Henry Flynt would organize, along with Maciunas, a 1963 demonstration against "serious culture" (directed at the Metropolitan Museum of Art, Lincoln Center, and the Museum of Modern Art), suggesting that high art had already fallen prey to the logic of late capitalism, a logic that could potentially be fought with the weapon of nonseriousness.

31 For the ethical problematic of much 1960s and 1970s performance, see Frazer David Ward, "False Intimacies, Open Secrets: Public and Private in the Performance Art of Vito Acconci and Chris Burden" (PhD diss., Cornell University, 2000). See also Miwon Kwon's "Exchange Rate: On Obligation and Reciprocity in Some Art of the 1960s and After," in Molesworth, *Work Ethic*, 83–97.

32 Herbert Marcuse was the most influential thinker of the postwar period regarding issues of work, leisure, and creativity. In *Eros and Civilization* (1955), he argued that "the play impulse is the vehicle of liberation." Linking libidinal urges and play urges, he advocated a desublimation of work's repressive tendencies. See Marcuse, *Eros and Civilization: A Philosophical Inquiry into Freud* (Boston: Beacon Press, 1966), 171. See also Chris Gilbert's essay on Marcuse's theories of leisure, "Herbie Goes Bananas: Fantasies of Leisure and Labor from the New Left to the New Economy," in Molesworth, *Work Ethic*, 67–81.

33 Michael Hardt and Antonio Negri, *Empire* (Cambridge, MA: Harvard University Press, 2000), 275.

34 Ibid., 293.

35 Ibid., 275; emphasis in the original.

36 On the repetition of Dada strategies throughout the postwar period, see Helen Molesworth, "From Dada to Neo-Dada and Back Again," *October* 105 (Summer 2003): 177–81.

37 For an expansion on this dichotomy in museological practice, see Nicholas Serota, *Experience or Interpretation: The Dilemma of Museums of Modern Art* (New York: Thames & Hudson, 1997).

Rrose Sélavy Goes Shopping
pages 61–73

1 Marcel Duchamp, quoted in "The Art of Assemblage: Transcript of the Symposium," in *Essays on Assemblage*, Studies in Modern Art, ed. John Elderfield (New York: Museum of Modern Art, 1992), 135.
2 Marcel Duchamp, "À l'Infinitif," in *The Writings of Marcel Duchamp*, ed. Michel Sanouillet and Elmer Peterson (New York: Da Capo Press, 1973), 74.
3 Ibid.
4 "The Richard Mutt Case," *The Blind Man*, no. 2 (May 1917): 5.
5 Beatrice Wood, "Marcel," in *Marcel Duchamp: Artist of the Century*, ed. Rudolf E. Kuenzli and Francis M. Naumann (Cambridge, MA: MIT Press, 1989), 14.
6 Pierre Bourdieu, *Distinction: A Social Critique of the Judgement of Taste*, trans. Richard Nice (Cambridge, MA: Harvard University Press, 1984), 56.
7 Hence, I imagine myself as someone who prefers Volkswagens to Audis, in part because I am someone who can afford a Volkswagen and not an Audi. Rather than feel badly about my inability to buy an Audi, I develop a fondness for Volkswagens as such, aided, without a doubt, by their hipster ad campaign that "speaks" to my generation.
8 Bourdieu, *Distinction*, 175.
9 Duchamp, "À l'Infinitif," 74.
10 Neil Harris, "Museums, Merchandising, and Popular Taste: The Struggle for Influence," in *Material Culture and the Study of American Life*, ed. Ian M. G. Quimby (New York: Norton, 1978), 154. Harris argues that the three elements of public taste are "knowledgeability, experience, and preference patterns."
11 John Wanamaker, *Golden Book of the Wanamaker Stories: Jubilee Year, 1861–1911* (Philadelphia: Forgotten Books, 2018), 245–46.
12 William Leach, *Land of Desire: Merchants, Power, and the Rise of a New American Culture* (New York: Vintage, 1994), 170.
13 Ibid., 167.
14 Ibid., 168.
15 John Cotton Dana, *The Gloom of the Museum* (Woodstock, VT: Elm Tree Press, 1917), 21.
16 See Carol Duncan, "John Cotton Dana's Progressive Museum," in *Self and History: A Tribute to Linda Nochlin*, ed. Aruna D'Souza (London: Thames & Hudson, 2001).
17 Bettina Berch, "Scientific Management in the Home: The Empress's New Clothes," *Journal of American Culture* 3, no. 3 (Fall 1980): 443.
18 On the shift from the production of daily goods such as soap and clothing and women's new role in sorting through the vagaries of ready-made goods, see Susan Strasser, *Satisfaction Guaranteed: The Making of the American Mass Market* (New York: Smithsonian Books, 1989); on the effect of department stores on women's shopping behavior, see Gail Reekie, *Temptations: Sex, Selling and the Department Store* (Sydney: Allen & Unwin, 1993), and Elaine S. Abelson, *When Ladies Go A-Thieving: Middle-Class Shoplifters in the Victorian Department Store* (New York: Oxford University Press, 1989); on the rise and proliferation of the genre of advice to women, on everything from shopping to mothering, see Barbara Ehrenreich and Deirdre English, *For Her Own Good: 150 Years of the Experts' Advice to Women* (Garden City, NY: Anchor Press, 1978).
19 *Webster's New Collegiate Dictionary*, 1977, s.v. "trademark."
20 This is the primary difference between my argument and Molly Nesbit's in "Ready-Made Originals: The Duchamp Model." Nesbit argues that Duchamp uses the "language of the industry," as typified by mechanical drawing taught in French schools, as a way to think about the "modern model of repetition's relationship to mass-production." In Nesbit's account, Duchamp tried to negotiate the "interrogation of shop windows" by reintroducing the "culture of the patent," meaning the values of the artisan and the original, to fight the "culture of the copyright," meaning the logic of repetition, mass production, and the commodity. While sympathetic to this persuasive argument, I have one fundamental reservation: the logic of the trademark more accurately describes the part of Duchamp's work that is invested in consumption as an activity, particularly with regard to his later discourse about taste and his early disclosure of choice. The logic of the copyright, as described by Nesbit, accurately describes his relation to the "exclusively" art-related issues of originality and the copy but does not account for his meditation on mass consumption as opposed to mass production. See Molly Nesbit, "Ready-Made Originals: The Duchamp Model," *October* 37 (Summer 1986): 53–64.
21 Strasser, *Satisfaction Guaranteed*, 6–7.
22 See William A. Camfield, *Marcel Duchamp: Fountain* (Houston: Houston Fine Art Press, 1989).
23 This transcription is part of Duchamp's larger play with complicating the notion of temporality in art history, for this "signature" was first used on the *Boîte-en-valise (Box in a Suitcase)* (1935–41),

the work in which Duchamp staged his own retrospective in miniature.
24 Bourdieu, *Distinction*, 56.
25 See Francis M. Naumann, "The Independents," in *New York Dada: 1915–23* (New York: Harry N. Abrams, 1994), 176–91.
26 On the other hand, a urinal is literally tasteless, without taste or class markings; "Now Mr. Mutt's fountain is not immoral, that is absurd, no more than a bath tub is immoral."
27 Wood, "Marcel," 14.
28 Camfield, *Marcel Duchamp: Fountain*, 30–31.
29 Wood, "Marcel," 12–13.
30 The two best histories of the exhibition of the readymades are Camfield's *Marcel Duchamp: Fountain* and Thierry de Duve's *Kant after Duchamp* (Cambridge, MA: MIT Press, 1996), especially chapter 2. Our knowledge of the readymades from this period comes almost exclusively from the famous photographs of Duchamp's studio, personal accounts of visits to the studio, letters, and the Stieglitz photograph of *Fountain*.
31 See Benjamin H. D. Buchloh, "Readymade, Objet Trouvé, Idée Reçue," in *Dissent: The Issue of Modern Art in Boston* (Boston: Institute of Contemporary Art, 1985), 111, and Rosalind E. Krauss, "Notes on the Index," in *The Originality of the Avant-Garde and Other Modernist Myths* (Cambridge, MA: MIT Press, 1985).
32 This argument is seen most clearly (and most reductively) in Robert Rauschenberg's understanding of the performative utterance. When asked by art patron Iris Clert for a portrait, Rauschenberg replied by sending a telegram that read: "This is a portrait of Iris Clert if I say so."
33 *Mary Sisler Collection* (1964), n.p., Philadelphia Museum of Art, object file.
34 Bourdieu, *Distinction*, 57.

My Funny Valentine: *Étant donnés*
pages 74–83

1 Benjamin H. D. Buchloh, "Introduction," *October* 70 (Autumn 1994): 4.
2 Michael R. Taylor, *Marcel Duchamp: Étant donnés* (Philadelphia: Philadelphia Museum of Art; New Haven, CT: Yale University Press, 2009).
3 Jean-François Lyotard, *Les Transformateurs Duchamp* (Paris: Galilée, 1977), 138.
4 Rosalind E. Krauss, *The Optical Unconscious* (Cambridge, MA: MIT Press, 1993), 113.
5 Pierre Cabanne, *Dialogues with Marcel Duchamp*, trans. Ron Padgett (New York: Da Capo Press, 1987), 88.
6 Marcel Duchamp, letter to Maria Martins, October 12, 1948, in Taylor, *Étant donnés*, 409.
7 Marcel Duchamp, letter to Maria Martins, April 7, 1949, in ibid.
8 Leo Bersani, *The Freudian Body: Psychoanalysis and Art* (New York: Columbia University Press, 1986), 60.

House Work and Art Work
pages 88–105

1 In the past few years, numerous exhibitions have taken place, to name but a few: Mary Kelly's *Post-Partum Document* was reassembled in its entirety by the Generali Foundation in Vienna (September 25–December 20, 1998); Martha Rosler is the subject of a traveling retrospective organized by Ikon Gallery in Birmingham, UK; Mierle Laderman Ukeles's *Maintenance Art* series was shown in its entirety at the Ronald Feldman Gallery, New York; Judy Chicago's *The Dinner Party* was the centerpiece of an exhibit curated by Amelia Jones at the Hammer Museum, Los Angeles (*Sexual Politics: Judy Chicago's* Dinner Party *in Feminist Art History*, April 24–August 18, 1996); *Division of Labor: "Women's Work" in Contemporary Art* was held at the Bronx Museum of the Arts (February 17–June 11, 1995); and the *Bad Girls* exhibition took place at the New Museum, New York (January 14–February 27 and March 5–April 10, 1994). So, too, books and journals have proliferated: *October* dedicated an entire issue to the question of feminism, replete with a questionnaire and a round table (*October* 71 [Winter 1995]); Laura Cottingham produced *Not for Sale* (1998), a video essay designed for teaching feminist art; *Feminism and Contemporary Art: The Revolutionary Power of Women's Laughter* by Jo Anna Isaak appeared in 1996 (London: Routledge); Mira Schor's award-winning *Wet: On Painting, Feminism, and Art Culture* (Durham, NC: Duke University Press, 1997) also appeared recently; and *The Power of Feminist Art* brought together in one volume a commanding overview of American feminist art of the 1970s (New York: Harry N. Abrams, 1994).
2 Under the umbrella of "essentialism," I am referring to artists and critics such as Norma Broude, Judy Chicago, Mary D. Garrard, Harmony Hammond, Suzanne Lacy, Lucy Lippard, Ana Mendieta, Faith Ringgold, Miriam Schapiro, Mira Schor, Faith Wilding, the artists involved in *Womanhouse* and the Feminist Art Program. And with regard to poststructuralism, I'm thinking here of the work of Victor Burgin, Mary Kelly, Silvia Kolbowski, Barbara Kruger, Kate

Linker, Laura Mulvey, Griselda Pollock, Cindy Sherman, and Lisa Tickner.

3 For a more elaborated account of this debate, see my "Cleaning Up in the 1970s: The Work of Judy Chicago, Mary Kelly and Mierle Laderman Ukeles," in *Rewriting Conceptual Art*, ed. Michael Newman and Jon Bird (London: Reaktion Books, 1999), 107–22.

4 Given that the works were made during the same period, clearly this is not the case. However, they were made in different geographical locations within which extremely different types of feminist discussions were taking place. See Mary Kelly's remarks to this effect in "A Conversation on Recent Feminist Art Practices," *October* 71 (Winter 1995): 49–69.

5 Lisa Tickner in ibid., 44.

6 Griselda Pollock, "Painting, Feminism, History," in *Destabilizing Theory: Contemporary Feminist Debates*, ed. Michèle Barrett and Anne Phillips (Stanford, CA: Stanford University Press, 1992), 154.

7 Faith Wilding, "The Feminist Programs at Fresno and CalArts, 1970–75," in *The Power of Feminist Art: The American Movement of the 1970s, History and Impact*, ed. Norma Broude and Mary D. Garrard (New York: Harry N. Abrams, 1994), 35.

8 Mary Kelly has frequently argued against the category "feminist art." Arguing against the notion of a cohesive "style" of feminist art, she proposes instead the notion of art "informed by feminism." See the exchange between Kelly and Silvia Kolbowski in "A Conversation on Recent Feminist Art Practices."

9 This is the effect of Laura Cottingham's video essay, designed for pedagogical purposes, *Not for Sale*. This tape's structure is based on that of the art history survey: it casts a wide net, includes a barrage of artists without explanation or justification for their inclusion (save their gender), the effect of which is that we are left with an alternative "canon." The separatist quality of the tape means that the practice of many artists is radically decontextualized and the work of nearly all the artists is ghettoized. For more on this tape, see my "Not for Sale" in *frieze*, no. 41 (Summer 1998): 91–92.

10 My thanks to Janet Kraynak for a discussion of this point.

11 Moira Gatens, *Feminism and Philosophy: Perspectives on Difference and Equality* (Bloomington: Indiana University Press, 1991).

12 Moira Gatens, "Powers, Bodies, and Difference," in Barrett and Phillips, *Destabilizing Theory*, 124.

13 Gatens, *Feminism and Philosophy*, 138.

14 Ibid., 124–25.

15 Ibid., 122–23.

16 For an elaboration of this argument, see Carole Pateman's *The Sexual Contract* (Stanford, CA: Stanford University Press, 1988). This critique elaborates on the problem of "equality" within liberal thought that is based in part on the inability of capitalism to function without the unpaid labor of maintenance. This subsequently permits a critique of democracy's historical dependence upon slavery. Here the implications of political theory are indispensable for thinking through the perennial blind spot of both Anglo-American and continental feminism, the problem of racial and ethnic difference.

17 Gatens, "Powers, Bodies, and Difference," 131.

18 Ibid., 128.

19 Ibid., 135.

20 Additionally, the essentialism/theory debate may also have restricted feminist discourse to notions of the subject that reside (rhetorically) outside of the dominant structure of capitalism, hence further marginalizing the political potential of feminism; and art that operates within its concerns.

21 For a reprint of Ukeles's "Maintenance Art Manifesto" in its entirety, see "Artist Project: Mierle Laderman Ukeles Maintenance Art Activity (1973) with Responses from Miwon Kwon and Helen Molesworth," *Documents*, no. 10 (Fall 1997): 5–22.

22 It is Ukeles's insistence on the structural aspect of everyday maintenance labor, as opposed to a fetishized notion of the "everyday," that distinguishes her performances from recent practices that merely represent or stage the everyday, such as Rirkrit Tiravanija's recent exhibition in which he placed a facsimile of his apartment in the gallery and allowed visitors to use the space as they saw fit. For instance, part of the "Maintenance Art Manifesto" included an exhibition proposal called "Care," in which Ukeles proposed to do the following: "live in the museum as I customarily do at home with my husband and my baby, for the duration of the exhibition, (Right? or if you don't want me around at night I would come in every day) and do all these things as public Art activities: I will sweep and wax the floors, dust everything, wash the walls (i.e., 'floor paintings, dust works, soap sculpture, wall paintings'), cook, invite people to eat, make agglomerations and dispositions of all functional refuse. The exhibition area might look 'empty' of art, but it will be maintained in full public view. MY WORKING WILL BE THE WORK." Needless to say, no one ever accepted this proposal. For an account

of Tiravanija's practice, see Janet Kraynak, "Rirkrit Tiravanija's Liability," *Documents*, no. 13 13 (Fall 1998): 26–40.

23 Griselda Pollock has argued that the "radical reconceptualization of the function of artistic activity—its procedures, personnel, and institutional sites—is the major legacy of feminist interventions in culture since the late sixties." See Pollock, "Painting, Feminism, History," 155.

24 For instance, no women artists are discussed in Benjamin H. D. Buchloh's "Conceptual Art 1962-1969: From the Aesthetic of Administration to the Critique of Institutions," *October* 55 (Winter 1990), although Hilla Becher and Hanne Darboven are mentioned in passing. More recently, Ann Goldstein and Anne Rorimer, *Reconsidering the Object of Art: 1965–1975* (Los Angeles: Museum of Contemporary Art; Cambridge, MA: MIT Press, 1995), included only eight women out of a total of fifty-six artists. More recently, however, this seems to have changed. For example, Peter Wollen included numerous women artists in the North American section of the 1999 exhibition *Global Conceptualism: Points of Origin, 1950s–1980s*.

25 Rosalyn Deutsche, *Evictions: Art and Spatial Politics* (Cambridge, MA: MIT Press, 1996), 273.

26 Pateman, *The Sexual Contract*, 144.

27 For an account of Chicago's early work and *The Dinner Party*'s fetishism of surface see Laura Meyer, "From Finish Fetish to Feminism: Judy Chicago's *Dinner Party* in California Art History," in *Sexual Politics: Judy Chicago's* Dinner Party *in Feminist Art History*, ed. Amelia Jones (Los Angeles: UCLA at the Armand Hammer Museum of Art and Cultural Center; Berkeley: University of California Press, 1996), 46–74.

28 *The Dinner Party*, it should be noted, is always exhibited accompanied by documentary photographs of the massive groups and collectives of women who worked on the project. In this regard, the labor of making *The Dinner Party* is always registered, but in a peripheral, supporting role. *The Dinner Party* effaces the marks of labor within its boundaries, and in so doing presents itself like a traditional museum-oriented art object: the result of creative genius as opposed to manual labor (a distinction that perpetuates the power relations between the artist and those who work in his or her atelier), and, furthermore, the result of artistic labor only, not the maintenance labor that supports such labor.

29 For an account of Minimalism that argues that the sculptures pressured the terms of what is and is not sculpture, see Rosalind E. Krauss, "Sculpture in the Expanded Field," in *The Originality and the Avant-Garde and Other Modernist Myths* (Cambridge, MA: MIT Press, 1985).

30 The exhibition *Women and Work* was curated by Margaret Harrison, Kay Hunt, and Mary Kelly; *Nightcleaners* was made by the Berwick Street Film Collective: Mark Karlin, Mary Kelly, James Scott, and Humphrey Trevelyan. For the best account of Kelly's early practice, see Judith Matsai, ed., *Social Process/Collaborative Action: Mary Kelly 1970–75* (Vancouver: Charles H. Scott Gallery, Emily Carr Institute of Art and Design, 1997).

31 Buchloh, "Conceptual Art 1962-1969," 107.

32 Frazer Ward, "Some Relations between Conceptual and Performance Art," *Art Journal* 56, no. 4 (Winter 1997): 39.

33 In this light, Kelly's *PPD* can be seen as a direct attack against the Conceptual art of someone like Joseph Kosuth, for instance, but not, say, the work of Hans Haacke. However, Kelly's work also does serve to problematize the dominant reception of Conceptual art as defined by male artists. For more on the historical context of the *Post-Partum Document*, see Juli Carson, "(Re)Viewing Mary Kelly's *Post-Partum Document*," *Documents*, no. 13 (Fall 1998): 41–60.

34 Mary Kelly, *Post-Partum Document* (London: Routledge & Kegan Paul, 1985), xvi.

35 I do not want to place these artists so firmly within specific categories that their work is seen to be either only an instance of that "style" of work, nor do I want to suggest that these "styles" are in any way internally coherent. Rather, I want to emphasize the ways in which these works are in conscious and explicit dialogue with the predominant movements of critical art of their period.

36 Frazer Ward, "The Haunted Museum: Institutional Critique and Publicity," *October* 73 (Summer 1995): 83.

37 The phrase "aesthetic of administration" is taken from Buchloh's definitive "Conceptual Art 1962-1969."

38 The tape is called this in the descriptive list of Rosler's works found in *Martha Rosler: Positions in the Life World*, ed. Catherine de Zegher (Birmingham, UK: Ikon Gallery; Vienna: Generali Foundation, 1998).

39 This is perhaps why *Vital Statistics* and *The Bowery* are her best-known works, in that each could be disseminated more easily in the form of photography, and hence traveled better through the distribution network of art magazines, etc. (For instance, *Vital Statistics* is usually represented as a photograph, while the video is not often shown.)

40 Rosler in de Zegher, *Martha Rosler: Positions in the Life World*, 31.
41 Benjamin H. D. Buchloh, "A Conversation with Martha Rosler," in ibid.
42 For more on the charge of kitsch launched against *The Dinner Party*, see Amelia Jones's "The 'Sexual Politics' of *The Dinner Party*: A Critical Context," in Jones, *Sexual Politics*, 82–118.
43 Conversation with the artist, summer 1997. See Miwon Kwon, "In Appreciation of Invisible Work: Mierle Laderman Ukeles and the Maintenance of the 'White Cube,'" *Documents*, no. 10 (Fall 1997): 15–18.
44 Fredric Jameson, "Periodizing the 1960s," in *The Sixties without Apology*, ed. Sohnya Sayres, Anders Stephanson, Stanley Aronowitz, and Fredric Jameson (Minneapolis: University of Minnesota Press, 1984), 79. Additionally, Martha Rosler has said of her own work, "Everything I have ever done I've thought of 'as if': Every single thing I have offered to the public has been offered as a suggestion of a work . . . which is that my work is a sketch, a line of thinking, a possibility." Buchloh, "A Conversation," 31.
45 For more on the importance of privacy, see Drucilla Cornell, *At the Heart of Freedom: Feminism, Sex, and Equality* (Princeton, NJ: Princeton University Press, 1998). Cornell despatializes privacy by insisting on the idea of an imaginary domain. The imaginary domain is a site (both imagined and actualized), where persons are free to articulate their desires with the historical protections of the idea of "privacy." By despatializing privacy, she is able to unhinge it from notions of private property, notions which have been legally disadvantageous for women (with regard to domestic violence, for instance).
46 Gatens, *Feminism and Philosophy*, 129.
47 Cornell, *At the Heart of Freedom*, 24.

Painting with Ambivalence
pages 106–17

1 There are numerous feminisms. For the sake of clarification, in my argument, I maintain that a feminist methodology offers two incisive gestures. The first is a paraphrase of Peggy Phelan's definition of feminism: it is a challenge to the persistent organization of the world through the category of gender that consistently privileges men. The second is that feminism privileges self-criticality (as opposed to self-expression, per se) in political, aesthetic, and intellectual practice.
2 Anne Middleton Wagner, *Three Artists (Three Women): Modernism and the Art of Hesse, Krasner, and O'Keeffe* (Berkeley: University of California Press, 1996), 16.
3 Of course only certain artists and critics, but those who held the purchase of the avant-garde or "advanced" art practices. Although many male artists continued to paint, it is historically fair to argue that the cultural and aesthetic value of painting slipped considerably as the hierarchies of media were radically reorganized as a result of the ascendancy of sculpture, photography, and the reception of the Duchampian readymade.
4 Phelan, survey for *Art and Feminism*, ed. Helena Reckitt (London: Phaidon Press, 2001), 32–34. I recently experienced this "rejection as trauma" acutely as I clung to the edge of my university quad on the day the undergraduates set up their "Take Back the Night" rally. To my horror, the other women participating in this staging of judgment ("How pathetic" practically audible as we silently walked by) were sorority girls. Of course, I thought, why would any of us want to walk into a space that asks us to identify with the trauma of rape? But where was I, between the sorority girls and today's nascent generation of feminists?
5 Lucy R. Lippard, introduction to *From the Center: Feminist Essays on Women's Art* (New York: E. P. Dutton, 1976), 3–4. The coalition Lippard refers to is the Art Workers' Coalition, of which she was a founding member.
6 Linda Nochlin argued that women were not permitted the same training as men, most notably when it came to learning to draw from the live nude. Without this crucial aspect of representational painting, how, she asked, could women artists ever have equaled their male counterparts? "Why Have There Been No Great Women Artists?," *ARTnews*, January 1971, 22–39, 67.
7 In her catalogue essay for "Ten Artists (Who Also Happen to Be Women)," reprinted as part of "Prefaces to Catalogues of Women's Exhibitions" in *From the Center*, Lippard wrote: "I continued to go to men's studios and either disregard or matronize the women artists who worked in the corners of their husband's spaces, or in the bedroom, even in the kitchen" (47). Mary Heilmann and Joan Snyder were included in this exhibition.
8 Elaine de Kooning with Rosalyn Drexler, "Dialogue," *ARTnews*, January 1971, 40.
9 *Mary Heilmann: The All Night Movie* (Zurich: Offizin Verlag, 1999), 40.
10 Clement Greenberg, "After Abstract Expressionism," originally published in *Art*

International 6, no. 8 (October 1962); revised and published in Henry Geldzahler, *New York Painting and Sculpture: 1940–1970* (New York: E. P. Dutton and Metropolitan Museum of Art, 1969), 369.

11 Lisa Saltzman, "Reconsidering the Stain: On Gender and the Body in Helen Frankenthaler's Painting," in *Reclaiming Female Agency: Feminist Art History after Postmodernism*, ed. Norma Broude and Mary D. Garrard (Berkeley: University of California Press, 2005), 379.

12 Lynn F. Miller and Sally S. Swenson, interview with Howardena Pindell, in *Lives and Works: Talks with Women Artists* (Metuchen, NJ: Scarecrow Press, 1981), 134.

13 Harold Rosenberg, "The American Action Painters," originally published in *ARTnews*, September 1952; reprinted in Geldzahler, *New York Painting and Sculpture*, 342.

14 Ibid.

15 Ibid., 346.

16 Ibid., 347.

17 Hayden Herrera, *Joan Snyder: Seven Years of Work* (Purchase, NY: Neuberger Museum, State University of New York, 1978), 2.

18 Maureen Mullarkey, "Following Her Instincts: Joan Snyder's Womanart at Alexandre Gallery and Betty Cuningham Gallery," *New York Sun*, November 18, 2004.

19 T. J. Clark, *Farewell to an Idea: Episodes from a History of Modernism* (New Haven, CT: Yale University Press, 1999), 374.

20 Ibid., 389.

21 Ibid., 397.

22 Lucy R. Lippard, "Top to Bottom, Left to Right," in *Grids* (Philadelphia: Institute of Contemporary Art, 1972); excerpt reprinted in Lucy R. Lippard, *The Pink Glass Swan: Selected Feminist Essays on Art* (New York: The New Press, 1995), 68.

23 Rosalind E. Krauss, "Grids" (1978), in *The Originality of the Avant-Garde and Other Modernist Myths* (Cambridge, MA: MIT Press, 1985), 9.

24 Ibid., 17.

25 Roland Barthes, "The Photographic Message" (1961), in *Image Music Text*, trans. Stephen Heath (New York: Hill & Wang, 1977), 25.

26 Ibid., 30.

How to Install Art as a Feminist
pages 118–29

1 Eli Zaretsky, *Capitalism, the Family, and Personal Life* (New York: Harper & Row, 1976), 1.

2 Each of these exhibitions was accompanied by an important catalogue: Hayden Herrera, *Joan Snyder* (New York: Harry N. Abrams, 2005); Adam Szymczyk, ed., *Lee Lozano: Win First Dont Last Win Last Dont Care* (Basel: Schwabe AG, 2006); Elizabeth A. T. Smith, *Lee Bontecou: A Retrospective* (Chicago: Museum of Contemporary Art; Los Angeles: UCLA Hammer Museum); and Cornelia Butler and Lisa Gabrielle Mark, eds., *WACK!: Art and the Feminist Revolution* (Los Angeles: Museum of Contemporary Art; Cambridge, MA: MIT Press, 2007).

3 I place "feminist art" in quotes because I don't believe in it as a designation of style. I prefer "art made by feminists" or "art made under the influence of feminism"—both are awkward formulations but nonetheless speak to the inherent limitations of rendering a political stance into a matter of style or preference.

4 It bears noting that despite the powerfully gendered quality of these narratives of influence, they are structural, available to either sex; some male painters have been taught via oral tradition, and some female artists have staged Oedipal rebellions. See Lisa Tickner's "Mediating Generation: The Mother-Daughter Plot," in *Women Artists at the Millennium*, ed. Carol Armstrong and Catherine de Zegher (Cambridge, MA: MIT Press, 2006), 85–120. Tickner suggests that it is better to think of "the question of attachment or rupture not as a gendered distinction, but in terms of a historical contrast in modes of production" (89).

5 Ibid., 91.

6 "Family—a code word referring to gays or the gay community, as in, 'Ellen DeGeneres is Family.'" Rebecca Scott, "A Brief Dictionary of Queer Slang and Culture," www.geocitrus.com/WestHollywood/Stonewall/4219.

7 Gilles Deleuze and Félix Guattari, *A Thousand Plateaus: Capitalism and Schizophrenia*, trans. Brian Massumi (London: Athlone Press, 1988), 25; quoted in Tickner, "Mediating Generation," 91–92.

8 Walter Benjamin, "Theses on the Philosophy of History" (1950), in *Illuminations*, ed. Hannah Arendt, trans. Harry Zohn (New York: Schocken Books, 1969), 255.

9 Mignon Nixon, "O + X," *October* 119 (Winter 2007): 6–20.

10 Juliet Mitchell, *Siblings: Sex and Violence* (Cambridge, UK: Polity Press, 2003).

11. Mignon Nixon, "Child Drawing," in *Eva Hesse Drawing*, ed. Catherine de Zegher (New York: Drawing Center; New Haven, CT: Yale University Press, 2006), 27–56.

12 Mitchell, *Siblings*, 16–17.

13 Miwon Kwon, "Promiscuity of Space: Some

Thoughts on Jessica Stockholder's Scenographic Compositions," *Grey Room*, no. 18 (Winter 2005): 52–63. The quotes appear on pages 54, 58, and 59.

14 George Baker, "Film Beyond Its Limits," *Grey Room*, no. 25 (Fall 2006): 92–125.

15 See in particular Briony Fer's chapter on Eva Hesse, "Studio," in her book *An Infinite Line: Remaking Art after Modernism* (New Haven, CT: Yale University Press, 2004), 116–43.

16 Tickner, "Mediating Generation," 94.

Louise Lawler: Just the Facts
pages 132–43

1 Achim Hochdörfer, "Louise Lawler: Preliminary Remarks on a 'Phenomenology of Cuts,'" *Camera Austria*, no. 92 (2005): 21.

2 Bruce Hainley, "Mata Hari Takes a Picture," *frieze*, no. 85 (September 2004): 85.

3 Jack Bankowsky, *Investigations 1988: Louise Lawler* (Philadelphia: Institute of Contemporary Art, University of Pennsylvania, 1988), n.p.

4 Johannes Meinhardt, "The Places of Art—The Photography of Louise Lawler," in *Hugo-Erfurth-Preis* (Leverkusen, Germany: Museum Morsbroich, 1991), 26.

5 See Benjamin H. D. Buchloh, "Allegorical Procedures: Appropriation and Montage in Contemporary Art," *Artforum*, September 1982, 43–56, and Hal Foster, "Re: Post," in *Art after Modernism: Rethinking Representation*, ed. Brian Wallis (New York: New Museum of Contemporary Art, 1984), 189–201. Among more recent publications, see Isabelle Graw's rethinking of the positive valence of appropriation in "Dedication Replacing Appropriation: Fascination, Subversion, and Dispossession in Appropriation Art," in *Louise Lawler and Others*, ed. Philipp Kaiser (Basel: Kunstmuseum Basel, Museum für Gegenwartskunst; Ostfildern-Ruit, Germany: Hatje Cantz, 2004), 45–64.

6 Graw, "Dedication Replacing Appropriation," 45.

7 See especially "Prominence Given, Authority Taken: An Interview with Louise Lawler by Douglas Crimp," in *Louise Lawler: An Arrangement of Pictures* (New York: Assouline, 2000), n.p. See also Jack Bankowsky, "Does Louise Lawler Make You Cry?," and George Baker and Andrea Fraser, "Displacement and Condensation: A Conversation on the Work of Louise Lawler," both in Kaiser, *Louise Lawler and Others*, 75–90 and 105–43.

8 Andrea Fraser, "In and Out of Place," *Art in America*, June 1985, 124.

9 Baker and Fraser, "Displacement and Condensation," 141.

10 Jack Bankowsky focuses specifically on Lawler's photographs of art by Andy Warhol in "Does Louise Lawler Make You Cry?"

11 "Prominence Given, Authority Taken," n.p.

12 See Rosalyn Deutsche's "Louise Lawler's Rude Museum," in *Twice Untitled and Other Pictures (looking back)*, ed. Helen Molesworth (Columbus, OH: Wexner Center for the Arts; Cambridge, MA: MIT Press, 2006), 123–32.

13 My thanks to Catherine Evans, chief curator, Columbus Museum of Art, for this information.

14 Jacqueline Rose, "Why War?," in *Why War?: Psychoanalysis, Politics and the Return of Melanie Klein* (Oxford: Blackwell, 1993), 16. My thanks to Rosalyn Deutsche for sharing this text with me.

15 Ibid., 34.

Klara Lidén: In Memory of Static
pages 144–53

1 John Kelsey mentions Keaton in passing in his catalogue essay "Klara's Moves," in *Klara Lidén* (Stockholm: Moderna Museet; London: Serpentine Gallery and Koenig Books, 2010), 15.

2 Roland Barthes, *The Neutral*, trans. Rosalind E. Krauss and Denis Hollier (New York: Columbia University Press, 2005), 22. My gratitude to Marina van Zuylen for knowing that I needed to read this lecture.

3 Ibid., 23.

4 Ibid., 27.

Jim Hodges: The Whole World Is Watching
pages 154–62

1 Quoted in Judith H. Dobrzynski, "Artist at Work: Taking the Ordinary and Finding the Beautiful," *New York Times*, March 24, 1999.

2 *Untitled* was made in collaboration with Encke King and Carlos Marques da Cruz, and was originally distributed for the 2011 World AIDS Day/Day With(out) Art by Visual AIDS.

3 Artpace in San Antonio organized a Texas-wide comprehensive survey exhibition of thirteen billboards created by Felix Gonzalez-Torres between 1989 and 1995.

4 June Howard, "What Is Sentimentality?," *American Literary History* 11, no. 1 (Spring 1999): 65–66.

5 Ibid., 70. Howard argues that recent scholarship has begun to articulate the links between

sentimentality and citizenship, seeing lines of affiliation between sympathy and empathy—so necessary to the democratic project—and sentimentality. Hence, without an awareness of the public and shared nature of our emotional social life as such and citizenship in particular are impossible.

6 Ibid.

7 See Richard Dyer, "In Defense of Disco," *Gay Left*, Summer 1979, 20–22.

8 Lauren Berlant and Michael Warner, "Sex in Public," *Critical Inquiry* 24, no. 2 (Winter 1998): 559.

9 At the time, ACT UP actions such as the 1989 "kiss-in" in front of St. Vincent's Hospital and Gran Fury's 1988 wheat-pasted posters of a hot sailor couple kissing exuded the kind of sex-positive "we're here, we're queer, get used to it" attitude designed to tear down the neoliberal language of "tolerance" and put in its place a fully articulated version of citizenship in which one's desiring identity had a firm status in the public sphere.

10 Susan Sontag, "Notes on Camp," in *Against Interpretation and Other Essays* (New York: Farrar, Straus and Giroux, 1966), 275.

11 "'Speech Is Blind': Jacques Derrida on 'Echo and Narcissus,'" YouTube, January 27, 2007, https://www.youtube.com/watch?v=ya46wfeWqJk; clip from *Derrida*, directed by Kirby Dick and Amy Ziering (New York: Zeitgeist Films, 2002).

12 ACT UP was rigorous in its critique of pharmaceutical companies' exploitation of the crisis in the name of profit, calling media attention to the exorbitant price of AIDS/HIV medications. This rhymes with the antiwar and Occupy movements' attacks on high oil and gas prices and the profit margins of companies such as Halliburton, which have benefited economically from a decade of war.

13 For instance, even though there have been more than six hundred thousand deaths in the United States due to AIDS-related causes, there is no memorial to those who have died. This seems to constitute "proof" of an inability to properly identify, recognize, and mourn segments of American culture that were decimated by the disease. See Sarah Schulman, *The Gentrification of the Mind: Witness to a Lost Imagination* (Berkeley: University of California Press, 2012).

14 One of my favorite installation shots of Hodges's work is published in the catalogue for the 2007 exhibition *I Remember Heaven: Jim Hodges and Andy Warhol*, curated by Susan Cahan for the Contemporary Art Museum St. Louis. It shows two of Warhol's camouflage self-portraits reflected in one of Hodges's camouflage mirror mosaics.

15 Judith Butler, *Precarious Life: The Powers of Mourning and Violence* (London: Verso, 2006), 30.

Doris Salcedo: Readymade Time
pages 163–73

1 Monica Amor, "Doris Salcedo," *Artforum*, February 2009, 191.

2 Nancy Princenthal, "Silence Seen," in *Doris Salcedo*, Contemporary Artist Series (London: Phaidon Press, 2000), 40.

3 Marcel Duchamp, "Apropos of Readymades," in *The Writings of Marcel Duchamp*, ed. Michel Sanouillet and Elmer Peterson (New York: Da Capo Press, 1989), 141.

4 "Interview with Charles Merewether 1998," in *Doris Salcedo*, 134.

5 Amor, "Doris Salcedo," 191.

6 Mieke Bal, "Earth Aches: The Aesthetics of the Cut," in *Doris Salcedo: Shibboleth* (London: Tate, 2007), 61.

7 Marcel Duchamp, "The Creative Act," in Sanouillet and Peterson, *The Writings of Marcel Duchamp*, 138.

8 Later on in "The Creative Act," Duchamp writes: "The creative act is not performed by the artist alone; the spectator brings the work into contact with the external world by deciphering and interpreting its inner qualifications and thus adds his contribution to the creative act." Ibid., 140.

9 Marcel Duchamp, "The Green Box," in Sanouillet and Peterson, *The Writings of Marcel Duchamp*, 26.

10 On the proliferation of the readymades, see William Camfield's excellent *Marcel Duchamp: Fountain* (Houston: Houston Fine Art Press, 1989). For more on the logic of the handmade readymade and its many twentieth-century practitioners, see my *Part Object Part Sculpture* (Columbus, OH: Wexner Center for the Arts; University Park: Pennsylvania State University Press, 2005).

11 For more on Duchamp and a critique of consumption (rather than production), see my "Rrose Sélavy Goes Shopping," in *The Dada Seminars*, ed. Leah Dickerman (Washington, DC: National Gallery of Art; New York: D.A.P./Distributed Art Publishers, 2005).

12 Bal, "Earth Aches," 55.

13 My thanks to artist Steve Locke for discussions about the violence of neutrality, particularly the violence of the white wall in the modernist museum.

14 "Interview with Charles Merewether 1998," 140.

15 Olga M. Viso, "Doris Salcedo: The Dynamic of Violence," in Neal Benezra and Olga M. Viso, *Distemper: Dissonant Themes in the Art of the 1990s* (Washington, DC: Hirshhorn Museum and Sculpture Garden, Smithsonian Institution; New York: D.A.P./Distributed Art Publishers, 1996), 94.
16 Bal, "Earth Aches," 55
17 See Duchamp, "The Green Box," 26.
18 This is the now standard critique of hallmark feminist works such as Judy Chicago's *The Dinner Party* (1974–79).
19 Doris Salcedo, "Traces of Memory: Art and Remembrance in Colombia," *ReVista* 2, no. 3 (Spring 2003): 28–30.
20 Ibid.
21 George Kubler, *The Shape of Time: Remarks on the History of Things* (New Haven, CT: Yale University Press, 1962), 19.
22 Salcedo, "Traces of Memory," 30.

Deana Lawson: *Nation*
pages 182–84

1 Michael Beschloss, "George Washington's Weakness: His Teeth," *New York Times*, April 28, 2014, https://www.nytimes.com/2014/04/29/upshot/george-washingtons-weakness-his-teeth.html.

Ruth Asawa: "San Francisco Housewife and Mother"
pages 185–92

1 Sarah Archer, "Maker to Market: Ruth Asawa Reappraised," *Journal of Modern Craft* 8, no. 2 (July 2015): 146.
2 Emily K. Doman Jennings, "Critiquing the Critique," in *The Sculpture of Ruth Asawa: Contours in the Air*, ed. Daniell Cornell (San Francisco: Fine Arts Museums of San Francisco; Berkeley: University of California Press, 2006), 137.
3 In this essay I focus almost exclusively on the role of mother due to an interest in the ways in which being a mother and being an artist are typically offered as an antinomy. This isn't to deny the intersectionality that structures Asawa's person and her work, but rather to continue an avenue of inquiry that began with the figure of the "artist mother" in my essay on the work of Anna Maria Maiolino, "Mother Knowledge," in *Anna Maria Maiolino* (Los Angeles: Museum of Contemporary Art; New York: DelMonico Books/Prestel, 2017), 164–71.
4 The single most sustained effort to think through the problem of the Mother-Artist dyad comes in Moyra Davey's edited volume *Mother Reader: Essential Writings on Motherhood* (New York: Seven Stories Press, 2001). See in particular Susan Rubin Suleiman's "Writing and Motherhood," 113–38, and Nancy Huston's "Novels and Navels," 211–24.
5 Much of my thinking about the logic of sameness and difference and its relation to siblings comes from Juliet Mitchell's *Siblings: Sex and Violence* (Cambridge, UK: Polity Press, 2003).
6 In his essay on Asawa, John Yau writes that "Robert Smithson's description of Hesse's work as 'psychic models of a very interior person' seems equally applicable to Asawa's wire constructions." I think my questions here are in this spirit: to see in the formal the structure of subjectivity and its intelligences rather than a one-to-one correspondence between identity and subject matter. John Yau, "Ruth Asawa: Shifting the Terms of Sculpture," in *Ruth Asawa: Objects and Apparitions* (New York: Christie's, 2013), 20.
7 For more on Albers and form, see my essay "Imaginary Landscape," in Helen Molesworth, *Leap Before You Look: Black Mountain College, 1933–1957* (Boston: Institute of Contemporary Art; New Haven: Yale University Press, 2016), 25–73.
8 For more on Asawa's work in San Francisco public schools, see Sally B. Woodbridge, "The Alvarado Art Workshop, 1968–1973," in Cornell, *The Sculpture of Ruth Asawa*, 222–26.
9 Cathleen Rountree, ed., *On Women Turning 70: Honoring the Voices of Wisdom* (San Francisco: Jossey-Bass, 1999), 83.

Lee Lozano: Drawings
pages 193–99

1 Lee Lozano, *Seek the Extremes!* (Nuremberg, Germany: Verlag für moderne Kunst Nürnberg, 2006), 50.

Catherine Opie: Politics
pages 200–207

1 Harvey Milk, "Gay Freedom Day Speech," reprinted speech, *Bay Area Reporter*, June 25, 1978, in *An Archive of Hope: Harvey Milk's Speeches and Writings*, ed. Jason Edward Black and Charles E. Morris III (Berkeley: University of California Press, 2013), 219.

Luc Tuymans: Painting the Banality of Evil
pages 211–23

1 Walter Benjamin, "Theses on the Philosophy of History," in *Illuminations*, ed. Hannah Arendt, trans. Harry Zohn (New York: Schocken Books, 1969), 257.
2 Hannah Arendt, *Eichmann in Jerusalem: A Report on the Banality of Evil* (London: Faber & Faber, 1963), 22.
3 Ibid., 231.
4 Benjamin Buchloh has argued forcefully that history painting as such is a defunct genre, writing: "But the history of history painting is itself a history of the withdrawal of a subject from painting's ability to represent, a withdrawal that ultimately generated the modernist tradition of aesthetic autonomy." See Benjamin H. D. Buchloh, "A Note on Gerhard Richter's *October 18, 1977*," *October* 48 (Spring 1989): 93. Curator Robert Storr takes issue with Buchloh's analysis, arguing instead for the persistence of history painting in *Gerhard Richter: October 18, 1977* (New York: Museum of Modern Art, 2000). Tuymans's oeuvre could arguably be described accurately by either critic's assessment.
5 So, too, Tuymans's oeuvre is continually discussed, equally inevitably, in the darkness cast by the long shadow of Gerhard Richter. Certainly Richter's importance cannot be denied, but given the logic of the archive, which I elucidate here, Oedipal dramas are a less convincing hermeneutic.
6 Hal Foster, "An Archival Impulse," *October* 110 (Autumn 2004): 21.
7 For a discussion of the strength of Tuymans's style and its effect on a younger generation of European painters, see Jordan Kantor, "The Tuymans Effect," *Artforum*, November 2004, 164–71.
8 This stroke was the hallmark of Tuymans's early style. By the late 1990s, his brushwork became quite expansive and heterogeneous.
9 Yve-Alain Bois, "Painting and the Task of Mourning," in *Painting as Model* (Cambridge, MA: MIT Press, 1990), 241.
10. Ulrich Loock, "On layers of sign-relations, in the light of mechanically reproduced pictures, from ten years of exhibitions," in Ulrich Loock et al., *Luc Tuymans*, Contemporary Artist Series (London: Phaidon Press, 1996), 38.
11 Tuymans has noted the influence of television several times. In an interview with Eric Suchere, he states: "I grew up with television. I am a part of a television generation. I mean that I grew up much more with images than with experience." See "Luc Tuymans: More than a Medium," trans. C. Penwarden, *Art Press*, no. 281 (July-August 2002): 26-31. Or again in an interview with Juan Vicente Aliaga: "For my generation, television is very important. There's a huge amount of visual information which can never be experienced but which can be seen, and its impact is enormous." "Juan Vicente Aliaga in Conversation with Luc Tuymans," in Loock et al., *Luc Tuymans*, 12.
12 This lack of legibility is so pronounced that it prompted the title of an essay by Montserrat Albores Gleason, "I Still Don't Get It," in *Luc Tuymans: I Don't Get It*, ed. Gerrit Vermeiren (Ghent, Belgium: Ludion Press, 2007), 169-75.
13 Yve-Alain Bois, Denis Hollier, and Rosalind Krauss, "A Conversation with Hubert Damisch," *October* 85 (Summer 1998): 3-17.
14 Susan Sontag, *On Photography* (New York: Farrar, Straus & Giroux, 1977), 166.
15 Erwin Panofsky, *Perspective as Symbolic Form*, trans. Christopher S. Wood (New York: Zone Books, 1991), 61, 57, 66.
16 See Roland Barthes, *Camera Lucida: Reflections on Photography*, trans. Richard Howard (New York: Hill & Wang, 1981).
17 For an excellent example of this phenomenon, as well as a very interesting essay, see Gerrit Vermeiren, "Proper," in *Luc Tuymans: Proper* (New York: David Zwirner, 2005), 3-7.
18 Loock, "On layers of sign-relations," 42-44. Loock talks about this as a kind of failure. I see it as exemplifying Tuymans's participation in the logic of the archive, in which a supplementary discourse is presumed due to the fragmentary nature of the material. It is only painting's myth of totality that imagines presentation and interpretation happening otherwise.
19 Ibid., 93n4.
20 And as such Derrida's conception of the archive is bound up with Freud's concept of repetition-compulsion and the death drive, elaborated in *Beyond the Pleasure Principle*. See Jacques Derrida, *Archive Fever: A Freudian Impression*, trans. Eric Prenowitz (Chicago: University of Chicago Press, 1996).
21 Ibid., 36.
22 Panofsky, *Perspective as Symbolic Form*, 59.
23 *Gaskamer*'s first iteration was a watercolor drawing that Tuymans made on site in Dachau in 1986. He has stated that he had no real intention of making a painting of a gas chamber at that time, for it was simply "not done." For years the watercolor floated around the studio. During the same period, Tuymans saw photographs of the very gas chamber he had drawn in a book on the camps by a Belgian inmate. What struck

Tuymans was that this black-and-white photograph and his watercolor—now completely yellowed—deployed the exact same angle of composition. Hence, *Gaskamer* is the product of several layers of mediation, as the original watercolor, the passage of time, and photographic source material all coalesced to form this impossible image (Tuymans, phone interview with the author, May 1, 2009).

24 For a more detailed account of Tuymans's use of filmic strategies, see Bill Horrigan's essay "Cinema, Belgium, Tuymans: A Note," as well as Prudence Peiffer's account of Tuymans's exhibition *At Random*, both in *Luc Tuymans*, ed. Madeleine Grynsztejn and Helen Molesworth (San Francisco: Museum of Modern Art; Columbus, OH: Wexner Center for the Arts; New York: Distributed Art Publishers, 2009), 59–65, 121–23.

25 This is a significant difference between Tuymans and Richter: Richter's blur connotes the finished quality of an event, as in a photograph, whereas the liquid quality of a Tuymans painting argues more for the ongoingness of an event—both forward and backward.

26 Curator Emma Dexter argues that the "category of still life seems to be at the core of Tuymans' practice." Dexter, "The Interconnectedness of All Things: Between History, Still Life, and the Uncanny," in *Luc Tuymans*, ed. Emma Dexter and Julian Heynen (London: Tate Publishing, 2004), 18.

27 Norman Bryson, *Looking at the Overlooked: Four Essays on Still Life Painting* (Cambridge, MA: Harvard University Press, 1990), 60.

28 Hannah Arendt, *On Violence* (New York: Harcourt, Brace & World, 1970), 63.

Manny Farber: One Day at a Time
pages 228–45

1 Patricia Patterson, "aran kitchens, aran sweaters," *Heresies* 1, no. 4 (Winter 1978): 89–92.

2 Manny Farber, "White Elephant Art vs. Termite Art," in *Negative Space: Manny Farber on the Movies*, ed. Robert Walsh, rev. ed. (New York: Da Capo Press, 1998), 134–44.

3 Ibid., 135.

4 Ibid., 137.

5 Ibid., 135–36.

6 Manny Farber, introduction to Walsh, *Negative Space*, 10.

7 Jean-Pierre Gorin, "Proposal for a Tussle" (2007), in *Essays on the Essay Film*, ed. Nora M. Alter and Timothy Corrigan (New York: Columbia University Press, 2017), 273.

8 "Jean-Pierre Gorin by Lynne Tillman," *BOMB*, no. 23 (Spring 1988), https://bombmagazine.org/articles/jeanne-pierre-gorin/.

9 Patricia Patterson and Manny Farber, "Kitchen without Kitsch," *Film Comment* 13, no. 6 (November–December 1977): 48.

10. Kevin Parker, "The Termite and All-Over Meaning," in *Manny Farber*, ed. Howard Singerman (Los Angeles: Museum of Contemporary Art, 1985), 56–62. See also Michel de Certeau, *The Practice of Everyday Life*, trans. Steven Rendall (Berkeley: University of California Press, 2011).

11 Christopher Lehmann-Haupt, "Elizabeth Hardwick, Critic, Novelist, and Restless Woman of Letters, Is Dead at 91," *New York Times*, December 4, 2007, A29.

12 Elizabeth Hardwick, introduction to *The Best American Essays 1986*, ed. Elizabeth Hardwick (New York: Ticknor & Fields, 1986), xiv–xvi.

13 Jonathan Crary, "Manny Farber: The Garden of Earthly Routines," in *Manny Farber: About Face* (San Diego: Museum of Contemporary Art San Diego, 2003), 129.

14 Ibid., 130.

15 Hardwick, *Best American Essays*, xviii.

16 Fielding Dawson's class notes from Olson's course at Black Mountain College, in Dawson, *The Black Mountain Book* (Rocky Mount: North Carolina Wesleyan College Press, 1991), 98.

17 Georges Perec, "Approaches to What?" (1973), in *Species of Spaces and Other Pieces*, ed. and trans. John Sturrock (London: Penguin Classics, 1998), 211.

18 Charles Olson, "The Kingfishers" (1953), in *In Cold Hell, in Thicket* (San Francisco: Four Seasons Foundation, 1967), 11.

Lari Pittman: Décor, the Decorative, Decorum
pages 246–56

1 Pat Kirkham, "Humanizing Modernism," in *The Design History Reader*, ed. Grace Lees-Maffei and Rebecca Houze (London: Bloomsbury, 2010), 360.

2 At the time of writing, the checklist for the exhibition *Lari Pittman: Declaration of Independence* (Hammer Museum, Los Angeles, September 29, 2019–January 5, 2020) indicated that these gourds were all in private collections, and that many of their owners are friends and acquaintances of Pittman.

3 Pittman has commented on the influence of feminism on his practice: "Although I wasn't allowed to be in the feminist program at CalArts,

because I was a man, I was certainly welcomed under its umbrella by my fellow artists. . . . The scent, the perfume, of the feminist art program really was pronounced and invaded, in the best sense, the whole department at the moment when we would look at all sorts of debased cultural moments of production that were given no value." "A Conversation with Helen Molesworth and Lari Pittman," in *Lari Pittman* (New York: Skira Rizzoli, 2011), 211.

4 Adolf Loos, "Ornament and Crime," in Lees-Maffei and Houze, *The Design History Reader*, 98, 100.

5 "A Conversation with Helen Molesworth and Lari Pittman," 206.

6 Quoted in Wayne Koestenbaum, "The Brute Force of High Tea," in *Lari Pittman*, 9.

7 Tea is a late-afternoon meal served as a means to bridge the long gap between lunch at noon and dinner at eight. The meal was typically taken by members of the upper classes. With the advent of industrialized labor, working-class people added meat or fish to tea and began to have the meal as their terminal meal of the day. A tea that has the addition of a more substantial protein, rather than the typical sweet, is called high tea.

8 "A Conversation with Helen Molesworth and Lari Pittman," 207.

9 Ibid., 208.

10 T. J. Clark, "In Defense of Abstract Expressionism," in *Farewell to an Idea: Episodes from a History of Modernism* (New Haven, CT: Yale University Press, 1999), 389.

Noah Davis: The Forest and the Trees
pages 269–75

1 The Underground Museum closed its doors on March 15, 2022. For more information about the Underground Museum and its closure, see "Dedicated to the Underground: A Conversation with Thomas Lax, Glenn Ligon, Julie Mehretu, and Fred Moten," in *Noah Davis: In Detail* (New York: David Zwirner Books, 2023), 88–107.

INDEX

Page references for illustrations appear in *italics*

ACKNOWLEDGMENTS

Acknowledgments are a form of cartography—they sketch the writer's horizon of possibility. Artists have always been my ideal reader, and hence these essays are for you, my beloved artists, my favorite category of person. I offer them with love and gratitude.

A bear hug of thanks is due to Donna Wingate, my editor of many years. This book was her idea, and I'm so glad she convinced me to do it. Thanks to Deborah Aaronson and Simon Hunegs at Phaidon for believing in it, and to Naomi Misuzaki and João Mota for their wonderful design work. A very special thanks to the artist Dike Blair for his beautiful painting that graces this book's cover.

Because the essays in this volume were written over three decades, they span several institutional jobs, cities, and groups of friends. My graduate school days in New York City and Ithaca, New York were shaped by lively and loving conversations with Doug Ashford, Peter Brunt, Leah Dickerman, Chris Hoover, Janet Kraynak, Miwon Kwon, and Frazer Ward, and I still see traces of them in the earliest texts. I was blessed with some of the best teachers a person could have. My unflinching gratitude goes to Susan Buck-Morss, Ron Clark, Hal Foster, and Rosalind Krauss.

The Columbus, Ohio years were extraordinary in every way, thanks in large measure to Jill Davis and Fred Dirkse, Lisa Florman, Bill Horrigan, Jan and Ben Maiden, Nancy and Dave Gill, and Ruthie and Stephen Melville.

My ten years in Cambridge and Boston were indelibly shaped by talking, thinking, and feeling with Chris Barrett, Taylor Davis, Ruth Erickson, Claire Grace, Melissa Franklin, Steve Locke, Jill Medvedow, Amy Sillman, Sue Schardt, Marina van Zuylen, and Stephan Wolohojian. Los Angeles was mind and heart-expanding due to my Underground Museum crew: Mark Ankner, Onye Anyanwu, Karon Davis, Noah Davis, Daniel DeSure, Aileen Getty, Kahlil Joseph, Justen LeRoy, and Megan Steinman.

Thank you to everyone who commissioned these essays. I'm especially indebted to my dear friend Connie Butler for her many invitations to write. The editors at *Artforum* and *October*, Brendan Dugan at Karma, and Lucas Zwirner at David Zwirner gave me access to wide audiences, and while everyone in this august coterie has my sincere gratitude, Michelle Kuo gets a special shout-out.

When the road was far from straight and the path forward not at all clear, three women appeared: thank you Kristy Edmunds, Pamela Rosenau, and Sue Hostetler Wrigley.

Over the past thirty years it has been my profound good fortune to have a posse that has sustained me in ways that exceed my vocabulary. My gratitude for these folks is bone deep: Chris Barrett, Gregg Bordowitz, Cheryl Lynn Bruce, Connie Butler, Gerry Dackerman, Moyra Davey, Jill Davis, Karon Davis, Taylor Davis, Fred Dirkse, Madeleine Grynsztejn, Catherine Lord, Kerry James Marshall, Josiah McElheny, James Molesworth, Catherine Opie, Barry Rosen, Sue Schardt, Tom Shapiro, Jason Simon, and Kim Thompson.

My middle-aged life was indelibly shaped by two deaths and one marriage. John Dackerman and Jason Fusco left the party early. Fusco was the first person who treated me like a storyteller; I still write as if he were the reader. John didn't give a hoot about my professional success, he only cared that I loved his sister, Susan Dackerman, who remains my favorite person of all time.

In memoriam
John Dackerman (February 19, 1966–April 2, 2007)
Jason Fusco (April 11, 1968–February 2, 2019)

Energy cannot be created or destroyed; it can only be changed from one form to another.
—Albert Einstein

IMAGE CREDITS

Cover, 225, 227: © Dike Blair. Courtesy the artist and Karma; 11: Photo © The Courtauld / Bridgeman Images; 17: © Robert Rauschenberg Foundation/ VAGA at ARS, NY and DACS, London 2023. Courtesy San Francisco Museum of Modern Art, purchase through a gift of Phyllis C. Wattis. Photo: Don Ross; 18: © Robert Rauschenberg Foundation/ VAGA at ARS, NY and DACS, London 2023. Digital image © The Museum of Modern Art, New York/ Scala, Florence; 35, 37: © Kerry James Marshall. Courtesy the artist and Jack Shainman Gallery, New York; 45: © Dawoud Bey, courtesy Sean Kelly. Digital image © The Museum of Modern Art, New York/Scala, Florence; 59: © Yoko Ono. Photo: John Bigelow Taylor; 75, 77: © Association Marcel Duchamp / ADAGP, Paris and DACS, London 2023. Courtesy Philadelphia Museum of Art, gift of the Cassandra Foundation, 1969, 1969-41-1; 89: © Judy Chicago. ARS, NY and DACS, London 2023. Photo © Donald Woodman, courtesy Judy Chicago / Art Resource, NY; 91: © Mary Kelly 2023. Image courtesy the artist and Pippy Houldsworth Gallery, London; 93: © Mierle Laderman Ukeles, courtesy the artist and Ronald Feldman Gallery, New York; 95: © Martha Rosler. Courtesy the artist and Mitchell-Innes & Nash, New York; 107: Courtesy the artist; 113: Courtesy the artist and Garth Greenan Gallery, New York. Digital Image © The Museum of Modern Art/Licensed by SCALA / Art Resource, NY; 116: © Mary Heilmann. Courtesy the artist, 303 Gallery, New York, and Hauser & Wirth. Photo: Stephen White; 119: © Dana Schutz. Courtesy the artist and David Zwirner; 123: © Amy Sillman. Courtesy the artist and Gladstone Gallery; 128: © Wangechi Mutu. Digital image © The Museum of Modern Art, New York/Scala, Florence; 139, 141: Courtesy the artist and Sprüth Magers; 149: © Klara Lidén. Courtesy the artist; Reena Spaulings Fine Art, New York; and Sadie Coles HQ, London; 155, 161: © Jim Hodges. Courtesy the artist and Gladstone Gallery; 165: Photo © Tate; 179: © Simone Leigh, courtesy Matthew Marks Gallery; 183: © Deana Lawson. Courtesy the artist, David Kordansky Gallery, and Gagosian; 187: Photo © 2023 Imogen Cunningham Trust / www.imogencunningham.com. Artwork © 2023 Ruth Asawa Lanier, Inc./Artists Rights Society (ARS), New York and DACS, London. Courtesy David Zwirner; 191: © 2023 Ruth Asawa Lanier, Inc./Artists Rights Society (ARS), New York and DACS, London. Courtesy David Zwirner. Photo: Kerry McFate; 195: Image © Estate of Hollis Frampton. Photo: Tom Loonan, Buffalo AKG Art Museum/Art Resource, NY/Scala, Florence; 197: © The Estate of Lee Lozano. Courtesy Hauser & Wirth; 198: © The Estate of Lee Lozano. Courtesy Hauser & Wirth. Photo: Barbora Gerny; 203, 206: © Catherine Opie. Courtesy Regen Projects, Los Angeles and Lehmann Maupin, New York, Seoul, and Hong Kong; 219: © Studio Luc Tuymans, courtesy Zeno X Gallery, Antwerp; 235, 244: © Manny Farber Estate. Photo: Brian Lockhart; 241: Courtesy Galerie Buchholz; 251: © Lari Pittman. Courtesy Lehmann Maupin, New York, Hong Kong, and Seoul; 259: © Lisa Yuskavage, courtesy the artist and David Zwirner. Image courtesy Image & Book Archive, Institute of Contemporary Art, University of Pennsylvania; 263: © Lisa Yuskavage. Courtesy the artist and David Zwirner; 271, 273: © The Estate of Noah Davis. Courtesy the Estate of Noah Davis and David Zwirner.

Phaidon Press Limited
2 Cooperage Yard
London E15 2QR

Phaidon Press Inc.
65 Bleecker Street
New York, NY 10012

phaidon.com

First published 2023

ISBN 978 1 83866 605 7

A CIP catalogue record for this book is available
from the British Library and the Library of Congress.

Edited by Donna Wingate, with Marc Joseph Berg

Commissioning Editor: Deborah Aaronson
Project Editor: Simon Hunegs
Production Controller: Andie Trainer
Design: Naomi Misuzaki, Supermarket

Printed in Italy

Cover: Dike Blair, *Untitled*, 2017, oil on wood panel,
12 x 9 in. (30.5 x 22.9 cm)